Disaster, Conflict and Society in Crises

Humanitarian crises – resulting from conflict, natural disaster or political collapse – are usually perceived as a complete break from normality, spurring special emergency policies and interventions. In reality, there are many continuities and discontinuities between crisis and normality. What does this mean for our understanding of politics, aid and local institutions during crises? This book examines this question from a socio-political perspective.

Emphasising the importance of everyday politics and practice, this book unravels the working of crises in society. The first part of the book deals with the multiple ways in which crises can be understood and acted upon. This is done through – among others – a discourse analysis of peace narratives in Sri Lanka and everyday climate change adaptation politics in Mozambique. The second part deals with the question of how local institutions fare under, and transform in response to, crises. Conflicts and disasters are breakpoints of social order, but they are also marked by processes of continuity and re-ordering, or the creation of new institutions and linkages. It focuses on institutions varying from inter-ethnic marriage patterns in Sri Lanka to 'big men' in the mining sector of Congo to situations of institutional multiplicity in Angola. Finally, the social and political realities of different arenas of interventions in crisis are examined, including humanitarian aid, peacebuilding and disaster risk reduction.

This book gives an invaluable wealth of case studies and a unique socio-political analysis of the humanitarian studies field, for both students and researchers in humanitarian studies, disaster studies, conflict and peace studies, as well as for humanitarian and military practitioners.

Dorothea Hilhorst is Professor of Humanitarian Aid and Reconstruction at Wageningen University. Her research concerns the *aidnography* of humanitarian crises and fragile states. Her publications focus on the everyday politics and practices of humanitarian aid, disaster risk reduction, climate change adaptation, reconstruction and peacebuilding.

Routledge Humanitarian Studies Series

Series editors: Dorothea Hilhorst and Alex de Waal
Editorial board: Mihir Bhatt, Dennis Dijkzeul, Wendy Fenton,
Kirsten Johnson, Julia Steets, Peter Walker

The Routledge Humanitarian Studies series in collaboration with the International Humanitarian Studies Association (IHSA) takes a comprehensive approach to the growing field of expertise that is humanitarian studies. This field is concerned with humanitarian crises caused by natural disaster, conflict or political instability and deals with the study of how humanitarian crises evolve, how they affect people and their institutions and societies, and the responses they trigger.

We invite book proposals that address, among other topics, questions of aid delivery, institutional aspects of service provision, the dynamics of rebel wars, state building after war, the international architecture of peacekeeping, the ways in which ordinary people continue to make a living throughout crises, and the effect of crises on gender relations.

This interdisciplinary series draws on and is relevant to a range of disciplines, including development studies, international relations, international law, anthropology, peace and conflict studies, public health and migration studies.

1. Disaster, Conflict and Society in Crises

Everyday politics of crisis response
Edited by Dorothea Hilhorst

This volume is a testament to how the study of disaster has come of age. It is a stimulating and innovative set of studies of the intersection of everyday politics with global issues including natural hazards, armed conflict and international assistance policy. Case studies from four continents and thematic chapters draw upon history, anthropology and political science, to integrate the understanding of governance, development and conflict. This book will be an important resource for students and practitioners alike.

Alex de Waal, World Peace Foundation at the Fletcher School, USA

This is a very useful collection. Each chapter draws important theoretical and policy conclusions from granular ethnographic cases. Together, they unravel a variety of ways that people and institutions engage effectively (or not) to frame and overcome the challenges of survival and governance in disaster, conflict and post-conflict crises.

Hugo Slim, University of Oxford, UK

Disaster, Conflict and Society in Crises is a timely, important and thematically diverse anthology that brings a holistic perspective to the study of international interventions. It covers policy and practice in the humanitarian arena, and offers a rich array of analysis. Both academics and practitioners will find much to stimulate their thinking in this book.

Sultan Barakat, University of York, UK

Dorothea Hilhorst tells us this book describes the everyday politics of disasters, but it does far more than that. It gets right down into the weeds of the way disasters and crises change society and people's lives. It delves into the ebb and flow of local power, the ways in which governance changes, and how love and deep relationships are shaped. This book provides a beautifully human portrayal of disasters, but with all the rigor of science.

Peter Walker, Tufts University, USA

This book brings together a timely sociological study of humanitarian crises and aid. It adds value to our understanding of post-conflict/disaster transitions by exploring how local institutions and communities recover. Drawing upon a wide range of case studies, it challenges a number of common assumptions that drive policy and practice.

David Connolly, University of York, UK

Disaster, Conflict and Society in Crises

Everyday politics of crisis response

Edited by Dorothea Hilhorst

Routledge
Taylor & Francis Group

LONDON AND NEW YORK

First published 2013
by Routledge
2 Park Square, Milton Park, Abingdon, Oxon OX14 4RN

Simultaneously published in the US and Canada
by Routledge
711 Third Avenue, New York, NY 10017

Routledge is an imprint of the Taylor & Francis Group, an informa business

British Library Cataloguing in Publication Data
A catalogue record for this book is available from the British Library

Library of Congress Cataloging-in-Publication Data
Disaster, conflict and society in crises : everyday politics of crisis response /
   edited by Dorothea Hilhorst.
      pages cm. — (Routledge humanitarian studies series ; 1)
   Includes bibliographical references and index.
   ISBN 978–0–415–64081–7 (hardback : alk. paper) — ISBN
   978–0–415–64082–4 (pbk. : alk. paper) — ISBN 978–0–203–08246–1
   (e-book)   1. Disaster relief.   2. Emergency management.   3. Conflict
   management.   4. Economic assistance.   I. Hilhorst, Thea.
   HV553.D557 2013
   363.34'8—dc23

                                                            2012050434

ISBN13: 978–0–415–64081–7 (hbk)
ISBN13: 978–0–415–64082–4 (pbk)
ISBN13: 978–0–203–08246–1 (ebk)

Typeset in Baskerville
by RefineCatch Limited, Bungay, Suffolk

MIX
Paper from
responsible sources
FSC
www.fsc.org   FSC® C013604   Printed and bound by CPI Group (UK) Ltd, Croydon, CR0 4YY

Contents

Illustrations

Figures

Tables

Boxes

Contributors

Gemma Andriessen is a former student of Disaster Studies, Wageningen University, the Netherlands; she graduated for her MSc in 2012 with a thesis about mutual images of non-governmental organization (NGO) workers and project beneficiaries in water and sanitation projects in South Sudan. She also holds an MSc in Social and Organizational Psychology. Her fields of interest include civil society development in conflict/post-conflict settings and gender dimensions. Gemma is currently working as a Junior Programme Officer at Hivos, an international development organization, in the Gender and Human Rights programme. E-mail: gemma_andriessen@hotmail.com

Luís Artur holds a PhD in Sociology of Disasters from Wageningen University, an MSc in Rural Development Sociology and a BSc in Agronomy. His current position is lecturer and researcher at Eduardo Mondlane University in Maputo, Mozambique. Artur has published internationally and nationally in books, journals and newspapers. In disaster studies, his main interest is in interfaces between different actors in disaster management, and local adaptations to climate change. E-mail: lartur2000@yahoo.com

Jeroen Cuvelier holds a PhD in Social and Cultural Anthropology from the University of Leuven, Belgium. His dissertation dealt with the construction of masculine identities among artisanal miners in Katanga, the south-eastern province of the Democratic Republic of Congo (DRC). He has held research positions at the International Peace Information Service in Antwerp and the Royal Museum for Central Africa in Tervuren. Since January 2012, he has worked as a post-doctoral fellow for Disaster Studies at Wageningen University, as well as the Conflict Research Group of Ghent University, doing and coordinating research on the artisanal mining sector in eastern DRC. E-mail: jeroencuvelier@yahoo.co.uk

Hilde van Dijkhorst is Researcher at the Sociology and Anthropology of Development department of the Wageningen University. She holds an MSc in Management of Agro-ecological Knowledge and Social Change, for which she conducted fieldwork in Botswana on NGO use of indigenous knowledge in research on non-timber forest products. She has conducted research on gender and humanitarian aid, and organizational learning on peacebuilding policies and practices. In 2011 she finalized her PhD at Disaster Studies with research on post-conflict recovery processes in relation to rural livelihoods in Huíla province, Angola. E-mail: hilde.vandijkhorst@wur.nl

Georg Frerks holds the chair of Disaster Studies at Wageningen University, as well as a chair on Conflict Prevention and Conflict Management at Utrecht University, the Netherlands. As a sociologist and policy analyst, Professor Frerks focuses on conflict and disaster-induced vulnerabilities and local responses as well as on policies and interventions implemented at international and national levels. He acts as an advisor to several governmental and non-governmental organizations. He studied for his PhD in Sri Lanka in the early 1980s and has since worked on the conflict in Sri Lanka as well as on the tsunami and its aftermath. He has authored many academic publications and policy reports in the field of conflict and disaster studies, of which 32 are based on Sri Lanka. E-mail: georg.frerks@planet.nl

Timmo Gaasbeek is policy officer with ZOA, a Dutch humanitarian NGO. In this function, he provides support on livelihoods and food security, water and sanitation, and monitoring and evaluation to programmes in the countries where ZOA is operational. Before his return to the Netherlands, he spent nine years overseas, working in Cambodia, Sri Lanka, India, Ethiopia and Liberia. Timmo Gaasbeek completed his dissertation in 2010 on everyday inter-ethnic interaction in a multi-ethnic part of Sri Lanka's war zone, focusing on interaction around a shared irrigation system, interaction during periods of acute violence, and interaction in inter-ethnic marriages. E-mail: timmogaasbeek@gmail.com

Gemma van der Haar is Assistant Professor in Disaster Studies, Wageningen University. She has a background in development sociology and conflict studies. Between 1994 and 2004 she carried out extensive research on the Zapatista uprising in Chiapas, Mexico. Her current research interests include governance change in conflict and post-conflict contexts and everyday practices of state formation in post-conflict settings, with a particular focus on local government and on the governance of land and natural resources. E-mail: gemma.vanderhaar@wur.nl

Merel Heijke is consultant on the relationship between government and citizens at the Quality Institute for the Dutch Municipalities (KING). She obtained her BA in social science at Utrecht University, after which she did an MSc in International Development Studies, with a specialization in Disaster Studies. She wrote her thesis in 2010, on parallel local governance in Štrpce, Kosovo. After several projects on peacebuilding and local governance for the peace organization IKV Pax Christi, she currently explores the world of local governance in the Netherlands and is fascinated by the 'veranderopgave', the force for change, pressing on Dutch local governance. E-mail: merelheijke@hotmail.com

Annelies Heijmans is an independent researcher and consultant involved in interactive research with humanitarian aid agencies and governments in the field of disaster risk reduction, climate change, risk governance, resilience and conflict transformation. Annelies Heijmans completed her PhD dissertation in 2012 on the policy-practice gap of community-based disaster risk reduction approaches in conflict settings in Afghanistan, Indonesia and the Philippines (*Risky Encounters: Institutions and Interventions in Response to Recurrent Disasters and Conflict* http://edepot. wur.nl/202163). E-mail: annelies.heijmans@yahoo.com

Dorothea Hilhorst is professor of Humanitarian Aid and Reconstruction at Wageningen University. Her research concerns the aidnography of humanitarian crises and fragile states. Her publications focus on the everyday practices of humanitarian aid, disaster risk reduction, climate change adaptation, reconstruction and peacebuilding. She coordinates research programmes in Angola, DRC, Afghanistan, Ethiopia, Sudan, Mozambique and Uganda. Thea Hilhorst completed her dissertation in 2000 on a Philippine development NGO and its surrounding networks, clientele and donors (*The Real World of NGOs. Discourses, Diversity and Development*, Zedbooks). She is general secretary of the International Humanitarian Studies Association, www.ihsa.info. E-mail: thea.hilhorst@wur.nl

Bram J. Jansen is an anthropologist and assistant professor at Wageningen University. He has worked on humanitarian, conflict and refugee studies. In the past ten years he conducted fieldwork in East Africa and the Horn of Africa, mostly Kenya, Uganda and South Sudan. He holds a PhD based on a study of social ordering processes in protracted refugee situations in Kenya. He is currently working on a two-year research on humanitarian governance and decision-making processes in South Sudan. E-mail: bramj.jansen@wur.nl

Lotte Kemkens obtained a Bachelor's Degree in Socio-Cultural Anthropology at Utrecht University. She holds a cum laude Master's Degree in International Development Studies from Wageningen University. As part of her Master's Degree, she specialized in disaster studies. Lotte Kemkens has conducted anthropological research in Indonesia and Uganda. Her research focus is on religion, human-nature relationships, development aid, humanitarian aid and disasters. She is currently pursuing a career in development and humanitarian aid.

Mathijs van Leeuwen is Assistant Professor at the Centre for International Conflict – Analysis and Management (CICAM), Institute of Management Research, at the Radboud University Nijmegen, and researcher at the African Studies Centre at Leiden University, both in the Netherlands. His research interests include post-conflict peacebuilding and development; land conflicts and local governance reform; reconciliation and reintegration of former refugees, internally displaced persons (IDPs) and ex-combatants. Mathijs worked on and off for the Wageningen Disaster Studies department during 1999–2008. In 2008 he completed his PhD dissertation on discourses and practices of civil society peacebuilding and their international support (*Partners in Peace*, Ashgate). E-mail: m.vanleeuwen@fm.ru.nl

Maliana Serrano obtained her PhD from Wageningen University in 2012, on the interactions between aid and local institutions during and after Angola's conflict. She has published on the humanitarian arena in Angola, and on policy and practices of institution-building in Angola's conflict and reconstruction periods. Maliana Serrano has worked with international NGOs such as Fondo Índigena (Latin America and the Caribbean), EuronAid (Network of European Food Aid and Food Security NGOs), and CARE International UK. She is currently the director of the Polytechnic Institute PANGEIA in Lubango, Southern Angola. E-mail: maliana_serrano@hotmail.com

Jan-Gerrit van Uffelen is the Research Coordinator of the Linking Emergency Aid to Food Security programme at Disaster Studies, Wageningen University. His research focuses on the discourse on food crises and the resulting programme options by global and national actors. Jan-Gerrit has extensive experience in relief and rehabilitation programming and, as an international consultant, provides advice to a variety of organizations working in conflict and post-conflict settings. His dissertation is on war-affected displacement and improved management, and design of return and repatriation programmes and processes (*Return after Flight: Exploring the Decision Making Process of War Displaced People by Employing an Extended Version of the Theory of Reasoned Action*, Lambert Academic Publishing). E-mail: gjvuff@xs4all.nl

Jeroen Warner is Assistant Professor of Disaster Studies at Wageningen University, where he also took his PhD. Trained in International Relations at the University of Amsterdam, his current interest is in the politics of disasters, risk and security. More generally he specializes in issues of (water) resource conflict, participation and governance. Jeroen is a core member of the London Water Issues Group, co-editor of the *International Journal of Water Governance* and sits on the Editorial Board of *Ambiente e Sociedade*. He has (co)published six books and many international peer-reviewed articles. E-mail: jeroen.warner@wur.nl

Loes Weijers is a research analyst with the international peace organization Pragmora. Her Masters thesis research was on the relationship between aid workers and refugees in the Bhutanese refugee camps in East Nepal. She has also worked for the Netherlands Red Cross. E-mail: weijersloes@gmail.com

Acknowledgements

This volume was produced on the occasion of 15 years of Disaster Studies at Wageningen University. In these years, we have developed our approach to study disaster, conflict and disaster response as social phenomena, and, importantly, we have been able to ground this in a number of ethnographic research programmes.

I am very grateful to the research-granting organization Science for Global Development (WOTRO) of the Netherlands Organization for Scientific Research (NWO) that enabled most of these researches: on aid in Angola, floods in Mozambique, peacebuilding in Guatemala and Burundi, artisanal mining in the Democractic Republic of the Congo, food security in Ethiopia and refugee camps in Kenya.

I gratefully acknowledge the invaluable assistance of Bart Weijs to the production of this volume, the wonderful support of Lucie van Zaalen and Wendy Ömerköylu-van Dijk, the detailed language editing of Dorothy Myers and the patience of Khanam Virjee and her colleagues at Routledge. I especially acknowledge the contribution of Georg Frerks, Gemma van der Haar, Bram J. Jansen and my PhD candidates to the core ideas of the book, the fond memories of fieldwork with Luís Artur, Mathijs van Leeuwen, Maliana Serrano and Jan-Gerrit van Uffelen and the inspiration and friendship extended by Norman Long and Paul Richards. Special thanks – as always – to Fred Claasen and our children Iana, Don, Franka and Ellis.

1 Disaster, conflict and society
Everyday politics of crisis response

Dorothea Hilhorst

Natural disasters and conflicts have always occupied people's nightmares and lived experiences. In our times, natural disasters appear to be on the increase. Although there are fewer conflicts than in previous decades, conflicts tend to be prolonged and often recur within years of achieving peace. Some of the plagues of yesteryears have virtually disappeared or have become more manageable, but other crises have become more intense. Modern communications bring crises to everybody's home and they continue to be very much part of everybody's mindsets.

Our times are also marked by the rapid development of international response mechanisms. Humanitarian aid started its modern history in the nineteenth century, yet has been evolving and restructuring considerably in the last twenty years. Peacebuilding initiatives have become more robust since the end of the Cold War, and are increasingly framed in languages of human rights or human security. Disaster response has increasingly become proactive, with attention to disaster risk reduction mechanisms that aim to reduce people's vulnerability to natural hazards.

This book unravels the everyday politics of conflict and disaster and crisis response. Everyday politics – like every type of politics – concern the control, allocation, production and use of resources and the values and ideas underlying those activities (Kerkvliet 2009: 227). Everyday politics are about

> the deliberate or implicit political dimensions of everyday life, involving people that embrace, comply with, adjusting and contesting, and contesting norms and rules regarding authority over, production of, or allocation of resources and doing so in quiet, mundane, and subtle expressions and acts that are rarely organised and direct.
>
> (ibid.: 232)

Everyday politics are different from official politics that involve people with authoritative positions in organisations, and they are different from advocacy politics that involve direct and concerted efforts to support, criticise and oppose authorities, their policies and programmes. In reality, the boundaries between these different kinds of politics are not clear, and we will find reference to all of them throughout this book. Nonetheless, we like to emphasise the importance of focusing on everyday politics in conflict and disaster.

This notion of everyday politics is broad and can encompass all kinds of activities. The key is that we are not looking for specific activities, yet aim to identify the political dimensions and implications of everyday practice. Casting a vote on election day can be said to be a purely political act. Distributing food aid is more complex and multi-dimensional: it is an act of humanity, requires skill and organisation, and is moreover political. Food aid may acquire symbolic meaning in international relations, allowing a level of access and control to international actors, and it can have profound local political consequences, ranging from changing levels and scope of displacement to abuses of aid that co-determine the outcome of a violent conflict (Macrae and Zwi 1992). Disaster management can be analysed from a technocratic point of view, where research aims to improve protocols, mechanisms and logistics. However, it also has political properties. The same elements can be studied for their everyday politics: the selection of risks to be addressed, the allocation of burdens brought about by particular risks, the intentions and interactions of different actors, the choices to apply certain techniques over others and their implications for the generation and allocation of knowledge and resources.

Disaster, conflict and humanitarian crises

This book takes the perspective that disasters and conflict, and the responses they trigger, are *social phenomena*. Natural disasters are the outcome of social vulnerabilities, are differently understood and trigger different responses among local people, bureaucrats, politicians and disaster managers. Conflicts are not just the outcome of social processes: they penetrate deep into society where the causes and manifestations of conflict are locally altered, and where doing conflict becomes a practice, that can be studied as any other form of social practice. Interventions seek to bring about change into societies, yet are themselves populated by actors who socially negotiate the meaning and effects of their programmes.

Disaster, conflict, crisis and crisis response are socially constituted as much as they affect society. They can never be understood as separate from the societies in which they occur. This may be read as a truism, because everything that involves human beings is a social phenomenon. One of the tasks this book therefore sets out to achieve is to show that, in fact, most common understandings and responses to crises display a different view. Disasters are usually perceived as radical disruptions of development and conflict, as a societal state that is totally different from peace. Likewise, interventions around conflict and disaster are often conceptualised as insulated from the crises they operate on, in or around.

The social nature of humanitarian crises starts with the question: how do we define crises? Definitions of disaster and conflict may centre on the number of people who die, the havoc they wreak, or their overwhelming effects (such as used in the EMDAT database: www.emdat.be). There are many sophisticated mechanisms by which to define, for example, the different stages of food insecurity building up to a famine (www.fews.net). However, these definitions have very little relevance in predicting societal response to events. Some risks are easily elevated to the status of 'crisis', while others that may be equally or more devastating are considered normal. As Douglas and Wildavsky argued, societies selectively choose risks for attention and this choice reflects beliefs about values, social institutions, nature and moral behaviour (Douglas and Wildavsky 1982). There are in the end no objective criteria by which to measure a crisis. This means that an inquiry into conflict, disaster and crisis always has to start with the question of *who* defined the crisis and *how* its response came about.

Natural hazards

Natural hazards are on the increase. The number of disasters triggered by natural hazards has been sharply increasing over recent decades, due to a combination of factors including worldwide population growth (there are more people to be exposed to hazards), urbanisation, environmental degradation, climate change and increasing vulnerabilities. Interestingly, while we see a trend of increasing numbers of affected people and damage done, the number of people who die from disasters has decreased. This can be attributed to the world's increased capacity to forewarn disasters, reduce their risks and provide relief to their victims. Reducing disaster risks has been incorporated into international policy agendas and governance bodies. The United Nation's Hyogo Framework of Action of 2005 has rendered Disaster Risk Reduction (DRR) one of the global concerns that individual countries increasingly institutionalise and report progress on annually.

Disaster studies often make a distinction between natural hazards and disasters to recognise the social nature of disasters. Since the 1980s, disasters have not been regarded as purely physical happenings requiring largely technological solutions but, primarily, as the result of human actions (O'Keefe *et al.* 1976, Hewitt 1983, Anderson and Woodrow 1989, Wisner *et al.* 2004). Social processes generate unequal exposure to risk by making some people more prone to disaster than others and these inequalities are largely a function of the power relations operative in every society. This can be understood in terms of the vulnerability of an individual, household, community or society (Hilhorst and Bankoff 2004). Since the 1990s, moreover, even the natural origin of hazards is increasingly questioned. Hazards intensify under the pressures of environmental degradation and climate change, which makes the relation between hazards and society increasingly mutual (Oliver-Smith 1999). The vulnerability angle brings in a different perspective on time and space interpretations of disasters, as their genesis can be traced to long-term, sometimes world-scale, processes.

Different actors 'see' disasters as different types of events and as a result they prepare for, manage and record them in very different ways (Bankoff and Hilhorst 2009). What risks are worth considering, what measures will be taken, and who is eligible to their benefits, are questions that constitute the everyday politics of disaster and can have far-reaching effects for people's room for manoeuvre and chances of survival. Contrasting responses to food insecurity in Niger and Malawi can illustrate this point. A food shortage in Niger in 2005 was responded to by massive humanitarian assistance. The response became controversial when many actors, from Niger and internationally, claimed that the so-called crisis in fact concerned a 'normal' situation that could have been addressed by minor interventions. The response was aptly labelled by Paul Howe as too-much-too-late (Howe 2009). In contrast, Stephen Devereux (2009) demonstrated convincingly that a food shortage in Malawi in 2002 that genuinely deserved to be treated as a crisis on account of a range of indicators – including excess mortality – remained unrecognised and, as a result, policy responses only made matters worse.

One of the intriguing questions concerns the effect of disaster on processes of social change. Some disasters are remembered for toppling governments, such as the 1975 earthquake in Mexico, or for enabling breaking through a conflict impasse, such as the 1994 tsunami that enhanced the peace process in Aceh. If disasters provide a window for change, the question is: who can effectively reap these opportunities? Pelling and Dill (2009), after reviewing a number of cases, conclude that disaster shocks can be tipping points to open up political space, resulting in the contestation of political power, but more often lead to the opposite: the consolidation of the powers-that-be. Where states do not respond adequately to disaster, this may create opportunities for social and political change. Where states are contested, disaster events can become the platform for contesting parties to gain legitimation and constituency. Power politics, in these cases, easily interfere with disaster response. After the Marmara earthquake in Turkey, for example, displaced residents were provided shelter in camps. A number of these camps were run by the communist party. Within days after the disaster, however, the Turkish government claimed these camps, an act which was generally understood as an attempt to abort possible political gains for the communist party by their camp management. In the Philippines, we found that the government and oppositional non-governmental organisations (NGOs) ran parallel disaster response mechanisms, including programmes for DRR. The two systems did not interact or coordinate, and were basically competing claims to the support of the population (Bankoff and Hilhorst 2009).

Conflict and development

Conflict studies have always been mainly associated with what Kerkvliet calls 'official politics' and 'advocacy politics'. Everyday practices and lived experience of conflict, in comparison, were mainly given attention in domains of literary representations (books and movies), personal interest, solidarity or morality. Recently, we have seen the emergence of conflict theory that accords central importance to everyday practices and politics.

From decolonisation until the early 1990s, conflicts were mainly analysed in terms of Cold War superpower rivalry. Since the 1990s, scholarly attention shifted to the local dynamics of the intra-state wars that broke out after the end of the Cold War (Kaldor 1999). Causes of conflict had to be found within societies: the different status of social groups, historically grown relations between ethnicities and the control over resources. The 1990s saw debate over the generalised root causes of such conflicts. Was greed or grievance dominant in generating conflict? Was conflict the result of resource scarcity or of resource abundance? These debates have given way to a recognition that conflicts are multi-causal and that the roots of specific conflict have to be understood in their own contexts and histories. Kalyvas (2003) points out how conflict plays out locally as 'convergence between local motives and supra-local imperatives, spanning the divide between the political and the private, the collective and the individual'. This view places everyday politics in the heart of conflict theory and analysis: conflict comes about and is being played out as the amalgam of these localised dynamics.

Conflict and peace are sometimes clear-cut situations, but more often they are labels that are socially constructed. Violent conflict has an enormous and traumatising impact on people and societies, and people know the difference between war and peace very well. They resent researchers who sanitise their situation and euphemistically speak of conflict, food insecurity and gender-based violence when they really mean war, hunger and rape. But acknowledging the suffering of war does not make the distinction between war and peace easier to draw. Conflict does not operate according to a single logic, and its drivers, interests and practices are redefined by actors creating their own localised and largely unintended conflict dynamics of varying intensity (Kalyvas 2006). This volume's understanding of conflict breaks through the binary of conflict and peace, and focuses instead of the everyday practices by which conflicts and peace are being 'done'.

Paul Richards (2005) argues that conflict is just one social project among many. Conflict situations are not the negative of peace, and there are many continuities and discontinuities within crisis situations. The transition from normality to crisis and back entails new ways of ordering and disordering of spaces, power, ritual, regulation and interaction. While much has been written, for example, about the economies of war, where the production, mobilisation and allocation of resources are organised to sustain the violence, there is a flip-side of this in the continuation of the normality of economies of production, transactions and distributions that we may call the economies of survival during crises. People hold on to normality as much as they can and continue planting their fields and trading their products. The different kinds of economies are deeply intertwined, and most activities are multi-faceted, creating new forms of economic life (Nordstrom 2004). Such social dynamics are crucial to the ways that conflicts evolve, alter and resolve and they can be unearthed through a focus on everyday practice. By studying everyday practices, it becomes apparent how the logics of violence, survival and reconciliation are renegotiated in their local context and how they work upon one another. It allows us to document these dynamics, explain their contradictions and bring the different stories of local actors' perceptions, interests and concerns to the surface.

Responses to crises

Crisis response often appears to be a matter of science, technology and the appropriate resources. However, under that surface we find that crisis response is social and highly political. It is shaped by the people, institutions and history of the context in which crises happen. Apart from the often controversial questions about whether there is indeed a crisis, what its causes are and what can be done about it, a most pertinent question is: *whose* crisis is it? Who has the authority to act? Most of the definitions of disaster incorporate the notion that disasters are situations that are too big to be handled by the directly affected (Alexander 1997). We are thus used to defining crisis as requiring extraordinary measures and often outside interventions. Within countries, crisis response is likely to create tensions between central authorities and the population. On the one hand, the protection of people can be seen as a core responsibility of governments. A lack of proper response evokes protests and can occasionally lead to revolution. On the other hand, we also see that central authorities use crises to enhance their legitimacy and to strengthen their grip over territories and populations, in ways that have little to do with the urgency of the situation.

In cases of political conflict, the dividing lines between legitimate authorities dealing with unruly rebels, and contested authorities who are challenged by equally legitimate opponents is very thin. While the international community considers the governments of the Democratic Republic of Congo (DRC) and Afghanistan as the legitimate authorities, this perspective may be different for local people who see little difference between government army atrocities and those of rebels or the Taliban. In the case of disasters caused by natural hazards, responses that are steered by state authorities often have a sub-text in aiming to modernise local communities or re-order their access. Mexican authorities tried to use the 1975 earthquake to drive poor people away from the city centre. *Sena* people living for centuries along the Zambezi river have found that their way of life has become unacceptable to authorities that use the recurring floods to impose a far-reaching resettlement programme (Artur and Hilhorst 2012). Since the establishment of the United Nations in 1948, and increasingly since the end of the Cold War, these questions are being reproduced at the level of the international community in relation to nation states. While the United Nations system provides individual countries with an umbrella to invoke when overcome by crises, this often turns into a reality where assistance becomes uninvited interference beyond the immediacy of the crisis.

International responses have strongly evolved in the past decades. International humanitarian aid, which dates back to 1859, has grown tremendously since 1989, in terms of volume, number of organisations and systems for information and communication (Walker and Maxwell 2009). Humanitarian aid has become very effective in saving lives. Famine in the twentieth century accounted, according to conservative estimates, for 130 million perished lives. Nowadays, a combination of measures for DRR and humanitarian response have led to a sharp reduction in the number of fatalities caused by humanitarian crises. At the same time, humanitarian aid is being criticised as never before. The problem is not with the core function of saving lives, but criticism abounds about the way that humanitarian aid is politicised, how transitions to development continue to be complicated, and how humanitarian organisations let organisational politics and competition interfere with their humanitarian principles.

How to find the appropriate response from among the enormous toolkit available internationally? Peacekeeping operations have evolved from restricted post-conflict monitoring to invasive operations where blue helmets or international troops actively engage in combat. The basic human rights conventions of 1948 are constantly evolving towards a complicated architecture of resolutions and implementing mechanisms, and the recent idea of the Responsibility to Protect and the International Criminal Court have further internationalised crisis response. Development politics have moved to more mature partnerships between countries, yet an increasingly large category of 'fragile states' continues to be subject to donor-driven interventions. Many of the political complications follow from different interpretations of situations and the appropriateness of different measures for these situations. The international community takes increasing responsibility for the human security of people over the responsibility of their national authorities. At the same time, we can ask fundamental questions about the power that the international community can muster to effectuate these functions (Chandler 2003). As we will elaborate below, the multiple realities of interventions are shaped by the context in which they occur and the interaction of a multitude of actors who socially negotiate, challenge, transform or accommodate the policies and programmes that aim to intervene in crisis situations.

Studying policy, institutions and interventions

This book deals with policy, institutions and interventions of conflict, disaster and societies in crisis. Its chapters are written by members of the Disaster Studies Group of Wageningen University, the Netherlands, on the occasion of the fifteenth anniversary of the group. Although we represent different backgrounds, expertise and interests, our approaches have much in common. We share our emphasis on everyday practice and politics and most of the chapters are based on empirical research in crisis-affected countries, mainly in Africa and Asia. To enhance the quality of our inquiries, we never rely solely on qualitative interviews coupled with quantitative data gathering. We find it essential to *observe* everyday practices, to enable us to detect the contradictions between the discursive claims of actors and the multiple realities created in everyday life. For the chapters of this book, data are therefore mainly gathered by ethnographic methods. Our focus on everyday practices allows research to be symmetrical and to break through dichotomies. We don't make a priori distinctions, for example, between powerful and power-less, between thinkers and implementers, or between technology and culture. Instead we find it important to establish empirically how power constellations are negotiated and how they are subject to change, what the social properties are of the formulation and implementation of policy and how both local knowledge and expert knowledge are specific and cultured.

As we want to follow the everyday politics of disaster, conflict and societies in crisis, the research underlying the chapters of this book is usually multi-sited. Multi-sited ethnography is designed to study contemporary local changes in culture and society (Marcus 1995). It acknowledges that such changes are being multiply produced in different sites. This resonates well with our domain of inquiry into how disasters are understood and acted upon, and how conflict evolves in interaction between local, national and international processes. Most of the chapters of this book are examples of multi-sited ethnographic research. The book can also be understood as one multi-sited ethnographic endeavour, as the chapters together weave a narrative of the social nature of disaster, conflict and crisis response. The book is divided into three parts, that focus on the everyday politics of policy practice; the institutional multiplicity of societies in crisis, and interventions meant to address disaster and conflict.

Policy speak and practice

Crises are social phenomena. There are always multiple ways in which crises can be understood and acted upon. This means that humanitarian crises attain their specific realities through the language and practices in which actors negotiate their meaning, communicate about them and develop and implement responses. Our field of interest is full of narratives: high-riding principles, political sound-bites, elaborate policies and apocalyptic media representations. Understanding the working of discourses of crises and crises response is therefore an indispensable element for analysing how people overcome humanitarian crises.

The chapters in this book all deal with policies and principles as socially negotiated. Humanitarian principles, for example, are interpreted differently by different actors and are more contextual than universal (Leader 2002, Minear 1999). They only become real through the way in which service providers interpret them and use them in their everyday practice (Hilhorst and Schmiemann 2002). Policies for peacekeeping, DRR, relief and reconstruction are the outcome of negotiating the definition of crisis and its solutions. Policy is the result of interaction between different stakeholders, who try to make policy fit their own perspectives of the problem and goals. Its implementation rarely follows the logic of the policy cycle model that views policy as the systematic pursuit of goals and the end result of a purposive course of action (Colebatch 2002). Instead, we view policies as processes (Mosse 2005) or emergent properties: the outcome of social negotiation in which involved actors aim to appropriate the project according to their own understanding, interests and ambitions.

This first part of the book comprises four chapters. Chapter 2 by Georg Frerks deals with the question of how competing definitions of war and peace have turned the conflict in Sri Lanka into a discursive battle that underpinned the violent encounters. This chapter, based on accumulated research of decades, outlines a discursive approach to war and peace based on prevailing discourses on the Sri Lankan conflict. After the Liberation Tigers of Tamil Eelam (LTTE's) defeat, the discursive battle continued on the nature of the future peace. Both the attempt to impose a victor's peace by the government and the struggle in the international arena over alleged war crimes became linked to contested notions of terrorism, self-determination, and human rights. The resulting discursive continuity between war and peace narratives complicated the government's policies for peacebuilding.

Chapter 3 by Luis Artur reconstructs the historical relationship between disaster and socio-political and economic realities in Mozambique. It asks how disasters and disaster responses co-shaped, or have been co-shaped by, the political and socio-economic agendas of the different actors involved. Building on an original reinterpretation of history, it argues that disasters played a crucial role in the formation and dissolution of traditional kingdoms, in shaping the colonial policies and interventions, and in keeping the Mozambique Liberation Front (Frente de Libertação de Moçambique, FRELIMO) in power. The chapter further analyses the current change in disaster management practice that resulted in paying attention to climate change.

Chapter 4 by Jan-Gerrit van Uffelen provides another historical account of politics of crisis in a specific context. It argues that the four decades-long quest for food security in Ethiopia has resulted in the de-disasterisation of Ethiopia's protracted food crisis. De-disasterisation refers to the process by which structural or recurrent crises become 'normalised' and are no longer framed or perceived as disasters. The chapter explores whether this de-disasterisation brings about ritual-ised policy that recycles responses to food insecurity by always presenting the same old wine in new bottles, or whether it brings about a structural change in policies to end the country's famine vulnerability and recurrent food crises. It concludes that Ethiopia's current Food Security Programme reflects important structural change but the disappointing rate of graduation – people who have successfully escaped food insecurity – suggests that additional structural change is needed in the form of a long term social protection strategy.

Chapter 5 by Jeroen Warner elaborates the themes put forward in the other chapters and contains an essay that builds on Ophir's (2010) notion of the politics of catastrophisation. The chapter applies 'securitisation' theory to the domain of disasters which are seen as a successful publicly accepted declaration of a vital threat. This is analysed in the context of the 'social contract' between authorities and citizens. The nature of political relations between state and society influence whether an event is declared a disaster, and what modality this will take, ranging from perceived heavy-handed interventionism to neglect. A disaster tests the resilience of political relations after a shock event and may lead to new contract terms.

Institutions and institutional multiplicity

Crises and their responses are institutionalised in very many and often conflicting ways. We view conflicts and disasters as breakpoints of social order, with a consid-erable degree of chaos and disruption, but they are also marked by processes of continuity and re-ordering, or the creation of new institutions and linkages. The institutionalised character of crises and responses is not always taken for granted. Starting with Anderson and Woodrow (1989), disaster response has for a long time been criticised for being premised on the total breakdown of local institutions and the supposed passivity of affected victims. Conflict policies have assumed that local economies and institutions are either destroyed or subsumed in the logic of violence and war. This idea that institutions cease to exist during conflict, leads to the notion that reconstruction can start with a *tabula rasa* or what Cramer (2006) aptly calls the 'great post-conflict makeover fantasy'. A primary reason to focus on institutions is thus to acknowledge that they should be taken into account as the basis for responses to crises. At the same time, we also need to acknowledge that the resilience of local institutions may be gravely undermined by prolonged crises, warning against overly romanticised ideas of local coping practices that would result in early withdrawal of support to the detriment of people's life chances (Serrano 2012).

During crisis situations, institutions may become more in flux, because of different factors that may include changing conditions as a result of violence and displacement, emerging new problems that cannot be resolved with existing mechanisms, a lack of legitimate state institutions, or rivalry between different sources of power.

In many crisis-affected areas, institutional and personal engagement are the same. Where states are weak or operate in so-called neo-patrimonial fashion, state functions are impersonalised and used for enabling and maintaining power bases around social networks. Contrary to the widely held belief that conflict-affected states are characterised by a lack of institutions, current insight reveals that the poor development of state-monopolised institutions leads to situations where multiple normative systems prevail and hybrid institutions evolve. Post-conflict societies often feature intense forms of institutional multiplicity (DiJohn 2008) in which state-endorsed institutions figure in a complex and fragmented landscape inhabited also by traditional institutions, citizen arrangements, armed groups and political movements contesting the state. The multiplicity of institutions may involve conflict, yet it also potentially affords local populations room to negotiate institutional arrangements.

Chapter 6 by Gemma van der Haar and Merel Heijke takes up the question of how such institutional multiplicity works out in practice, and what the social effects are that it produces on the ground. It focuses on a particular form of institutional multiplicity, namely 'parallel governance': those situations where two distinct sets of institutions exist, associated with competing political agendas, usually between states and their competitors. The chapter draws on two case studies of parallel governance in southern Kosovo and eastern Chiapas, Mexico. It shows, first, how the interaction of separate sets of institutions involves dynamics of confrontation as well as accommodation and mutual adjustment, and second, how the political agendas associated with, and embodied in, the parallel systems work out in the local governance arena.

Importantly, we consider international aid organisations and their interventions as part of the local institutional landscape. They do not operate outside of societies but are embedded in local realities. They '*exist in an arena of social actors with competing interests and strategies*' (Bakewell 2000: 104). Aid interlocks with social, economic and political processes in society, co-shaping local institutions and institutional transformation processes by working through, competing with or reinforcing them (Serrano 2012). Chapter 7 by Bram J. Jansen takes this up for the case of Kakuma refugee camp. Refugee camps are seen as seclusion sites in which refugees are little more than victims or cunning beneficiaries of aid, with little room to manoeuvre vis-à-vis the camp authorities. This image neglects processes of social organisation that take place among refugees within refugee camps. In Kakuma refugee camp, forms of parallel governance emerged, among different national and ethnic groups, with regard to various domains such as the camp economy, dispute resolution, politics, education, and other forms of camp-community based self-organisation. This chapter explores the development and emergence of multiple authorities that seek to contest, adapt or build on camp organisation.

Chapter 8 by Jeroen Cuvelier focuses on the 'social life of policies' in cases of institutional multiplicity. It deals with the unexpected outcomes of initiatives that aimed at breaking the link between mining and armed conflict in eastern DRC. It demonstrates that the processes of extracting and trading mineral resources are still shaped by what Utas (2005) has described as the politics of 'bigmanity'. Non-military strongmen at the local level have managed to retain the upper hand in the struggle for Kivu's mineral riches by developing multiple strategies and by drawing on multiple sources of power in an environment characterised by institutional multiplicity and hybrid political orders.

Chapter 9 by Maliana Serrano continues with the theme of interventions in situations of institutional multiplicity. It addresses the often neglected domain of intervention by churches or other religious institutions. It provides a case study of a local church in Bunjei in Angola and sheds light on the institutional arrange-ments besides formal state institutions that co-exist and are involved in addressing the needs of local people, from conflict resolution to basic service delivery. The chapter focuses on the prominent role of a local church – the Evangelical Congregational Church in Angola (IECA) – in local reconstruction and develop-ment processes. It shows that IECA's local position constantly evolves through legitimisation and de-legitimisation dynamics. These are affected by IECA's organisational characteristics and practices, and by those of alternative actors involved in the governance of social services, including other aid organisations and state institutions.

The last of this part, Chapter 10 by Timmo Gaasbeek, explores how conflict affects personal relations and may lead to changes in the institution of marriage. Drawing on extensive ethnographic research, the chapter looks at inter-ethnic marriages in a part of Sri Lanka's war zone. Mixed couples exemplify how ethnicity works at its margins. Unexpectedly, intermarriage has increased during conflict, mainly the result of conflict-induced mobility. Often under suspicion, mixed couples actively downplay their inter-ethnic nature and stay 'below the radar'. Most wives even change ethnicities. By highlighting this everyday pragma-tism, the chapter underscores the importance of looking at the smaller spaces of relationships and interactions which both link to, and depart from, wider contexts of conflict and disaster.

Arenas of interventions

The final part of the book deals with arenas of intervention. Conflict and disaster situations are usually dense with interventions, ranging from actions by local authorities, charity organisations, rescue workers, international aid agencies, military, journalists and even fortune seekers. This book conceives of aid as an integrated part of these everyday realities of crisis and post-crisis situations. Although aid volumes usually make up a very minor part of the resource flows in societies, in the locales of implementation, aid can strongly affect local power relations and (re)ordering processes. Aid interventions cannot be seen as the chain of implementation of pre-defined plans but the negotiated product of a series of interfaces between different social fields (Long and van der Ploeg 1989). As programmes gain meaning throughout formulation and implementation processes, they increasingly become part of local realities in many intended and unintended ways.

It is important to stretch the analyses of aid beyond single programmes, and study the effect of the *ensemble* of aid establishments and interventions (Hilhorst 2003). We are used to conceiving of the make-up of society as the relations between state, civil society, private sector and popular participation. The international aid establishments are left out of the equation, even though they have a strong and rather permanent presence in many places. Aid has become – in the words of Mark Duffield (2002) – a form of governance, and it is hard to tell how the negotiations over power and social contracts would evolve without international actors playing an intermediary or engineering role.

The final part starts with Chapter 11 by Dorothea Hilhorst and Bram J. Jansen which introduces the notion of humanitarian space as arena and elaborates our perspective on the everyday politics of aid. 'Humanitarian space' denotes the physical or symbolic space which humanitarian agents need in order to deliver their services according to the principles they uphold. This concept, which separates humanitarian action from its politicised environment, is widely used in policy documents and academic texts, even though empirical evidence abounds that this space is in fact highly politicised. This chapter explores how different actors use the concept and the language of humanitarian space and principles in the everyday politics of aid delivery and is based on two cases: a protracted refugee camp in Kenya and the tsunami response in Sri Lanka. It maintains that the humanitarian space is an arena where a multitude of actors, including humanitarians and recipients, shape humanitarian action.

Chapter 12, by Mathijs van Leeuwen, continues with this theme and focuses on the politics and practices of civil-society efforts for peacebuilding. Contemporary practices of peacebuilding through strengthening civil society are often criticised for failing to take account of the politics involved: they remain ambiguous on whose interests and what societal transformation they want to promote, yet implicitly underwrite particular development agendas, or unwittingly take sides in conflict. This chapter explores how peacebuilding interventions actually become political in everyday organising practices and the practices of interpreting conflict and defining interventions. If this politicisation is intentional, it not only originates from political and ideological choices vis-à-vis the context of conflict in which organisations operate, but as much from organisational politics of legitimisation.

Chapter 13 by Annelies Heijmans analyses the everyday politics of disaster risk reduction in Central Java, Indonesia. It deals with the internationally widely advocated domain of Community-Based Disaster Risk Reduction (CBDRR) where the knowledge and commitment of local people forms the backbone of efforts to render communities safe and resilient. The chapter argues that interpreting disasters and identifying risk reduction measures are negotiated and political processes. It concludes that there is no such thing as *the* CBDRR approach, but that one has to look beyond the binaries of top-down and bottom-up approaches to understand how in the 'political arena' DRR-actors negotiate the principles and meaning of their CBDRR approach.

Chapter 14 by Hilde van Dijkhorst dwells on another popular theme of aid interventions: Linking Relief Rehabilitation to Development (LRRD). The chapter analyses the multiple post-conflict recovery and LRRD approaches and processes in Angola, which do not necessarily build on one another, even running counter to one another. The chapter brings out that whereas LRRD approaches are based on the notion that post-conflict recovery follows a linear move from crisis to normality, in the case of Angola this linearity is not present. LRRD in Angola has overwhelmingly and uncritically been approached through seeds and tools interventions, displaying a narrow understanding of rural livelihood dynamics.

Aid agencies are part of the field of actors that together constitute the realities of crisis and survival, and the motives and attitudes of agencies deserve the same attention as the lifeworlds of local actors. This is taken up in the final chapter of this volume. Chapter 15 by Dorothea Hilhorst, Gemma Andriessen, Lotte Kemkens and Loes Weijers deals with mutual imaging of aid workers and aid recipients and the effects this has on aid legitimacy. The chapter explores how mutual imaging of aid workers and aid recipients in Nepal, Uganda and South Sudan affects aid legitimacy. Consistent with a perspective of aid as socially negotiated, the contextual and interactionist concept of imaging is used, rather than labelling (done to people), or perceptions (located in people's head). The chapter uses a Q-methodology that symmetrically researches different groups of actors by posing the same questions. It concludes that distinctions between aid workers and recipients are not clear-cut, that imaging is indeed important for legitimacy, and highlights the distinctive, ambiguous roles of community volunteers and incentive workers.

References

Alexander, D. (1997) 'The Study of Natural Disasters, 1977–1997; Some Reflections on a Changing Field of Knowledge'. *Disasters*, 21(4): 283–304.

Anderson, M. B. and P. J. Woodrow (1989) *Rising from the Ashes; Development Strategies in Times of Disaster*, Boulder: Westview Press.

Artur, L. and D. Hilhorst (2012) 'Everyday Realities of Climate Change Adaptation in Mozambique'. *Global Environmental Change*, 22: 529–536.

Bakewell, O. (2000) 'Uncovering Local Perspectives on Humanitarian Assistance and Its Outcomes'. *Disasters*, 24: 103–116.

Bankoff, G. and D. Hilhorst (2009) 'The Politics of Risk in the Philippines: Comparing State and NGO Perceptions of Disaster Management'. *Disasters* 33(4): 686–704.

Chandler, D. (2003) 'New Rights for Old? Cosmopolitan Citizenship and the Critique of State Sovereignty'. *Political Studies*, 51: 332–349.

Colebatch, H.K. (2002) *Policy (second edition). Concepts from the Social Sciences*. Buckingham: Open University Press.

Cramer, C. (2006) *Civil War is not a Stupid Thing. Accounting for Violence in Developing Countries*. London: Hurst & Co.

Devereux, S. (2009) 'The Malawi Famine of 2002'. *IDS Bulletin*, 33(4): 70–78.

DiJohn, J. (2008) *Conceptualising the Causes and Consequences of Failed States: A Critical Review of the Literature*, working paper Crisis States Research Centre.

Douglas, M. and A. Wildavsky (1982) *Risk and Culture. An Essay on the Selection of Technological and Environmental Dangers*. Berkeley/Los Angeles/London: University of California Press.

Duffield, M. (2002) 'Social Reconstruction and the Radicalisation of Development: Aid as a Relation of Global Liberal Goverance'. *Development and Change*, 33(5): 1049–1071.

Hewitt, K. (1983) *Interpretations of Calamity from the Viewpoint of Human Ecology*, The Risks and Hazards Series. Sydney: Allen & Unwin Inc.

Hilhorst, D. (2003) *The Real World of NGOs: Discourses, Diverstiy and Development*. London: Zed Books.

Hilhorst, D. and G. Bankoff (2004) 'Mapping Vulnerability'. In G. Bankoff, G. Frerks and D. Hilhorst (eds) *Mapping Vulnerability: Disaster, Development and People*, pp. 1–10. London: Earthscan.

Hilhorst, D. and N. Schmiemann (2002) 'Humanitarian Principles and Organizational Culture: Everyday Practice in Médicins Sans Frontières-Holland', *Development in Practice* 12(3/4): 490–500.

Howe, P. (2009) 'Archetypes of Famine and Response'. *Disasters*, 34(1): 30–54.

Kaldor, M. (1999) *New & Old Wars. Organized Violence in a Global Era*. Oxford: Polity Press.

Kalyvas, S. (2003) 'The Ontology of "Political Violence": Action and Identity in Civil Wars'. *Perspectives on Politics*, 1: 475–494.

Kalyvas, S. (2006) *The Logic of Violence in Civil War*. Cambridge: Cambridge University Press.

Kerkvliet, B. (2009) 'Everyday Politics in Peasant Societies (and ours)'. *Journal of Peasant Studies*, 36(1): 227–243.

Leader, Nicholas (2002) *The Politics of Principle: The Principles of Humanitarian Action in Practice*. London: Humanitarian Practice Network.

Long, N. and J.D. van der Ploeg (1989) 'Demythologizing Planned Intervention: An Actor Perspective', *Sociologia Ruralis*, XXIX, 3/4: 226–49.

Macrae, J. and A. Zwi (1992). 'Food as an Instrument of War in Contemporary African Famines: A Review of the Evidence'. *Disasters*, 16(4): 299–321.

Marcus, G. (1995) 'Ethnography in/of the World System: The Emergence of Multi-Sites Ethnography'. *Annual Review of Anthropology*, 24: 95–117.

Minear, Larry (1999) 'The Theory and Practice of Neutrality: Some Thoughts on the Tensions'. *International Review of the Red Cross*, 81(833): 63–71.

Mosse, D. (2005) *Cultivating Development: An Ethnography of Aid Policy and Practice*. London: Pluto Press.

Nordstrom, C. (2004) *Shadows of War. Violence, Power and International Profiteering in the Twenty-First Century*. Berkeley/Los Angeles: California University Press, 119–139.

O'Keefe, P., K. Westgate and B. Wisner (1976) 'Taking the "Natural" out of "Natural Disasters"'. *Nature*, 260 (15 April): 566–567.

Oliver-Smith, A. (1999) 'What is a Disaster?: Anthropological Perspectives on a Persistent Question', in A. Oliver-Smith and S. M. Hoffman (eds) *The Angry Earth: Disaster in Anthropological Perspective*, pp. 18–34. Routledge: London.

Ophir, A. (2010) 'Politics of Catastrophization. Roundtable: Research Architecture: A Laboratory for Critical Spatial Practices'. Online: http://roundtable.kein.org/node/1094 (Accessed 25 June 2012).

Pelling, M. and K. Dill, (2009) 'Disaster Politics: Tipping Points for Change in the Adaptation of Sociopolitical Regimes'. *Progress in Human Geography*, 1–17.

Richards, P. (2005) 'New War: An Ethnographic Approach'. In P. Richards (ed.) *No Peace, No War: An Anthropology of Contemporary Armed Conflicts*, pp. 1–21. Oxford, Ohio: James Currey, Ohio University Press.

Serrano, M. (2012) *Strengthening Institutions or Institutionalising Weaknesses? Interactions between Aid and Institutions in Huíla Province, Angola*, PhD thesis, Wageningen University.

Utas, M. (2005) 'Victimcy, Girlfriending, Soldiering: Tactic Agency in a Young Women's Social Navigation of the Liberian War Zone.' *Anthropological Quarterly*, 78(2): 403–430.

Walker, P. and D. Maxwell (2009) *Shaping the Humanitarian World*. London/New York: Routledge.

Wisner, B., P. Blaikie, T. Cannon and I. Davis (2004) *At Risk: Natural Hazards, People's Vulnerability and Disasters* (2nd edn). London: Routledge.

Part I
Policy speak and practice

2 Discourses on war, peace and peacebuilding in Sri Lanka

Georg Frerks

Introduction

Wars are not only fought with arms but also – and sometimes more importantly – with words. The successful discursive justification of war is crucial for the mobilisation of fighters, followers and those financing the war, as well as for gaining international recognition and support. Just as wars are fought in the discursive arena, so is peace. Peace is often heavily contested and controversial. 'What peace? Whose peace? Peace on what terms?' These are questions that come to mind.

This chapter advocates the relevance of a discursive approach to peace and war, and presents case study data on Sri Lanka. First, it introduces the discursive approach to conflict and gives a brief historical overview of the Sri Lankan conflict. Then, it summarises the multiplicity of discourses that have always accompanied the war between the Government of Sri Lanka (GoSL) and the Liberation Tigers of Tamil Eelam (LTTE).

After the defeat of the LTTE in May 2009, the Sri Lankan government has tried to promote its own particular interpretation of the LTTE's struggle and of the role of the international community and non-governmental organisations (NGOs) during the war. It also outlined a particular vision of Sri Lanka's future in peace, and the peacebuilding process needed to achieve it. Though promoted with the massive power and political predominance of the current government, this vision failed to convince all stakeholders. In effect, despite the radically changed military and political situation on the ground, there seems to be a fair continuity of discourse from the war period up to the present. In that sense, the government's attempt to attain discursive hegemony over competing discourses backfired. The same applied to the international arena, where a discursive struggle was fought over the end of the war and alleged war crimes and crimes against humanity. Though the discourses discussed have local origins, they are linked to international debates, such as those concerning terrorism, self-determination and human rights. This has complicated the government's efforts to promote its own storyline, despite its attempts to call into question the motives of the international and local actors that engaged in the debates with them.

Discursive approaches to conflict

Emergence of discourse in conflict studies

Derived from linguistics, the notion of discourse has been adopted in philosophy, social sciences and conflict studies. 'Conflict as constructed discourse' has become one significant way of understanding conflict. Early work on social movements and mobilisation already underlined the importance of framing to achieve collective action (McAdam *et al.* 1996). The book *Discourses on Violence: Conflict Analysis Reconsidered* by Jabri (1996) has put the 'discursive structuration and legitimation of war' and the idea of 'exclusionary discourse' firmly on the agenda of conflict studies. Apter's edited volume on the legitimisation of violence (1997) and the idea of 'violent imaginaries' coined by Schmidt and Schröder (2001) have also been important contributions to the discursive analysis of conflict. Bhatia showed how the 'politics of naming' worked, and 'how words were seen to be of equal power to bombs' by movements and governments (2005: 6).

The Sri Lankan conflict through the lens of discourse

In this chapter, I look at conflict and peace in Sri Lanka as socially constructed phenomena that are, to a significant degree, based on perceptions and discourses. Discourse, as a system of representation, attributes meaning and frames how actors understand and relate to the world around them. I look at how actors in Sri Lanka or 'discursive communities' manufactured representations of 'reality' and used discourse in the articulation of political grievances, for mobilising support for armed struggles and for legitimising them. Through discourse, they have interpreted and reinterpreted the past, defined the image of the enemy, and reshaped social identities and boundaries.

For example, the designation, by a series of mainly western states and the GoSL, of the LTTE from a militant movement into a terrorist organisation during the so-called War on Terror has affected its political stature, fundraising and room for manoeuvre. Nadarajah and Sriskandarajah (2005) describe the 'politics of naming' by the Sri Lankan state that created an opportunity to denounce the Tamil discourse and to criminalise the LTTE. On the other hand, the discursive construction of the *Eelam* homeland and the right to self-determination by the LTTE can very well be analysed discursively.

Discourse and peacebuilding

Discourse analysis has also been used to analyse policy making, including by Hansen (2006) on the Western debate on Bosnia, by Frerks (2007, 2008) on donor policies on the Diplomacy, Defence and Development (3-D) or 'comprehensive' approach and on human security, and by Bastian (2007) on the politics of foreign aid in Sri Lanka. Similarly, peacebuilding operations by donors and NGO activities are subject to discursive manufacturing and contestation (Bush 2004,

Chandler 2009, Duffield 2007). This has been obvious in the case of the so-called 'liberal peace' in countries ranging from Sierra Leone, Burundi, Iraq and Afghanistan to Sri Lanka, to mention only a few (Goodhand *et al.* 2011, Stokke and Uyangoda 2011). 'Western' or 'imperialist intentions' behind such 'aid' and 'peacebuilding' efforts were 'exposed', suspicions of religious conversion and financial malpractices raised, and general xenophobia and hostility promoted. In Sri Lanka, NGOs have been accused of 'recolonising' the country (Goonatilaka 2006). The attempts of the United Nations to discuss the end of the war and the post-war efforts in Sri Lanka have raised vehement protests by the GoSL. On 15 March 2012, thousands of protesters flocked onto the streets of Colombo shouting slogans against the UN. There has also been an academic debate on those issues. Talentino (2007) shows how negative perceptions and resentments against externally enforced change have developed in the context of peace-building. The Sri Lankan author Rajasingham-Senanayake (2003) has criticised the 'post-conflict industry' in relation to the conflict in Sri Lanka.

Discourse in action

Fairclough (2005) demonstrates how discourses help constitute and consolidate economic and political systems. His critical discourse analysis highlights the performative aspect of discourse and the power it engenders. Critical discourse analysis enables us to see 'what discourse does', or, as Jones and Norris (2005) have called it, 'discourse as action'. Discourse does not only operate at an abstract level, as 'representations' or 'discourse reduced to discourses' (Fairclough 2005: 58). On the contrary, discourse constitutes 'power-to-define' and is translated into concrete social actions. As Jabri (1996: 94–95) has highlighted,

> Social texts do not merely reflect or mirror objects, events and categories pre-existing in the social and natural world. Rather they actively construct a version of those things. They do not describe things, they do things. And being active, they have social and political implications.

The performative aspect of discourse can be studied by analysing how local actors translate international or national discourses in practice and how these are appropriated, contested and reframed in local settings. In this way, discourse analysis can, for example, help us understand how the post-conflict situation is organised and why it succeeds or fails. Discourse analysis may also help design strategies to deal with entrenched exclusionary discourses, for example, by bridging differences between opponents, identifying emergent alternative discourses or reframing the original conflict in a peaceful direction (Frerks and Klem 2005: 43–44).

So far, little empirical work exists on discursive practices in post-conflict situations and peacebuilding. While there is some insight as to how discourse helps manufacture war, the capability of discourse analysis for designing peaceful strategies is still in its infancy.

An overview of the Sri Lankan conflict

Though the conflict between the GoSL and the LTTE had long historical roots in pre-colonial, colonial and post-independence developments and government policies (Silva 2005), it surfaced as an overt violent conflict in July 1983, when 13 Sinhalese soldiers were ambushed by the LTTE in Tirunelveli in north Sri Lanka. Riots broke out in Colombo killing hundreds, if not thousands, of Tamils, and damaging the homes and livelihoods of many more. The violence in Colombo was planned with the participation of politicians and government staff, and with the use of government vehicles. The rioters also had voters' lists and the addresses of Tamil house and shop-owners (Tambiah 1996: 94–97). This episode started a full-blown war that was to last more than 25 years and ended with the defeat of the LTTE on 17 May 2009.

Political background to the conflict

The violent conflict was a culmination of the growing tensions between consecutive Sinhalese-dominated governments and increasingly radicalising Tamil groups that started to fight for an independent state for the Tamil population, called *Tamil Eelam,* from the mid-1970s onwards. Though Tamil political parties had demanded a federal system from 1949, no tangible progress had been achieved. In fact, several pacts concluded between the Tamil Federal Party (FP) leader Chelvanayakam and subsequent Sri Lankan prime ministers were withdrawn due to Sinhalese resistance. The idea of a separate Tamil state arose especially in response to the 1972 Constitution that provided primacy to the Sinhalese language and Buddhist religion. In 1976 the Tamil United Liberation Front (TULF) resolved at its first national convention, held in Vaddukoddai,

> that the restoration and reconstitution of the Free, Sovereign, Secular, Socialist state of *Tamil Eelam* based on the right of self-determination inherent in every nation has become inevitable in order to safeguard the very existence of the Tamil nation in this country.
>
> (Satchi 1983: 185, quoted in Sitrampalam 2005: 205)

Escalation towards armed militancy

Disillusionment with the ineffectual elder Tamil leadership, diminished prospects for education and employment and grievances originating from discriminatory government measures, had led to a quick radicalisation and organisation of Tamil youths. Militant factions had acquired arms and guerrilla training, reportedly with the help of India. Over the years the LTTE forcefully gained dominance over the other Tamil militant groups to the point where it claimed to be 'the sole representative of the Tamil-speaking population'. It started to engage in armed skirmishes on a significant scale with the Sri Lankan army from the late seventies onwards, and President Jayewardene proscribed the movement in 1978.

He passed the Prevention of Terrorism Act in 1979, giving extraordinary powers to the police and army, which reportedly led to extra-judicial killings and disappearances.

Indian involvement (1985–1990)

After failed Indian mediation initiatives in Thimpu, Bhutan and Bangalore, the Indian and Sri Lankan governments under the leadership of Prime Minister Rajiv Gandhi and President Jayewardene concluded the Indo-Lanka Accord in 1987, leading to the deployment of an Indian Peace Keeping Force (IPKF) to enforce a ceasefire. The militant Tamil groups were, however, not party to the Accord, and only reluctantly agreed. Yet, as soon as the Indian forces arrived, they came to be seen as enemies by the movement. Alleged abuses by the IPKF led to resentment among the Tamil population, while it was unable to counter the LTTE's guerrilla warfare. The Indian presence was also unpopular among many Sinhalese, and in 1988 Ranasinghe Premadasa was elected president on an anti-IPKF ticket. He requested the Indians to leave the country while secretly arming the Tigers to fight the IPKF. The IPKF ended in failure and the last Indian forces left the country in 1990, leaving large caches of weapons and ammunition that fell into the hands of the LTTE.

Continuation of violent conflict (1990–2002)

However, tensions between the LTTE and the Premadasa government grew quickly, marking the start of 'Eelam War II' by the LTTE. The government commenced a counter-insurgency campaign, including the bombing of Jaffna. The LTTE now also began targeting Muslims, the forced expulsion of about 120,000 Muslims from the Northern Province in 1990 being the most dramatic example. The LTTE killed Indian Prime Minister Rajiv Gandhi in 1991, in a notorious attack by female suicide bomber Dhanu. The LTTE also assassinated several Sri Lankan ministers and ex-ministers. The violence worsened, with countless massacres, disappearances and political killings in which both sides seemed to be equally involved. In 1993 a suicide bomber killed Prime Minister Premadasa.

Though Chandrika Bandaranaike Kumaratunga won the 1994 presidential elections on a peace agenda, talks between the government and the LTTE failed in April 1995, and 'Eelam War III' started. The Government answered with its 'War for Peace', including an all-out attack on Jaffna city, leading to massive displacement of the local population. The 'War for Peace' aimed at forcing the LTTE to the negotiation table while formulating a devolution package to address the political differences. However, the proposed constitutional reform was never able to get the required parliamentary support from the opposition, while its 'diluted' contents were also rejected by the LTTE. In the meantime, violence between the parties continued during the second half of the 1990s, with the LTTE able to recapture parts of the areas lost in 1995, including the strategic Elephant

Pass. In areas under its control, the LTTE had set up its own administrative structures in key sectors, such as the police, the judiciary and tax collection, while allowing the continuation of the Sri Lankan state services in the general administration and the provision of social services. These state services, however, functioned in close collaboration with, if not under the complete control of, the LTTE.

Ceasefire Agreement (2002–2008)

A Ceasefire Agreement (CFA) was brokered on 23 February 2002 by the Norwegian Government and monitored by the Sri Lanka Monitoring Mission (SLMM). The new government under United National Party (UNP) Prime Minister Ranil Wickramasinghe de-proscribed the LTTE and engaged in peace talks with the movement. Within a year, six rounds of peace talks were held in various parts of the world. In April 2003, however, the LTTE suspended its participation in the talks, citing its exclusion from a donor meeting in Washington (the LTTE was proscribed in the US) and the lack of sincerity on behalf of the government as the main reasons. Instead, the LTTE presented its own proposal on an Interim Self-Governing Authority (ISGA) for the north-east in October 2003, which raised fury and anxiety among the Sinhalese. After a tumultuous political period, the UNP government collapsed and lost the subsequent parliamentary elections to Mahinda Rajapakse who became Prime Minister in 2004 and was elected President in 2005. Rajapakse realised that the 'War on Terror' had reframed the conflict and how the LTTE was perceived internationally (irrespective of its having no factual link to 9/11) and he capitalised on this by systematically referring to them again as 'terrorists'.

The CFA was in the meantime characterised by numerous violations. Amidst protracted violence in the east, the tsunami hit the Sri Lankan shores on 26 December 2004. The unprecedented disaster seemed to have a brief fraternalising effect, but then relief and reconstruction aid became subject to political manoeuvering. The envisaged joint government-LTTE mechanism for the administration of tsunami aid in the north and east, the so-called Post-Tsunami Operational Management Structure (PTOMS), was never implemented due to constitutional constraints and opposition from the extreme nationalistic JanathaVimukthi Peramuna (JVP, People's Liberation Front). In the end, the tsunami experience deepened rather than helped overcome the political conflict (Frerks and Klem 2011).

Military closure of the war (2009)

After the defection of Karuna and his followers from the LTTE in 2004, the balance of power in the eastern part of the island shifted to the GoSL. In 2007, President Rajapakse was able to regain military control of the East and evict the LTTE and after that, the tables turned against the LTTE. The GoSL formally abrogated the CFA and the associated SLMM to pursue a military solution to the conflict. A bloody military campaign with high military and civilian losses led finally to the defeat of the LTTE and the complete extinction of its military and political leadership in May 2009, including its leader Vellapullai Prabhakaran. Total victory was claimed by President Rajapakse and a post-conflict period of reconstruction was ushered in that was to deal with the political and military exigencies of the situation and the socio-economic reconstruction of the war-affected areas. Meanwhile, an intense debate had erupted between the GoSL, international NGOs and the international community on whether the Sri Lankan army engaged in war crimes or crimes against humanity (see page 30).

The last period of the war resulted in possibly 40,000 casualties and about 300,000 internally displaced persons (IDPs), mainly Tamils from the North fleeing from the violence. They were housed in so-called welfare camps in the Vavuniya District, while being checked on their affiliation with the LTTE. The GoSL provided basic needs such as temporary shelter, food, water, sanitation and medicine, but came under international criticism for the alleged deficiency of the aid provided and the time it took to conduct the security screening. Also the cash grant for the returnees was considered inadequate for the recovery of lost assets. The government started de-mining the war-affected areas, clearing the ground for resettlement and the resumption of agriculture. Children and young people forcibly conscripted by the LTTE were rehabilitated in centres around the country. The majority were released back to their families at the completion of their rehabilitation period.

Cost of war

The war caused more than 80,000 casualties, of which 27,000 were soldiers from the Sri Lankan armed forces, one million people fled the country, and some 800,000 people were internally displaced. The conflict also undermined the economic stability and development of the conflict areas and of the country as a whole. It has been calculated that Sri Lanka's Gross Domestic Product (GDP) per capita could have been about US$ 500 higher if there had been no war. The war further affected Sri Lanka's erstwhile good human rights record and led to the militarisation of society (Mel 2007). It also led to increased ethnic and social divisions and mutual distrust, as well as economic disparities between the war zones and the rest of the country.

Discourses on the Sri Lankan conflict

Apart from these historic facts and events per se, there is a variety of explanatory discourses on the conflict. Frerks and Klem and their research partners at four Sri Lankan universities collected studies, articles and stories on the Sri Lankan conflict (Frerks and Klem 2005) and organised workshops where these were discussed. These materials represent the major prevailing narratives on the conflict in the country. I briefly summarise below the nine main discourses on the Sri Lankan conflict that were distinguished in this publication.[1]

The 'Duttagamini' discourse

The history of Sri Lankan Buddhism is described in mythological accounts and chronicles. The most famous of these chronicles, the *Mahavamsa* (Geiger 2003), describes the succession of Sinhalese kings from the sixth century BC to the fourth century AD. The task of those kings is the protection of Buddhism against invasions from the Indian peninsula. The 'heroic' resistance and victory of King Duttagamini over King Elara and 30 other Tamil princes are archetypical for Sinhala-Buddhism. 'When he had thus overpowered thirty-two Damila kings, Duttagamini ruled over Lanka in single sovereignty' (Mahavamsa, Chapter XXV, 'The Victory of Duttagamini'). The *Mahavamsa* narrative has a large influence on contemporary Sri Lankan politics and imaginaries of conflict, where Tamils are perceived as the current equivalent of King Elara. Giving in to Tamil demands for autonomy would undo the heroic deeds of Duttagamini and other Sinhalese kings. The guardian role for Sinhala-Buddhism has now been taken up by the *Sangha* (Buddhist clergy) and Sinhalese politicians. Quoting Tambiah, Gunasekera (2005: 82) observes that Buddhism thus gradually developed into a political force that limited friendly engagement with other religions and strongly opposed concessions towards the Tamils.

The Sinhalese grievances discourse

This discourse focuses on the grievances of the Sinhalese, asserting that colonial rulers gave preference to the Tamil minority in order to dominate the majority in a game of divide and rule. The over-representation of the Tamils in the colonial bureaucracy and their high educational standards are quoted as examples. Putting Sinhalese first in post-independence government policy is, therefore, only considered a fair and logical consequence of past injustices. This discourse also emphasises that innocent Sinhalese suffered from terrorist attacks at the hands of Tamil rebels and were killed, intimidated or driven away from their homes. All in all, this discourse, among others, promoted by the JVP, attributes the conflict to groundless claims by the Tamil minority and posits a legitimate attempt of the majority to defend their rights and correct wrongs of the past.

The failed nation-building discourse

This discourse, prevailing among moderate intellectual sections of all ethnic groups, attributes the conflict to the failure to establish a Sri Lankan nation. In the establishment of the independent Sri Lankan state, ethnic identities prevailed over an encompassing Sri Lankan nationalism. Political agendas came to be drawn along ethnic lines and symbols – such as the flag, the anthem, national holidays and festivals – came to be a reflection of Sinhalese culture. The language policy which declared Sinhalese as the only official language in 1956 further alienated the minorities, and was compounded by educational, land and economic policies. This provided a breeding ground for resistance, Tamil militancy and ultimately war. The rivalry between the two major political parties – the United National Party (UNP) and the Sri Lanka Freedom Party (SLFP) – also prevented a moderate approach as they vied for support among the same Sinhalese electorate and allied with more radical parties and Buddhist elements that demanded a strong pro-Sinhalese agenda.

The neo-colonialism and state terrorism discourse

Rather than the unfortunate mismanagement of the ethnic issue, many Tamils saw the situation described above as a 'master-minded' attempt by Sinhalese-dominated governments to occupy, exploit and oppress them. For them, 'independence' was only the replacement of one colonial power – the British – by another – the Sinhalese. S.J.V. Chelvanayakam, a leading Tamil politician, described Sinhalese-dominated rule as 'neo-colonialism'. He blamed the government for inflicting violence, starvation and death on the Tamils. In 1974 he concluded that

> The Tamils have traversed a long road and are now at the end of their tether. When two nations cannot get on together they come to the parting of ways. Has the parting come? That is the problem of the Tamils of Ceylon.
> (Chelvanayakam 2005: 279)

The LTTE argued that oppression by the state left them no alternative but armed struggle. 'The Tamil struggle for self-determination took a monumental turn from a pacifist Gandhian non-violent agitation [. . .] into a radical revolutionary armed campaign' (LTTE 2005: 295). The LTTE stated further that 'The oppression practised against the Tamils by the Sri Lankan regimes can only be characterised as a blatant form of genocide' (LTTE 2005: 294). The Tigers assigned to the government a conscious intention to eradicate the Tamils. 'The oppression was not simply an expression of racial prejudice, but a well-calculated genocidal plan aimed at the gradual and systematic destruction of the basic foundations of the Tamil national formation' (LTTE 2005: 293). The LTTE framed state governance as deliberate aggression and referred to notions such as 'self-determination', 'genocide' and 'state terrorism' to provide justification for the 'armed resistance'.

The homeland discourse

Tamil writers refer to the age-old presence of Tamils on the island and the historic existence of the separate kingdom of Jaffna, while using notions such as 'homeland' and 'self-determination'. In this larger picture, the unity of Sri Lanka is no more than a historic interlude in a long period of a separate Tamil entity. Documents written by colonial authors are used to prove that both the Portuguese and Dutch administrations acknowledged the separate identity of the Tamils and respected their independence until the British subordinated the Tamil entity to the larger whole of Sri Lanka:

> [The kingdoms of Kotte, Kandy and Jaffna] which were isolated from each other and administered as separate areas, were brought together into one

administrative unit by the British in 1833. This was done for reasons of administrative convenience without the consent of the peoples of the island. [. . .] In this way they brought together two peoples who had lived separately through the ages.

(Chelvanayakam 2005: 276)

The LTTE embraced a similar view:

We have a homeland, a historically constituted habitation with a well-defined territory embracing the Northern and Eastern Provinces, a distinct language, a rich culture and tradition, a unique economic life and a lengthy history extending to over three thousand years.

(LTTE 2005: 299)

This historic discourse propagates the view that independence is an *inherent* and *inalienable* right of the Tamil people. The frequently cited term 'self-determination' is essential in this account. In the words of the LTTE, this principle 'upholds the sacred right of a nation to decide its own political destiny, a universal principle enshrined in the UN Charter that guarantees the right of a people to political independence' (LTTE 2005: 292).

The Muslim discourse

The arrival of Arabic settlers in Sri Lanka is dated from the fifth century onwards. After the birth and death of 'the Prophet', these traders became Muslims. In the north and east, they married Tamil women and still share many social character-istics with the Tamils, such as the dowry system and the Tamil language. Given the extensive integration of the Muslims in the Tamil community, they even have been described as 'Islamic Tamils' (Abdullah 2005: 187).

Muslim authors, however, view the Muslims as a distinct group. With the ethnici-sation of politics after independence and the escalation of violence since 1983, a true Muslim discourse has emerged. The Muslims have allied themselves both with the Sri Lankan government and with militant Tamil groups. Like the Tamils, the Muslims experienced damaging government policies in the fields of education, language, employment, distribution of development assets and the colonisation of lands. In the early years of Tamil militancy, young Muslims even joined the ranks of those rebel groups. The Muslims, however, also faced hostility from the LTTE, such as in the Kaththankudi and Eravur incidents where Muslims were killed by Tamil militants while praying in their mosque. The large-scale expulsion of Muslims in 1990 from the Northern Province also has left a deep historical scar and was experi-enced as 'ethnic cleansing' (Ismail *et al.* 2005: 196). Having suffered both from govern-ment discrimination and Tamil aggression, the Muslims felt caught between the two. Suspicious of both sides, their sense of ethnic identity has strengthened and they started to organise themselves politically to the point of advocating relative autonomy for the areas they inhabited under the banner of self-determination (Fazil 2005).

The 'Batticaloa discourse'

Though often lumped together with the Tamils in general, the Eastern Tamils seem to have their own perspective. The defection of Karuna – former LTTE commander in the east – and his supporters from the movement was more than a political incident. The Batticaloa Tamils distinguish themselves from the Jaffna Tamils with a somewhat different dialect, a more agrarian culture and differences in caste. The perceived domination by the Jaffna Tamils is a historical grievance among the eastern Tamils. The eastern grievances ultimately have worked their way into the LTTE, even though they have been suppressed for a long time. The extensive recruitment of combatants in the east, the numerous losses of young eastern Tamils in northern battles and the very limited number of eastern Tamils occupying leading positions in the movement (one out of thirty) further reinforced the 'Batticaloa discourse' of exploitation, suffering and sacrifice.

Discourses of social revolution

All the discourses above had a salient ethnic dimension. Other discourses are grounded in non-ethnic ideologies of social injustice and political change. The JVP asserts that there is no conflict of ethnicity. The grievances are one and the same for all people of the country and they see it as 'a crisis of the capitalist system itself' (Ranaweera and Abeyratne 2005: 62). The Sri Lankan Marxist movement originally cut across ethnic divisions as well. The movement involved both the Sinhalese masses and the plantation Tamils of the hill country.

Similar to the JVP, the LTTE has also propagated a 'social revolution'. Though deeply entrenched in Tamil culture and history, the LTTE voiced its commitment to the 'total eradication' of the 'oppressive [caste] system', a 'social evil that perpetuates inequality and inhumanity' (LTTE 2005: 300). In addition, the movement propagated the emancipation of women and progressive environmental policies. They publicly denunciated the dowry system and promoted equality of women and their inclusion in the cadre structure of the movement.

It has been suggested that the JVP and the LTTE are very similar, as both have adopted an agenda of socio-economic revolution and engaged in violent combat with the government. Both movements consisted largely of dissatisfied youths who have denounced the politics of the elitist representation as ineffective and unjust. In this connection, traditional culture, including the caste system and hierarchical family relations, the important role of student unions, limited social mobility and high unemployment are all relevant factors in understanding the LTTE and the JVP.

The peace and harmony discourse

Donors and NGOs, such as development organisations and religious movements, were strong advocates of this discourse. Their view is that peaceful solutions are better and more rational than violent solutions. They argue that misunderstanding, lack of respect and mistrust are the crucial problem. This can be overcome through exchange, cultural festivals, reconciliation workshops and the teaching of non-violent principles. However, there is a potential tension between the underlying principles of the peace discourse and existing grievances and injustice. The agencies involved tend to avoid questions regarding rights and injustice. These issues are subordinated to the greater goal: peace. As a result, the mantra of peace, respect and harmony may take on the character of peace propaganda.

The peace discourse is, to a large extent, grounded in traditional and religious principles. The Hindu principle of Ahimsa, the Buddhist philosophy of non-violence, Islamic views of peaceful co-existence and Christian compassion are often mentioned as the inspiring source of peace initiatives. Supporters of the peace discourse emphasise the commonalities between religions and highlight that the different ethnic groups of the island were traditionally peace-loving people who lived in harmony at local level. These sentiments were echoed during our field research by a number of local-level civil society organisations that stressed that the conflict and ethnic disharmony were brought to their villages from outside, especially by 'politicians promoting their own interests'.

The peace movement seems to have revived during the conflict, as the devastating impact of the war led to a search of non-violent alternatives. In addition, the role of external organisations and donors has been vital. During the 1990s, and especially during the CFA period, peacebuilding became a popular field of activity among donors with substantial funding made available for agencies in this field. Techniques such as non-violent communication and non-violent conflict resolution were introduced to Sri Lanka.

Discourses on peace and peacebuilding in Sri Lanka

The Government of Sri Lanka defeated the LTTE on 17 May 2009. Though some theoreticians state that military defeat produces a more stable situation than a negotiated peace, others claim that a 'victor's peace' imposed by one side sows the seeds for recurring conflict. Whatever the case may be, recent data show that three-quarters of all conflicts of the last ten years have been recurrences of earlier conflicts (Hewitt *et al.* 2010: 1). Whereas post-war moments can be a window of opportunity for establishing stability, justice, reconciliation and development, this opportunity is often squandered. As Darby and McGinty (2000, 2008) show, the 'management of peace' is full of obstacles. Factors contributing to failure include ignoring fundamental conflict issues and key actors, weak institutions, flawed reconstruction programmes, continuation of corrosive violence, lack of economic development, and failure to enter into negotiations and strike deals (Darby and McGinty 2008: 352–372).

For the Sri Lankan government, the issue is straightforward. A democratically elected government was attacked by a group of separatist terrorists and had the full right to defend itself and the country. Now, with the LTTE defeated and its leadership killed, there is, in the government's view, no problem left. In an address to the Inter-Parliamentary Union (IPU), Sri Lanka's Irrigation and Water Resources Management Minister, Nimal Siripala de Silva, said:

All Sri Lankans are now enjoying the benefits of peace [that] dawned after defeating the ruthless terrorism and assured that Sri Lanka will not allow to raise the ugly head of terrorism again in this beautiful island in the Indian ocean.[2]

The thing to be done now, according to the government, is the development of the war-affected areas, the resettlement of the displaced population and the rehabilitation and reintegration of ex-LTTE fighters, which it claims to be doing energetically. Sri Lanka's Minister of External Affairs stated:

In light of the results already achieved on the ground in respect of a wide range of issues including resettlement of internally displaced persons, the rehabilitation of ex-combatants, and the revival of the economy of those parts of the country specially affected by the conflict, these represent a degree of progress which far exceeds what has been accomplished in comparable post-conflict situations in other regions of the world.[3]

The government reintegrated 10,375 former combatants into society, out of the total of 11,700 LTTE cadres that have surrendered to, or were arrested by, the security forces.[4]

The government has promoted its own discourse vehemently, both nationally and internationally, and has rejected the allegations that have been raised about the way the Sri Lankan troops concluded the war. A Panel of Experts was appointed by the UN Secretary General to look into the alleged violations of international humanitarian and human rights law during the final stages of the armed conflict in Sri Lanka and to advise him on an accountability process according to international standards; it has asserted that the allegations of human rights violations (by both sides to the conflict) are credible, and therefore called for further investigation both of the Sri Lankan government and the LTTE (UN 2011). The Sri Lankan authorities have totally rejected the UN Panel report and claimed that any further steps on the basis of recommendations of the report would undermine reconciliation and endanger the peace that has reigned on the island over the past two years. The government alleged that the report was not based on credible information sources. It has also rejected several other accusations that have been expressed by the donor community, national and international NGOs, and observers and journalists from Sri Lanka and abroad. In fact, the government has criticised foreign NGOs and donors for being partial in the conflict, sometimes even suggesting a 'western conspiracy' against the country and its government.

In April 2012, it mobilised all its diplomatic resources to prevent the acceptance of a US-sponsored Resolution at the UN Human Rights Council in the face of what Mahinda Samarasinghe, the President's Special Envoy on Human Rights, called a 'a systematic and organised campaign aimed at distorting and misinforming this Council and the outside world of the situation in Sri Lanka'.[5] In his address to the IPU, Minister de Silva said that:

> While the government is taking every possible step to speed up economic development, restore human rights and democracy after the war's end, the LTTE diaspora has launched a campaign to discredit the government in the eyes of the international community

and he urged the IPU delegates not to be deceived by the misleading and malicious campaign against Sri Lanka by the LTTE rump.[6] Domestically, as well, the government did not allow much criticism. Human rights defenders were attacked in the state media and have felt intimidated and threatened.[7] Offices of critical newspapers were attacked or set ablaze, but no culprits were identified or arrested.

Despite all the government's efforts to impose its own discourse vis-à-vis the course of events in the three years after the LTTE's defeat, several alternative discourses have sprung up, some of them being in fact continuations of the discourses on the Sri Lankan conflict that I reviewed in the earlier section of this chapter.

The various alternative discourses state that the victorious government in Sri Lanka has behaved in a too triumphant manner and hardly reached out to the Tamil (or Muslim) minority. Because the government has refused to look seriously into the alleged war crimes, it is felt that impunity reigns and no clean beginning for reconciliation can be achieved. Neither has the government shown initiative to redress any of the root causes and grievances underlying the original conflict. In this context it is argued that the government denies the complex historical genesis of the conflict and exonerates past and present Sinhalese-dominated governments from any wrongdoing. Others have argued that no significant post-conflict reconstruction has started in many conflict-affected areas, and that many families are still living under difficult, if not desperate, conditions. Investments have centred on physical infrastructure and less on economic development and the restoration of livelihoods. The hoped-for peace dividends are still far removed from actual experience, it is argued.

Duffield (2007) states that western interventionist discourses emanate from a metropolitan desire to rule the world. He argues that western humanitarian and peace interventions are primarily technologies of power aimed at controlling people living on the margins of global society. The more radical criticisms with regard to Sri Lanka state that the peacebuilding efforts of the government are in effect a tool for control and domination, reminding us of Duffield's critiques on western-imposed peacebuilding in so-called 'borderlands' and 'fragile states', but applied here to the domestic scene.

The current criticisms of the Sri Lankan government largely reflect the state terrorism and neo-colonialism discourses that I mentioned above and suggest that the victorious government is trying to establish full Sinhalese domination in the northern and eastern Tamil and Muslim areas by a variety of measures. Based on interviews in Sri Lanka, the International Crisis Group (ICG) refers, for example, to the military presence in those areas that reportedly amounts to a serious militarisation of society, installing full Sinhalese control and surveillance over the administration and civil society, and leading to a climate of fear (International Crisis Group 2012a and 2012b), something the President has denied in his address at the 3rd Victory Day parade on 19 May 2012 (*Sunday Observer* 2012: 13). Another ICG report has outlined the alleged consequences of this military presence for local women (International Crisis Group 2011). Also it mentions that those areas are governed increasingly by Sinhalese civil servants, often hand-picked by the highest political authority. Further allegations include the changing of the demographic composition of the area by stimulating the settlement of Sinhalese or condoning the occupation of land in the north and east by Sinhalese. The ICG refers to a strategy of changing 'the facts on the ground' (International Crisis Group 2012a: I, 19). It also has been observed that contracts and invest-ments in the area are largely in the hands of Sinhalese businessmen or military personnel and not with local Tamils or Muslims. The ICG finally mentions a systematic 'Sinhalisation' policy in the cultural and symbolic domain, for example, by rendering Tamil names of villages and streets in Sinhalese, putting up war monuments and erecting Buddha statues (International Crisis Group 2012a: 17–18).

Conclusion

It can easily be seen that the words and acts of the current government are feeding into a number of counter-discourses. Its own storyline is a Duttagamini-type of discourse that claims that Sri Lanka is first of all, an undivided Sinhala-Buddhist country, with the Sinhalese having the historical right to settle anywhere in the country. In addition, government sources state that the minorities have similar rights, referring, for example, to the sizeable Tamil population in Colombo. Contrary to this discourse, we find a variety of narratives that remind us of earlier state terrorism and Sinhala colonialism discourses prevailing under Tamil militancy, and other discourses that refer to minority rights.

It is clear from recent developments that the government's discourse is more than text, and that it 'does things', as observed by Jabri in her work on discourse. This performative aspect is reinforced by the government's 'power-to-define' and its capability to implement whatever measures are deemed necessary, by force if need be. Sections of the minorities complain that their views are not taken into consideration and that, on this basis, it is impossible to talk about meaningful peacebuilding or reconciliation. Some observers fear that peace and stability are illusory under such conditions, and that there may even be a risk of resumption of violence in the future.

At the moment Sri Lanka finds itself at a crucial crossroads in its history. Half of its existence as an independent country has been relatively peaceful, but the other half has seen full-blown war. Can the country emerge from this situation now that the military conflict has ended? Can it overcome the divisions, suffering and loss the war implied? What does this require from those in charge of the management of the post-conflict process and the reconstruc-tion of the country? And what discourse should accompany and support such goals?

Knowledge of the existence and workings of different local, national and international discourses is helpful in understanding the stances of the different stakeholders and in informing peacebuilding strategies, conflict transformation and reconciliation. Criticisms of international conflict resolution and peace-building attempts in the past have characteristically centred on the lack of cultural, historical and local understanding. Acquiring knowledge on the prevailing discourses can help to offset such criticisms. But what does it mean when such criticisms are levelled against one of the local protagonist parties now allegedly imposing a hegemonising victor's peace?

In a transition from war to peace, people and parties to the conflict have to adopt different ways of looking at the world. In consequence, the discourses that they use must change or adopt new elements. It implies a gradual shift from radical, exclusionist and violent discourses to more moderate, inclusive and accommodating types of discourse that induce peaceful settlement and a shared future. Whereas in armed conflict, enemy images and related war rhetoric are predominant, in transitions to peace, other messages need to be conveyed to the former opponents, to the constituency and to the outside world. At the current juncture, Sri Lanka's victor's peace provides a different transition scenario from the one where agreements emerged after negotiations or a compromise. It is highly important to gauge what space exists for conflict transformation under this victor's peace. I hope I have shown not only how discursive positioning and continuities are important entry points in understanding ongoing events and dynamics, but also how these may impede a sustained and consolidated peace. In the counter-narratives that I have outlined, there were perhaps too many of Darby and McGinty's problematic obstacles to peace to be sure of a conflict-free Sri Lanka in the future. Hopefully, there is still time and scope to deal with them.

Acknowledgements

Thanks to Luís Artur, Mathijs van Leeuwen, Jonathan Spencer and Kalinga Tudor Silva for their constructive comments on an earlier draft of this chapter. All responsibility remains with the author.

Notes

1   I thank Bart Klem for his permission to draw upon our joint chapter in this publication (Frerks and Klem 2005: 1–46).
2   http://www.priu.gov.lk/news_update/Current_Affairs/ca201204/20120408sl_ taking_unique_steps_to_expedite_reconciliation.htm
3   http://www.priu.gov.lk/news_update/Current_Affairs/ca201203/20120301 external_intervention_gravely_ hamper_srilankan_process.htm, accessed 29 April 2012.
4   http://www.priu.gov.lk/news_update/Current_Affairs/ca201203/20120302loans_ facilities_rehabilitated_ltte_cadres.htm, accessed 29 April 2012.
5   http://www.priu.gov.lk/news_update/Current_Affairs/ca201203/20120323us_ move_misconceived_unwarranted_ill_timed.htm, accessed 29 April 2012.

6   http://www.priu.gov.lk/news_update/Current_Affairs/ca201204/20120408sl_
    taking_unique_steps_to_expedite_reconciliation.htm, accessed 29 April 2012.
7   See: joint statement: Sunila Abeysekara, Nimalka Fernando and Dr. Paikiasothy
    Saravanamuttu, 23 March 2012, Colombo, Sri Lanka.

References

Abdullah, R. (2005) 'Ethnic Harmony in Eastern Sri Lanka', in G. Frerks and
    B. Klem (eds) *Dealing with Diversity, Sri Lankan Discourses on Peace and Conflict*. The Hague:
    Netherlands Institute of International Relations 'Clingendael'. 183–190.
Apter, D. (ed.) (1997) *The Legitimization of Violence*. New York: New York University
    Press.
Bastian, S. (2007) *The Politics of Foreign Aid in Sri Lanka, Promoting Markets and Supporting Peace*.
    Colombo: International Centre for Ethnic Studies.
Bhatia, M.V. (2005) 'Fighting Words: Naming Terrorists, Bandits, Rebels and other
    Violent Actors', *Third World Quarterly* (Vol. 26), 1: 5–22.
Bush, K. (2004) 'Commodification, Compartmentalization, and Militarization of Peace-
    building', in T. Keating and W.A. Knight (eds) *Building Sustainable Peace*. Edmonton:
    University of Alberta Press, 23–45.
Chandler, D. (2009) *Statebuilding and Intervention. Policies, Practices and Paradigms*. London and
    New York: Routledge.
Chelvanayakam, S.J.V. (2005) 'A Memorandum from the Tamils of Ceylon to all
    Delegates attending the 20th Commonwealth Conference in Sri Lanka', in G. Frerks
    and B. Klem (eds) *Dealing with Diversity, Sri Lankan Discourses on Peace and Conflict*. The
    Hague: Netherlands Institute of International Relations 'Clingendael', 275–290.
Darby, J. and R. McGinty (2000) 'Conclusion: The Management of Peace', in J. Darby
    and R. McGinty (eds) *The Management of Peace Processes*. London: McMillan Press Ltd,
    228–261.
Darby, J. and R. McGinty (2008) *Contemporary Peacemaking, Conflict, Peace Processes and
    Post-War Reconstruction* (2nd edn). Basingstoke: Palgrave Macmillan.
Duffield, M. (2007) *Development, Security and Unending War: Governing the World of Peoples*.
    Cambridge: Polity Press.
Fairclough, N. (2005) 'Critical Discourse Analysis in Transdisciplinary Research', in
    R. Wodak and P. Chilton (eds) *A New Agenda in Critical Discourse Analysis*. Amsterdam/
    Philadelphia: John Benjamins Publishing Company, 53–70.
Fazil, M.M. (2005) 'The Muslim Factor in the Sri Lankan Conflict', in G. Frerks and
    B. Klem (eds) *Dealing with Diversity, Sri Lankan Discourses on Peace and Conflict*. The Hague:
    Netherlands Institute of International Relations 'Clingendael', 161–182.
Frerks, G. (2007) 'Conflict, Development and Discourse', in G. Frerks and B. Klein
    Goldewijk (eds) *Human Security and International Security*. Wageningen: Wageningen
    Academic Publishers, 45–63.
Frerks, G. (2008) 'Human Security as a Discourse and Counter-discourse', *Security and
    Human Rights*, 19(1): 8–14.
Frerks, G. and B. Klem (eds) (2005) *Dealing with Diversity, Sri Lankan Discourses on
    Peace and Conflict*. The Hague: Netherlands Institute of International Relations
    'Clingendael'.
Frerks, G. and B. Klem (2011) 'Muddling the Peace Process. The Political Dynamics of the
    Tsunami, Aid and Conflict', in J. Goodhand, B. Korf and J. Spencer (eds) *Conflict and Peace-
    building in Sri Lanka. Caught in the Peace Trap?* London and New York: Routledge, 168–182.

Geiger, W. (2003) *The Mahavamsa or The Great Chronicle of Ceylon*, translated by Wilhelm Geiger, and from the German into English by Mabel Haynes Bode. New Dehli/Chennai: Asian Educational Services.

Goodhand, J., B. Korf and J. Spencer (eds) (2011) *Conflict and Peacebuilding in Sri Lanka. Caught in the Peace Trap?* London and New York: Routledge.

Goonatilaka, S. (2006) *Recolonisation, Foreign Funded NGOs in Sri Lanka*. New Delhi/Thousand Oaks/London: Sage Publications.

Gunasekera, S. (2005) 'Sri Lanka's Historical Failure to Accommodate Ethnic Diversity', in G. Frerks and B. Klem (eds) *Dealing with Diversity, Sri Lankan Discourses on Peace and Conflict*. The Hague: Netherlands Institute of International Relations 'Clingendael', 73–84.

Hansen, L. (2006) *Security as Practice. Discourse Analysis and the Bosnian War*. Abingdon: Routledge.

Hewitt, J.J., J. Wilkenfeld and T.R. Gurr (2010) *Peace and Conflict 2010, Executive Summary*. University of Maryland. Boulder, CO: Paradigm Publishers.

International Crisis Group (2011) *Sri Lanka: Women's Insecurity in the North and East*. Asia Report No. 217 – 20 December 2011. Colombo/Brussels: International Crisis Group.

International Crisis Group (2012a) *Sri Lanka's North I: The Denial of Minority Rights*. Asia Report No. 219 – 16 March 2012. Colombo/Brussels: International Crisis Group.

International Crisis Group (2012b) *Sri Lanka's North II: Rebuilding Under the Military*. Asia Report No. 220 – 16 March 2012. Colombo/Brussels: International Crisis Group.

Ismail, M., R. Abdullah and M.M. Fazil (2005) 'Muslim Perspectives from the East', in G. Frerks and B. Klem (eds) *Dealing with Diversity, Sri Lankan Discourses on Peace and Conflict*. The Hague: Netherlands Institute of International Relations 'Clingendael', 152–159.

Jabri, V. (1996) *Discourses on Violence: Conflict Analysis Reconsidered*. Manchester and New York: Manchester University Press.

Jones, R.H. and S. Norris (2005) 'Discourse as Action/Discourse in Action', in S. Norris and R.H. Jones (eds) *Discourse in Action. Introducing mediated discourse analysis*, Abingdon: Routledge, 3–14.

Lessons Learnt and Reconciliation Commission (2011) *Report of Sri Lanka's Lessons Learnt and Reconciliation Commission*, 16 December 2011.

LTTE (Liberation Tigers of Tamil Eelam) (2005) 'Socialist Tamil Eelam: Political Programme of the LTTE', in G. Frerks and B. Klem (eds) *Dealing with Diversity, Sri Lankan Discourses on Peace and Conflict*. The Hague: Netherlands Institute of International Relations 'Clingendael', 291–306.

McAdam, D., J.D. McCarthy and M.N. Zald (1996) 'Introduction: Opportunities, Mobilizing Structures and Framing Processes – toward a Synthetic, Comparative Perspective on Social Movements', in D. McAdam, J.D. McCarthy and M.N. Zald (eds) *Comparative Perspectives on Social Movements. Political pportunities, Mobilizing Structure and Cultural Framings*, 1–20. Cambridge: Cambridge University Press.

Mel, N. de (2007) *Militarizing Sri Lanka, Popular Culture, Memory and Narrative in the Armed Conflict*. Los Angeles/London/New Dehli/Singapore: Sage Publications.

Nadarajah, S. and D. Sriskandarajah (2005) 'Liberation Struggle or Terrorism? The Politics of Naming the LTTE'. *Third World Quarterly*, 26 (1): 87–100.

Rajasingham-Senanayake, D. (2003) 'The International Post-Conflict Industry: Myths, Rituals, Market Imperfections and the Need for a New Paradigm'. *Polity*, 1(3) July-August: 9–15.

Ranaweera Banda, R.M. and U. Abeyratne (2005) 'Perspectives from the South', in G. Frerks and B. Klem (eds) *Dealing with Diversity, Sri Lankan Discourses on Peace and Conflict*. The Hague: Netherlands Institute of International Relations 'Clingendael', 49–71.

Schmidt, B.E. and I.W. Schröder (eds) (2001) *Anthropology of Violence and Conflict*. London/ New York: Routledge.

Silva, K.M. de (2005) *A History of Sri Lanka*. Colombo: Vijitha Yapa Publications.

Sitrampalam, S.K. (2005) 'Perspectives from the North', in G. Frerks and B. Klem (eds) *Dealing with Diversity, Sri Lankan Discourses on Peace and Conflict*. The Hague: Netherlands Institute of International Relations 'Clingendael', 203–230.

Stokke, K. and J. Uyangoda (eds) (2011) *Liberal Peace in Question. Politics of State and Market Reform in Sri Lanka*. London/New York/Dehli: Anthem Press.

Sunday Observer (2012) 'Freedom sans Fear and Mistrust – President'. *Sunday Observer*, 20 May 2012: 13.

Talentino (2007) 'Perceptions of Peacebuilding: The Dynamic of Imposer and Imposed Upon'. *International Studies Perspectives*, 8: 152–171.

Tambiah, S. (1996) *Leveling Crowds: Ethnonationalist Conflicts and Collective Violence in South Asia*. Berkeley/Los Angeles: University of California Press.

UN (2011) *Report of the Secretary General's Panel of Experts on Accountability in Sri Lanka*, 30 March.

3 The political history of disaster management in Mozambique

Luís Artur

Introduction

Climate change and the search for effective disaster risk reduction measures are inviting us to revisit history. Climatologists and statisticians alike are busy examining weather patterns of the past, in order to establish whether climate change is real and different from climate variability, and to assess its impact compared with past events. It has become normal to proclaim that climate change will exacerbate disaster events worldwide in an unprecedented manner.

While natural scientists with their global and downscaled models are reconstructing world history, social scientists are also increasingly called upon to understand systematically how societies have structured themselves to cope, adapt and take advantage of crisis situations, and how these mechanisms have continued or changed overtime. Many publications, such as the Hyogo Framework of Action, IPCC (2007), UNDP (2008), Webster *et al.* (2008) and IFRC (2009), among others, have consistently called for the need to grasp the societal ordering of climate change and disasters. Although climate change is a global phenomenon, its manifestations, impacts and adaptation mechanisms are local. This chapter is a contribution toward understanding this, through a case study of the history of disaster and climate change management in Mozambique.

In this chapter, I aim to reconstruct the historical relationship between disasters and the socio-political and economic agendas of the actors concerned. The chapter asks how disasters, and responses to them by different actors have been co-shaped by the political and socio-economic agendas of the actors involved. In particular, I will focus on the ways in which, first the pre-colonial, then the Portuguese colonial authorities, and later the Mozambican government, organized disaster management. By doing so, I want to make the case that disaster response has been one of the constitutive elements in shaping the state and state-society relations in Mozambique.

I will start the chapter by providing an overview of major natural hazards affecting Mozambique and how they are presented in the mainstream literature. Following this, I reconstruct the historical relationship between disasters and the socio-political and economic contexts. The last section of the chapter addresses specifically the interfaces of actors in the arena of climate change response.

With regard to the pre-colonial and colonial history in particular, however, I have to make a disclaimer. I am not a historian and did not have time or the skills to study original historical archives. Instead, I have based my analysis on secondary sources, re-interpreting some of the claims authors have made. I do not pretend to provide the ultimate history of disaster management, and parts of this chapter may be better read as an evolving narrative on the history and politics of disaster management that invites other scholars to further substantiate, elaborate or refute in future debate. The chapter is based on fieldwork and material collected through literature review, interviews and observations, over a period of 18 months in Mozambique, as part of the author's PhD programme at Wageningen Disaster Studies department (2006–2010). Conceptually, the chapter resonates with claims that understanding of the political history is crucial to grasping the societal ordering of climate change and disasters (cf. Blaikie *et al.* 1994, Bankoff 2003, Oliver-Smith 2005).

Natural hazards and disasters in Mozambique: an overview

Mozambique is a disaster-prone country. The country has 1,700 kilometres of coastline along the Indian Ocean which is affected every year by cyclones of different intensities. Mozambique is also the lower riparian country of ten international rivers that drain their waters into the Indian Ocean. Excessive rainfall allied with the mismanagement of rivers and dams as well as environmental degradation has produced a history of flooding of different magnitudes. Further, some of the regions of the country have a semi-arid climate, and drought has historically been part of people's everyday life. Droughts, flooding and cyclones are three major natural hazards which, allied with the poverty and high vulnerability of the affected people, has produced disasters in Mozambique: it has on average, one disaster per year (INGC *et al.* 2003: 7) and ranks third on global weather-related damage, following Bangladesh and Ethiopia (Buys *et al.* 2007: 38).

Natural hazards and disasters manifest themselves differently across the country and produce differentiated responses. Drought hits mainly southern Mozambique, flooding affects the central region, while cyclones tend to make landfall mostly in northern Mozambique. Southern Mozambique is characterized mainly by low rainfall patterns (in the range of 400–600 mm/year) and soils of lower fertility with limited water retention capacity. This leads to cyclical drought, limited agricultural production and food insecurity among rain-fed agriculture-dependent households. On average, household agricultural production from rain-fed agriculture provides food security for four to five months, especially in the interior of Gaza and Inhambane provinces (De Matteis *et al.* 2006).

Central Mozambique is flood-prone. The region is characterized by high precipitation and large flat areas, especially along the Zambezi basin (the largest basin in Mozambique). Annual rainfall in central Mozambique ranges between 800 and 1200 mm/year, becoming exceptionally high (around 1500 mm/year) in the Zambezia and Tete plateaus (Santos and Henriques 1999: 6). Further, of the ten international rivers, five (Zambezi, Shire, Pungue, Buzi and Save) cross Mozambique in the central area. This context leads to recurrent flooding in the region, especially along the Zambezi delta.

Cyclones affect the northern provinces of Nampula and Cabo-Delgado particularly badly. Mozambique is, on average, hit by one cyclone and three to four tropical depressions every year (INGC *et al.* 2003: 12). Hewitt created a record in 1969 of natural hazards all over the world, and he found records of cyclone in Mozambique for the year which claimed 110 lives (Hewitt 1969). Since then, 17 disasters resulting from cyclones have been recorded to date, half over the last ten years. Cyclones and tropical depressions link to flooding and droughts, as they are accompanied by rainfall. The 2000 flooding was related to three cyclones: Eline, Gloria and Hudah.

The above overview shows that natural hazards have been part of the history of many Mozambicans. The number of people affected and killed by natural hazards dictates to a large extent the call for relief aid, but this needs to be treated with extreme caution for a variety of reasons. These include poor collection methods, such as the use of different units of measurement (individual, households, communities), and, importantly, omission and deliberate distortion by those involved in data collection and analysis. Moreover, data may be out of date. In Mozambique, numbers play a political role and embed different discourses. During the 1980s, when the government needed much international aid, it stressed how the South African apartheid-backed civil war in Mozambique had devastating impacts, and so presenting higher numbers of the affected and killed was not a major concern for the government. In the 1980s, data provided by the government were, in most cases, questioned by donors, and verification missions were deployed to the affected areas to determine the real number of people requiring aid relief (Barnes 1998).

Conversely, the government has recently been attempting to demonstrate its commitment and efficiency in disaster management, and so there is a tendency to downplay the numbers. In recent years, the government has not only tended to present the lowest figures from amongst the different sources but also often disputed higher figures provided by external sources; this included UN agencies which formerly used to question government numbers. For example, during the 2007 flooding in the Zambezi delta, the government estimated that 163,045 people were displaced, while the World Food Programme (WFP) estimated 285,000 and the United States Agency for International Development (USAID) 331,500.

There is little dispute, as we shall see, that the government response to disasters has improved, but the production of figures needs to be viewed within the broader national and international context. Government data have been critically questioned by some authors, and Hanlon (2007) disputed the claim that poverty has reduced in Mozambique by 15 per cent between 1997 and 2003. Given the above, data on disasters in Mozambique may be viewed, at best, as estimates of a general magnitude.

Continuities and changes in the occurrence of natural hazards and disasters

Natural hazards are on the rise in Mozambique. Since 1970, Mozambique has been hit by 77 disasters, of which 41 (53 per cent) occurred within the last 10 years (2000–2009). The number of people killed has more than tripled compared with the previous decade, and there is an increase of nearly 50 per cent in the number of people affected by natural hazards. In 2005, an estimated 94 per cent of the population in Mozambique was affected by natural hazards (Mafambissa 2007: 5).

The increase may partly reflect an improved capacity for data collection. It may also reflect increased vulnerability to disaster. A growing population, environmental degradation and limited alternative sources of livelihood tend to increase people's vulnerability to disasters. There is mounting evidence that poverty reduction programmes have failed to reach the poorest segments of society (Hanlon 2007; UNICEF 2007). Climate change is also exacerbating this trend. INGC (2009) suggests that increases in the frequency and intensity of natural hazards in Mozambique are related to climate change which will continue to become manifest.

While disasters are increasing in general, there have been changes in the main hazards producing disasters. Droughts have historically been the major natural hazard, claiming more than a hundred thousand lives and affecting nearly 23 million since 1970. Nonetheless, flooding has become the major natural hazard over the last ten years (Figure 3.1).

Disaster management practices: a historical perspective

Disaster management practices have undergone different transformations in response to changing characteristics of the disasters themselves but also to the political and economic interests of the actors involved. In this section, I consider eight major periods of disaster management in Mozambique. Although, within each period, disaster management practices were diverse and dynamic, they were marked by some common elements which allow them to be clustered according to these periods. Amongst other elements, they were marked by particular interfaces between the international, national and local domains of disaster management that differentiate one period from the other.

The 'kingdomination' of disasters: pre-colonial disaster management practices

Before colonization, Mozambique was administered through lineages, chieftaincies and a very complex system of kingdoms. Kingdoms encompassed different

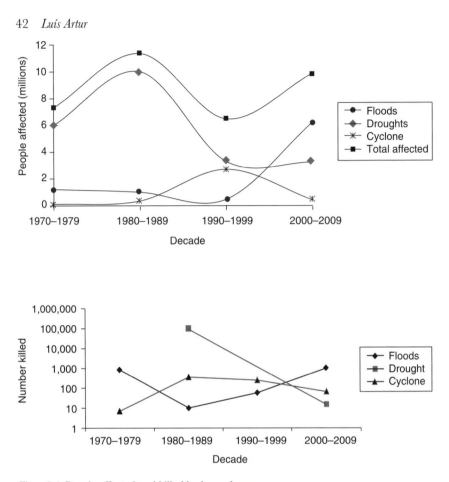

Figure 3.1 People affected and killed by hazard type.

Source: author based on EM database

chieftaincies and lineages; there were dozens before Portugal conquered the last one (the Gaza kingdom ruled by Ngungunhana) in 1895. The set up, expansion, retreat or dissolution of these kingdoms was highly influenced by natural hazards and disasters. Different historical records highlight this. Newitt (1988: 18–19) found that, from the 1750s, climatic changes made droughts and crop failure a growing problem until the 1830s. In extreme cases, entire regions became depopulated as hunger was succeeded by epidemics that killed off or dispersed the population. Settled life became impossible, agriculture and trade ceased and accumulated reserves emptied. To illustrate this, Serra (2000: 88) points out that southern Mozambique had about 20 kingdoms in 1770. The drought and its consequent famine resulted in widespread migration, warfare and a massive dissolution and retreat of many kingdoms. In 1815 only two kingdoms (Nduandue and Mtetua) remained. Droughts and floods were used, in the pre-colonial period, as trigger factors to conquer new areas or forge alliances with other kingdoms. This was a practice in southern Mozambique, between South African and Mozambican kingdoms, but also along the Zambezi basin in central Mozambique, between Zimbabwean, Malawian and Mozambican kingdoms (Liesagang 1970).

Hence, the kingdoms had to control/dominate the disasters in order to exist. Two major levels of disaster management may be distinguished in the kingdoms, namely, at the individual household and at the general kingdom levels.

At the individual household level disaster management practices varied across regions. In the south, households tended to craft their livelihoods taking drought into account. Sorghum and millet, both drought-resistant crops, and later on cassava, which is also drought resistant, were the major crops in their farming systems (Junod 1996). Additionally, as in many other drought regions, cattle became an integral part of the farming system.[1] Furthermore, to compensate for the low agricultural production levels, households tended to increase the production areas and this influenced the birth rates and polygamy practices. Having more children and wives provided labour to open up larger fields and increase production. Livestock played a role in polygamy. The dowry, *lobolo*, generally involved cattle (Hedges 1977: 190). Hence, cattle, agricultural production and drought became integrated into the everyday practices of local people. In central Mozambique, a more flood-prone region, canoes and fishing arts have long played a role in livelihood and disaster management. Canoes were, and are still, used for evacuation from the flood affected areas. Records suggest that flooding and the use of canoes on the Zambezi delta, central Mozambique, dates as far back as 1548 (Chidiamassamba and Liesegang 1997).

At the kingdom level, the focus was on addressing the root causes of drought and disasters. As these were perceived as natural problems influenced by the ancestors, the focus was on seeking the connection with the ancestors, asking for their protection, and asking them to bring rain. Rainmakers and mediums became an integral part of the ruling class (Newitt 1995: 32). Rituals and offerings to ancestors were performed by rainmakers and mediums before the rainy season, so that the ancestors could bring rain and good harvests. Over time, the rainmakers and mediums expanded their roles and became involved in conflict resolution, in choosing the kings and the wives for the kings, and by 'guiding' practices that people were expected to follow in order to make ancestors happy and bring fortune instead of disasters. Kings that were not rainmakers or mediums, or were not backed by rainmakers and mediums, tended to have weaker authority and shorter mandates (Liesagang 1970: 323, Newitt 1995: 33). Hence, disaster management through rainmakers and mediums played a socio-political role in the kingdoms and the 'kingdomination' of disasters. Disaster management became embedded in the everyday practices of the kingdoms and in shaping the relationship between the rulers and the ruled.

The 'colonization' of disasters: disaster management practices during the colonial period

Literature on disaster management during the colonial period is scarce, and the existing literature is dominated by the view that the colonial authorities were not interested in disaster management as it affected mainly the poor native people living in the countryside (Wisner 1979, Bolton 1983). This view is based on two arguments. First, despite recurrent natural hazards in Mozambique, the Portuguese authorities were not able to establish a disaster management institution during nearly 500 years' presence in Mozambique. Second, the cruelty and brutality with which the colonial rulers treated the native people supports the argument. Portugal's colonization of Mozambique was one of the most brutal in the world, involving slavery, forced labour, forced cash crop production and coercive taxation (Vail and White 1978, Isaacman 1996, Rocha *et al.* 1999).

I would like to qualify these observations. Although I concur that the colonial policies have increased people's vulnerability to disaster, these accounts do not recognize practices that aimed to reduce disasters, or that were intended for other purposes but had, nonetheless, a positive effect on disaster risk reduction. There are oral and written records claiming that colonial authorities did, somehow, intervene during disasters. During the great famine of 1823–1831, Portuguese authorities organized, in some parts of the countryside, food for work programmes for the most destitute groups of native population (Newitt 1988: 29). Furthermore, after flooding, colonial authorities or private companies used to distribute agricultural seeds and tools so that the natives could resume agricultural production (Vail and White 1978: 250, Negrão 2001: 70). Life stories collected during the present study suggest that the authorities and private companies used to distribute humanitarian aid whenever they found people secluded. This included mainly food and clothes.[2]

Defending the view that the colonizers were not interested in disaster management would be to suggest that they would be indifferent if all the native people perished from disasters. But, given that colonizers depended on the natives for labour, food and cash crop production, and earned considerable resources from taxing native people (Rocha *et al.* 1999, Negrão 2001), it is hard to sustain such claims. I would like to conclude that the colonial authorities did pay attention to managing disasters, but this was mainly done in order to implement their colonial policies and to strengthen their political and economic position rather than from any truly philanthropic motives. To sustain this claim, I will briefly use the case of drought in the southern region.

Droughts are, as discussed above, a recurrent natural hazard in the south of Mozambique. This informed how Portuguese authorities in Mozambique administered this region. On the one hand, Portuguese people tended to refuse to settle unless a basic infrastructure for agricultural production, especially irrigation schemes, was provided by the government. Smith (1991: 502) noted that even the Portuguese troops who were sent to Mozambique during the 'scramble' era refused to remain as colonists; they preferred to leave Mozambique and migrate to Brazil and the United States. Emerging from this, and aligned with the colonization objective of settling Portuguese people in Mozambique, the Portuguese authorities built an irrigation scheme in Chokwe district where it established the first *colonato* (an organized Portuguese settlement). Comprising 30,000 hectares, the Chokwe irrigation scheme is the largest in Mozambique. Each colonist agreeing to stay was given 4 hectares of land on the irrigation scheme for agricultural production and 24 hectares for livestock grazing outside the scheme. They also had government technical support for their activities (Muchave 1998: 25). Hence, to colonize the region, the government first had to 'colonize' the drought.

On the other hand, for the native people, drought and Portuguese domination and the ways in which the domination was carried out, tended to weaken their social, economic and political structures, and migration to South Africa became increasingly the primary option for livelihoods (Covane 2001: 55). Rather than inhibiting the migration practices, the colonial authorities decided to profit from it. In 1897, Portugal and South Africa signed a treaty concerning the recruitment of labour from southern Mozambique for the mining industry in South Africa. In exchange, the Portuguese made demands including direct payment in gold, increased use of Maputo Port (called Delagoa Bay at that time) by South Africa and a payment of 13 shillings per individual, supposedly to cover administrative costs (Wuyts 1981: 37, Newitt 1995: 491).

To reinforce the treaty, the Portuguese authorities passed a law in 1907 under which 'illegal' emigration to South Africa was punished by up to twenty months of forced labour without payment (Serra 2000: 201). By 1952, nearly 250,000 Mozambicans were working in South Africa, and by 1967, the Portuguese earnings from those migrants were estimated to be around eight times the value of the marketed agricultural products of southern Mozambique (Murteira 2000, in Vaz and Zaag 2003: 10). Up to Independence in 1975, nearly one in five adult males from southern Mozambique was working in South Africa (Wuyts 1981: 35).

The policies on migration were not designed to reduce disaster, but had the consequence that people could enhance their protection against drought at the same time that Portugal earned financial resources and strengthened its position in Mozambique. Thus drought shaped, to a large extent, the colonization policy, especially in southern Mozambique and the relationship between colonial Portugal and South Africa.

1975–1979: the 'socialization' of disasters

The period 1975–1979 was marked by the inception of what would become Frente de Libertação de Moçambique's (FRELIMO) vision of a new Mozambique. Following Independence in 1975, the FRELIMO party declared socialism and Marxism-Leninism as its main political ideology. It proclaimed Mozambique a People's Republic which would be led by the working class (*classe operária*) and followed by the peasantry (*camponeses*). Agriculture was defined as the basis of the economy which would be strengthened through state farms and cooperatives. Individual property was abolished and assets reverted to the state in 1977.

Based on the socialist ideology, peasants who lived scattered in the countryside were forced to move to communal villages (*aldeias comunais*) under the slogan of 'socialization of the countryside' (*socialização do campo*). The government claimed that in communal villages development take-off would be quicker. By moving into the communal villages, hazards that scattered households tended to face individually now became socialized and they had to find ways to cope together with hazards and disasters.

While the *villagization* policy tended to 'socialize' disasters, disasters were in turn used to promote the *villagization* and socialization policy. In 1977, cyclone Emily struck the southern coast of Mozambique and, in conjunction with waters discharged from the Massingir dam in Gaza province, produced the worst flood in 60 years. The flooding killed 300 people and affected about 400,000 people (Wisner 1979). All displaced people were then forced to move into the communal villages.

In the national media, those declining the *villagization* were called *Xiconhocas* or 'enemies of the people', and labelled anti-revolutionary and anti-FRELIMO. They faced penalties which included jail or being sent to so-called re-education centres (*centros de re-edução*), established to educate the *Xiconhocas*. A further penalty was the exclusion from humanitarian aid. Aid was selectively provided to those embracing the *villagization* policy. As a consequence of these political measures, 26 communal villages were created in Gaza province along the Limpopo River, comprising about 200,000 people (Coelho 1993: 384). A similar approach was used in the Zambezi valley following the flood of 1978 which claimed the lives of 45 people and affected nearly 450,000 people.

1980–1986: disasters and the dissolution of Marxism

The period 1980–1986 was marked by a decline of the national economy. A complex emergency arising from policy failures, droughts and civil war was hitting Mozambique, and the government faced serious problems in addressing these.

Policy failures involved a range of ineffective interventions. The government used its limited financial resources and gold reserves to empower state farmers, to expand social services and to increase wages. As a result, by early 1982, the country's gold stock fell by over 80 per cent and, by 1983, the foreign reserves could pay barely a month of imports (Cravinho 1995: 163).

The political ideology of socialism, state farms and communal villages was also creating a considerable number of dissatisfied people. People were showing this in a number of ways: they burned houses in communal villages, refused to partici-pate in or even sabotaged state and cooperative farms, and increasingly deserted communal villages, taking seeds and agricultural implements with them (CEA 1979). In the end, the results of the investments fell far short of expectations and the economy shrank.

Besides the economic situation, Mozambique faced two parallel and intercon-nected events. The first was a drought. From 1980, the southern region started to face drought which became acute from 1983 to 1985, claiming the lives of 100,000 people and affecting more than five million. The second was the civil war (1976–1992) which left behind widespread devastation. It is estimated that almost 1 million people lost their lives, while 2 million were forced to find refuge in neighbouring countries and another 4 million were internally displaced (UNHCR 1996).

The outcome of the three major trigger factors (policy failure, drought and civil war) was that the country's social, economic, political and military position was seriously eroded. Mozambique's exports fell from 280.8 million US$ in 1980 to 79.1 million US$ in 1986; imports fell from 800 million US$ to 543 million US$, and the budget deficit escalated from 32.4 million US$ in 1980 to 488 million US$ in 1986 (Cravinho 1995: 187–188). From 1982 onwards, the country could no longer afford to pay its debts which had increased to 2.9 billion US$ by 1985. As a result, the government was having difficulty in accessing additional credits.

To overcome the problem, the government started approaching the West. In 1984, Mozambique joined the IMF, the World Bank and Lomé Convention (Adam 2005). Negotiations for the national Structural Adjustment Plan (SAP) dragged on until January 1987 when the agreement for disbursement was finally signed. The SAP signalled a clear detachment from the Marxist ideology to a more liberal and market-oriented economy. Since that time, international (Western) aid has started to flow.

1987–1994: 'un-neutral' aid – aid empowering FRELIMO

The period from 1987 to 1994 has been the most highlighted in the history of disaster management in Mozambique. This period was marked by an influx of international aid and represents the period of the emergence of the so-called dependency and begging mentality.

The year 1987 started with the disbursement agreement between IMF and the government in January and with an emergency appeal for 333 million US$ in February, launched by the UN Secretary General. By the end of 1987, international aid had increased by 58 per cent and in 1988 by 110 per cent, compared with 1986 (Figure 3.2). In 1989, international aid amounted to nine times the national revenues from exports and represented 66 per cent of the national GDP (Adam 2005: 180). From 1987 to 1994 emergency appeals totalled nearly 1.5 billion US$.

But aid to Mozambique was not neutral during that period. The Mozambican government managed, during the 1980s, to ride successfully on the mounting sentiments in the West against the apartheid regime of South Africa. Civil war backed, partly, by the apartheid regime became the major justification for the country's economic collapse. In April 1988, the US State Department released a report which pictured Resistência Nacional de Moçambique (RENAMO), backed by the apartheid regime, as a brutal movement of mass killing and rape (Barnes 1996: 6). Given the evidence of those times this was, to a large extent, correct. The report was released a few days before the launch of a UN-backed donor conference held in Maputo, 26–27 April 1988. During this conference, attended by representatives of 37 countries, 41 NGOs, 10 United Nations Agencies and 2 regional organizations,[3] the same message prevailed. In the conference, President Chissano stressed civil war and apartheid over internal policy failures.[4] This was echoed in the speeches from other prominent guests such as the UN Secretary General, the UN Under Secretary General for Special Political Issues and by the US Deputy Secretary of State for African Affairs, Roy Stacy.

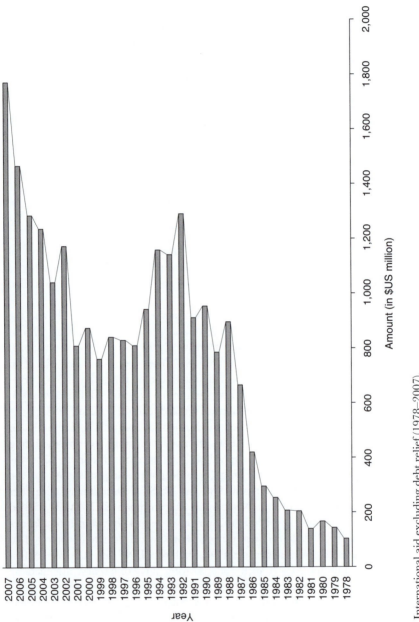

Figure 3.2 International aid excluding debt relief (1978–2007).

Source: author based on OECD database. Available at http://stats.oecd.org/index.aspx?datasetcode=csp2009

As the Mozambican government was perceived as an innocent victim, donors and NGOs alike did not invoke the principle of neutrality in humanitarian aid. Without discussion, they all worked through the government or with the government, to the extent that people at local level associated aid with the government. Governmental military force was involved in aid escorts, and received payments, fuel and food through international assistance (Vaux 2001: 105). By 1990, 56 per cent of humanitarian aid required governmental military escort (UN 1990: 14). The effect was the politicization of aid. The escorts were used to gather military intelligence, move military forces around districts and strengthen the position of the government with the local population. It also led to distribution of aid that was far from needs-based. Maier (1989) interviewed people fleeing RENAMO-controlled areas and most of them claimed that FRELIMO-controlled areas were far better off because they were given humanitarian aid that was absent in the RENAMO areas.

Additionally, as international humanitarian aid increased, the Mozambican government was literally exempted from its obligation of feeding and clothing its people and could afford to reinforce its military force either numerically, materially or financially. Up to 1990, the international community provided 90 per cent of total food requirements, both to the rural and urban population, and in 1989 donors funded the purchase and armour of 12 trucks to escort humanitarian aid (UN 1990: 2,7). As aid was being 'pumped' into the country, the government appointed a new military leadership in 1987 and sought additional military assistance from the UK, Italy and Portugal. By the end of 1987, the FRELIMO army had grown from 35,000 soldiers in 1985 to 65,000–70,000 soldiers (Weinstein and Francisco 2005: 170) and had started larger military operations in the provinces of Manica, Sofala, Zambezia and Tete. By 1989, the government regained control over the districts in Zambezia province which had been under RENAMO control. The government became so confident that it sent home the 3,000 Tanzanian troops that had been in Zambezia province (Maier 1989: 14).

1995–1999: aid withdrawal, restructuring and conflicts

The civil war ended in 1992 and the first multi-party elections were held in 1994. Up to then, there was still massive fund inflow. But from 1995, with the end of the UN peacekeeping mission, international funding dropped. Nonetheless, the emergency situation and funds channelled during the previous period had led to an increased number of staff and an accumulation of material assets. By 1997, the national department that assisted the affected population, Departamento de Prevenção e Combate as Calamidades Naturais (DPCCN), had nearly 900 workers, about 700 vehicles and dozens of warehouses (DPCCN 1997: 12). Most of the logistics and monetary incentives for DPCCN qualified staff were provided by the international community. With the decrease of international funding, the government had to cut the staff and withdraw the incentives provided previously. A restructuring process took place to reduce the number of staff and amend the role of DPCCN for a development context. DPCCN was finally abolished in 1999 and, in its place, the National Institute for Disaster Management (INGC) was created. INGC had places for only 200 of the previous 900 people, and many of the former DPCCN assets such as cars and warehouses were put up for sale. Other organizations undertook similar measures. The Mozambican Red Cross, for instance, had to reduce its staff from nearly 500 to about 150 and sell some of its assets.

The process was contentious, with different conflicts over who stays and who goes, and who takes what and where. Some experienced and qualified staff left the government to join international organizations that offered better conditions. Organizations such as World Food Programme (WFP), the Food and Agriculture Organization (FAO) and Christian Action Research and Education (CARE) were accused by the government of poaching its most qualified staff (Adam 2005: 47). Some people were dismissed without compensation and some took institutions such as the Mozambican Red Cross and DPCCN to court.[5]

2000–2004: floods and the re-emergence of humanitarian aid

In 2000 and 2001, Mozambique was hit by two successive floods which had a massive impact. Together, they claimed the lives of 813 people; 2.7 million people were directly affected, of whom 767,000 had to be evacuated. Nearly 250,000 hectares with different crops were lost and about 18,600 fishermen lost their tools (Negrão 2001: 14–15). Losses were estimated to be more than 750 million US$. To address the emergency situation, the government appealed for international aid. By the end of April 2000, more than 160 million US$ were offered to the government of Mozambique through different channels (Christie and Hanlon 2001: 64). In May, the government made a reconstruction appeal in Rome asking for almost 450 million US$, and donors promised almost 453 million US$. In 2001, the government appealed for 30 million US$ for emergency operations, while different organizations such as the UN, the Red Cross Society and others, made their own appeals.

The appeals in 2000 and 2001 marked the resurgence of humanitarian appeals after an interlude of nearly ten years. Figure 3.2 above shows the rise in aid following the great flood of 2000. Christie and Hanlon (2001) analysed the response to the 2000 flood and claimed that, given the magnitude of the flooding, Mozambique would not have been able to manage the response by itself. An international response was needed and resulted in many lives saved and livelihoods reconstructed. The two floods were also used to claim climate change impacts in Mozambique, hence feeding the emerging national discourse on climate change discussed next.

From 2005 onwards: strengthening national capacity for disaster and climate change management

In 2005, Armando Guebuza replaced Joaquim Chissano as the Head of State. In his inaugural speech, Guebuza mentioned corruption, lack of self-reliance and self-esteem (*auto estima*), and *laissez-faire* (*deixa andar*) as the three major factors that contributed to the prevailing high rates of national poverty and vulnerability. These he intended to fight.

Regarding disaster management, the INGC traditional attachment to the Ministry of Foreign Affairs illustrated its dependency on the international community and weakened national sovereignty, self-reliance and self-esteem. There were also claims that INGC inherited a corrupt staff from the previous DPCCN, and a corruption scandal involving the General Director of the INGC leaked to the media in 2005. Both aspects forced, to some extent, changes within INGC. In December 2005, INGC was moved from the Ministry of Foreign Affairs to the Ministry of State Administration by the decree 27/2005 of 1 December 2005. In 2006, a new Director General of INGC was appointed and some former staff were sacked or reassigned elsewhere. New staff were contracted and, by 2009, the number of staff had nearly tripled as compared with 2006. It employed 380 people, as compared with 134 when INGC was attached to the Ministry of Foreign Affairs.[6]

In 2006, the government approved an 80 million US$, 10-year Master Plan focusing on disaster risk and vulnerability reduction. In 2007, the mandate of INGC had been modified to accommodate new responsibilities. Rather than disaster prevention and response, INGC was now charged with the authority for coordinating the development of drought prone areas and for coordinating reconstruction following disasters. New agencies and departments were created within the INGC, which started operating in 2007. Three National Emergency Operative Centres *Centro Nacional Operativo de Emergência* (CENOE) were established; a Unit for Civil Protection (UNAPROC) was created, as well as a Cabinet for the Coordination of Reconstruction (GACOR). Funding had also improved considerably. INGC is given annually about 120 million meticais (nearly 4.5 million US$) for contingency planning.

One of the major reasons for the need to strengthen INGC in recent years relates to climate change and disaster management. A report by INGC (2009) takes stock of climate change processes in Mozambique. Over the last fifty years, the average temperature in Mozambique has increased by 1.6°C, the rainfall season has started later and there has been an increase in the length of dry spells. By the year 2100, temperatures are expected to increase by up to 6°C, with further consequences including long droughts and heavy flooding. Although climate data are highly imprecise and scarce in Mozambique, the report sheds light on climate change and variability and resonates with earlier claims (Christie and Hanlon 2001; World Bank 2005). In the section that follows, I want to address how the government is responding to climate change, and also how the different actors in the climate change arena interact.

Government response to climate change: between economic growth and environmental concerns

Following the Rio Summit in 1992, Mozambique has gradually developed a legal framework for coping with climate change. Under the coordination of the

Ministry for Coordination of Environmental Action (MICOA), different regulatory tools have been established and a number of interventions on climate change carried out.

Despite the legal tools and interventions, the overall achievement of environmental sustainability (Millennium Development Goal 7: MDG 7) is unlikely to be achieved by 2015 (GoM and UN 2005). It turns out that, in practice, the government is focusing more on MDG 1 (to halve the proportion of people living in extreme poverty). It appears that economic growth competes with environmental concerns.

A major economic policy has been to encourage private foreign investments using different incentives such as limited taxation. Although some of these seem climate-friendly – for instance, investments in hydro-power dams – others will certainly increase greenhouse emissions in the years to come. These include the granting of 256,680 hectares for coal exploration to the Australian mining company Riversdale.[7] Similarly, the Brazilian company Vale do Rio Doce will extract about 2.4 billion tonnes of coal over a period of 25 years, which may be extended for a longer time.[8] Both companies are planning to produce electricity by burning coal. Forests, in the meantime, are being depleted by the export of wood, mainly to China, ironically referred to by some as the 'Chinese takeaway' (Mackenzie 2006).

Given the extreme poverty, lack of employment and basic infrastructure, it is understandable that the government is preoccupied with development concerns rather than investment in tackling climate change where the returns may only be visible in the long run. The effect is, however, that climate change mitigation and adaptation become competing claims in the allocation of budgets and investment decisions by the government. The hopeful suggestion that climate change adaptation may lead to economic growth and that economic growth can provide the resources for adaptation (UNDP 2008) cannot prevent the current situation in which decision-making often entails a negotiation between the two interests.

Actors and stakeholders in climate change in Mozambique: power struggles and strategies

Increased concerns about climate change and disasters are leading to an increased amount of projects on Disaster Risk Reduction (DRR), climate change mitigation and adaptation. Data from MICOA show that more than 60 projects and programmes on DRR, climate change adaptation and mitigation have been or are being implemented in Mozambique.[9] This has led to competition among government bodies for handling them. As mentioned above, MICOA was initially the coordinating body for climate change. Development agencies have questioned MICOA's authority by claiming that climate change is a development more than an environmental problem. In 2005, the government of Mozambique created a Ministry for Planning and Development (MPD). In order to mainstream climate change adaptation in the national development process, this Ministry has started to claim the coordination of adaptation measures. Another player is the Ministry for Science and Technology (MCT) which has the mandate to handle interventions regarding science and technology. This Ministry created a working group on climate change in 2007 and claims climate change interventions as well.

The disaster management community in Mozambique, notably the INGC, also has increased its stake in climate change adaptation programmes. INGC has broadened its mandate by incorporating prevention, vulnerability reduction, reconstruction and development of drought-prone areas. INGC has also produced the first national study on climate change. At the launch of the study in Maputo in May 2009, which I attended, the issue of coordination of climate change became a major bone of contention, and many guests from competing institutions perceived the initiative as an attempt by INGC to claim the leadership.

Municipalities are also emerging as actors in the climate change arena. When UN-Habitat launched a project aiming to develop mitigation and adaptation mechanisms in two cities of Mozambique, representatives of the municipalities were keen to defend the point that they had the lawful duty to develop any intervention in their areas of jurisdiction. Development agencies, such as the Mozambican Red Cross, Care international, the German Development Agency (GIZ) and World Vision, are also unilaterally or in partnerships implementing climate change related projects. And lastly, the private sector is stepping into the climate change arena. The Matola Gas Company (MGC), the Cimentos de Moçambique (CM) and the Electricity Company (EDM) have all asked for certificates to access funds under the Clean Development Mechanism.[10]

The main feature emerging from this unfolding arena is the lack of a coherent strategy and leadership for dealing with climate change. This leads to disparate projects, efforts and funds. It is unclear what the outcomes of these disparate initiatives will be for adapting to climate change at the local level. Actors use the room for manoeuvre created by the lack of coordination for developing and implementing climate change interventions, according to their own understanding, needs and rules. INGC assumes that millions of US$ are being pledged annually for disaster and climate change in Mozambique, but the government is not aware of how many organizations and donors are working on the issues and where.[11] Hence, government claims of sovereignty and capacity to coordinate or control the multiple actors is in practice being reshaped and appropriated by different actors within the governance domain and outside it.

Conclusions

This chapter reconstructed the historical relationship between disaster and socio-political and economic relations and processes in Mozambique. It discussed disaster management as part of state formation that embedded discourse and power relations. In the pre-colonial period, disasters played a crucial role in the formation and dissolution of the kingdoms. Droughts led to migrations and the conquering of new lands, or coalition building between different kingdoms. In the colonial period, the Portuguese authorities used drought to reinforce their presence, either by building irrigation schemes or by legislating migrations to South Africa by the native people. After Independence, droughts and floods, with particular focus on the latter, were used to promote the *villagization* policy and the Marxist-Leninist ideology.

The management of the disaster resulting from civil war, drought and policy failure in the 1980s, involved a 'powerlessness and victimization by Apartheid' approach on the part of the state, riding successfully on the mounting sentiments in the West against the apartheid regime of South Africa. This approach empowered FRELIMO and tended to weaken the RENAMO guerrilla movement.

In recent years, disaster management in Mozambique has tended to follow a rather contrary pattern. Instead of powerlessness, the government is keen to demonstrate self-reliance and effective disaster response.

A current change in disaster management practice has resulted from attention to climate change and its presumed effects involving increased disaster risks. Climate change has become an arena of power struggles where different actors dispute resources, including knowledge. In analysing climate change and actor interfaces, the conclusion is that there is a lack of a coherent framework for climate change response. This lack of a coherent framework is an emerging feature of the situation in which complex power struggles between different ministries (and other actors) for leading and coordinating the response take place.

The political history of disaster management laid out here shows that pathways have developed historically that condition and delineate current responses. Disaster responses, as this chapter demonstrates, have always been selective and organized in such a way that they served the vested interests of authorities in reinforcing their position. When central authorities are contested or fragmented, as is often the case, disaster practices become a battlefield for different interests and discourses. The emerging disaster and climate change response practices result from building coalitions and the ability of the individual actors to take advantage of the dominant discourse. History teaches us to become more realistic about the feasibility of addressing the urgent problems posed by climate change and of proposing effective responses.

Acknowledgements

My deepest gratitude to the Netherlands Organization for Scientific Research (NWO) for funding the research. I am also thankful to Andrew Collins, Peter Walker and to the Disaster Studies Group at Wageningen University in the Netherlands for their valuable comments on earlier version of this chapter.

Notes

1 These practices are still recognizable today. By 2000, the south of Mozambique, comprising Maputo, Gaza and Inhambane provinces, championed cattle production with a stock of 338,589 heads representing 46 per cent of the national cattle herd (INE 2002). A new livestock census was underway in 2010 but the data, to be released by 2012, may not change this historical pattern radically.

2 Interview with Fernando Chapo, 63 years old, Inhangoma-Mutarara, 11 September 2008; interview with chief *regulo* Cocorico, 24 September 2007, and chief *regulo* Chamanga, Mopeia, 7 May 2008.
3 CENE and DPCCN (1988).
4 In his speech of seven pages, Chissano mentioned 15 times war perpetuated by the apartheid regime, only 3 times natural hazards and made no reference to policies. Speech accessed at the Centro dos Estudos Africanos, Maputo.
5 Interview with Fernanda Teixeira, Mozambican Red Cross General Secretary, 11 October 2008.
6 Interview with Dr. Bonifácio Antonio, INGC Chief Coordinator, 28 May 2009.
7 www.riverdalemining.com.au/content/19/ accessed 16 October 2009.
8 www.vale.com/vale/moatize accessed 18 October 2009.
9 Information taken from a MICOA database (2011) on programmes on DRR and Climate Change.
10 Interview with Felício Fernando from MICOA on 27 May 2009.
11 Interview on 28 May 2009 with Dr. Bonifácio Antonio, Coordinator Officer Manager INGC and Felicio Fernando from MICOA.

References

Adam, Y. (2005) *Escapar aos Dentes do Crocodilo e Cair na Boca do Leopardo*. Maputo: Promedia.
Bankoff, G. (2003) *Cultures of Disaster: Society and Natural Hazard in the Philippines*. London and New York: Routledge Press.
Barnes, S. (1996) *Humanitarian Assistance as a Factor in the Peace Negotiations 1990–1992 in Mozambique*. Uppsala, Sweden: Nordiska Afrikainstituten.
Barnes, S. (1998) *Humanitarian Aid Coordination during War and Peace in Mozambique: 1985–1995*. Uppsala, Sweden: Nordiska Afrikainstituten. Studies on Emergencies and Disaster Relief. Report # 7.
Blaikie, P., T. Cannon, I. Davis and B. Wisner (1994) *At Risk: Natural Hazards, People's Vulnerability and Disasters*. London and New York: Routledge Press.
Bolton, P. (1983) 'Social and Environmental Changes Associated with the Cahora Bassa Project'. In: *The Regulation of the Zambezi in Mozambique. A Study of Origins and the Impacts of the Cahora Bassa Project*. PhD Thesis, University of Edinburgh, Chapter 6, 343–406.
Buys, P., U. Deichmann, C. Meisner, T. That and D. Wheeler (2007) *Country Stakes in Climate Change Negotiations: Two Dimensions of Vulnerability*. Washington, DC: World Bank.
CEA (1979) *Problemas de Transformação Rural na Provincia de Gaza. Um Estudo Sobre Articulacao Entre Aldeias Comunais Seleccionadas, Cooperativas Agrícolas e Unidades de Produção do Baixo Limpopo*. Governo da Republica de Moçambique, Maputo.
CENE and DPCCN (1988) *Rising to the Challenge. Dealing With Emergency in Mozambique. An Inside view*. Governo da Republica de Moçambique, Maputo.
Chidiamassamba, C. and G. Liesegang (1997) *Dados Historicos sobre ocorrencia e tipos de cheias no vale do Zambeze*. Paper presented at the workshop on sustainable use of Cahora Bassa dam and Zambezi Valley, Songo, 29 September to 2 October 1997.
Christie, F. and J. Hanlon (2001) *Mozambique and the Great Flood of 2000*. African issues, London: Long House Publications.
Coelho, J. (1993) *Protected Villages and Communal Villages in the Mozambican Province of Tete (1968–1982). A History of State Resettlement Policies, Development and War*. PhD Thesis, University of Bradford.
Covane, L. (2001) 'Southern Mozambique: Migrant Labour and Post-Independency Challenges'. In: C. Wet and R. Fox (eds) *Transforming Settlement in Southern Africa*. Edinburgh: Edinburgh University Press, 48–64.

56   *Luís Artur*

Cravinho, J. (1995) *Modernizing Mozambique. Frelimo Ideology and the Frelimo State.* PhD thesis, University of Oxford, UK.

De Matteis, A., L. Oliveira, P. Martill and J. Correia (2006) *Baseline Survey of Food Security and Nutrition in Mozambique.* Maputo: SETSAN.

DPCCN (1997) *Projecto de Reajustamento de DPCCN e a Criação de Reserva Financeira para a Prevenção de Calamidades.* Governo da Republica de Moçambique, Maputo.

GoM and UN (2005) *Report on the Millennium Development Goals.* Governo da Republica de Moçambique, Maputo.

Hanlon, J. (2007) *Is Poverty Decreasing in Mozambique?* IESE, Maputo, Conference paper # 14.

Hedges, D. (1977) *Trade and Politics in Southern Mozambique.* PhD thesis, University of London.

Hewitt, K. (1969) *Natural Hazard Research. A Pilot Survey of Global Natural Disasters of the Past Twenty Years.* University of Toronto, Working paper # 11.

IFRC (2009) *World Disaster Report 2009.* Geneva: IFRC.

INE (2002) *Censo Agro-Pecuário 1999–2000.* Apresentação Sumária dos Resultados. Maputo: INE.

INGC (2009) *Synthesis report. INGC Climate Change Report: Study on the Impacts of Climate Change on Disaster Risk in Mozambique,* van Logchem, B. and Brito, R. (eds). Maputo: INGC.

INGC, UEM and Fewsnet (2003) *Atlas for Disaster Preparedness and Response in the Limpopo Basin.* Maputo: INGC, UEM and Fewsnet.

IFRC (2009) *World Disaster Report 2009.* Geneva: IFRC.

IPCC (2007) *Fourth Assessment on Climate Change.* Cambridge: Cambridge University Press.

Isaacman, A. (1996) *Cotton is the Mother of Poverty. Peasants, Work, and Rural Struggles in Colonial Mozambique, 1938–1961.* London: James Currey.

Junod, H. (1996) *Usos e Costumes Bantu.* Maputo: Arquivo Histórico de Moçambique.

Liesagang, G. (1970) 'Nguni Migration Between Delagoa Bay and the Zambezi, 1821–1839'. *African Historical Studies,* 3: 317–337.

Mackenzie, C. (2006) *Forestry Governance in Zambézia, Mozambique: Chinese Takeaway!* Report prepared for FONGZA, Quelimane, Mozambique.

Mafambissa, F. (2007) *Efeitos dos Desastres Naturais na Produção Agrícola de Culturas Alimentares e na Segurança Alimentar.* IESE, Maputo, Conference paper #21.

Maier, K. (1989) 'The Battle for Zambezia'. *Africa Report,* March-April: 13–16.

Muchave, P. (1998) *Estratégias de Produção e Comercialização Agrícola no Perímetro Irrigado de Chokwe.* Maputo: Tese de licenciatura, FAEF.

Negrão, J. (2001) *O Impacto Socioeconómico das Cheias.* Oração de Sapiência por Ocasião da Abertura do Ano Lectivo 2001–2002. Maputo, Moçambique.

Newitt, M. (1988) 'Drought in Mozambique 1823–1831'. *Journal of Southern African Studies,* 15(1): 15–35.

Newitt, M. (1995) *A History of Mozambique.* London: Hurst & Company.

Oliver-Smith, A. (2005) 'Communities after Catastrophe. Reconstructing the Material, Reconstructing the Social'. In S. Hyland (ed.) *Community Building in the Twenty-First Century.* School of American Research Press, 45–70.

Rocha, A., D. Hedges, E. Medeiros and G. Liesagang (1999) 'A História de Moçambique 1885–1930'. In D. Hedges (ed.) *Historia de Moçambique, Volume 2: Moçambique no auge do colonialismo, 1930–1961.* Maputo: Livraria Univeristaria, Universidade Eduardo Mondlane, 1: 34.

Santos, M. and G. Henriques (1999) *Characterization of Meteorological Drought in Mozambican.* International Conference on Integrated Drought Management-Lessons for Sub-Saharan Africa. Pretoria 20–22 September.

Serra, C. (2000) *Historia de Moçambique.* Volume I. Maputo: Livraria Universitária.

Smith, A. (1991) 'The Idea of Mozambique and Its Enemies, c. 1890–1930'. *Journal of Southern African Studies,* 17(3): 496–524.

UN (1990) *The Emergency Situation in Mozambique. Priority Requirements for the Period 1990–1991.* New York: United Nations.

UNDP (2008) *Human Development Report 2007/2008. Fighting Climate Change: Human Solidarity in a Divided World.* New York: UNOP.

UNHCR (1996) *Evaluation of UNHCR's repatriation operation to Mozambique.* Geneva.

UNICEF (2007) *Childhood Poverty in Mozambique and Budgetary Allocations.* New York: UNICEF.

Vail, L. and L. White (1978) 'Tawani, Machambero: Forced Cotton and Rice Growing on the Zambezi'. *The Journal of African History,* 19(2): 239–263.

Vaux, T. (2001) *The Selfish Altruist. Relief Work in Famine and War.* London and Sterling, VA: Earthscan Publications.

Vaz, A. and P. van der Zaag (2003) *Sharing the Incomati Waters. Cooperation and Competition in the Balance.* Paris, France: UNESCO.

Webster, M., J. Ginnetti, P. Walker, D. Coppard and R. Kent (2008) *The Humanitarian Costs of Climate Change.* Feinstein International Center. Medford, MA: Tufts University.

Weinstein, J. and L. Francisco (2005) 'The Civil War in Mozambique. The Balance between Internal and External Influences'. In Collier, P. and N. Sambanis (eds) *Understanding Civil War – Africa.* Washington, DC: World Bank Publications.

Wisner, B. (1979) 'Flood Prevention and Mitigation in the People's Republic of Mozambique'. *Disasters,* 3(3): 293–306.

World Bank (2005) *Learning Lessons from Disaster Recovery: The Case of Mozambique.* Working Paper # 12. The World Bank Group: Washington DC, USA.

Wuyts, M. (1981) 'Sul do Save: Estabilização da força de Trabalho'. In: *Estudos Moçambicanos* 3: 33–44, CEA, Maputo, Mozambique.

4 The de-disasterisation of food crises

Structural reproduction or change in policy development and response options? A case study from Ethiopia

Jan-Gerrit van Uffelen

Introduction

Addressing hunger and food insecurity in protracted crisis

The reduction of hunger and food insecurity worldwide is a matter of great urgency. The number of hungry people today is higher than in 1996 when world leaders at the World Food Summit set the target to reduce the number of hungry by half by 2015. Though the prevalence of hunger in terms of undernourishment has declined significantly over the past decades, the number of hungry people rose to 906 million in 2010 (FAO 2010a).

Hunger is a measure of undernourishment and indicates that a person's caloric intake is below the minimum dietary energy requirement. The absence of hunger is closely related to food security, which is commonly defined as a situation where 'all people, at all times, have physical, social and economic access to sufficient, safe and nutritious food to meet their dietary needs and food preferences for an active and healthy life' (FAO 1996). A precise operational definition of food security does not exist. It is generally acknowledged, however, that food security has four dimensions relevant to food security programming: production of food, access to food (either via informal or formal networks such as markets), the utilisation of food, and the stability of the food system.

Addressing hunger and food insecurity in protracted crisis situations presents one of the most challenging contexts for the international community. Protracted crises have been defined as environments in which 'a significant proportion of the population is acutely vulnerable to death, disease and disruption of livelihoods over a prolonged period of time' (Harmer and Macrae 2004). Protracted crises differ across various contexts but share some of the following characteristics: duration or longevity of the crisis, conflict, weak governance or public administration, unsustainable livelihood systems and poor food security outcomes, and a breakdown of local institutions (FAO 2010b). Positive food security outcomes in such situations often need improvements in all four dimensions of food security. This requires a balance between relief and development-oriented activities. Linking the divided relief and development domains has, however, been a challenge for decades and has never been operationalised as a programmatic framework (Maxwell *et al.* 2010).

Crises, both at a global as well as a local level, pose significant risks to poor and vulnerable households, often with serious consequences for their food security. Particularly in countries characterised by protracted food crises, these may turn into catastrophic famines when a shortage of food or purchasing power leads, in the absence of a timely and appropriate response by the government or international community, to excess mortality from starvation or hunger-related diseases. Traditionally, the provision of food aid has been central in addressing hunger and food insecurity. Its use in humanitarian aid and development assistance has, however, come under increased scrutiny both from food policy makers and practitioners in the delivery of the humanitarian response (Barrett and Maxwell 2005, Maxwell *et al.* 2010). Central to this debate is how positive food security outcomes in countries prone to food crises can be realised through the globalisation of relief, better food aid governance, development assistance, and economic progress. The occurrence of famine and outcomes of food crises are known to be as much a function of the conditions that cause such crises as the policy response (Ó Gráda 2009: 3). This places food security policy making at the heart of the debate in efforts to effectively address transitory or chronic food insecurity, or combinations of both.

The case of Ethiopia

This chapter looks at the policy-making process and the response to tackling hunger and food insecurity. In doing so, I focus on Ethiopia's protracted food crisis and trace the evolution of changing interpretation frames and response options amongst the successive governments of Ethiopia and its international partners in dealing with past famines, current famine vulnerability, and recurrent food crises. Ethiopia's decades' long quest to promote food security has culminated in the Productive Safety Net Programme (PSNP) which is the key component of the country's current Food Security Programme (FSP). Both globally and in Ethiopia, the PSNP is presented as the result of a structural change in food security policy.

The de-disasterisation of famine vulnerability and recurrent food crises

My interpretation, based on a review of relevant literature and interviews with senior policy makers at both national and international level, is that, in essence, Ethiopia's food security policy-making process has resulted in the 'de-disasterisation' of the country's famine vulnerability and recurrent food crises. With the term 'de-disasterisation', I mean the process by which structural or recurrent crises become 'normalised' and are no longer framed or perceived as disasters. De-disasterisation can be negative, when it leads to the *de facto* acceptance of high levels of acute or chronic food insecurity that used to be considered disastrous, with the result that affected people are not receiving the support they need for immediate survival or covering their basic food needs. On the other hand, de-disasterisation can be positive, in cases where it results in structural changes in policies that aim to address the root causes of the disaster.

Structure of this chapter

The structure of this chapter is as follows. After this Introduction, the next section presents the methodology, followed by a short overview of the history of food crises in Ethiopia in section three. The fourth section narrates the history of food security policy making by looking at the changing perspectives and interpretation frames of successive Ethiopian governments and their international partners in dealing with hunger and food insecurity. The fifth section looks at the Productive Safety Net Programme, the key component of the country's Food Security Programme and the culmination of Ethiopia's decades' long quest for food security. The last section presents the Summary and Conclusions.

Methodology

To characterise the evolution of food security policies promoted by successive Ethiopian governments and their international partners, I trace the history of the different interpretation frameworks of the major stakeholders. I concentrate on Ethiopia's key famine periods 1972–1973, 1984–1985 and the food crises of 1999–2000, 2002–2003, 2008 and 2011. I am particularly interested in showing how food security response has, and still is, evolving, and whether food security policies are structurally reproducing response options or represent a fundamental break from the past that allows for new programmes to emerge.

Ethiopia is used as an exemplar, since the country has had a long history of food crises, with the international community increasingly involved in the management of the food crises and disaster responses following the famines of 1972–1973 and 1984–1985. Following the Great Ethiopian Famine of 1984–1985, the country has remained vulnerable to famine (the 2000 crisis in the Somali Region and the 'localised famine' of 2002–2003) and chronically food insecure, with an average of five million Ethiopians requiring food aid every year since the mid-1980s (GoE 2003, IFPRI 2009a, 2009b).

The United Nation's Food and Agriculture Organization (FAO) labels Ethiopia as a country facing a protracted crisis. This is because of the frequency of its recurrent food crises (Ethiopia reports a food crisis almost every year since the 1984–1985 famine), the high percentage of the population being undernourished (41 per cent in the period 2005–2007), the high proportion of humanitarian assistance as a share of total assistance since 2008 (21 per cent) and because Ethiopia is on the list of Low-Income Food-Deficit countries due to its poor economic and food security status (FAO 2010b).

The policy response to protracted food crises: structural reproduction or change?

Countries in protracted food crisis make for difficult contexts for the international community to work in. This is because of the different ways in which the relief and development community perceive and interpret protracted crises, understand its relationship to the development process, and provide aid to address such crises (FAO 2010b).

Three main interpretation frameworks may be distinguished. These are (1) the humanitarian discourse, (2) the development discourse, and (3) the social protection discourse. The humanitarian discourse problematises hunger and food insecurity as the result of a disaster or crisis which necessitates a needs-based emergency response to deal with acute hunger and food insecurity (Barrett 2006, Maxwell *et al.* 2010). The developmental discourse explains hunger and food insecurity as a result of poverty, and typically prescribes a market-based response that often emphasises the need for agricultural production and economic growth (Barrett 2008, Maxwell *et al.* 2010). The social protection discourse explains hunger and food insecurity as a result of vulnerability and risk to shocks, and suggests initiatives to protect the vulnerable against livelihood risks, such as safety nets (Devereux and Sabates-Wheeler 2004, McCord and Slater 2009, FAO 2010b). These discourses reflect different styles of governance that not only promote different solutions and response options but may also compete with one another.

My understanding is that, when a particular discourse is prominent in the policy-making process, food security policy is characterised by a structural reproduction of response options which can be of a cyclical or cumulative nature. It is cyclical when merely reproducing a given response option such as, for example, provision of food relief following drought. It is cumulative when making gradual improvements in the way response options are delivered, such as improvements in targeting and the timely provision of emergency relief resources to beneficiaries. The policy process is characterised by structural change when an alternative discourse gains prominence in the policy domain and promotes new types of programmatic response. Structural changes often reflect a fundamental rethinking of explanations of hunger and food insecurity and can result in alternative solutions and new response options that constitute a break from the past.

The research questions

In looking at Ethiopia as a case, we focus on how successive Ethiopian governments and their international partners understand and frame food crises and promote response options. We do this in the light of three research questions:

1   How have global and national food security actors framed and responded to Ethiopia's recurrent food crises?
2   Do the resulting policies promote structural reproduction of programmatic response options or promote structural change and produce new response options?

3   Is there a need for additional structural change in Ethiopia's food security policy to end the country's protracted food crisis?

Key policy documents of the main global and national food security actors in Ethiopia's food security policy-making process were reviewed, including literature on famine and food crisis response as relevant to the Ethiopian case. Senior staff of the main agencies involved in food security policy making in Ethiopia and at their international headquarters were interviewed[1] to solicit their views and opinions regarding the evolution of policy, the resulting response options, their impact, and the implications for future policies aimed at solving Ethiopia's protracted food crisis.

Famine and food crisis in Ethiopia

Famines and food crises are not new phenomena to Ethiopia. Famine in Ethiopia was first recorded in the ninth century, with ten major famines occurring in the fifteenth to seventeenth centuries (Pankhurst 1985, Hoben 1995). The great famine of 1888–1889 caused widespread death and devastation, with more localised, but no less lethal, famines occurring in 1916–1920, 1927–1928, and 1934–1935 (Hoben 1995). In recent times, Ethiopia has experienced famine in 1972–1973 and in 1984–1985, causing an estimated excess mortality of 60,000 and 500,000, respectively (de Waal 1997, Devereux 2000, 2006). Recent food crises were recorded in 1999–2000 (Hammond and Maxwell 2002, White 2005, Devereux 2009), 2003 (Kehler 2004, Lautze and Raven-Roberts 2004), 2008 (OCHA 2008), and 2011. Following the famine of 1984–1985 a minimum of five million Ethiopians have required food aid annually (FDRE 2003), peaking at close to thirteen million people in 2003 (GoE 2003, WFP 2004). The recent 2011 crisis in the Horn has resulted in 13.3 million people in need of humanitarian assistance, of whom 4.6 million were Ethiopians (OCHA 2011), in addition to those covered by the PSNP programme.

Analysts of food insecurity in Ethiopia can be divided into two camps: the 'physical ecology cluster', who focus on population growth, declining soil fertility, and drought, and the 'political economy' cluster, who blame government policies, weak markets, and institutional failure (Devereux 2000). The role of conflict in the decline of food security and livelihoods has been mentioned by various authors as a contributing factor, tipping local food shortages into catastrophic droughts (de Waal 1997, White 2005). Many of the major famines of the twentieth century, the Ethiopian famines of 1972–1973 and 1984–1985 being no exception, were linked to either civil strife or warfare, with human action greatly exacerbating 'acts of nature' (Ó Gráda 2009).

In Ethiopia, local food crises are typically triggered by erratic weather conditions, in particular drought, with rural overpopulation and land degradation commonly being mentioned as underlying causes. People's survival strategies are forced responses to structural food deficits (Rahmato 1991, Sharp *et al.* 2003). Livelihoods of Ethiopia's overwhelmingly rural population are heavily reliant on peasant agriculture in the highlands and agro-pastoralism in the lowlands (Sharp *et al.* 2003, White 2005). Rural Ethiopia is unusually undifferentiated, with small farmers accounting for 90 per cent of the total crop area and agricultural output (Bollinger *et al.* 1999). In much of Ethiopia's highlands, increasing population pressure has reduced landholdings that are becoming too small to provide subsistence under current farming systems. High population growth, averaging around 3 per cent annually, reduces landholdings to 'starvation plots' and drives agricultural expansion onto hillsides and grazing lands, thus contributing to degradation (Rahmato 1994, White 2005). People's food and income strategies are further reduced, as off-farm employment opportunities are limited in both availability and income-generating potential (Devereux 2000).

Both the 'physical ecology' as well as the 'political economy' interpretation lenses have merit as partial explanations of Ethiopia's famine vulnerability and food insecurity, but neither are thought to be sufficient in themselves (Devereux 2000). In their landmark publication *Famine and Food Insecurity in Ethiopia*, Webb and von Braun (1994) stated that Ethiopia's food-secure future without famine must rest on three pillars: active emergency preparedness, sound growth policies, and good governance. This highlights the centrality of the food security policy-making process in Ethiopia and the crucial importance of appropriate programmatic response options for the country to become structurally food secure.

Ethiopia's food crises and the evolution of response

Countries in protracted crisis present many challenges for the aid apparatus, particularly in relation to the complex interrelationship between humanitarian aid and development assistance. This section looks at how global and national food security actors have framed Ethiopia's recurrent food crises and defined policies and response options accordingly.

Famine as disaster: the 1972–1973 and 1984–1985 famines, and the institutionalisation of emergency relief aid

The Sahel drought of 1968–1973 caused a serious decline in food availability in parts of northern Ethiopia. Localised food shortages turned into a crisis, causing mass displacement and starvation that claimed an estimated 40,000 to 80,000 deaths in 1972–1973 (Ó Gráda 2009). Authorities initially sought to suppress news of the crisis, but when a BBC documentary reported on the 'unknown famine', it quickly became the focus of an international relief effort by mid-October 1973. Ethiopia's 1972–1973 famine eroded Emperor Haile Selassie's legitimacy and became one of the few famines known to have triggered regime change (Ó Gráda 2009). The Dergue government (1974–1991) discredited the Imperial regime, blaming responsibility for the famine on its feudal land policies and practices, with the Dergue's socialism presented as an anti-famine political contract. The 1972–1973 famine contributed to a strong growth of UN and non-governmental organisation (NGO) disaster relief institutions in Ethiopia and resulted in the creation of the Relief and Rehabilitation Commission (RRC) in 1974.

Return of serious droughts in the Sahel during the mid-1980s caused harvest failures in northern Ethiopia, particularly in Tigray and Wollo. Harvest failures in 1983 and 1984 were exacerbated by the war waged by the Dergue against secessionists in Tigray, resulting in famine. The situation was compounded by the Dergue's ill-advised economic policies which reduced the private food trade and undermined agricultural output because of low prices and forced collectivisation (Wolde Mariam 1985, Rahmato 1991, Webb and von Braun 1994). By showing images of Ethiopians dying from starvation, 1984 BBC news coverage revealed the dimensions of the 'greatest humanitarian disaster of the late 20th century'. It caused a global public outcry which transformed the 'face of aid' (Gill 2010). The 1984–1985 famine left almost one-fifth of Ethiopia's population in need of aid, with an estimated mortality of 500,000 people (Ó Gráda 2009).

International news coverage of the 1972–1973 and the 1984–1985 food crises exposed government inaction versus the action by the international community. By declaring both crises a famine, the international community initiated large-scale emergency relief operations. The Imperial Ethiopian government's inaction and the ability of famine to trigger regime change served as 'an historical fact of which subsequent officials and politicians have remained intensely aware' (Lautze *et al.* 2009). It made the management of disaster response and food crises central to Ethiopian politics. However, the response to the 1984–1985 crisis was late, with the RRC claiming a catastrophic drought by May 1984 (RRC 1984). Its 'early' warning was met by limited donor response, as the RRC was increasingly seen as being politicised. When international aid did arrive, it was instrumental in saving lives; it was also clear, however, that the Dergue used the international relief presence to its economic, diplomatic, and military advantage (de Waal 1997).

In the aftermath of Ethiopia's 1984–1985 famine, the provision of longer-term developmental aid by western donors for the Ethiopian government was not an option, particularly so on account of the Dergue's Marxist ideology and with the West seeing the government to be 'violating human rights, pursuing a protracted civil war in the north, following bad economic policies and aligned with the Soviet Union' (Hoben 1995). In order not to be blamed for merely alleviating the symptoms of the crisis by providing continued emergency food aid, donors adopted the 'physical ecology' lens, framing the underlying causes of Ethiopia's famine and famine vulnerability as environmental degradation due to population increase, poverty, and poor farming practice (Hoben 1995). This structural change in policy made new programmatic response options possible in the form of large-scale land reclamation programmes, in particular, soil and water conservation works. These were implemented through Food-for-Work (FFW) activities which were seen as the 'least bad development-oriented intervention option' (Hoben 1995: 1013). Applying the physical ecology lens meant a fundamental break from emergency food aid to putting food distributions to productive use in the form of Food-for-Work. But while there was convergence between the government and its predominantly western donors to use food aid in a productive manner by promoting

FFW, there was at the same time divergence with the Dergue's formal policy on resettlement as a developmentalist approach in promoting durable solutions to famine and food insecurity (Clay and Holcomb 1986).

As a result of the 1972–1973 and 1984–1985 famines, the humanitarian discourse became central to the food security policy-making process, albeit with an important break from food aid to Food-for-Work, and contributed to the institutionalisation of emergency relief aid. This saved lives and suppressed Ethiopia's famine vulnerability. Food insecurity, however, remained both widespread, as well as persistent, as clearly shown by the re-occurrence of food crises in 1999–2000 and 2002–2003.

Famine vulnerability as a disgrace: the food crises of 1999–2000 and 2002–2003 as a key transition period

Following the downfall of the Dergue, the Transitional Government of Ethiopia (1991–1995) adopted a more liberal market model in line with its Economic Development Strategy. On the basis of its 1993 National Policy on Disaster Prevention and Management (NPDPM), the government sought a stronger coordination with the international community, requesting NGOs to focus on Disaster Risk Reduction. The government also decided to replace all remaining free food distributions with Food-for-Work under the Employment Generation Scheme, with the aim of rebuilding productive assets. The programme had, however, serious flaws: relief food was unreliable (often too little and coming too late) and essential complementary inputs, such as tools, equipment, and supplies, were largely unavailable (Kehler 2004).

In 1995, the government replaced the Relief and Rehabilitation Commission as its disaster management utility with the Disaster Prevention and Preparedness Committee (DPPC), whose aim was to prevent disaster, reduce its impact, and ensure timely assistance to disaster victims. This institutional reform underlined a shifting emphasis from addressing the consequences of food crises to preventing such crises happening in the first place. In 1995, the Federal Democratic Republic of Ethiopia (FDRE) was established and, following a number of years with favourable weather conditions and good harvests, the issue of famine vulnerability and food insecurity became less salient. The government decided to reduce its disaster response capacity, even though more than two million Ethiopians needed food aid during the bumper harvest year of 1996. But instead of an improvement in the situation, food shortages became more frequent in Ethiopia, affecting more people. Towards the end of the millennium, Ethiopia's food security had steadily worsened despite the country being the largest recipient of emergency aid per capita in Africa, and despite thirty years of food aid (Kehler 2004).

In 1999–2000, Ethiopia faced another serious drought, with international donors opting for a 'food aid bias'. They focused on short-term humanitarian needs rather than longer-term support for food security, in part because of serious international concerns about the 1998–2000 Ethiopian-Eritrean war (White 2005). The mass mortality of the 1999–2000 crisis in Ethiopia's Somali Region was less than that of the 'Great Ethiopian Famine' of 1984–1985, but still claimed between 72,000 and 123,000 lives (Salama *et al.* 2001).

Yet, the beginning of the third millennium also proved to be a key transition period, with food security actors framing Ethiopia's recurrent food crises and persistent food insecurity in new ways. In 1981, Sen, in his seminal work on poverty and famines, had already shown that famine was not created by the absence of food *per se* but by the lack of people's entitlement to access food (Sen 1981). At an international level, critical rethinking of the humanitarian response to food insecurity had reconceptualised famine vulnerability as the outcome of a process rendering people vulnerable to external shocks, rather than the outcome of a sudden event. Food crises in southern and eastern Africa during the early 2000s stimulated a further radical rethinking of the humanitarian response to food insecurity and hunger in Africa. This led to the recognition that hunger and food insecurity, far from being unpredictable emergencies, were essentially a reflection of chronic poverty and vulnerability and, thus, predictable (McCord and Slater 2009).

At the same time, there was a recognition that food aid was no solution to Ethiopia's chronic food insecurity, as evidenced by declining per capita food production since the beginning of the 1970s (Devereux 2000). Food aid to combat chronic or acute food insecurity in Ethiopia saved lives, but it did not succeed in halting a decline in people's livelihood assets, improving malnutrition or mitigating people's vulnerability to shocks (Kehler 2004). This was dramatically demonstrated by the drought of 2002–2003, which required 'exceptional food assistance' for well over 13 million Ethiopians, with acute malnutrition peaking at 52 per cent (WFP 2004, MoARD 2009). The 2002–2003 crisis exposed once again the weakness of the humanitarian needs-based approach, which had consistently prioritised the use of food aid in dealing with Ethiopia's recurrent food crises. The crisis highlighted that, in protracted crisis situations, interventions that maintain food entitlement of affected populations must extend beyond ensuring immediate human survival (Flores *et al.* 2005). While emergency food aid is often a necessary part of humanitarian response to acute food security, it is not sufficient to build the foundations of longer-term food security (Barrett 2006, FAO 2010b).

The 2002–2003 crisis also highlighted the fact that declaring a famine is a political act (de Waal 1997) and that who declares famine has implications for international versus national responsibility in dealing with it and its effects. While the government downplayed the scale and seriousness of the situation on the ground in 2003, a group of international specialists visiting the Gode area stated that, 'you have a widespread livelihood crisis leading to emergency levels of malnutrition, morbidity, mortality, with alarming implications for destitution: that for us is a famine' (Lautze and Raven-Roberts 2004).The reluctance to declare the 2002–2003 food crisis a famine was clearly associated with political vulnerability on the part of the Ethiopian government as well as its international donors, in particular the US (Lautze and Raven-Robert 2004). The compromise, according to Lautze and Raven-Roberts, was for the US Agency for International Development (USAID) to refer to the crisis as a 'localised famine', implying 'that the situation was serious, but not unmanageable'.

In a sense, the 2002–2003 food crisis made clear that Ethiopia's famine vulnerability was perceived as a disgrace, something bad and to be ashamed of, both by national politicians as well as the international community, and something to be addressed at all cost. In the aftermath of the crisis, Ethiopia's Prime Minister, Meles Zenawi, demonstrating significant political commitment, declared food security a top national priority and voiced the government's commitment to break the decade-long dependency on external aid. Following the Prime Minister's declaration, humanitarian and development actors in Ethiopia joined hands as part of the New Coalition for Food Security formed in 2003. This initiative sought to find ways to 'reduce dependency on foreign emergency food aid' and to 'phase out the use of food aid altogether' (MoARD 2009). The coalition recommended a gradual transition from humanitarian assistance to a system of productive safety nets as a bridge between emergency and development in disaster-prone food-insecure areas. The WFP supported this transition, in line with its new policy guidelines which promoted the use of safety nets as more central to the aid system 'to safeguard in the event of shocks, assist those in need and ensure that livelihoods are built upon' (WFP 2004). Donors and development partners also underlined the need to shift from food aid as a resource transfer to cash, which the government supported. The World Food Programme also underlined the need for complementary interventions besides cash or food for work as the solution to Ethiopia's chronic food insecurity. By boosting local production to replace imported food aid with purchase of locally produced crops and capacity building to enable a reliable cash transfer programme, Ethiopia would, according to the WFP in 2004, 'graduate from relief aid by 2015' (Kehler 2004).

In conclusion, the 1999–2000 and 2002–2003 food crises made it clear that the institutionalised humanitarian response, albeit with food aid increasingly provided in the form of Food-for-Work in non-crisis years to address production failures, suppressed Ethiopia's famine vulnerability but did little to end hunger and food insecurity. This shifted the focus and interpretation frames of the major stakeholders not only to Disaster Risk Reduction (in line with the NPDPM) but even more so towards a focus on poverty reduction to address food entitlement or exchange failures.

The critique on the hegemony of the humanitarian needs-based discourse that dominated Ethiopia's food security programming during the last decades of the twentieth century was that, though it did save lives, it failed to save livelihoods. Ethiopia's new Food Security Strategy was designed to do both – thus representing, in theory at least, a structural and fundamental change in food security policies.

The end of famine vulnerability and food insecurity? Ethiopia's current Food Security Programme

The 'localised famine' of 2002–2003 signalled a change in approach to famine, away from the humanitarian discourse towards a more development-oriented discourse. The focus broadened from the use of relief food aid and food-for-work in response to food production failures to a focus on poverty reduction and liveli-hood diversification to address food entitlement failure. This paved the way for Ethiopia's 2005–2009 Food Security Programme (FSP) that aimed to transform the institutionalised relief-oriented emergency system into a more developmental-oriented predictable safety net. The resulting programmes, the donor-funded Productive Safety Net Programme (PSNP) and the government-funded so-called Other Food Security Programmes (OFSPs), were designed to break the circle of food aid dependency. The third component of the FSP, the government-funded Voluntary Resettlement Programme (VRP), is in response to the 'physical ecology' explanation of famine vulnerability, which the government and its development partners shared. However, unlike the government, its international partners never considered the government's developmentalist perspective on resettlement as a lasting and sustainable solution to end food insecurity and hunger. The VRP has also been criticised as a strategy to make the poorest of the poor invisible through their participation in the programme (Hammond 2008, Bishop and Hilhorst 2010).

The PSNP is the main component of the FSP and receives by far the largest budget allocation of the three FSP components. As such, the PSNP does not reflect a structural change in policy, as its design of Public Works and Direct Support is identical to the system in the 1990s, with Food-for-Work for chroni-cally food-insecure households with labour capacity and Gratuities Relief for labour-constrained households. Most of the Public Works activities are also similar to the Food-for-Work activities of the 1990s. The PSNP thus structurally repro-duces response options, but these do reflect an important cumulative change in nature on at least four accounts. First, resource transfers are no longer based on unpredictable annual emergency needs assessment and appeals but PSNP beneficiaries receive, at least in theory, resource transfers for a five-year period. Beneficiaries are engaged in community asset building (such as soil and water conservation works, road construction) and in return receive resource transfers for which predictability and timeliness are seen as key to the success of the programme (MoARD 2004). Also, cash has been introduced as a resource transfer and currently represents around 5 per cent of all resource transfers. Second, the WFP as the main provider of resource transfers to the PSNP, has started to procure food in Ethiopia (through its Purchase for Progress projects) and regionally. Third, in terms of targeting, the PSNP distinguishes between the chronically food insecure and the transitory food insecure. The first group is covered by the safety net func-tion of the PSNP and the second group by the PSNP's contingency budget for addressing acute needs following an external shock. And fourth, the PSNP has benefitted from gradual improvements in WFP's 'Project 2488' and the MERET programme (short for Managing Environmental Resources to Enable Transitions to More Sustainable Livelihoods) which succeeded it in 1999. MERET has adopted a community-based participatory watershed development approach, by using resource transfers to pay for disaster risk reduction. Rehabilitation of degraded lands is complemented with a range of income-generating activities (such as horticulture, animal husbandry, and beekeeping) and productivity improvement, including low-cost soil fertility management and small-scale irrigation (Nedessa and Wickrema 2010).

The combination of the PSNP and the OFSP reflect an important structural change in policies, enabling new types of programming and programmatic linkages. The PSNP and OFSPs were designed to link, in new and innovative ways, relief to development by harnessing the humanitarian and developmental discourses in a multi-annual timeframe. In essence, the PSNP and OFSP comprise three strategies: addressing acute humanitarian emergencies in the event of external weather-related shocks, in particular drought (the PSNP's emergency utility function); the provision of a safety net for consumption smoothing and asset protection for the chronically food insecure; and asset-building among the chronically poor as a pathway out of the safety net and poverty (graduation). The PSNP and its emergency utility thus address chronic and transitory food insecurity aimed at consumption smoothing and asset protection, and is seen as conditional for the OFSPs. The OFSPs are aimed at increasing poor people's productive assets (both to enhance production and exchange entitlement) by increasing agricultural productivity and promoting livelihood diversification through on- and off-farm productive investments, such as the provision of agricultural production packages, small-scale irrigation and rainwater harvesting projects, and the provision of credit.

The de-disasterisation of Ethiopia's protracted food crisis

The evolution of responses to Ethiopia's recurrent food crises show significant changes in the ways in which the Ethiopian state and its international partners have interpreted and framed Ethiopia's famines and food crises.

My contention is that the food security policy process in Ethiopia has, in effect, resulted in the de-disasterisation of Ethiopia's protracted food crisis. The 1972–1973 and 1984–1985 food crisis were declared famine disasters by the international community and it responded with emergency food relief – which became quickly institutionalised. Following these disasters, famine prevention became more central to food security policy. The 1999–2000 and 2002–2003 food crises, however, exposed Ethiopia's continuing famine vulnerability which was seen as a disgrace, with both crises being downplayed and the 2002–2003 crisis described as a 'localised famine', underscoring that 'the situation was serious, but not unmanageable'. These two crises paved the way for Ethiopia's 2005–2009 Food Security Strategy which aimed to transform the institutionalised relief-oriented emergency system into a development-oriented safety net. The government is of the opinion that Ethiopia's famine vulnerability and food insecurity is now under control and that its current 2010–2014 FSP and highly ambitious broader growth-oriented policies[2] will end Ethiopia's dependency on international emergency food aid and food assistance. The government therefore regards the PSNP (the major component both of the 2005–2009 and the 2010–2014 FSP) as a short-term mechanism for achieving rural development and graduation out of food insecurity and poverty.

So, after nearly forty years of famine relief and structural approaches to address food insecurity, Ethiopia's recurrent food crises and famine vulnerability are seen as a developmental challenge rather than an emergency. The boundaries between crisis and normality have faded, with emergencies being 'normalised' in terms of policies and programmes. The question is whether the current policies that are institutionalising this de-disasterisation are 'normalising' the crisis or contributing to a lasting solution of Ethiopia's protracted food crisis. The answer to this question crucially depends on the success or failure of households' 'graduation' from the PSNP and OFSP.

The PSNP as a lasting solution to Ethiopia's protracted food crisis?

The impact of the Food Security Programme

The expected results of the combined impact of the PSNP and OFSP's were very ambitious. The aim of Ethiopia's 2005–2009 FSP was to 'enable the 8.29 million chronically food insecure people to attain food security within a five year period' and to 'improve significantly the food security situation of the remaining 6.71 million facing transitory food insecurity problems' (MoFED 2006). This high ambition is a reflection of the objective of the Coalition for Food Security which, when established in 2003, was to 'achieve a major turn-around of the food insecurity challenges within the timeframe of three to five years' (MoARD 2009).

Evaluations of the PSNP and OFSPs demonstrate significant programmatic impact. A number of evaluations found explicit evidence of the PSNP smoothing consumption and protecting assets (IDL 2006, 2010, Devereux *et al.* 2008, IFPRI 2008, SCF 2009). In areas where the PSNP and OFSPs were implemented well, and where the two programmes were combined, household asset holdings increased and crop production improved (Gilligan *et al.* 2009). Progress towards graduation from the safety net has, however, been disappointing with only 56,895 households graduated by April 2009 or less than 10 per cent of all PSNP households (MoARD 2009). Graduation at the scale expected by the Ethiopian government did not happen. Senior staff of the government's main international partners, both in Ethiopia and at international headquarters, expressed the view that achieving livelihood diversification proved a far more complex and time-consuming process than initially anticipated. In explaining why graduation fell short of expectations, they stated capacity and implementation challenges rather than design faults. For example, only a quarter of the PSNP beneficiaries were covered by the OFSPs in the period 2005–2009, which was seen as compromising households' ability to graduate from the safety net. Concern was also expressed regarding the quality of the Public Works (the 'productive' element of the PSNP). Soil and water conservation activities, for example, were not logically sequenced but instead 'doing bits and pieces of everything with the work being rushed' and with resource transfers not made conditional on the quality of work done or the level of transformation taking place.[3]

The risk management utility of the PSNP was put to the test in 2008 when drought hit parts of northern Ethiopia. By the time additional resources were required to deal with the drought, both the PSNP's contingency budget (20 per cent of the overall PSNP budget is reserved as risk management utility to deal with 'sudden disaster' or 'situations of immediate need') and Ethiopia's Emergency Food Security Reserve were already depleted. This raised questions amongst agencies such as the World Bank and the WFP over whether the safety net was overstretched and fundamentally under-resourced.[4] The 2008 drought coincided with high inflation rates in Ethiopia, which eroded the food purchasing power of households receiving cash transfers (around 5 per cent of all households). Both donors and the government were confronted with large budget increases to raise PSNP wages.

Contestation of the graduation narrative

With graduation seen as central to the FSP's success but falling way short of the government's expectations, differences between the government and its donors and development partners are becoming increasingly apparent. The government of Ethiopia aims to end the PSNP in 2014, arguing that after ten years of Public Works, participants should have graduated, though some Direct Support households might receive some ongoing assistance. But while the government plans graduation at scale before the end of 2014, and demands regional governments such as, for example, Amhara Regional State to graduate all Public Works PSNP beneficiaries by 2013, the government's development partners expect that most PSNP beneficiaries will not achieve 'self-reliance' by 2014. They therefore think that the PSNP should continue in some form.

The graduation narrative is, therefore, at risk of becoming contested, with international partners of the government fearing that PSNP beneficiaries will be graduated for political reasons, to achieve the government's pre-established targets to end people's dependency on aid, rather than on the basis of real improvement in people's livelihoods. This would mean that many of the households that 'graduate' are left as vulnerable and food insecure as before the start of the programme in 2005. If that happens, the de-disasterisation of Ethiopia's recurrent food crises signifies the 'normalisation' of such crises, resulting in the structural reproduction of the humanitarian needs-based response to addressing people's acute food needs, rather than the envisaged structural changes in policy to find a lasting solution to end Ethiopia's recurrent food crises.

The praxis of graduation is central in bridging the emerging divide between the government and its international partners. It is, therefore, essential that households graduate on the basis of real improvement in their livelihoods. This requires a more fundamental debate about what can be regarded as the holy grail of the graduation narrative: the level of assets required for chronically food-insecure households to become food secure and graduate from the safety net.

Findings and conclusion

Based on a review of key literature, interviews with senior government officials and staff of international food security actors, this chapter has examined how Ethiopia's famines and food crises have informed the making of food security policy.

My contention is that Ethiopia's four decades-long quest for food security has resulted in the de-disasterisation of its famine vulnerability and recurrent food crises. The key issue is whether this de-disasterisation is driven by policies that structurally reproduce particular response options (such as emergency aid as promoted by the humanitarian discourse) resulting in the 'normalisation' of crises, or by a structural change in policy that allows for new types of response options that hold out a promise to end famine vulnerability and recurrent food crises.

Emergency food relief was the response to the 1972–1973 and 1984–1985 famines, as in the humanitarian discourse. In the wake of the 1984–1985 famine, the Dergue government and its western donors initiated a structural change in policy by converging on the idea of putting food aid to productive use. Policy developments by the Transitional Government of Ethiopia and the Federal Democratic Republic of Ethiopia in the 1990s resulted in structural reproduction of the Dergue's programmatic response options, albeit characterised by an important cumulative change, in particular by seeking improvements in the quality of Food-for-Work activities. The food crises of 1999–2000 and 2002–2003 led to the recognition that, far from being unpredictable emergencies, hunger and food insecurity were also a reflection of chronic poverty and thus, predictable (McCord and Slater 2009). This resulted in a structural change in policy in 2005 that promoted new types of programmes aimed at seeking an end to Ethiopia's recurrent food crises. In addressing food insecurity, Ethiopia's 2005–2009 FSP and its 2009–2014 FSP link, in new and innovative ways, the humanitarian and developmental discourse and regard the PSNP and OFSPs as essential and complementary for people to become food secure and to graduate from the safety net.

Graduation from the safety net, seen as central to the success of the PSNP and OFSP, has so far fallen short of expectations, which has contributed to the contestation and politicisation of the graduation narrative. This highlights the different perspectives and expectations between the government and its partners in the PSNP. The government has a 'developmental' vision and sees the PNSP as a temporary mechanism for achieving rural development and graduation-at-scale out of food insecurity. The government's developmental partners see the PSNP as a safety net that should be institutionalised to provide permanent social protection against future external shocks, in particular drought, as such shocks are not only seen as inevitable but are also seen as highly likely to push people back into poverty and food insecurity, given the highly risky livelihood context in large parts of rural Ethiopia.

Experience of graduation on the basis of real improvement in people's livelihoods will tell whether there is a need for a further structural change in Ethiopia's food security policy. Evidence so far strongly suggests that there is a need to institutionalise social protection as a permanent and integral part of Ethiopia's food security and wider policy environment. Such an additional structural change in policy would mean that the de-disasterisation of Ethiopia's famine vulnerability and recurrent food crises addresses the root causes of the manifestations of disaster.

Acknowledgements

The author wishes to thank Annelies Heijmans, Jeroen Warner, Stephen Devereux, and Peter Oosterveer for their constructive comments on an earlier version of this chapter. All responsibility remains with the author.

Notes

1 Interviews were held in February 2009 in Rome with the World Food Programme (WFP), FAO, and International Fund for Agricultural Development (IFAD) and in Washington with International Forestry Resources and Institutions (IFPRI) and the World Bank (WB) in June 2011. Meetings in Addis with the WFP, FAO, WB, and IFPRI were held twice a year in the period 2009–2011. During the same period, Ethiopian government officials at federal level were met once a year in Addis and twice a year at a regional level in Bahir Dar.
2 Its current five-year poverty-reduction paper, the Growth and Transformation Plan.
3 Interview WFP, Addis Ababa, Ethiopia (January 2011).
4 Interview WFP and World Bank, Addis Ababa, Ethiopia (January 2011) and World Bank in Washington DC (June 2011).

References

Barrett, C.B. (2006) *Food Aid in Response to Acute Food Insecurity*, ESA Working Paper Nos. 06–10, Rome: Agricultural and Development Economics Division, Food and Agriculture Organisation of the United Nations.

Barrett, C.B. (2008) 'Smallholder Market Participation: Concepts and Evidence from Eastern and Southern Africa', *Food Policy*, 33 (4): 299–317.

Barrett, C.B. and Maxwell, D.G. (2005) *Food Aid After Fifty Years: Recasting its Role*. London: Routledge.

Bishop, C. and Hilhorst, D. (2010) 'From Food Aid to Food Security: The Case of the Safety Net Policy in Ethiopia', *Journal of Modern African Studies*, 48 (2): 181–202.

Bollinger, L., Stover, J. and Seyoum, E. (1999) *The Economic Impact of AIDS in Ethiopia*. Washington, DC: Futures Group International.

Clay, J.W. and Holcomb, B.K. (1986) 'Politics and the Ethiopian Famine 1984–85', Occasional Paper 20, *Cultural Survival*, Cambridge, MA: Cultural Survival, Inc.

Devereux, S. (2000) *Famine in the Twentieth Century*. Working Paper 105, Brighton: Institute of Development Studies.

Devereux, S. (2006) *The New Famines: Why Famine Persists in an Era of Globalisation*. London: Routledge.

Devereux, S. (2009) Why Does Famine Persist in Africa? *Food Security*, 1: 25–35.

Devereux, S. and Sabates-Wheeler, R. (2004) *Transformative Social Protection*. Working Paper 232, Brighton: Institute for Development Studies.

Devereux, S., Sabates-Wheeler, R., Slater, R., Tefera, M., Brown, T. and Teshome, A. (2008) *Ethiopia's Productive Safety Net Programme (PSNP): 2008 Assessment Report*. Brighton: Institute for Development Studies.

de Waal, A. (1997) *Famine Crimes: Politics and the Disaster Relief Industry in Africa*. Oxford: James Currey.

FAO (1996) *Declaration on World Food Security*, Rome: World Food Summit, FAO.

FAO (2010a) *Global Hunger Declining, but Still Unacceptably High: International Hunger Targets Difficult to Reach*. Rome: Economic and Social Development Department, Food and Agriculture Organisation of the United Nations.

FAO (2010b) *The State of the Food Insecurity in the World: Addressing Food Insecurity in Protracted Crises*. Rome: Food and Agriculture Organisation of the United Nations.

FDRE (Federal Democratic Republic of Ethiopia) (2003) *The New Coalition for Food Security Ethiopia, Vol. I – Food Security Programme*, Addis Ababa: Government of Ethiopia.

Flores, M., Khawaja, Y. and White, P. (2005) 'Food Security in Protracted Crises: Building More Effective Policy Frameworks', *Disasters*, 29 (suppl.): S25–S51.

Gill, P. (2010) *Famine and Foreigners: Ethiopia Since Live Aid*. Oxford: Oxford University Press.

Gilligan D.O., Hoddinot, J. and Taffesse, A.S. (2009) *The Impact of Ethiopia's Productive Safety Net Programme and its Linkages*. IFPRI Discussion Paper 00839. Washington, DC: International Food Policy Research Institute (IFPRI).

GoE (2003) *Update on the Current Situation and Assistance Requirements*. Addis Ababa: Joint Government – UN Addendum, March 14, 2003.

Hammond, L. (2008) 'Strategies of Invisibilization: How Ethiopia's Resettlement Programme Hides the Poorest of the Poor', *Journal of Refugee Studies* 21 (4): 517–536.

Hammond, L. and Maxwell, D. (2002) 'The Ethiopian Crisis of 1999–2000: Lessons Learned, Questions Unanswered', *Disasters*, 26 (3): 262–279.

Harmer, A. and Macrae, J. (eds.) (2004) *Beyond the Continuum: Aid Policy in Protracted Crises*, HPG Report 18, London: Overseas Development Institute.

Hoben, A (1995) 'Paradigms and Politics: the Cultural Construction of Environmental Policy in Ethiopia', *World Development*, 23 (6): 1007–1021.

IDL (2006) *Ethiopia's Productive Safety Net Programme: PSNP Policy, Programme and Institutional Linkages*. Final Report, Bristol: Overseas Development Institute.

IDL (2010) *Ethiopia Productive Safety Net Programme: Assessment of Graduation Report*. Bristol: The IDL group, Overseas Development Institute.

IFPRI (2008) *An Analysis of Ethiopia's Productive Safety Net Programme and Its Linkages*. Washington, DC: International Food Policy Research Institute.

IFPRI (2009a) *Global Hunger Index 2009*. Washington, DC: International Food Policy Research Institute.

IFPRI (2009b) *A Sub-National Hunger Index for Ethiopia: Assessing Progress in Region-Level Outcomes*. Washington, DC: International Food Policy Research Institute.

Kehler (2004) 'When will Ethiopia Stop Asking for Food Aid?' *Humanitarian Practice Network*, No 27, July 2004. London: Humanitarian Policy Group, Overseas Development Institute.

Lautze, S. and Raven-Roberts, A. (2004) 'Famine (Again) in Ethiopia'. *Humanitarian Practice Network*, No 27, July 2004. London: Humanitarian Policy Group, Overseas Development Institute.

Lautze, S., Raven-Roberts, A. and Erkineh, T. (2009) *Humanitarian Governance in the New Millennium: An Ethiopian Case Study*. London: Humanitarian Policy Group, Overseas Development Institute.

McCord, A. and Slater, R. (2009) *Social Protection, Rural Development and Food Security, Issues Paper on the Role of Social Protection in Rural Development*. ODI Working Paper. London: Overseas Development Institute.

Maxwell, D., Webb P., Coates, J. and Wirth, J. (2010) 'Fit for Purpose? Rethinking Food Security Responses in Protracted Humanitarian Crises', *Food Policy*, 35 (2).

MoARD (2004) *Productive Safety Net Programme: Programme Implementation Manual*. Addis Ababa: Ministry of Agriculture and Rural Development.

MoARD (2009) *Food Security Programme 2010–2014.* Addis Ababa: Ministry of Agriculture and Rural Development.

MoFED (2006) *Ethiopia: Building on Progress: A plan for Accelerated and Sustained Development to End Poverty (PASDEP)* Volume I: Main Text. Addis Ababa: Ministry of Finance and Economic Development.

Nedessa, B. and Wickrema, S. (2010) 'Disaster Risk Reduction: Experience from the MERET Project in Ethiopia'. In Omamo, S.W., Gentilini, U. and Sandström, S. (eds) *Revolution: From Food Aid to Food Assistance, Innovations in Overcoming Hunger.* Rome: World Food Programme.

OCHA (2008) *Situation Report 11th August 2008: Drought/Food Crisis in Ethiopia.* United Nations Office for the Coordination of Humanitarian Affairs. http://ochaonline.un.org/ethiopia

OCHA (2011) *Horn of Africa: Humanitarian Snapshot (as of 20 September 2011).* United Nations Office for the Coordination of Humanitarian Affairs. www.unocha.org

Ó Gráda, C. (2009) *Famine: A Short History,* Princeton: Princeton University Press.

Pankhurst, R. (1985) *The History of Famine and Epidemics in Ethiopia Prior to the Twentieth Century.* Addis Ababa: Relief and Rehabilitation Commission.

Rahmato, D. (1991) *Famine and Survival Strategies,* Uppsala: The Scandinavian Institute of African Studies.

Rahmato, D. (1994) 'Land Policy in Ethiopia at the Crossroads'. In Desalegn Rahmato (ed.) *Land Tenure and Land Policy in Ethiopia after the Derg.* Proceedings of the Second Workshop of the Land Tenure Project, Working Papers on Ethiopian Development 8, Centre for Environment and Development (SMU), Trondheim: University of Traondheim, 1–20.

RRC (1984) *The Belg Rain Failure and its Effect on Food Production.* Special report May, Addis Ababa: Relief and Rehabilitation Commission.

Salama, P., Assefa, F., Spiegel, P., van der Veen, A. and Gotway, C. (2001) 'Malnutrition, Measles, Mortality, and the Humanitarian Response During a Famine in Ethiopia', *JAMA* 286 (5): 563–571.

SCF (2009) *Cash, Food, Payment and Risk, A Review of the Productive Safety Net Programme.* London: The Save the Children Fund, UK.

Sen, A. (1981) *Poverty and Famines: An Essay on Entitlement and Deprivation.* Oxford: Oxford University Press.

Sharp, K., Devereux, S. and Amare, Y. (2003) *Destitution in Ethiopia's Northeast Highlands.* Brighton: Institute for Development Studies.

Webb, P. and von Braun, J. (1994) *Famine and Food Security in Ethiopia Lessons for Africa,* The International Food Policy Research Institute, London: John Wiley and Sons.

WFP (2004) *WFP and Food-Based Safety Nets: Concepts, Experiences and Future Programming Opportunities,* WFP, Executive Board, Third Regular Session, October 2004, Policy Issues, Agenda Item 4.

White, P. (2005) 'War and Food Security in Eritrea and Ethiopia, 1998–2000', *Disasters,* (29) s92–113.

Wolde Mariam, M. (1985) 'The Social Consequences of Famine', in Fasil Gebre Kiros (ed.) *Challenging Rural Poverty.* Trenton: Africa World Press.

5 The politics of 'catastrophization'

Jeroen Warner

Introduction

In March 2010 Jaap Smit, Director of a Dutch non-governmental organization (NGO) in aid of victims (*Slachtofferhulp*), lamented the increasing tendency to call unfortunate events 'disasters'. He noted a worrying inflation of the 'disaster' label; a decreasing acceptance that, as his colleague Leferink and Sardemann (2010) has it, 'shit happens'; and the overblown demand that, when it happens, 'never again'. Smit strongly argued for the deflation of catastrophic discourse: we need to put 'disasters' into perspective. By international standards, he claimed, the Turkish Airlines crash in the Netherlands in February 2010, killing seven, was more like a major traffic accident, not a disaster.

The difference between labelling a calamitous event 'bad luck' or 'injustice', Leferink and Sardemann (2010) notes, is a political one; the formal or informal declaration of a disaster has a material impact that can be quite counter-productive to its victims. Olson (2000), likewise, notes that a disaster is political from the start, as both public sector and NGO sectors have a tendency to place the political aspects in the background, in light of the overriding humanitarian interest in restoring order and stability. However, political scientists and security specialists are strangely silent about disaster; they tend to focus on its managerial side. As a result, the nexus between disaster and politics has largely been the domain of political ecology.

This Chapter applies a constructivist interpretation of security studies to crisis and disaster. While constructivism is still marginal in disaster studies (Tierney 2007),[1] I propose that applying the concept of 'securitization', the speech act[2] invoking a vital threat (Buzan *et al.* 1998) to disaster, can be analytically productive. Like disaster, security relates to a vital threat, crisis, emergency or urgent situation. It will be shown that the debate on the construction of crisis, which has now quietly entered the humanitarian domain, can easily be extended into disaster declaration and, potentially, the whole disaster life cycle, from prevention to reconstruction.

This realization leads me into a brief discussion of literature advocating and widening the emergency logic to ever more domains, taking stock (albeit non-exhaustively) of arguments about why manifest and potential hazards should or should not be treated as disastrous. The contribution links 'securitization' with a close cousin, known from psychology: 'catastrophization' – the tendency to always fear the worst. Introducing catastrophization into the field of humanitarianism, Adi Ophir (2010) adds multiple dimensions to the discursive one, connecting speech and audience with the relationship to the danger itself.

To define something as a security problem needs a context – it is possible only within a wider political framework of ideas, norms and values which give it a meaning and legitimacy (Kaygusuz 2007). I surmise that this context is expressed in a political deal: the social contract legitimizing a protection arrangement. The acceptance of a disaster declaration, and of the extraordinary measures taken on its basis, depends on the prior social contract. Indeed, the *ex-post* evaluation of these measures can change the social contract, as disaster managers are held to account for their action or inaction; where the social contract is not consolidated and different actors may have different perceptions of what is in the imputed social contract and what it legitimizes, disaster response can lead to conflict. I therefore propose to enhance the securitization model, especially in its application to disaster handling, its social marketing in targeting audiences needed for legitimization, and its subsequent evaluation in light of the social contract. While basically a conceptual essay, the paper is informed by the author's research on the politics of disaster risk reduction projects in five countries (Warner 2011) and a subsequent field study in the Netherlands (Velotti *et al.* 2011).

Disaster as a political construct

A long-standing puzzlement informing the present contribution is that the declaration of disasters, by media or political voices – even ambassadors[3] – seems to bear little relation to 'expert' definitions of disaster. Definitions abound; there are no hard and fast universal rules to this. Some disaster studies experts stipulate that, for an event to be a disaster, there needs to be a minimum number of victims (Dombrowsky or Sheeham, in López-Ibor 2005), injuries and losses, and non-routine interventions and coordination between different organizations are required.

At the policy level, however, emergency management initiatives do not mesh well with what disaster experts and managers would call a disaster. Not all major events are labelled catastrophe, and not all publicly declared catastrophes are major events. For example, when a flood threatened the Netherlands in 1995, the Dutch parliament enacted emergency legislation, despite nobody having drowned – the only person who perished slid off a truck during evacuation. Conversely, the low-level response to Q fever in the Netherlands, which has so far claimed 24 victims and hundreds of sick people in the South Netherlands in the past few years (Commissie-van Dijk 2010, www.nu.nl/binnenland/2751994/minstens-24-doden-q-koorts.html) could be cited as an example of the opposite situation. The denial of an AIDS epidemic in South Africa by the Mbeki government is another case (Fassin and Vazques 2005). Some threats are successfully incorporated into emergency politics even though no death or injury is unequivocally attributable to it, such as climate

Table 5.1 Match between technical and political disaster security: a catastrophization matrix

		Declaration of national disaster	
		Yes	No
Event meets disaster criteria	Yes	Yes, yes Example: 1953 coastal flood	Yes, no 1995 river flood (NL)
	No	No, yes Q fever	No, no 2010 river flood (NL)

Note: It is likely that some cases travel through different cells in the matrix over time.

change (Brauch 2009). Some would call traffic an undeclared disaster, given its staggering daily death toll worldwide. A heuristic two-by-two matrix with Dutch examples (Table 5.1) can be drawn to illustrate the phenomenon:

There is no disaster without it being declared as such by an authoritative source – an event is 'only actually a disaster when someone who is authorized to say that it is does so' (Green 2000). Calling a crisis is an exceptional administrative act, suspending normal rights, controls and procedures for the sake of national security, and redistributing security among stakeholders (Ophir 2010). It defines a lethal threat, legitimizing emergency legislation that legitimizes extraordinary measures. Disaster, catastrophe or crisis (treated here as near-synonyms) is thus a discursive construction of a situation or an event, with serious social and policy implications. Declaring something a disaster is tantamount to declaring something a vital threat, with one difference: a threat has not happened yet, while a disaster has happened, and is an admission that something is too overwhelming to deal with in routine mode. In setting aside normal rights and procedures and checks and balances, it accepts infringements on individual local or national sovereign rights.

Security speech, humanitarianism and disaster

Securitization

The constructed and instrumentalized nature of an attempted declaration of disaster noted here is strongly reminiscent of the speech act of 'securitization' (Buzan *et al.* 1998). This currently hegemonic tradition in European security studies, known as the Copenhagen School, argues that security is not a response to an objective reality, but a successful political 'speech act' – a publicly accepted declaration of a vital threat. A declaration of disaster shares with securitization a sense of urgency and priority that, as noted above, may be totally out of step with expert definitions.

After the fall of the Berlin Wall, the Copenhagen School joined those who observed a widening of the security domain beyond its traditional concern with territory. Fossil fuels, oil, drugs, economic competition, the environment and terrorism could all be elevated to national security concerns and, in so doing, legitimize special measures, such as the deployment of the military and the suspension of civil rights. The Copenhagen School's crucial innovation, however, was that they saw vital threats to security as social constructions rather than objective facts, and noted that an issue only becomes a security concern when it is authoritatively declared to be one. Security 'dramatizes' an issue and imbues it with absolute priority, presenting it as an absolute threat (Buzan *et al.* 1998: 108). Once declared, crisis situations are dealt with in the 'logic-of-war' mode (Table 5.2, left-hand side) where normal rights and rules no longer apply: their life-and-death nature legitimizes extraordinary measures. What Buzan *et al.* (1998) have called the 'securitization' of a core value makes legal what in normal circumstances would be illegal. A state of 'exception' means the suspension of formal and essential order and normal sources of authority. 'Securitization', likewise, overrules other speech acts such as threats and promises, which become irrelevant in the face of annihilation.

A security speech act calls for the 'neutralization, elimination or constraint of that person, group, object or condition which engenders fear' (Dillon, 1996). Dillon's inclusion of a fearful 'condition' suggests that, as with the securitization of climate change (e.g. Youngs 2009, Trombetta 2008, Brito 2009), the absence of a clearly definable enemy does not deter a securitizer from declaring an emergency. It therefore seems strange that disasters are not mentioned in the securitization literature, as both disaster and security studies deal with the domain of emergency and life-and-death decisions. Disasters have received surprisingly little attention in the security studies literature, although Buzan *et al.* (1998) in passing mention disasters and particularly single out the Dutch obsession with floods.

Perhaps this lack of attention is because the focus of the research and debate on securitization is very much concentrated on European security issues[4] (though see

Table 5.2 Ideal-typical securitized and non-securitized policy making (Warner 2011, after Buzan *et al.* 1998)

Logic of securitization *('war', 'crisis', 'exception')*	*Logic of non-securitized policy making* *('peace', 'routine', 'normality')*
For extraordinary, urgent events	For ongoing concerns
Vertical (top-down management, patronage in protection)	Horizontal (co-management, negotiation among autonomous actors)
Bypassing of democracy and stakeholder participation	Stakeholder participation
Bypassing of market mechanism and cost–benefit analysis	Market for security goods and services
Compliance through force and rules	Compliance through marketing of security
Secrecy, information distribution on need-to-know basis	Openness, public accountability
Army, experts	Public services, democratic fora

Wilkinson, 2007). Disaster studies, for its part, has long focused on developing countries and suffered from the fallacy of 'tropicality' (Bankoff, 2004): disasters are not supposed to be 'over here' in the North, but 'out there' in the South, in 'the area of otherness . . . unsafe for westerners'. It risks being a form of developmentalist 'governmentality'. Hurricane Katrina in 2005 as well as, more recently, the Japanese tsunami and mega-earthquakes of 2011 and Hurricane Sandy in 2012, however, remind us that wealthy 'developed' societies are not immune to disaster.

Securitization analysis has, of late, been applied to disaster management's closest relation, humanitarianism. UN organizations, governments, NGOs, may proclaim a humanitarian crisis, create an image of disaster as an exceptional event, legitimizing exceptional measures. The exception may mean military intervention and the release of unprecedented funds: the Asian tsunami response, for example, secured an almost blank cheque for humanitarian aid (Watson 2011).

Security creates a 'defining other' (Ignatieff 1993); in a catastrophe, the 'humanitarian state of exception' does not address a threat to public security, but a widely supported need to aid disaster victims (Fassin and Vazques 2005). In humanitarianism, humanity as a whole is the referent of security. The depoliticization of disaster means there is no 'us and them' between ourselves: if we are all victims of the outside force of nature, this strengthens the humanitarian appeal for assistance (Watson 2012). Like climate change, this makes humanitarian crisis a special domain of emergency, that of 'threats without enemies' (Prins 1993).

Disasters, however, are not automatically security issues. Epidemics, even the Spanish flu epidemic of 1918–19, were not considered security threats and, likewise, not treated in an exceptional mode. While there has been a progressive 'securitization' of health-related disaster and humanitarian assistance since the nineteenth century (Fidler 2007), Deudney (1990) could still note twenty years ago that, 'we speak about "natural disasters" or designate "national disaster areas" but we do not speak about such events threatening "national security"'. There is thus nothing 'natural' about the declaration of natural disasters as exceptional issues.

In fact Deudney (1990) denied that natural calamities are threats to national security, as the security sector is concerned with organized violence, not well-being. Other critical thinkers join Deudney in lamenting the militarization of non-traditional domains of security, including the attaching of security criteria to humanitarian aid (e.g. Duffield 2010).

They are challenged by those who argue that a widening of security could also reflexively change the meaning and practices of security (Trombetta 2008). In this vein, Biswas (2011) argues that the practices of the military have evolved, developing capacities for providing humanitarian services in relief and recovery, sometimes in some form of cooperation with non-governmental organizations.

Meanwhile, Fassin and Vazques (2005) note that the state of emergency is not a matter of 'all or nothing'. New forms are emerging that leave basic rights intact but create partial exceptions, such as the indefinite detention of supposed terrorist at Guantanamo Bay, while in Venezuela's *Tragedia de Vargas*, a torrent of floods and mudslides wreaking havoc in 1998, the military lent assistance, but remained in its barracks. While previously state and society were estranged, joint hardship strengthened the bond between the two. The evidence that several 'saviours' committed criminal acts in the process did not impede a new-found sense of unity of state and society (Fassin and Vazques 2005). Humanitarian 'catastrophization', therefore, can stand a government in good stead. Miggiano (2009) goes so far as to say that securitization of migration does not so much serve a societal but a political security concern.

Unfortunately, the Copenhagen School has not been very clear on what 'extraordinary measures' means. Seeking to remedy this gap, Brito (2009) suggests Gramsci's 'extraordinary politics', which creates whole new structures, and Peter Hall's (1993) 'paradigm shift' in social learning may be viable candidates for extraordinariness. Watson (2011) notes we should contextualize the normal and the exceptional – while, for example, in liberal democracies, the deployment of the army has become unusual, in authoritarian states this would be nothing special. This question can easily be extended to the exceptionality of disastrous hazards in different contexts (cf. Hilhorst and Warner 2009).

What is exceptional, then, depends on social, cultural and political expectations of what is normal. Like fire brigades, humanitarian agencies do not need exceptional measures, only exceptional circumstances. Even among the exceptionality of disaster situations, there are normal routines, normal interventions based on consensus between sender and recipient of aid, on invitation or passive consent of the recipient state – although this welcome may not be echoed by the supposed beneficiaries or other stakeholders. Only when humanitarian values are invoked to legitimize extraordinary means (such as the non-consensual violation of *normal* domestic or international norms, say the sanctity of sovereignty), we may note a humanitarian exception. Intervention by consensus and invitation would not qualify as exceptional (Watson 2011).

A society's historic engagement with a threat makes the security mode easier to invoke. In the Netherlands, saying 'dikes', one also implicitly says 'security and priority' (Buzan *et al.* 1998: 27–28). A reference to floods easily opens a security window, legitimizing the appearance of, for example, military reservists, the surveillance of abandoned properties and the availability of an 'emergency fund' to compensate flood victims. This, however, is not exceptional; the deployment of such a public disaster response may be more or less what citizens expect from government, as our interviews in the regularly flooded south of Limburg in the Dutch South suggest (Velotti *et al.* 2011). Issues arise when an emergency is invoked to push aside not only formal but also informal arrangements and expectations, to restore order. In the Dutch South, for example, the compulsory expropriation of land (the designation of 'eminent domain' for flood protection) under the 1995 Delta Emergency Law is not experienced by the farmers involved as a legitimate exception, and continues to be resented and resisted by affected farmers (see e.g. Warner 2011). Extraordinary measures, then, are not a necessary requirement for securitization; the key condition is their acceptance, or not, by the people affected (Brito 2009). As a result of a reflexive process of the securitization process and the threat, measures taken may not be seen anymore as extraordinary (Trombetta 2008).

Later on, I will argue that the interpretation of normality and legitimate exceptionality, as well as its acceptance, also stems from an implicit 'social contract' in operation within (and between) states.

Catastrophization

Let's now see how the application of 'securitization' to the realm of humanitarianism and disasters can be linked with Ophir's work on 'catastrophization'. Ophir's catastrophization is at once a discursive speech act, a diagnosis and a material process. In psychology, to 'catastrophize' is to invoke the spectre of a catastrophe. Without some form of action, a threshold will be crossed and a disastrous future will come about: something terrible will happen (Ophir 2007). Such a patient suffers from pathological exaggeration of their situation. Catastrophization designates an 'anxiety disorder' in which one interprets 'a specific, mildly negative event as having global and negative implications for one's view of the self and/or one's future'. 'Catastrophization is a process in which catastrophe is imminent. However, what is imminent has not happened yet . . . [moreover] the catastrophe [is all the more effective because it] is suspended' (Ophir 2010).

Catastrophization in individuals is a curable affliction. Ophir (2010) however sees catastrophization as an ingrained *societal* phenomenon, even as a strategy to promote an agenda. Catastrophization legitimizes fast-tracking unpopular and possibly lopsided distribution politics (see also Klein 2007). While Ophir never refers to the Copenhagen School, catastrophization-as-discourse closely resembles the scholarship on 'securitization'. To invoke exceptionality, agents in the humanitarian realm are prone to 'catastrophizing'. They then seek to mitigate the catastrophe, a practice known as Disaster Risk Reduction (DRR). But they cannot, or will not, eliminate the catastrophe, rather, they keep it 'in suspense'. Keeping catastrophe in suspense creates the condition for collaboration between the actual catastrophizing forces and the agents of catastrophizing discourse that seemingly oppose them (Ophir 2010). These choices may even mean 'collaborating, purposefully or not, with the forces that have operationalized catastrophization and use it as measured, calculated, and controlled means of governance'.

The actors creating the risk are not necessarily the same ones as those fighting it. But there is a symbiotic relationship between them – a plausible threat has to be created to legitimize controlling it. For this to work, the spectre of catastrophe needs to be invoked: the discursive creation, or exaggeration, of mortal danger.

In sum, Ophir's concept of catastrophization is three-pronged:

- framing an event or situation as a catastrophe in which the state has to take the lead; discursive catastrophization, introduced above
- induces the reduction/mitigation of the risk (DRR)
- holds the danger in suspense (political ecology): not letting the catastrophe happen but also not removing the cause.

The application of 'catatsrophization' to natural hazard and disaster lands us in similar territory as 'securitization'; the debate between those who believe 'widening' the exceptional is a good thing and those who do not. The next sections go into the arguments for each side.

Against catastrophization?

The Copenhagen School tends to take the liberal view that 'security mode' decision-making should be an exception to be avoided,[5] and a more or less explicit agenda of de-securitization should be pursued. Other critical voices in security studies, such as Welsh (Wyn-Jones) and French (Bigo) security scholars, suggest that security sectors have a vested interest in presenting everything as a security issue. They have pointed out that national security and human security often work at cross-purposes.

Contrary to Leiss and Chociolko (1994), states may actively seek responsibility in tackling disasters and disaster potential. Disasters bring political capital: a disaster enhances state legitimacy and legitimizes violence and expropriation of so-called 'eminent domain'. States in a sense depend on disaster, the exception, for its legitimacy. A state needs the barbarians at the gates out to desecrate the 'home' (Miggiano 2009) to legitimize a state of emergency and exploit refugees as non-citizens.

Seeking to have a situation or event declared a disaster may serve humanitarian but also utilitarian political instrumentality: to tackle the deficiencies in the *status quo ante* and to enable measures that are unfeasible in normal times (Boin *et al.* 2009). The fragmented political infrastructure in liberal democracies may impel political actors to spread a 'sense of crisis' to forge a winning coalition to get things done (Béland 2005). They may bank on the narrow political time window a crisis procures a government to fast-track large-scale, costly and potentially controversial measures in a narrow time window. As the memory of disaster, especially floods, quickly fades, authorities catastrophize to elicit support for painful interventions. Besides, invoking humanitarian catastrophe can also be powerful for actors wishing to securitize a referent that otherwise does not command a high priority (Vaughn 2009).[6]

The increasing tendency for emergency policy making and risk management has also been widely researched, and its impact on civil rights and liberties lamented. As many liberal observers of security studies have noticed, this tendency legitimizes ever more invasive interventions to restrict people's behaviour within bounds. The expansion of the security sphere to the 'security chain' comprising all the links of the DRR chain (prevention, mitigation, response, reconstruction) makes it harder to define where security starts and normality ends – all the more since the four phases do not come to pass sequentially. This means a blurring of the spheres of normality and exception.[7]

Emergency politics is the politics of fear and urgency. Fear creates *demand* for protection and delivery which those who claim to be able to *supply* security – defence forces, insurance companies, security services, civil engineers – are happy to provide. Similar to other advertisers, their job is to make people aware of latent needs and they are interested in playing on those fears. While social demand does not expect the private sector to eliminate all individual security risks, it does call for the public sector to take care of macro-risks (Krahmann 2008). Authorities therefore feel impelled to respond, symbolically (Cook 2010, see next page) or materially.

The 'nationalization' of a risk management issue can prove beneficial to states, as shown by the Ecuadorian example earlier, and it can also attract lower-level stakeholders. In the rural Dutch province of Limburg, for example, a long but ultimately successful battle was fought to have flood protection infrastructure included in the national flood security framework (Wesselink *et al.* 2012). Different actors, then, may push for a new social contract between core and periphery.

However, states are not always keen to declare an exception. It doesn't necessarily look good for a government to admit that the normal system is overwhelmed, and that the military and/or outside support is needed to overcome the crisis situation. China used to routinely under-report disasters. Disasters may be opportunistically *relabelled*. For example, city authorities reframed the calamitous San Francisco Earthquake of 1906 as a fire hazard, to downplay the earthquake risk in the San Francisco bay (Tierney 2007). Events and chains of events that claim thousands of victims each year are not catastrophized at all, including traffic, alcohol and creeping famine.

Bureaucracies, moreover, are often poorly equipped for emergency action (Rosenthal 1984). Called on to respond to a political demand for security, state apparatuses are not at all keen to switch to crisis mode. Addressing a routine situation with a non-routine course of action is far harder for bureaucracies than routine courses of action, and may need strong persuasion. One way of addressing political demand for security is a symbolic response, aimed at influencing public perception (Helsloot 2007). We cannot automatically assume a match between speech and action. While there may either be non-verbalized or covert emergency action, security speech may be merely symbolic (Cook 2010) which paves the way for declaring a security crisis. The securitization of climate change by the EU in 2008 is an example: after moving climate into the security domain, not much has happened since.

Finally, we are witnessing a trend to reduce the role of the state, including in security provision. The post-welfare ('post-providential') state stresses self-reliance and divests itself of pretences to cradle-to-grave safety nets. This observation, more generally pertinent to security provision has, however, been challenged by critical scholars who observe more covert forms of securitization. These opposing observations will be discussed in more detail in the next section in the context of the currently dominant trend of DRR.

Acceptance of catastrophization and the social contract

Disaster events and also their handling tend to create social disturbance, amplified by the media, leading to political questions about risk and responsibility. If there is a disagreement about the timing and intensity of security measures, authorities will be held to account, as illustrated by the case of Hurricane Katrina in the US. When Katrina hit landfall, natural hazards were 'out-securitized' by the war on Iraq. The budget for operation, maintenance and reinforcement of flood defence works had been cut in 2004 (Lewis 2007: 307). When the government changed its mind and declared a disaster, a lack of funding was over-compensated for by military presence, treating citizens as refugees, as 'non-citizens'. The response was generally assessed as too much, too late, as citizens escaping the flood were stopped at the border like refugees or criminals, like 'non-citizens' falling outside the normal protection of civil rights. It gave a sense of abandonment and then of over-reaction on the part of the state.

To assess the *resilience of political relations*, we can investigate what happens during and after a shock event. As flood memory fades, are disaster managers eventually called to account? Or does the state call its people to account? If a disaster fails to be declared, politicians may be taken to task for negligence. If a disaster is declared, what happens after the window of non-accountability closes? Are disaster managers called to account after a certain time elapses, like the Roman dictators of old?

The consequences of '(non-)catastrophization' of a flood event raise the issue of post-disaster *accountability and legitimacy*. It is eminently possible that a symbolic response satisfies the intended constituency in certain cases. In others, however, disaster managers are held accountable for the handling, or not, of the disaster event and for subsequent disaster risk reduction. Since it entails the loss of civic rights, and open political debate (de-politicization) and (after a time) accountability may be demanded, as the cases show, it may only mean a stay of execution. A crisis may strengthen the legitimacy of the ruling government (Fassin and Vazques 2005) but also lead to protest, instability, even revolution, if a society is disappointed about the ways in which a disaster was handled. Disasters have strong 'magnifying effects on unstable polities' (Drury and Olson 1998). In Nicaragua (1972) and Mexico (1985), revolutions have been attributed to the poor handling of disasters (Pelling and Dill 2009). Poor or heavy-handed handling of a disaster can make the state look like the real threat.

Under- and over-catastrophization and the social contract

In the early days of the Copenhagen school, Buzan and Waever referred to 'undersecuritization'. The local reticence to do something about the spread of AIDS, for example, 'in the face of a palpable existential threat . . .' (Buzan and Waever 2002: 252). Their use of these neologisms, however, suggested there was an absolute security imperative that should, objectively, have been met. I propose to reinstate this concept from a constructivist perspective: the enunciator claims, and finds resonance for this claim from a crucial audience, that there should have been more protection. This may be contrasted with 'oversecuritization' where an enunciator claims there is too much catastrophization. The concept was mentioned in passing in Warner (2003) and other scattered literature, such as Colombo and Tocci (2011) and Bendel (2006). The political evaluation of security policies can be expected to vary according to the historic context and political expectations. Unexpected natural events, and also their handling, tend to create social disturbance, amplified by the media, leading to political questions about risk and responsibility.

I propose to reintroduce the concepts of over- and under-securitization in light of the discussion on the *social contract* – the explicit (constitutional) but also implicit expectations, rights and obligations of state and society towards each other, the express expectations of protection against chaos and instability. Disaster-affected people, 'called on' to assume the subject position of the victim, may refuse to be 'hijacked' for others' benefit and/or resist being rescued and rehabilitated, thus surprising their supposed 'saviours' and advocates.

In this context, we may turn to Pelling and Dill's (2009) discussion of how disasters call into question the terms of the implicit social contract. The social contract is an analytical construct denoting how much power citizens are prepared to give the state and what they demand in return. An emergency, such as a flood, permits a liberal state to interpret the social contract temporarily as coercive rather than 'permissive' (Nugent 2010).

Catastrophization is not a priori better or worse than non-catastrophization, but rather it appears that, for disaster response to be accepted in society, it should be perceived as commensurate with the seriousness of the disaster. The acceptance or rejection of disaster discourse is a modality of the social contract. Its terms become more visible after a crisis in the emergence or absence of strong debate, protests and litigation. System instability after a crisis can mean the reassessment of the prior social contract.

The terms and flexibility of the 'social contract' influence whether or not a perceived crisis situation is declared a national security issue, a local security issue or none at all – in other words, what is considered 'normal' and what is 'exceptional'. If the social contract survives, this attests to what may be called the 'political resilience' of a social system (Järvelä 2007) after a shock. If not, regime instability ensues (Pelling and Dill 2009) that may tip into revolution or authoritarianism.

Disasters thus test the resilience of the social contract. Where the social contract is contested and reassessed post-disaster by the state, citizenry or subgroups, regime instability opens up, with scope for progressive and regressive change (Pelling and Dill 2009).

In this context, external humanitarian aid cuts right through existing, fragile or robust, social contracts. While traditional humanitarianism makes its recipients passive victims, social contract theory assumes the active involvement of citizens in the founding or refounding of government (Zack 2011). Thus, while De Waal (1996) noted the damage humanitarianism has done to existing social contracts in Africa, there is no deterministic reason why the 'clients' of humanitarianism are confined to passivity and broken social contracts. If the polity is not completely destroyed, a resilient social contract allows disaster-affected people to 'talk back' to their protectors and call them to account.

Taking this argument even further, we may note that, absent a capable or legitimate government, local actors can take centre stage. No matter what authorities do, in practice, shock events are first and foremost handled locally (Kirschenbaum 2004). The negative outlook on disaster, reinforced by the media, portrays an image of chaos and disorder. In the popular image of Hurricane Katrina, this chaos seemed to result less from the storm than from the reckless behaviour of the residents of New Orleans (Dynes and Rodriguez 2007). That image neglects the predominantly pro-social behaviour and social cohesion found in many disaster situations. Social solidarity networks and individuals need to be self-reliant to prepare for, respond to, and recover from the event while emergency services are unavailable. If expectations do not match measures, there may be a perceived *under-* or *over-catastrophization*, or indeed *counter-catastrophization*.

Not only can local disaster responders be expected to be held up to scrutiny, community representatives can also catastrophize, non-catastrophize or even counter-catastrophize. They may reject external intervention and DRR projects as intrusions on the 'good life'. In terms of subject positions, countersecuritization also reverses who is the hero and who is the villain in the disaster narrative employed. Countersecuritizers may project themselves as heroes and the state's disaster representatives, policies or interventions as villains. Both would-be hero and alleged villain, then, will have to work on their PR to convince their audience that there is a catastrophe in the making. Those fearing their opposition may therefore seek to preserve legitimacy by undertaking legitimizing communication strategies.[8]

The next section briefly explores this need for disaster discourse to be marketed and accepted, and how its take-up may relate to the pre-existing 'social contract'.

Selling security

The approach taken here highlights the observation that exceptional measures need to be promoted, sold, and marketed. Where securitizing agents perceive an 'imbalance of securitization between insiders and outsiders' (Buzan and Waever 2002), they can seek to influence the attitude of these outsiders to secure their (ongoing) support. The mobilization of an audience can, however, fail: securitization does not by necessity lead to exceptional action, and when it does, it will not necessarily go uncriticized. There is not necessarily an a priori audience willing and able to fund, implement or accept emergency measures. Funders called on to enable extraordinary measures do not always willingly rise to the occasion as 'heroes' in the storyline. Based on multiple cases in Europe and Asia, Warner (2011) found that flood security can be a hard sell when intended sponsors of DRR projects legitimized by securitization are located outside the securitized zone: they are not necessarily so easily persuaded to fund them.

Funders became nervous and projects ran into trouble when affected stakeholders mobilized powerful others. All six flood disaster risk reduction projects I researched in my dissertation research (Warner 2011) eventually ran up against social opposition, often using strong language and 'staging'[9] (Hajer 2002) to make their point and justify civil disobedience. Yet their opposition was not only a counterstrategy to disarm the emergency discourse, but also invoked a different threat, or labelled the remedy itself as a threat – that the disaster risk reduction strategy opted for by the state or private sector keeps disaster in suspense or actually constituted a disaster itself. This contradicts the great majority of securitization writings, which assume the speaker, speaking from a position of authority, to have the upper hand and use their superior social capital to 'speak security'. In this sense counter-catastrophization can even be emancipatory (cf. McDonald 2009).[10]

DRR and de-catastrophization

In light of the above discussion, let us turn to the currently fashionable and ubiquitous phenomenon of 'Disaster Risk Reduction' (DRR) or 'Disaster Risk Management' (DRM). Since the 1950s, a trend has developed aiming not to resist disaster but to accommodate it, reducing its risk without the hope of eliminating it. The DRR cycle implies total disaster risk can be reduced without external losses. However, as 'natural disasters' are always socially and politically mediated, we also add to our own catastrophization in a Beckian reflexivity. While there is a trend in liberal democracies towards renouncing state responsibility for disaster, risk management is enhanced. In this perspective, people's behaviour is the key source of risk, and DRR the way to reduce this risk across time and space.

The effect of this can go two ways: widening the security mode – total catastrophization (strengthening the Hobbesian mode), or narrowing it – total de-catastrophization (strengthening the Lockeian mode).

Our research at the Wageningen Disaster Studies group yields many recorded examples of local communities in Asia, Africa and Latin America where local people, exposed to recurrent natural events and regularly migrating or evacuating, do not perceive there to be any disaster, even when they sustain considerable human, material and immaterial losses. Heijmans (2012), moreover, notes that local people tend not to see themselves as vulnerable, or to identify natural hazards as dangers that overwhelm society and need special treatment – floods and earthquakes are part of life, as are poverty and violent conflict. Bringing DRR to such villages can, therefore, be like modern-day missionary work, persuading locals with comprehensive physical data that they are indeed in need of protection (Heijmans 2012). A quick learning curve leads to strategic subsequent local demands for protection, to work the humanitarian system in a way that produces security 'goodies'. The study by Weert (2009), for example, shows that Amazonian Bolivia regularly receives flood relief goods from NGOs such as CARE, but actually uses them for other ends that they deem more urgent.

We have noted the dangers of the catastrophization of everything (insecuritization) above. The practices of security in security domains such as terrorism and immigration treat all stages of risk management as within the security domain.

What about the alternative? 'De-catastrophization'[11] takes place when risks are considered 'manageable'. The official abandonment of the disaster category for recurring drought in Australia is an example (Botterill 2010). As noted, Bankoff (2004) has exposed disaster and vulnerability as largely Western exports. It is, however, unclear whether those affected by shocks and challenges are always better off without the resources made available by disaster declarations. Self-help and community-based disaster risk reduction then become a survival strategy, not a choice. The eligibility for the special resources released by the state as exception, however, is highly dependent on political relations between state and society, centre and periphery. This determines whether an area will be declared a disaster zone (Sylves 2008), and what modality the response will take, ranging from perceived heavy-handed interventionism to neglect (Warner 2011, Raleigh 2010). While self-help is celebrated in literature on community-based DRM, the failure to be recognized as an emergency area can lead to a sense of abandonment in flood-affected people (Warner and Oré 2006). Beleaguered people may have a sense of abandonment when they have no access to, or claim on, the state (Raleigh 2010). Strengthening local capacities to cope with the challenges can only go so far.

Conclusion

In his film *The Inconvenient Truth* (2005), Al Gore labelled climate change a 'global emergency'. Climate change, Gore maintained, 'is not a political issue, it is a moral issue'. Gore depoliticized a threat (the 'climate crisis') by labelling it something higher than politics.

A crisis, however, is quintessentially political, exposing dormant political divides that may call into question the existing social contract and test its resilience. A 'crisis', redefined as a successful representation of urgency, can break the closure, legitimized by something bigger than politics, with important political and institutional consequences. It is therefore attractive for those seeking to break the *status quo* to push for the declaration of a disaster.

The proclamation of disasters, or the threat of disasters, opens windows of opportunity for military response, unauthorized interventions, blank cheques, suspending civil rights and indeed DRR projects. Often such projects, however, redistribute rather than reduce risks between stakeholders and 'keep catastrophe in suspension'. After all, disasters, and their management, do not impact societies across the board, but redistribute vulnerabilities and capacities, and thus security, among stakeholders (Ophir 2010). This is not only a function of their pre-disaster vulnerability but also the way disasters are managed.

Deliberate economic or political gain can incite actors to ignore or collude with forces that undermine the social and environmental capacity to cope with disaster risk they purport to reduce. But also, without conscious action, the redistribution and political opportunism inherent in disaster risk reduction measures may actually add to the potential of catastrophe, by precipitating the incidence of floods and droughts, and more so, the consequences.

Faced with calamity, governments need to create a balance between the extremes of stifling control and total abandonment, protection and freedom. The state, then, is also the target audience for socially expressed catastrophizing moves. Also, external donors may be target 'audiences' and vulnerable to reputational risk from 'backing the wrong horse'. The assumption that securitizers automatically have the initiative and the upper hand is, therefore, questionable.

The trend in securitizing the DRR cycle may go either way: towards total securitization or total desecuritization. While the current political trend is towards smaller states and offloading security tasks, more unobtrusive 'amorphous' forms of security provision may take the place of explicit public protection. To avoid the securitization of everything, non-direct response phases of the disaster cycle might be dealt with more deliberatively and accountably (Hilhorst and Warner 2009).

This point should be taken with due regard to the social contract. Since budgets and mandates are neither unlimited nor unbiased, DRR often involves a form of risk distribution or risk displacement, keeping disaster in suspense. DRR, deliberately or accidentally, amounts to *triage*: who lives, who dies – who's in, who's out. It becomes a containment policy, discursively and/or materially cordoning off the place where the bad things are, to guarantee safety for some but not others – treating some like 'citizens' and others like 'non-citizens' (Ophir 2007, 2010). Where DRR becomes Disaster Risk Displacement, political feedback mechanisms to account for these choices may be in need of improvement.

Acknowledgments

The author thanks Georg Frerks, Bram J. Jansen, Naho Mirumachi and Julia Trombetta for their constructive comments on an earlier draft of this chapter. All responsibility remains with the author.

Notes

1 From a constructivist worldview, there is no need to pass judgement about whether there 'objectively' is a crisis, or whether a molehill has been blown up or photoshopped to look like a mountain. Many 'dangers' and 'crises' are ambiguous. In specific cases, a crisis situation can be created, manufactured or placed in the background. To a degree, crises can be constructed or manufactured through representing the event as catastrophic or non-catastrophic. This does not deny the reality and effects of, for example, a hurricane (Balzacq 2005, Vuori 2011), but the human action in preparation for them as Disaster Risk Reduction is seen as constructed.

 The limited appeal of constructivism in disaster studies may be to do with the inherent interventionism of much disaster scholarship (Cardona 2003). A constructivist approach is an alternative not only to the natural sciences, which tend to focus on the hazard only as an external factor, but also to both behaviourist (Burton, Kates) and structuralist (Hewitt, Blaikie) social-science approaches, which see disasters as an objective reality 'out there', to be identified, analysed and tackled. Psychologists, historians and some sociologists, however, point to the constructed nature of disasters. This subjectivity, of course, complicates any pretence of intervention (Cardona 2003).

2 According to pragmatics, a subdiscipline of social psychology, speakers can make an utterance from a position of authority in a specific setting that changes social reality. Classic examples are baptizing a ship and pronouncing a couple married.

3 US ambassadors can declare disasters in the nations to which they are posted. For example, the US ambassador to Kenya declared a famine in 2011 a disaster, thus releasing special resources.

4 The war on terror and migration are important themes that explain security concerns with Europe's 'near abroad'. Other popular research topics in this field are AIDS, arms trade, drugs, mass immigration.

5 Buzan *et al.* (1998) also maintain that sometimes securitization, such as that of AIDS, may actually have been a positive development which saved lives. In the domain of

disaster, the military has the best equipment to rescue and relocate people affected by an overwhelming event and to rebuild critical infrastructure at lightning speed.

6 Jocelyn Vaughn (2009: 264) highlights the 'instrumentality of the argumentation process by analyzing how securitizers reduce the legitimacy deficit of their chosen referent object . . . by linking it with referent objects that possess greater legitimacy.' Vaughn calls this an associative argument: A might not deserve protection but B does, and B cannot be protected without also protecting A. She cites the example of the very public attack on the Red Cross in Iraq; humanitarian organizations are supposed to be inviolable in the battlefield, but this was not respected.

7 In the context of the 'war against terror', Ignatieff (2004) has called for agreeing beforehand on a fixed time window for the state of exception, which can be managed under strict pre-agreed conditions.

8 Cho mentions the strategies of Avoidance/Deflection, Disclaimer, Image Enhancement (Cho 2009). But others (both public and non-public actors) may actively seek to change the contract, as did the Dutch water manager in 2003 when she publicly stated the government could no longer guarantee 100 per cent flood safety (Roth *et al.* 2006).

9 A speech act is not only a ritual, it is also a dramatization (or another form of play, such as comedy or satire, McDonald 2009, Hajer 2002) that helps pitch a security message to an intended audience.

10 'A range of (often marginal) actors contest dominant logics or discourses of security and threat through articulating alternative (even emancipatory) discourses of security and threat, rather than simply arguing for 'desecuritization' (MacDonald 2009: 575).

11 The Copenhagen security school discusses desecuritization, a logic of peace, as a situation in which the threat may still arise, but is not treated as acute. Likewise we may postulate decatastrophization as the discursive move claiming that an event or threat should not be treated in disaster mode, but denying or backgrounding the (potential for) disaster.

References

Balzacq, T. (2005) 'The Three Faces of Securitization: Political Agency, Audience and Context', *European Journal of International Relations* 111 (2): 171–201.

Bankoff, G. (2004) 'The Historical Geography of Disaster: "Vulnerability" and "Local Knowledge" in Western Discourse'. In Bankoff, G., Frerks, G. and Hilhorst, D.M.J. (eds) *Mapping Vulnerability, Disasters Development and People*, London: Earthscan, 25–36.

Béland, D. (2005) 'Insecurity, Citizenship, and Globalization: The Multiple Faces of State Protection', *Sociological Theory*, 22(1): 25–41.

Bendel, P. (2006) 'Migrations- und Integrationspolitik der Europäischen Union: Widersprüchliche Trends und ihre Hintergründe'. In Baringhorst, S., Hunger, W. and Schönwälder, K. (eds.) *Politische Steuerung von Integrationsprozessen: Intentionen und Wirkungen*, Wiesbaden: VS Verlag für Sozialwissenschaften, 95–120.

Biswas, N.R. (2011) 'Is the Environment a Security Threat?' *International Affairs Review*. Winter. Online: www.iar-wu.org/sites/default/files/articlepdfs/Niloy%20Biswas%20-%20Is%20the%20Environment%20a%20Security%20Threat.pdf (Accessed 25 June 2012).

Boin, A., 't Hart, P. and McConnell, A. (2009) 'Crisis Exploitation: Political and Policy Impacts of Framing Contests', *Journal of European Public Policy*, 16(1): 81–106.

Botterill, L. (2010) 'Risk Management as Policy. The Experience of Australia's National Drought Policy'. *Options Méditerranéennes A*, no. 95. Online: http://ressources.ciheam.org/om/pdf/a95/00801352.pdf (Accessed 25 June 2012).

Brauch, H.G. (2009) 'Securitizing Climate Change'. Paper presented at the annual meeting of the ISA's 50th Annual Convention 'Exploring the Past, Anticipating the

Future', New York Marriott Marquis, New York City, US, 15 February, http://www.allacademic.com/meta/p310532_index.html

Brito, R. de (2009) *Securitizing Climate Change: Process and Implications*, Master's thesis, Universidade de Coimbra, Portugal. Retrieved from https://estudogeral.sib.uc.pt/bitstream/10316/12089/1/Rafaela%20Brito%20-%20Securitizing%20Climate%20Change.pdf (18 February 2013).

Buzan, B. and Waever, O. (2002) *Regions and Powers: The Structure of International Security*. Cambridge: Cambridge University Press.

Buzan, B., Waever, O. and de Wilde, J. (1998) *Security. A New Framework*. London: Lynne Rienner.

Cardona, O. D. (2003) 'The Need for Rethinking the Concepts of Vulnerability and Risk from a Holistic Perspective: A Necessary Review and Criticism for Effective Risk Management'. In Bankoff, G., Frerks, G. and Hilhorst, D. (eds) *Mapping Vulnerability: Disasters, Development, and People*. London: Earthscan Publishers, pp. 37–51.

Cho, C.H. (2009) 'Legitimation Strategies Used in Response to Environmental Disaster: A French Case Study of Total S.A.'s *Erika* and AZF Incidents'. *European Accounting Review*, 18(1): 33–62.

Colombo, S. and Tocci, N. (eds) (2011) 'The Challenges of State Sustainability in the Mediterranean'. IAI research papers. Instituto Affari Internazionali. Edizioni Nuova Cultura, Rome.

Commissie-van Dijk (2010) 'Van verwerping tot verheffing, Evaluatie commissie Q Koorts'. Online: http://www.evaluatiecommissieqkoorts.nl/2010/11/rapport-q-koortsvan-verwerping-tot-verheffing/ (Accessed 25 June 2012).

Cook, A.H. (2010) 'Securitization of Disease in the United States: Globalization, Public Policy, and Pandemics'. *Risk, Hazards and Crisis in Public Policy*, 1(1): Article 3.

De Waal, A. (1996) 'Social Contract and Famine: First Thoughts'. *Disasters*, 20(3): 194–205.

Deudney, Daniel. (1990) 'The Case against Linking Environmental Degradation and National Security'. *Millennium*, 19(3): 461–476.

Dillon, M. (1996) *Politics of Security: Towards a Political Philosophy of Continental Thought*. London: Routledge.

Drury, A.C. and Olson, R.S. (1998) 'Disasters and Political Unrest: An Empirical Investigation'. *Journal of Contingencies and Crisis Management*, 6(3): 153–161.

Duffield, M. (2010) 'The Liberal Way of Development and the Development–Security Impasse: Exploring the Global Life-Chance Divide'. *Security Dialogue*, 41(1): 53–76.

Dynes, R.R. and Rodriguez, H. (2007) 'Finding and Framing Katrina. The Social Construction of Disaster'. In Brunsma, D.L., Overfelt, David and Picou, Steve J. (eds) *The Sociology of Katrina: Perspectives on a Modern Catastrophe* (2nd edn) New York: Rowman & Littlefield, pp. 23–34.

Fassin, D. and Vazques, P. (2005) 'Humanitarian Exception as the Rule: The Political Theology of the 1999 *Tragedia* in Venezuela'. *American Ethnologist*, 32 (3): 389–405.

Fidler, D.P. (2007) 'Governing Catastrophes: Security, Health and Humanitarian Assistance'. *Faculty Publications*. Maurer School of Law, University of Indiana. Paper 451. Retrieved from: http://www.repository.law.indiana.edu/facpub/451 (18 February 2013).

Green, W.G. (2000) 'What is a Disaster?' Paper presented at the 2000 Virginia Critical Incident Stress Management Conference https://facultystaff.richmond.edu/~wgreen/conf3.pdf

Hajer, M. (2002) 'Discourse Analysis and the Study of Policy Making'. *European Political Science*, 2 (1): 61–65.

Hall, P.A. (1993) 'Policy Paradigms, Social Learning, and the State: The Case of Economic Policymaking in Britain'. *Comparative Politics*, (25)3: 275–296.

Heijmans, A. (2012) *Risky Encounters. Institutions and Interventions in Response to Recurrent Disasters and Conflict*. PhD Dissertation. Wageningen: Wageningen University.

Helsloot, I. (2007) *Voorbij de Symboliek. Over de Noodzaak van een Rationeel Perspectief op fysiek Veiligheidsbeleid*. Inaugural address. Den Haag: Boom.

Hilhorst, D. and Warner, J. (2009) 'Normality and Exception: Linking up the Security Chain'. Paper presented during the 1st International Humanitarian Studies Association conference, Groningen, 1–3 February 2009.

Ignatieff, M. (1993) *Blood and Belonging: Journeys into the New Nationalism*. New York, NY: Farrar, Straus and Giroux.

Ignatieff, M. (2004) *The Lesser Evil: Political Ethics in an Age of Terror*, Edinburgh: Edinburgh University Press.

Järvelä, M. (2007) 'Introduction. Social Resilience, Urban Poverty and Sustainable Livelihood in Megacities of the South'. In Gould, J. and Siitonen, L. (eds.) *Anomalies of Aid. A Festschrift for Juhani Koponen*. Helsinki: Interkont Books #15, 244–268.

Kaygusuz, O. (2007) 'Securitization in the Context of Global Hegemony: US-Turkish Relations in Perspective'. Paper presented at the SGIR Pan-European Conference 2007, Turin. Standing Group in International Relations, European Consortium for Political Research (ECPR).

Kirschenbaum, A. (2004) 'Generic Sources of Disaster Communites: A Social Network Approach'. *International Journal of Sociology and Social Policy*, 24: 94–129.

Klein, N. (2007) *The Shock Doctrine. The Rise of Disaster Capitalism*. New York: Metropolitan Books.

Krahmann, E. (2008) 'The Commodification of Security in the Risk Society'. Working Paper No. 06–08. Bristol University, School of Sociology, Politics and International Studies, http://www.bristol.ac.uk/spais/research/workingpapers/wpspaisfiles/krahmann0608.pdf

Leferink, S. and Sardemann, R. (2010) 'Kramp na de Ramp. Een kritische beschouwing op de hulpverlening bij rampen'. Utrecht: Slachtofferhulp Nederland.

Leiss, W. and Chociolko, C. (1994) *Risk and Responsibility*. Montreal: McGill-Queens University Press.

Lewis, D. (2007) *Water Policy for Sustainable Development*, Baltimore, MD: JHU Press.

López-Ibor, J.J. (2005) 'What is a Disaster?' In López-Ibor, J., Christodoulou, G., Maj, M., Sartorius, N. and Okasha, A. *Disaster and Mental Health*. New York: John Wiley & Sons, 37–63.

McDonald, M. (2009) 'Securitization and the Construction of Security', *European Journal of International Relations*, 14(4): 563–587.

Miggiano, L. (2009) 'States of Exception: Securitization and Irregular Migration in the Mediterranean. New Issues in Refugee Research'. Research Paper No. 177. UNHCR. November. http://www.unhcr.org/4b167a5a9.pdf

Nugent, P. (2010) 'States and Social Contracts in Africa'. *New Left Review*, 63: 35–68.

Olson, R.S. (2000) 'Toward a Politics of Disaster: Losses, Values, Agendas, and Blame'. *International Journal of Mass Emergencies and Disasters*, 18 (August): 265–287.

Ophir, A. (2007) 'The Two-State Solution: Providence and Catastrophe'. Article 2. *Journal of Homeland Security and Emergency Management*, 4(1): 1–44.

Ophir, A. (2010) 'The Politics of Catastrophization. Roundtable: Research Architecture: A Laboratory for Critical Spatial Practices'. Online: http://roundtable.kein.org/node/1094 (Accessed 25 June 2012).

Pelling, M. and Dill, C. (2009) 'Disaster Politics: Tipping Points for Change in the Adaptation of Socio-political Regimes'. *Progress in Human Geography*, 34(1): 21–37.

Prins, G. (1993) *Threats Without Enemies. Facing Environmental Insecurity.* London: Earthscan.

Raleigh, C. (2010) 'Political Marginalization, Climate Change, and Conflict in African Sahel States'. *International Studies Review*, 12(1): 69–86.

Rosenthal, U. (1984) *Rampen, rellen, gijzelingen. Crisisbesluitvorming in Nederland.* Amsterdam/ Diemen: De Bataafsche Leeuw.

Roth, D., Warner, J. and Winnubst, M. (2006) *Een Noodverband voor Hoog Water.* Boundaries of Space series, Wageningen University.

Sylves, R. (2008) *Disaster Policy and Politics: Emergency Management and Homeland Security.* Washington, DC: CQ Press.

Tierney, J.J. (2007) 'From the Margins to the Mainstream? Disaster Research at the Crossroads'. *Annual Review of Sociology*, 33: 503–525.

Trombetta, M.J. (2008) 'Environmental Securitization and Climate Change: Analysing the Discourse'. *Cambridge Review of International Affairs*, 21(4): 585–602.

Vaughn, J. (2009) 'The Unlikely Securitizer: Humanitarian Organizations and the Securitization of Indistinctiveness', *Security Dialogue*, 40(3): 263–285. http://sdi.sagepub.com/content/40/3/263.full.pdf

Velotti, L., Engel, K., Warner, J. and Weijs, B. (2011) 'Meeting Communities where Communities Meet'. Borgharen and Itteren, Maastricht, The Netherlands. Miscellaneous Report #73, University of Delaware. Online: http://dspace.udel.edu:8080/dspace/bitstream/handle/19716/10384/Misc%2073.pdf?sequence=1 (Accessed 25 June 2012).

Vuori, J.A. (2011) 'How to do Security with Words. A Grammar of Securitization in the People's Republic of China'. Dissertation. University of Turku Humaniora department. Online: www.doria.fi/bitstream/handle/10024/70743/AnnalesB336Vuori.pdf?sequence=1 (Accessed 25 June 2012).

Warner, J. (2003) 'Risk Regime Change and Political Leadership: River Management in the Netherlands and Bangladesh'. In Pelling, M. (ed.) *Natural Disasters and Development in a Globalizing World.* London: Routledge, 185–198.

Warner, J. (2011) *Flood Planning. The Politics of Water Security.* London: I. B. Tauris.

Warner, J. and Oré, M.T. (2006) 'El Niño Platforms: Participatory Disaster Response in Peru'. *Disasters*, 30: 102–117.

Watson, S.D. (2011) 'The "Human" as Referent Object? Humanitarianism as Securitization'. *Security Dialogue*, 42(1) 3–20.

Watson, S.D. (2012) 'Framing' the Copenhagen School: Integrating the Literature on Threat Construction'. *Millennium. Journal of International Studies*, 40(2): 279–301.

Weert, S. (2009) 'In search of *tranquilidad*. A research on household livelihood security in the Northern Bolivian Amazon'. MSc thesis, Wageningen University.

Wesselink, A. Warner, J.F. and Kok, M. (2012) 'You Gain Some Funding, You Lose Some Freedom: The Ironies of Flood Protection in Limburg, the Netherlands'. *Environmental Science and Policy*. (Online first).

Wilkinson, C. (2007) 'The Copenhagen School on Tour in Kyrgyzstan: Is Securitization Theory Useable Outside Europe?' *Security Dialogue*, 38: 5–25.

Youngs, R. (2009) 'Beyond Copenhagen: Securitising climate change'. Policy brief #22. FRIDE, , Madrid.

Zack, R. (2011) *Ethics for Disaster.* Lanham, MD: Rowman and Littlefield.

Part II
Institutions and institutional multiplicity

6 Conflict, governance and institutional multiplicity

Parallel governance in Kosovo and Chiapas, Mexico

Gemma van der Haar and Merel Heijke

Introduction

A striking feature of situations of protracted conflict is the emergence of multiple structures of authority and regulation that operate next to, and sometimes in opposition to, state institutions. Though it is now clear that such 'institutional multiplicity' – as it was called in DiJohn (2008) – is pervasive in conflict and conflictive post-conflict ('no peace, no war', Richards 2005) settings, studies of the workings of institutional multiplicity are still limited. It is important, however, to get a better understanding of the kinds of dynamics involved in institutional multiplicity and the social effects it produces on the ground. This will further our understanding of how governance works in conflictive spaces and how local societies cope with, and respond to, conditions of conflict. It will also add to the argument, made in the context of the fragile states debate, that we need to move beyond understandings of conflict in terms of institutional *breakdown* to understand conflict instead as involving complex dynamics of institutional *change*.

A crucial aspect of institutional multiplicity is how the different sets of institutions relate to each other, and what the implications are of their interaction in shaping governance on the ground. How does institutional multiplicity affect order and security, public service provision, and the regulation of access and entitlements? How do people draw on, invest in, or mitigate institutional multiplicity? This chapter addresses these issues by focusing on a particular form of institutional multiplicity, referred to as 'parallel governance'. Parallel governance concerns those situations where two distinct sets of institutions exist, associated with competing political agendas, usually between states and their competitors. Parallel governance entails situations of circumscribed 'split sovereignty' (Pula 2004, in Van der Borgh 2012) and is marked by overt competition of claims to governance. In situations of parallel governance, the competing sets of institutions are framed as mutually exclusive, yet in practice, as this chapter will show, these institutions interact in a number of ways. The explicit competition and oppositional political framing is a distinct feature of parallel governance that is not necessarily found in all instances of institutional multiplicity. A particular concern in this chapter is to discuss how the workings and trajectories of parallel governance are shaped by the tension between these broader political agendas and local demands for service provision, security and order.

This chapter draws on two case studies of parallel governance in southern Kosovo and eastern Chiapas, Mexico. Both cases represent a protracted 'no peace, no war' situation in which the levels of overt violence are relatively low but considerable societal tensions persist. In both cases, also, post-conflict processes of reconstruction and state-building interact with a continued resistance to the state by groups in society who operate a distinct set of institutions (authorities, public service provision, administration of justice) as a core element of their resistance strategy. Despite the differences in setting, the two cases together are suggestive of the fact that institutional multiplicity is a core feature of 'no peace, no war' conflict dynamics, that has broader political significance and is felt directly in the everyday lives of local populations. Drawing on both cases, we are able to show, first, how the separate sets of institutions interact with each other involving dynamics of confrontation as well as accommodation and mutual adjustment, and second, how the political agendas associated with, and embodied in, the parallel systems work out in the local arena.

This text is structured as follows. After this introduction, the next section develops the theoretical argument around institutional multiplicity in conflict settings, in general, and parallel governance, in particular. This is followed by two sections that discuss the cases of Kosovo and Chiapas, drawing on fieldwork in particular sites (Štrpce/Shtërpcë municipality in Kosovo, Altamirano municipality in Chiapas). First, the emergence and development of parallel governance in both cases is outlined, paying attention to both the local needs and the political framing. Then, we discuss in more detail the interaction between the parallel sets of institutions, paying attention to issues of legitimation, the negotiation of boundaries, and how confrontation occurs alongside accommodation and negotiation.

This text is based on in-depth fieldwork in two localities. The case study in Chiapas, Mexico, focused on Altamirano municipality and took place during a period of eight months in 2003/2004. It was an exploratory study of the interaction dynamics between state institutions for local governance, on the one hand, and Zapatista-operated institutions on the other. The ideas generated from this work informed the three-month fieldwork in Štrpce/Shtërpcë municipality in Kosovo, that took place between November 2009 and February 2010. In both cases, the decision to focus on a specific locality was in line with the intent to unravel the dynamics of parallel governance on the ground. The methodology combined interviewing, participant observation and critical events analysis.

Institutional multiplicity in conflict and post-conflict spaces

This contribution is part of broader attempts at understanding governance and the workings of the state in settings of protracted conflict and post-conflict tension, going beyond the 'fragile states' perspective (Boege *et al.* 2009, Debiel and Lambach 2009, Heathershaw and Lambach 2008, Hagmann and Hoehne 2009,

Menkhaus 2006). We build on, and hope to further develop, the notion of 'institutional multiplicity' as it has been coined by the Crisis States Research Centre. In a paper by DiJohn (2008), institutional multiplicity is defined as follows:

> Institutional multiplicity is a situation in which different sets of rules of the game, often contradictory, coexist in the same territory, putting citizens and economic agents in complex, often unsolvable, situations, but at the same time offering them the possibility of switching strategically from one institutional universe to another (33).

For the purpose of this chapter, we take institutional multiplicity to refer to those situations in which multiple sets of institutions exist, emanating from the state, from customary systems, but also from insurgent groups, social movements or, in the context of a high density of aid provision, from non-governmental organisations (NGOs) (DiJohn 2008, Van der Haar 2012). In situations of institutional multiplicity, different claims to authority and regulation exist that are expressed in distinct sets of rules, 'offers' of public goods, sources of legitimation, enforcement mechanisms and, sometimes, administrative procedures.

The attractiveness of the concept of institutional multiplicity is its lack of normative and prescriptive connotation. It does not, a priori, privilege or dismiss any type of governance arrangement. It does not juxtapose institutions in binary terms, as state versus non-state, or 'formal' versus 'informal'. Institutional multiplicity finds governance not only beyond formal government, but also beyond the 'informal' or customary, and allows for the governing functions of NGOs and insurgent groups. In this way, it opens up the space to consider the structure, workings and impact of any source of authority and regulation, without predefined notions of what type of institutions should fulfil what functions or what principles should be expected to govern its operation. Researching institutional multiplicity, then, means to investigate empirically the make-up, reach, effectiveness and legitimation efforts of different institutional offers or claims to governance, in a field in which a multiplicity of such claims operate. It implies examining the way these different sets of institutions interact and influence one another, and the way this shapes social life.

Our approach to institutional multiplicity is closely related to, and builds on, the notion of 'hybrid political orders', coined by Boege *et al.* (2009) and defined as follows:

> [I]n hybrid political orders, diverse and competing authority structures, sets of rules, logics of order, and claims to power co-exist, overlap, interact and intertwine, combining elements of introduced Western models of governance and elements stemming from local indigenous traditions (2009: 17).

The emphasis in the work on hybrid political orders so far has been on the way in which the state interacts with customary forms of governance, though it is not necessarily restricted to that, and may be extended to other societal arrangements

(Kraushaar and Lambach 2009). A particular strength of the notion of hybrid political orders is the way it conceptualises the interaction between different regulatory orders. We draw on these insights in our approach to studying institutional multiplicity. Whereas the original formulation in DiJohn highlights the contradictions inherent in institutional multiplicity, the work on hybrid political orders extends our notion to forms of functional complementarity. The notion of hybridity conveys the idea that the different institutional orders intertwine and blend, or, as put by Boege *et al.*: 'these spheres do not exist in isolation from each other, but permeate each other' and the political orders arising from this are 'characterized by the closely interwoven texture of their separate sources of origin' (2009: 17). In the approach to institutional multiplicity developed in this chapter, the interactions between different sets of institutions are a core concern. We consider the dynamics of interaction to span a range of forms that may occur alongside each other: contradiction, confrontation and friction, as well as accommodation, mutual adjustment and negotiation. We understand intertwining and interpenetration as a possible, but not a necessary, occurrence in the process of interaction. The nature of the institutional and social boundaries between the different regulatory spheres, the degree and dynamics of their permeability as well as processes of boundary (de-) construction, are key issues for empirical study.

Our understanding of institutional multiplicity is informed by the broader field of legal pluralism, which studies the co-existence of multiple legal orders in the same social space. Classical approaches to legal pluralism tended to essentialise customary law, fixate it in time, and oppose it to state law (Kraushaar and Lambach 2009). More recently, legal pluralism has addressed the interrelatedness and mutual influence between different rule-sets and systems of authority, highlighting how social practice produces this interwining as it moves across and between the different legal orders. As we attempt to show in this text, social practice includes both strategic calculus and normative judgements about the (moral or political) righteousness of the different sets of institutions. Legal pluralism has traditionally been focused on the administration of justice, litigation and conflict resolution, but its approaches and insights hold relevance for the study of pluralism in governance, including civil administration and public service delivery.

Institutional multiplicity does not necessarily involve political contention or competition. Multiple institutions may simply operate next to each other in complementary fashion without explicit political meaning being attached to it. However, in practice, political contention may easily develop, including in cases where it is not present from the outset. Non-state institutional arrangements may emerge in a non-politicised fashion, in response to demands for specific 'gaps' in service delivery, the organisation of security, or conflict resolution. In the context of conflict or post-conflict contentious politics, such institutional arrangements may acquire a political meaning. Institutional multiplicity, then, comes to involve contention over the legitimacy of the state and moral arguments around the values and virtues of the different sets of institutions. Even when framed as administrative or technical, few institutions seem to exist without such normative or political meaning, and the challenge is to understand the way this plays out in settings of institutional multiplicity.

Parallel governance is a form of institutional multiplicity in which moral and political contestation is a crucial feature of the way the different sets of institutions relate. With 'parallel governance', we refer to governance organised and sustained as part of strategies of resistance to and critique of the state. As a consequence, the respective institutional orders are posited as clearly distinct from, and opposite to, each other. In the cases we consider in this chapter, the parallel institutions are operated from a minority position, representing a situation of *circumscribed* split sovereignty. The parallel institutions present a powerful political statement and locally constitute a competing power base, but are not strong enough to topple the state as such. In these settings, governance is a project, a claim, rather than an accomplished fact.

Parallel governance generally responds both to governance 'gaps' experienced on the ground and to political agendas. Many regions affected by protracted, violent conflict have also suffered from a limited investment of the central state in basic services, such as roads, potable water, and basic health care and education (Douma and van der Haar 2010). Strategies of resistance to the state may successfully frame the lack of state investment in terms of state neglect, marginalisation or (ethnic) exclusion, and partly build on these grievances. Investments in parallel service delivery then symbolise the failure of the state and stages the competing governance offer as 'the better alternative'. In practice, the pragmatic (governance-oriented) and the political dimensions of parallel governance do not always fit together smoothly, and tensions may arise between the ambitions to outcompete the state in service delivery and overarching political strategies (Heijke *et al.* 2012).

This contribution seeks to move beyond the notion of conflict as the domain of the ungoverned and instead to understand (protracted) conflict dynamics as involving multiple processes of institutional change: disruption and breakdown, as well as emergence, creation, re-definition. We argue that in some cases, such as those where parallel governance systems are created, rather than institutional breakdown, the contrary situation of a growing density of institutions may be found.

Resistance and institutions: trajectories of parallel governance in Chiapas and Kosovo

In this section we discuss two situations of parallel governance, one in rural Chiapas, in eastern Mexico, and the other in post-Milošević Kosovo. In Chiapas, parallel governance has become a core strategy in what has become known as the 'Zapatista uprising' of 1994, in which mostly indigenous peasants opposed the Mexican state at local and national levels and advocated respect and recognition of their rights. Zapatista autonomous structures are found especially in eastern Chiapas. Our fieldwork there concentrated on the region of Altamirano municipality where adherence to the Zapatista movement had been very strong in the 1990s but where a clear situation of split sovereignty has arisen. In Kosovo, Serb minorities maintained governance structures financed and operated from Belgrade as a sign of their refusal to recognise Kosovo as an autonomous entity and, as of 2008, as an independent state. Our discussion draws on fieldwork in Štrpce/ Shtërpcë municipality, where Serbs are a majority in a mixed municipality, while the remainder of the region is predominantly Kosovo Albanian. The section shows how parallel governance emerged in these two cases and outlines the basic structure of the 'split sovereignty' situation.

Zapatista autonomous governance in Chiapas

In Chiapas, in Southern Mexico, so-called 'autonomous municipalities' have been created as part of the political strategy of the EZLN (*Ejército Zapatista de Liberación Nacional*). The uprising of the EZLN, globally known as the Zapatista rebellion, started with a declaration of war on the Mexican government and the occupation of town halls in six towns in Chiapas in the night of 1 January 1994. This was followed by ten days of persecution by the Mexican army. In the years following 1994, the movement pursued a strategy of non-violent resistance to the Mexican state in which they came to rely strongly on the operation of parallel institutions. The situation since 1994 can be characterised as 'no peace, no war'; official peace negotiations remain interrupted since the late 1990s, and the situation on the ground has involved variable levels of tension and conflict (including factional violence), but no military confrontations.

The Zapatistas created so-called 'autonomous' structures of governance, at the level of communities, municipalities and regions. These structures started as a means to organise the civilian basis of the movement and link them to the military command structure. But with the breakdown of official peace talks in 1997, they were consolidated and became both the symbol and the practical organisation of Zapatista resistance to the Mexican state (Burguete 2003, Van der Haar 2005). As of 2003, the autonomous structures have become the main channels for the support of and interaction with a wide range of NGOs and sympathisers, as well as the press and researchers. The strategy of resistance has meant more concretely that the population that adheres to the EZLN does not recognise municipal and juridical authorities of the state, refuses to make use of state-organised services of healthcare and education, and declines government subsidies and social programmes. The Zapatista autonomous municipalities are organised not as territorial units but on the basis of political allegiance. Zapatista adherents respond to the 'autonomous' regulations and authorities and access 'autonomous' services. The people 'loyal to the government' or those that consider themselves neutral, on the other hand, respond to the official municipal structures and authorities, and access services provided by the state.

The Zapatistas made an effort to create all the basic attributes associated with the state at the local level and to provide a parallel offer of services in an effort to 'mirror' the state. The visible infrastructure comprises, among others, offices for the authorities, court rooms, schools and health posts. There are formalised positions of authority, institutionalised channels of representation and administrative procedures, a civil registry and committees for different areas of concern including administration of justice, development, land tenure and adjudication, education and healthcare, to name the most important. Some of these services are limited to the Zapatista adherents (such as the land administration office), others are open to the broader regional population (such as the justice system). The structures are sustained through voluntary labour contributions and cash contributions by the Zapatista population, as well as financial and other types of support from NGOs and solidarity groups from both within and beyond Mexico.

The Zapatista parallel institutions are supported by – and expressive of – a political agenda of indigenous autonomy, social justice and a critique of the Mexican state. The Zapatista movement has criticised the Mexican state for despotism and neglect, capturing the experience of political exclusion, injustice and institutionalised racism common to much of the poor and indigenous population in Mexico. The autonomous structures are framed as representing a responsible and responsive form of government, with high degrees of participation and accountability. In addition, the parallel structures are justified in relation to the right to indigenous autonomy, building on the international recognition of the rights of indigenous populations to organise themselves in accordance with their culture and traditions.[1] This way of framing Zapatista governance has resonated at national and global levels. At the same time, the parallel structures are key to maintaining the visibility of the Zapatista uprising and testifying to its viability.

In eastern Chiapas, the competition between the Zapatistas and the state for the loyalty of poor citizens has meant more state and more services. In response to the services created by the Zapatistas, and in an effort to pre-empt further claims of neglect and exclusion, the Mexican state intensified its material, functional and symbolic presence in Chiapas. It displayed intense efforts in the building of roads, clinics, schools and courts, public policies to support vulnerable populations, and in the visibility of state officials.

Serb parallel structures of government in Kosovo

In 1999 the international community took action to end the Serbian rule over Kosovo, turning the Serb population in Kosovo into a minority in a new, though undefined, political entity (not yet to be called a state) in which Albanians formed by far the majority. Under the Yugoslav regime, Kosovo had been a province within Serbia with some degree of autonomy. This was severely reduced under the Milošević regime which repressed the Albanian population of Kosovo. After the NATO intervention of 1999, Kosovo was placed under UN mandate while its future status remained unresolved. In 2008, Kosovo declared its independence from Serbia and established itself as an independent state, though this status has not been recognised by all other countries, even in Europe. Serbia never recognised the UN mandate (UNMIK) and continues to dispute Kosovo's status as an independent state. Similarly, much of the Serb population in Kosovo refuses to recognise Kosovo as a political entity and continued to consider Belgrade and at the time of writing the Serbian government as the legitimate government for the Kosovar territory. In regions with Serb population, Belgrade-sanctioned and financed municipal governments continued to function even when new municipal governments were installed, giving rise to a situation of parallel governance. Belgrade continues to finance the salaries of local officials, to pay for schools and hospitals and to operate some public services.

The influence of Serbia is especially strong in the northern part of Kosovo, where Serbs are a majority and where there is a direct proximity to the state of Serbia. In the centre and south of Kosovo, the situation is different.[2] Here, Serbs are a minority but are concentrated in a number of areas that have become known as 'enclaves'. They received special protection by the international military force Kosovo Force (KFOR) during years of considerable tension and violence against Serbs, and have remained segregated from the surrounding Albanian environment. Serbs in the southern half of Kosovo feel isolated and more marginalised from Serbia than those in the north of the country. There is a certain fear that Serbia might not keep up its commitment to Serbs in this part of Kosovo (also Van der Borgh 2012).

As in the case of Chiapas, parallel structures in Kosovo are found at the level of municipal government. In Kosovo, however, the Serb parallel institutions are not new creations but remnants of a state in the context of a new political entity. The Serb parallel structures include municipal and judicial authorities, schools and healthcare facilities, and municipal services such as garbage collection. The structures rely on the financial support (for salaries, operational costs) from Belgrade. Serb parallel governance in these conditions has both a material significance, and a symbolic one. They provide crucial services to the Serb population, such as education in Serbian, and they testify to Kosovo Serbs' allegiance to Serbia and the denial of the Kosovar independent state. The parallel structures also function as guardians of culture and tradition.

The decentralisation process in Kosovo has recently 'institutionalised' several former Serb enclaves as municipalities in their own right, and grants them a number of extra facilities (the so-called enhanced powers) on top of those granted to all Kosovar municipalities. In practice, this system allows for the continuation of financial support from Belgrade and the operation of schools and clinics under the Serbian framework.

'Split sovereignty' in Chiapas and Kosovo

In situations of parallel governance, rule-sets, authorities and entitlements apply not to a contiguous spatial territory but rather their validity is socially circumscribed to a group of adherents. The geographical overlap involved produces particularly complex dynamics. There is, in both in Chiapas and Kosovo, a degree of spatial segregation, with some villages being Zapatistas and others not (in the case of Chiapas), or some being Serb and others Albanian (in the southern part of Kosovo) and, in both cases, some villages being mixed. Yet, people of different political allegiances, with their associated institutional frameworks, share certain spaces and resources such as urban centres, access roads, central buildings and some essential services. In Altamirano municipality, two competing centres of governance are located at relatively close distance, the official municipal centre of Altamirano and the Zapatista seat of government in nearby Morelia (about 8 kilometres away). Access to the centre at Morelia for many Zapatistas is only possible by passing through Altamirano, where also the market is located and where both groups come to look for higher level health services. In Štrpce/Shtërpcë, up until the elections of 2009, the Belgrade-supported officials and those working for the Kosovar structure 'shared' the same building, as both continued to stake a claim to the town hall. The overlap in governance spheres means that neither one of the structures is hegemonic and can choose to ignore the other, at least not in practice.

In terms of social space, Štrpce/Shtërpcë in Kosovo was more segregated than the Altamirano region in Chiapas. In Altamirano, Zapatistas and non-Zapatistas continued to be connected through a common ancestry, family ties and religious bonds, as well as commercial networks. Though at some point these connections had been severed by the tense political situation, when polarisation eased, people started to re-connect. The situation was not without friction but there was regular and sometimes warm social interaction. In the context of Štrpce/Shtërpcë, this was found to be rather different: the ethnic and language divide was also a social divide and people lived largely in separate spheres. Culture and religion provided no cross-ethnic spaces, though commerce does to some degree (Heijke *et al.* 2012).

Competing claims to governance in practice: parallel governance between politics and pragmatism

In situations of parallel governance, multiple interfaces occur inevitably between the competing governance structures, despite the efforts to present them as mutually exclusive. Parallel governance, for that reason, involves complex dynamics of confrontation and friction, and – as we found during fieldwork – also of accommodation, negotiation and mutual adjustment. This section describes how these dynamics unfold in practice, drawing on material from the field studies in Chiapas and Kosovo. We draw attention to three core dimensions involved in the interrelation between the respective sets of institutions. First, we discuss local accommodation mechanisms that mitigate the confrontation that derives from the mutually exclusive political agendas. Second, we look at how adjustment between the different claims to governance occurs through critical events which test, and redefine, their respective boundaries. Finally, we look at how the co-existence between two competing offers involves a constant process of legitimation vis-à-vis local citizens, in which both sides oscillate between pressure for political loyalty and persuasion through better services.

Confrontation and accommodation

Both in Štrpce/Shtërpcë and in Altamirano, the parallel governance arrangements are closely tied to competing and ultimately incompatible political agendas. The political agendas underpinning the parallel sets of institutions deny the legitimate existence of the other. In Chiapas, the formal Zapatista standpoint is to dismiss the Mexican state as illegitimate, whereas the Mexican state considers Zapatista autonomy as unconstitutional, though it does not actively seek to dismantle the parallel structures. In Kosovo, the Serb position is to deny the legitimacy of an independent Kosovo, whereas the Kosovar agenda contests the continued Serb influence at the municipal level, though it has to accept certain levels of support in the newly created Serb-majority municipalities (affording the support a legal basis it previously lacked).

The political projects and discourses associated with parallel governance emphasise polarisation and incompatibility down to the local level. In fieldwork, we found that this was played out in instances of outright confrontation, sporadically involving violence and accompanied by a considerable degree of tension. Examples from Chiapas include Zapatista schools being shut down by non-Zapatistas, and disputes over land occupied under the Zapatista banner. At the same time, however, instances of accommodation and even negotiation could be identified. Sometimes, state authorities chose to de-escalate the conflict. Also, there were examples of local actors seeking to maintain a certain degree of stability and security at the local level. Though the incompatibility at the level of political projects was clearly understood by local actors, local mitigation mechanisms often worked to contain the situation, preventing outright escalation, a situation perhaps best described as one of 'mediated confrontation'.

In both cases, we identified some efforts aimed at coordination and negotiation between the different authorities. These tended to have very low visibility and to rely on personal contacts and a sense of responsibility of specific individuals. In Chiapas, ever since the suspended peace talks in 1997, the Zapatistas had followed a policy of 'no negotiation with the government'. This refusal to negotiate did not only apply to the central (federal) government, but also the state and the municipal governments, as well as officials in a wide range of state agencies. Though maintained very strictly in some years, this policy was eased in 2003, partly in response to the tensions between Zapatistas and non-Zapatistas at the local level. The Zapatista leadership then allowed for arrangements with formal (municipal) authorities around issues of local interest. In the Altamirano region, this meant that the autonomous Zapatista authorities (*Junta de Buen Gobierno*) and the formal municipal authorities would consult around issues concerning both their constituencies. This worked as follows: if projects of an infrastructural nature awarded to non-Zapatista villagers required that trucks with building materials would pass through a Zapatista community, this would be communicated in advance and the consent of the Zapatistas would be sought and, usually, given. (Sometimes something was asked in return, such as a small share of the materials transported.) This was locally felt, by authorities of the two sides as well as by local inhabitants, as a huge improvement compared with the previous situation when trucks with building materials or the entry of state officials were blocked by the Zapatistas which often led to confrontations.

The communication between Zapatista and official municipal authorities in the case of Altamirano was facilitated by the fact that the individuals involved knew one another and, to a certain degree, respected one another. The municipal administration at the time of fieldwork (2003–2004), had purposefully included some individuals who had previously been part of the Zapatista movement (1994–1997) hoping to be able, through them, to liaise with the Zapatistas, at least informally. This worked, though with considerable tension. Individuals on both sides were motivated by the sense that, despite the political differences, the negative impacts on people's daily lives should be reduced, and that it was in their common interest to keep tensions down and avoid unnecessary friction.

A similar interest in maintaining local order and the reliance on personal contacts to limit escalation and insecurity was found in Štrpce/Shtërpcë where this took place especially *among* the Serb population between those Serbs working in the formal Kosovar administration and those in the parallel Serb (Belgrade-supported) administration. Štrpce/Shtërpcë is a municipality with a Serb majority in an Albanian setting, with the town itself being mainly inhabited by Serbs and with some villages being Albanian, some Serb, and a few mixed. Both the parallel (Belgrade-supported) and the formal (Prishtina-supported) municipal governments were headed by Serb Mayors. The efforts had to stay below the radar because they contradicted the formal discourses of opposition and mutual lack of recognition. The encounters seem to have relied on very informal testing of the waters and keeping each other informed. Possibly the relative remoteness of Belgrade and the isolation of the Serb population in Štrpce/Shtërpcë and their sense of vulnerability created the room for manoeuvre and the incentive to invest in these relations (also Van der Borgh 2012).

Our fieldwork found that the Serb population in Štrpce/Shtërpcë was in a real dilemma. Should they continue to bet on Belgrade and, in a principled manner, continue to deny Kosovo as an independent state, or adopt a more pragmatic approach and start to accept their integration into Kosovo and make the best of it? This was clearly seen around the elections in autumn 2009. In the first round, many Serbs did not vote, as in earlier elections, as voting would imply recognition of the Kosovar state. When it became apparent that this would put an Albanian in office, and after lobbying by the Serb candidate for Mayor, the second round showed a strong increase in the number of Serb voters who, given their majority in the municipality, brought victory to the strongest Serb candidate. An Albanian, with whom the new Mayor was already on good terms, became vice-Mayor in some sort of power-sharing arrangement.

Boundary-testing, boundary-setting

Parallel governance implies that boundaries between the different sets of institutions need to be defined and a modus of articulation needs to be developed. In both cases studied, we found that boundary-testing and boundary-setting to mark the respective spheres of influence was an ongoing phenomenon. In our analysis, we followed specific events around which boundaries were put to the test, were re-negotiated and were temporarily fixed. These events were instructive for the researchers but similarly instructive to local observers: like us, ordinary citizens understood these events as tests of the relative strengths of the competing sets of institutions and the modus of articulation that had been forged. In the case of Štrpce/Shtërpcë the elections of autumn 2009 were such a critical event that showed – as discussed above – that pragmatism was gaining some ground amongst the Serb population and that they were willing to show a minimal degree of acceptance of the Kosovar state. The newly elected Serb Mayor pushed this further in an attempt to fix the limits to the Serb parallel structure. After years of uncomfortable co-existence of the Kosovar and Belgrade-supported personnel in the same municipal building, he apparently unilaterally changed the locks almost immediately after he was installed, issuing a message that could hardly be misunderstood. The act was risky but the new situation was not challenged: new boundaries were set and the Belgrade-supported structures were relegated to the margins of public life in Štrpce/Shtërpcë.

In Chiapas, in the Altamirano region, boundary-setting took place around the issue of the role of the Zapatista efforts in the administration of justice. As of 2003, the Zapatistas opened their justice services to any citizen who wished to make use of them. They were appealing to a widespread discontent and frustration with the way the official justice system worked. Many people resented not only a perceived ineffectiveness, meaning that their problems remained unresolved, but also had strong suspicions (or knowledge) of corrupt practices. The state legal system was, as in many places in the world, very inaccessible to poor citizens. Thus, the Zapatista offer was welcomed and, at least initially, attracted considerable numbers of people to the Zapatista seat of government. In the flow of the initial success, the Zapatistas also started to effectively pursue people that were sued in their system. If a woman came to sue her ex-husband for refusing to pay alimony (a right that had started to become recognised at the level of the town and was now being actively pursued by divorced women), and if an investigation carried out by the Zapatistas corroborated the situation, they would first call upon him to appear before their court. If the man refused to appear, they would proceed to actively pursue him and bring him to the seat of autonomous government. This was where the autonomous system hit a boundary. When the Zapatistas started to actively pursue people in the main town of the official municipality, they were understood to directly penetrate the sphere of power of formal municipal government. They were warned by the Mayor that this was a bridge too far. This was where the boundary came to be defined: the Zapatista institutions for the administration of justice were tolerated and left to operate, as long as they did not violate the sphere of the central town. This boundary was accepted by the Zapatista leadership at the time.

In both cases mentioned, it is unclear what role the potential threat of the use of force played in setting the boundaries, but it is clear that the Kosovo Serbs in the one case, and the Zapatistas in Chiapas in the other, had something to lose. In Altamirano as well as Štrpce/Shtërpcë, the Mayor could have employed the police to enforce the decision, unlike the competitor. It is unknown to what extent they would have been prepared, in either case, to use force or what the expectations were on the other side regarding that use of force. It was clear in both cases, however, that the non-acceptance of this boundary could threaten the relative leeway that the 'resistance' structures enjoyed. Challenging the boundary might be costly and result in a more reduced space of operation.

Competing legitimacies, conflicting loyalties

The existence of different sets of institutions in overlapping social spheres has, as a consequence, that multiple offers of services are visible to local citizens and compared by them. This implies an almost continuous contest for the loyalty of the local population.

In the cases studied, the local legitimacy of the competing sets of institutions is partly a given, as it derives from the political or social allegiance which they represent, organise and symbolise. Local legitimacy is, however, also related to the actual performance. During fieldwork in Chiapas, we found people to comment almost continuously on the different governance arrangements and assess the performance of 'their' governance against that of the other group. Comments concerned both the performance in service delivery – in terms of quality, sustainability, accessibility or costs – and governance practices – in terms of transparency, responsiveness and equity. Governance actors on both sides were acutely aware that political loyalties were not insensitive to performance. The need for a good governance 'offer' gave rise to the cross-over of norms, the intertwining between sets of institutions that Boege *et al.* refer to (2009). An example of this was found in the Chiapas fieldwork. During the electoral campaign for local office, the candidates for the official (i.e. state-based) municipality took up what were locally seen as the strong points of the Zapatista discourse, namely the respect for indigenous rights, financial transparency and equity.

Parallel governance may give rise to conflicting loyalties. Fieldwork revealed how people sometimes felt trapped between their needs and their political allegiances. We found some forum shopping, but this was never politically innocent. People felt tied to the political agenda of 'their' institutions, even when, in response to strongly felt needs they decided to resort to services of the 'others'. In Chiapas, this occurred in healthcare and administration of justice. In healthcare, people might resort to the health services of 'the other group' in pursuit of treatment and cure. Zapatistas who could not mobilise the cash required for the private hospital that was known to sympathise with the movement, might turn to the state clinic. Similarly, some non-Zapatistas put greater confidence in the private clinic or, exceptionally, accessed the Zapatista health worker in their locality, if there was no other possibility. In the case of administration of justice, as mentioned, there were many cases of non-Zapatistas who accessed the Zapatista local justice system desperate to find a solution for their situation. Examples ranged from divorce issues with ex-husbands who were refusing to pay alimony, taxi drivers involved in a conflict over permits, and a local church group seeking to legalise a property they had been bequeathed. Decisions to shift forum were not taken lightly, as the symbolic meaning of these choices was clearly understood. People weighed the costs (in terms of strengthening the political competitor) and the personal benefits.

We also found that there was considerable acceptance for this kind of choice, especially in situations of desperation.

In Štrpce/Shtërpcë, the cases of forum shopping seemed more limited, but a certain degree of pragmatism was also found there. Local actors made strategic choices in order to 'get things done'. We found instances of cooperation between Serb and Albanian companies for, for example, road construction, with the funds coming from Belgrade but Albanian companies being sub-contracted to do the job with a view to speed and cost-effectiveness (Heijke 2010). There were also cases where this pragmatism meant that both local governments were by-passed and the request was directly made to NGOs, as people expected a more effective response there. But the main concern was a more generalised worry over the future of the Serb community and trying to assess what, in the long run, they might expect from either Belgrade or Prishtina.

In both cases studied, citizens and local governance actors alike reported a degree of confusion related to the fact that it is not always clear who governs what and by what rules. An example comes from Kosovo and relates to tax payment: the lack of clarity about which of the local governments in Štrpce/Shtërpcë was to collect property tax, in practice meant that people would not pay these taxes at all. In response, the Kosovar local government of Štrpce/Shtërpcë then decided to only issue identity papers after payment of the taxes that were due. An issue of great concern in Štrpce/Shtërpcë was the future of a ski centre that had been constructed in the Yugoslav era. Potential investments in the centre were stalled due to disputes over the property relations between Kosovo and Serbia. As it became one of the few remaining issues that Serbia could exert leverage over, the stakes went beyond the mere economic benefits involved. In Chiapas, uncertainty pertained mostly to the longer-term consequences of the rules and entitlements established under autonomy: for example, would birth certificates or primary school diplomas issued by the Zapatistas be respected by the Mexican state or would these rights be annulled?

In Štrpce/Shtërpcë, the parallel systems sometimes created gaps in service delivery, as when a road would be started but not finished, because it was unclear who was responsible for what part of the job. In other cases, it meant that the job was done twice, meaning a waste of resources. However, it also sometimes meant that there were two chances to get something organised, increasing the probability that it might actually happen. As in Chiapas, in one of the villages where a water pump broke and both the Zapatista half of the village and the non-Zapatista half of the village agreed to try and get a new pump through their respective channels (in the first case an NGO they were connected to, in the second case the municipal government) to see which solution would work first.

Despite the difficulties observed, the competition between the governance systems for legitimacy and for proving their worth to their respective constituencies, is not necessarily negative for local citizens. In both cases, but perhaps more strongly so in Chiapas, the conditions of parallelism have raised citizens' awareness about governance, both in the exercise of power and in the outcomes it produces. Actors on both sides have responded by raising their standards.

Similarly, the situation has created room for innovation. The parallel structures often resonate with broader discontent with the state, which those actors in formal local government who want to innovate and break way from 'old politics' can use to create more leverage.

Conclusion

This chapter has discussed the workings of parallel governance in the cases of Chiapas, Mexico, and Kosovo. By doing so, we have provided an example of what institutional multiplicity may mean in practice in the context of political conflict. We have shown how investing in institutions and stepping up the governance offer are ways to 'outcompete' the other party in conflict. Where this happens, a growing density of institutions rather than institutional breakdown and an intensified process of institutional change is the consequence.

We have shown that parallel governance, as it takes shape in the context of protracted conflict (including a conflictive 'post'-conflict phase), involves complex dynamics of contestation as well as accommodation and mutual adjustment. We have shown that parallel governance may involve the occurrence of governance gaps and fissures, namely, public goods that are not provided, governance demands that are not met, and also creates room for innovation and the emergence of new institutional solutions.

Parallel governance presents a structured situation with a high density of governance. One of the main tensions in parallel governance relates to the political agendas they are tied to, on the one hand, and local needs on the other hand. Competing claims to governance in the cases examined here, are related to, and expressions of, political agendas. They involve resistance to a state that is criticised for being illegitimate, and an effort of the established system to counter and pre-empt that claim. The political agendas in these cases are diametrically opposed. This carries with it the potential for considerable social conflict and disruption. In the cases examined, however, we saw that this threat was kept in check by locally worked out arrangements of accommodation and adjustment. In both cases individuals created some room for coordination and normalisation of local relations, based on their networks, and with a strong sense of public responsibility. Parallel institutions are caught up in competition but are not insensitive to local needs for order and the provision of public goods, often across the political divide. Whether the parallel systems will effectively contribute to these public goods depends on the degree to which the divisive political agendas to which they are tied are kept in check. We have shown that the inherent political competition in situations of parallel governance can be mitigated by local actors interested in creating room for manoeuvre for working out local solutions. However, these local solutions are vulnerable to broader political dynamics. When more political pressure is exerted on local actors, this limits the room for local solutions.

The study of institutional multiplicity moves beyond the analysis of the state-customary binary to focus on the emergence and evolvement of institutions tied to agendas of resistance within which the customary as such seems to play a minor role – and instead it is the make-up of the state that is disputed. The cases show how the dispute may not revolve around the content of the norms as much as they revolve around the question of who (which system) is allowed to exercise authority. Adherence to a specific set of rules, or accessing a specific service, then needs also to be understood in relation to the symbolic significance this has in terms of legitimising a specific authority and associated political project versus another (such as has been discussed by Sikor and Lund, 2010). Material and political interests may, from the perspective of the citizens, enter into contradiction. We found little evidence for purely pragmatic forum shopping, given the awareness of and sensitivity to the competing agendas that were in dispute. Rather, local citizens move between more principled and more pragmatic positions and show variable degrees of flexibility in navigating institutional multiplicity.

Acknowledgements

The authors are grateful for the comments received on earlier drafts by Mathijs van Leeuwen, Timmo Gaasbeek, Chris van der Borgh, Daniel Lambach and Dorothea Hilhorst who contributed to improving the arguments.

For the Chiapas research we acknowledge the financial support from WOTRO/NWO foundation, which funded a two-year post-doctoral research 'Governing in Dispute'. Gemma van der Haar acknowledges the support of the CIESAS in San Cristóbal de las Casas, which hosted her during the time of the fieldwork.

The fieldwork in Kosovo was part of an MSc-thesis project that took place in the framework of the Working Group on Local Governance of the Dutch Knowledge Network on Peace, Security and Development (see Heijke 2010; Heijke et al. 2012). We acknowledge the financial support received by the PSD network. We acknowledge the support and feedback of NGO Fractal, VNG International and IKV Pax Christi.

Notes

1 Tradition in itself is not drawn upon as a source of legitimacy, but the Zapatista structures and rule-sets do build on customary institutions in the region (such as community-level deliberation) which are common in local society, for Zapatistas and non-Zapatistas alike (Van der Haar 2005).
2 The divided city of Mitrovica presents a special situation. Literally located on the north-south division, marked by the river Ibar, it has a Serb quarter located north of the river and an Albanian quarter south of the river, each with their respective local governments.

References

Boege, V., A. Brown and K. Clements (2009) 'Hybrid Political Orders, not Fragile States', *Peace Review*, 21 (1): 13–21.
Burguete Cal y Mayor, A. (2003) 'The de facto Autonomous Process: New Jurisdictions and Parallel Governments in Rebellion', in Rus, J., R.A. Hernández Castillo and

S.L. Mattiace (eds) *Mayan Lives, Mayan Utopias: The Indigenous Peoples of Chiapas and the Zapatista Rebellion.* Lanham: Rowman and Littlefield Publishers.

Debiel, T. and D. Lambach (2009) 'How State-building Strategies miss Local Realities', *Peace Review*, 21 (1): 22–28.

DiJohn, J. (2008) 'Conceptualising the Causes and Consequences of Failed States: A Critical Review of the Literature', Working Paper no. 25, London: Crisis States Research Centre.

Douma, N. and G. van der Haar (2010) 'Basic Services, the State, and Development in Post-conflict Settings: Current Discourse', in M. Noor (ed.) *Multi-stakeholder Processes, Service Delivery and State Institutions, Theoretical Framework and Methodology.* Working paper, Dutch Knowledge Network on Peace, Security and Development, The Hague.

Hagmann, T. and M.V. Hoehne (2009) 'Failures of the State Failure Debate: Evidence from the Somali Territories', *Journal of International Development*, 21: 42–57.

Heathershaw, J. and D. Lambach (2008) 'Introduction: Post-conflict Spaces and Approaches to State-building', *Journal of Intervention and Statebuilding*, 2 (3): 269–289.

Heijke, M. (2010) *'Everything is Politicized'*, Competing governments in *Štrpce/Shtërpcë*. Master's thesis at Wageningen University.

Heijke, M., G. van der Haar and B. Weijs (2012) 'Between Politics and Pragmatism: "Parallel governance" in Štrpce/Shtërpcë, Kosovo, Case Studies on Local Governments in Post-Conflict States', working paper, Dutch Knowledge Network on Peace, Security and Development, The Hague.

Kraushaar, M. and D. Lambach (2009) 'Hybrid Political Orders: The Added Value of a New concept', Occasional paper series, Australian Centre for Peace and Conflict Studies, University of Queensland.

Menkhaus, K. (2006) 'Governance without Government in Somalia: Spolires, State-building and the Politics of Coping', *International Security*, 31 (3): 74–106.

Pula, B. (2004) 'The Emergence of the Kosovar Parallel State 1988–1992', *Nationalities Papers*, 32 (4): 797–826.

Richards, P (ed.) (2005) *No Peace, no War: Anthropology of Contemporary Armed Conflicts*, Oxford: Ohio University Press/James Curry.

Sikor, T. and C. Lund (eds) (2010) *The Politics of Possession: Property, Authority, and Access to Natural Resources*, Chichester: John Wiley & Sons.

Van der Borgh, Ch. (2012) 'Resisting International State Building in Kosovo', *Problems of Post-communism*, 59 (2): 31–42.

Van der Haar, G. (2005) 'Land Reform, the State and the Zapatista Uprising in Chiapas', *Journal of Peasant Studies*, special issue 'Rural Chiapas ten years after the Zapatista Uprising', 32 (3 & 4): 484–507.

Van der Haar, G. (2012) 'State Formation in Dispute: Local Government as an Arena in Chiapas, Mexico', in C. Dijkema, K. Gatelier, I. Samson and J. Tercinet (eds) *Rethinking the Foundations of the State, An Analysis of Post-crisis Situations*, Brussels: Bruylant.

7 Two decades of ordering refugees

The development of institutional multiplicity in Kenya's Kakuma refugee camp

Bram J. Jansen

Introduction

In academic and popular sources, refugee camps have been viewed as top-down governed structures associated with prison-like total institutions, 'warehouses' and seclusion sites, in which refugees are seen as little more than victims or cunning beneficiaries of aid, with little room to maneuver vis-à-vis the camp authorities (Horst 2006). This image neglects processes of social organization that take place among refugees within refugee camps. One of these developments is the emergence of multiple authorities that seek to contest, adapt or build on humanitarian governance and camp organization. In the past years, a modest emerging genre of refugee camp ethnographies shows how, instead, these human-itarian constructions include a multiplicity of institutions (Agier 2002, Horst 2006, Schechter 2004, Turner 2005, Jansen 2011). This chapter builds on that genre and analyzes the development of institutional multiplicity in Kakuma refugee camp in Kenya.

Instead of a refugee camp as a humanitarian necessity, I approach Kakuma camp as a large multicultural refugee town that has existed since 1992, located in the semi-desert of northern Kenya. With a varying population over time, most refugees came from Sudan, Somalia, Ethiopia, and smaller numbers from Uganda, Rwanda, the Democratic Republic of Congo, Burundi and Eritrea. The camp had a population of nearly 90,000 people during the main fieldwork period in 2005/6. This decreased in 2008 after the Sudanese peace prompted many to return to Sudan, but in 2012 the population is growing again, approaching 100,000 people due to a renewed influx of Sudanese and Somali refugees. Over the years, the humanitarian space of the camp has been inhabited by refugees with their own cultural backgrounds and social organization. In Kakuma, forms of parallel governance emerged, among different national and ethnic groups, but also with regard to various domains such as the camp economy, dispute resolution, politics, education and other forms of camp-community-based self-organization.

In this chapter I analyze how, in line with the analogy of the camp as an accidental city, the coming together of these multiple and converging institutions made the camp a dynamic social settlement, instead of a temporary humanitarian measure *per se*. This chapter is based on 18 months of ethnographic fieldwork between 2003 and 2010 in Kakuma refugee camp. A last visit was made in early 2012.

Ordering refugees/governing refugees

The protracted refugee camp is an ambiguous space. It is simultaneously a place where elaborate mechanisms of aid delivery assist vulnerable people in need, and a place where people's political status is suspended until a (hypothetical) return home. The refugee camp as an apolitical space is enshrined in refugee-hosting rationale, because refugee protection demands that the very politics that lie at the basis of flight do not continue to pose a threat for people once in refuge. The politicization and militarization of the refugee camps around Goma in the Democratic Republic of Congo (DRC) in the aftermath of the Rwandan genocide is illustrative of this principle: the genocide continued in moderate form under the very political leadership that organized the genocide in Rwanda (Lischer 2005, Terry 2002). The idea of the refugee camp as a top-down governed structure thus finds legitimacy here from a security prerogative of refugee-hosting organizations and governments. The very structure of the refugee camp demands docile beneficiaries, who will pick up their food on the given date, who will do what the host state or the refuge regime wants them to do. This is the image of refugees in protracted refugee situations as 'wasted life' (Bauman 2004), 'in limbo' or in 'debilitating dependence' (Adelman 2008: 8).

Simultaneously, critical statements have been made to the effect that the refugee is often framed as incapable of governing himself/herself, and hence dependent on outside assistance and care (Harrell-Bond 1986, Kaiser 2006). This, in turn, legitimizes humanitarians' cooperation – some would say complicity – with host states in agreeing to assist and even manage people in refugee camps, often in marginal areas where temporariness dictates the constituting of refugees as what Agamben (1998) refers to as 'bare life,' people beyond politics, in need of humanitarian care to manage their lives.

However, the very protractedness of many refugee situations makes it increasingly complicated to treat people as beneficiary-subjects who are temporarily beyond politics. As Hyndman writes: 'though camps are arguably a useful and acceptable short-term emergency measure, the second-rate status accorded to refugees in these "temporary cities" is problematic' (Hyndman 2000: 23). Similarly, De Waal notes that

> humanitarian action is paradigmatically regarded as a state of exception – it takes place beyond politics. In this sense, humanitarianism is seen as a moment at which history is suspended and pure humanity is briefly in focus. This is a necessary fiction for the humanitarian enterprise, but as emergencies become prolonged, it is a pretense that becomes harder to uphold.
>
> (De Waal 2010: 135)

Although emergency may have ended, Kakuma refugee camp represents a prolonged humanitarian emergency measure – it is referred to as a protracted refugee situation, defined as existing over five years and hosting more than 25,000 people (UNHCR 2008). The very location of the camp illustrates the government's purpose in attempting to keep refugees excluded from Kenyan society. Officially, refugees are not allowed to work and to move freely out of the camp. In it, almost all responsibilities for caring for the refugees are with international organizations and non-governmental organizations (NGOs). The United Nations High Commissioner for Refugees (UNHCR) acts like a pseudo-government of the camp. Every aspect of refugee camp governance, with the exception of security, is organized by UNHCR and their implementing partners: international and national NGOs such as the International Rescue Committee (IRC) and the Lutheran World Federation (LWF).

The refugees, then, are not so much governed by the Kenyan government but instead by international organizations with international rights-based mandates. These keep refugees within the limits of the camp while simultaneously seeking to uplift them. In practice, this means a negotiation between the refugee regime and the refugees. Turner observed in Lukole camp in Tanzania:

> [T]he refugees themselves seek to maneuver in this temporary space, thus creating pockets of sovereign power outside the reach of either the camp commandant's restrictions or UNHCR's benevolent control. Although they are positioned as bare life by the Tanzanian state, they are not paralyzed. And, likewise, as much as the bio-politics of UNHCR attempts to create moral apolitical beings, it never succeeds and history and politics strike back.
>
> (Turner 2005: 313–14)

My approach is not that of the camp as a problem to be solved *per se*, from either a refugee rights or humanitarian aid perspective. Instead I am interested in this ambiguous social phenomenon of the camp that, in social terms, grows into a human community, but in political terms remains a temporary humanitarian structure. Although the UNHCR and NGOs are seen as organizing the camp, I am interested in what ways refugees organize themselves and how emergent orders co-exist as multiple institutions or parallel authorities that give shape to the social organization of the camp.

Institutional multiplicity

Institutions are 'humanly devised rules that constrain or enable individual and collective behaviour' (Beall *et al.* 2004: 5). Institutions can refer to culture, social norms, values and traditions, but also policies, laws and judiciary systems (Heijmans 2012). They are socially embedded and subject to change and adaptation, and range from the informal to the formal. In the camp, institutions not only co-exist, they are also connected to each other. Institutional multiplicity, then, is not so much about parallel orders, institutions or authorities that co-exist independent of each other, but resemble what Boege *et al.* (2009) refer to as 'hybrid political orders':

> In hybrid political orders, diverse and competing authority structures, sets of rules, logics of order, and claims to power co-exist, overlap, interact, and intertwine, combining elements of introduced Western models of governance and elements stemming from local indigenous traditions of governance and politics, with further influences exerted by the forces of globalization and associated societal fragmentation (in various forms: ethnic, tribal, religious).
>
> (Boege *et al.* 2009: 17)

I have studied the interfaces between the refugee regime and refugee communities, and groups that emerged over the course of the camp's existence. These interfaces show competing claims for governance, and this is where negotiation over common interests takes place. Interface analysis then, following Long's (1989, 2001) suggestion, has led me to follow how people in the camp make their way in seeking room to maneuver and carve out pockets of authority. These people stand with one leg in the refugee-hosting apparatus, and the other in more autonomous orders inside the camp. They have been labeled as 'interface experts' (Hilhorst 2003) or 'liminal men' (Turner 2001) – people that are capable of negotiating along the interfaces between different institutional arrangements. Other leaders derive authority from tribal or ethnic affiliation, and co-exist in a more informal way, alongside other, NGO-approved, structures of governance. Yet others have the resources to circumvent policy and control. People have agency, interpret their surroundings, and act on that. In this sense, camps create social realities as a result of people's reactions to the environment. Malkki notes about the Tanzanian refugee camp for Burundians that 'as a technology of power, the camp ended up being much more than a device of containment and enclosure; it grew into a locus of continual creative subversion and transformation' (Malkki 1995: 236–37).

The development of institutional multiplicity is rooted in the historicity and specificity of the camp environment. In the cases I develop, I will hold to this chronology. I will argue that what represents such ambiguity for refugee hosting is, simultaneously, the result of the specific governing strategies that UNHCR and NGOs adopted over the years.

In the coming paragraphs, I will analyze forms of transformation, subversion and the adaptation of camp governance. I will highlight three broad developments as they emerged in the chronology of the camp's existence and the way they shaped and influenced the governing structure over the years. I frame these as social fields that are linked but also independent and, in the words of Sally Falk More, 'can generate rules and induce compliance to them [. . .] yet are also set into a larger social matrix which can, and does, affect and invade it' (Griffiths 1986: 29). The three fields I explore are: ethnic/tribal authority, refugee camp administrations and participation, and the camp economy. Broadly, these are competing claims for governance by muscle, competing claims for governance by cooperation, and competing claims for governance by economic resources.

After sketching the three broad developments, I analyze their working in the camp's history and present manifestation. By analyzing these developments as part of a chronological process, I highlight the development of the camp as a whole, and the ways people settle in a space deemed artificial and temporary.

'Rebelization' and ethnic orders

The first field concerns forms of ethnic or tribal organization that I regard as the most basic form of social grouping in the history of the camp. The very origin of Kakuma refugee camp lies in the arrival of the Lost Boys from Sudan. Nominally, they were referred to as the children separated from their parents in the chaos of armed conflict and who managed to escape the perils of war by finding their way to the Kenyan border, after having been expelled from the Ethiopian refugee camps where they were staying as refugees before. However, this is only one side of the story. The coming of the Lost Boys in fact constitutes the beginning of the association of the rebel movement with the refugee camp, from the camp's very inception.[1]

The 'Red Army' (*jaysh al-ahmar*) was the name given to the units of small boys that were (to be) trained in the Ethiopian camps by the Sudan People's Liberation Army (SPLA) to create future cadres for the war. In the Ethiopian Gambella region, the refugee camps Dimma, Itang and Fugnido were located near to the rebel camps Bongo and Bilpam. The smallest children would stay and go to school in the refugee camps where they received basic military training, while the older ones would commute between the rebel and the refugee camps. Ethiopia allowed and supported the military endeavors of the SPLA from their territory (Sommers 2005: 141). When the Ethiopian government fell in their own civil war, the camps were attacked by the victorious rebel army, and the refugees and the SPLA were expelled. The boys took off and started wandering through the Sudan in search of safety. After some time, some ended up on the border with Kenya in Lokichoggio, the main hub for the massive relief project, Operation Lifeline Sudan. That first group consisted of about 20,000 people, mostly young boys, who, instead of being new refugees who needed to adapt to refugee camp life, had already been in the camps in Gambella since the mid-1980s. As such they settled themselves, to a large degree, in the empty humanitarian space. The Sudanese placed those they deemed vulnerable with families in a sort of foster care, others were grouped together in small boys' units with an elder guardian. They started their own schools and their churches 'under the tree,' and called upon their kin to join them.

The number of Sudanese in Kakuma grew to more than 65,000 in 2005, making the Sudanese, and the Dinka tribe in particular, the largest and most powerful group in the camp. The presence of the Sudanese linked to, or part of, a rebel movement, influenced everyday governance. A good example to illustrate the above is to look at differences between the customs of refugees and UNHCR's rights-based policy, with respect to the understanding of what constitutes a crime. This is one of the areas where refugees' and UNHCR's orders meet. Which behavior is tolerated and condoned in a particular community, and which is not? Traditions, and the right to enact cultural norms, are claimed by refugees. Examples are issues that have to do with polygamy, child marriages, sexual and domestic violence, wife inheritance and circumcision.

Merry writes, following Foucault (1978), 'the making of subjectivity through law is a particular intimate locus for the operation of hegemony and resistance' (2003: 351). These subjectivities often revolved around the position of women, children and minorities and their treatment by men. This was an interesting area in terms of the interface. Rights-awareness campaigns primarily challenge the masculinity of men, particularly in patriarchal societies (ibid.: 352). The resistance against some of the social change programming of UNHCR and the NGOs was one locus where refugees sought to enact their own lifestyles and traditions, and this may even have strengthened ethnic identification and role models.

For instance, various communities had their own jails in the camp, most notably the Sudanese. These were actual cellblocks, where people could be detained awaiting a bench court trial. These jails, and the space that refugee communities have to enact their own customary ruling, form grey areas somewhere between UNHCR's desired order and authority and that of the refugees themselves. In Kakuma, sanctions and sometimes violent punishment could come at the hand of the refugees' own community, as well as from the Kenyan police and sometimes even UNHCR or NGOs. Non-criminal offenses were dealt with by the Sudanese community itself by the varying levels of bench courts, instead of being reported to the police and/or UNHCR for adjudication by Kenyan courts, as was officially required for cases defined as 'crimes' under Kenyan law. But the same held for theft and general aggression, and even murder. One of my informants was 'fined' 1,500 Kenyan Shillings by the Sudanese administration for reporting a crime to the Kenyan police. The argument for the fine was that he should have turned to 'his own' authorities: the Sudanese leadership. 'Sudan has its own morals, they don't believe in Kenyan justice,' he told me afterwards, an opinion that was widely shared.

In another example of how community leadership constitutes a bridge between autonomy and the refugee regime when one goes to report a crime, the Kenyan police demands the presence of a refugee representative, such as a chairman or a secretary, making the control by the Sudanese administration practically inescapable. The description of 'vulnerability' in the camp is what Hyndman refers to as the 'transfer point of power' (Hyndman 2000). Whereas the humanitarian staff could elevate a person into a resettlement scheme by identifying vulnerability, the refugee leadership could do the same, by withholding or forwarding claims.

In one case, an aunt of one of my informants died after having sustained injuries in a fight. Apparently she had been aggressive and abusive, and her neighbours sought to punish her or to stop her. According to her relative, who was my informant, the official Kenyan autopsy report in the hospital did not indicate violence as the result of her death. As such, the case ceased to be a police matter for the Kenyan authorities. The Sudanese authorities in the camp held a different opinion, however, and took the aunt to Sudan for a ruling Sudanese style. According to camp regulations, the Kenyan judiciary was to deal with murder cases in the camp. In this example, the Sudanese leadership evaded the official UNHCR/Government of Kenya regulations and decided to let tradition/custom prevail. The woman was, in effect, abducted from the camp. In general, marriage practices involved a practice referred to as 'elopement,' in which the prospective husband would take a woman by some degree of force until she would agree to be married to him. In practice, the evasion of the elders'/parents' consent resulted in punishment by the Sudanese administration.

There were several bench court systems in the camp, organized hierarchically starting with the community-level bench courts at the bottom, ultimately all the way up to the high court in South Sudan (see also Griek 2007: 123). Given that this is SPLA territory and SPLA jurisdiction, the workings of the bench courts can hardly be seen separately from the SPLA. Although the link is indirect, it is nonetheless strong. Some of the elders I knew were called upon in the bench court rulings. These men were SPLA, still 'serving' in the camp, while they were simultaneously refugees who held high positions in the official refugee-run administration of Kakuma. Here, space for maneuvering was sustained by the power of the SPLA to enact custom that often directly contravened UNHCR policy, through men who were part of the very same refugee-hosting apparatus. These are prime examples of the interfaces that are influential in the organization of the camp.

On other occasions, the weight of the Sudanese translated into violent attempts to change UNHCR policy in the camp. A famous example was a reaction to changes made to the food distribution system in the 1990s. In the first years of the camp's existence, food trucks visited each separate community and left food there to be subdivided by the communities themselves. The agencies changed the system, which did not allow them to control who received what, into a system that required refugees (except those in the protection area) to come to food distribution centres in the camp themselves to collect their rations. After negotiations with UNHCR bore no fruit, the then Dinka chairman ordered the Sudanese to torch the newly built distribution centres, and within a few hours they went up in flames. Although the centres were rebuilt and the new policy was implemented anyway, aid workers explained how the leadership of the camp and the SPLA were close, and that its power was large enough to be was easy for it to mobilize the Sudanese, and the Dinka in particular.

Other communities had different but similar administrations, based on nationality or ethnicity. Enactment of custom and local law also took place here. Among the Somalis, for instance, were the Sharia courts or *Maslaha* (similar to the Sudanese bench courts), and family relations were managed in those courts away from UNHCR's view. Although based on custom, the relative autonomy that refugee administrations claimed to settle issues such as wife inheritance, past crimes, gender and sexual violence, meant that some people in the camp ran additional risks according to international rights standards. The enactment of claims for self-governance in the above examples gains legitimacy through custom and tradition and the size of the refugee population. This is also manifested between different groups. The threatening of a Burundian teacher by a Sudanese youth after he challenged Sudanese pupils was condoned by the Sudanese leadership and, as a result, the teacher had to be transferred to another school in the camp. Other occasions played out between and within communities in similar ways, up to the level of violence that, although perceived by the NGOs as problematic and dysfunctional, can also be seen as manifestations of ordering. The Rwandan, the Congolese and the Ugandan communities similarly excluded people on the basis of tribal and ethnic affiliations – often on the basis of past conflict experiences.

Refugee empowerment and participation

The Sudanese were organized from the very beginning of their arrival. The Lost Boys were in effect brought by the SPLA and, although they did not recreate the militarization of the camp as in Ethiopia, they linked not only the Sudanese popu-lation to the SPLA, but also generated leadership out of that. Three men were illustrative of this. They were prominent Dinka elders who had influential posi-tions in many aspects of life in the camp. Two of them had come with the Lost Boys from Ethiopia. In Kakuma, they took up the care of the children. Over time, the Sudanese leadership became conflated with the UNHCR organized refugee camp leadership. This is where the second field of ordering becomes important: the participation and empowerment strategies of UNHCR and the NGOs with regard to the refugee population.

One of the three men became Director of IRCs childcare program and the other became Director of Education with LWF. The third man continued migrating between two other camps in Uganda, Kenya and South Sudan and organized recruitment and liaised between the refugees and the SPLA. All three were SPLA leaders who were also involved in the bench court system in the camp, as well as in other governance issues, as they were simply respected elders too. The first two men held high positions in the refugee regimes' participatory refugee administration system, and were paid for that. Yet, the men were also still members of SPLA, and in that capacity had one leg in another, parallel authority. As such, they were the quintessential interface experts, in that they were both in the rebel movement and in the refugee-hosting apparatus.

They exerted authority in the camp on various levels; this is where the label 'institutional multiplicity' becomes relevant. They were both figures in the rebel movement (all three of the men were, after the Sudanese peace agreement in 2005, 'rewarded' with various government positions in South Sudan), as well as in the refugee camp administration system. As a result of that combination, they were elders in a tribal social structure that yielded great influence over daily life, and ranged from formal to informal. This simultaneously represents a tension in the power of the official camp governors and in the empowerment of refugee leaders as a conflation between UNHCR and tribal ordering. Hyndman notes that the NGO CARE proposed refugee community participation projects in the Kenyan camps in the early 1990s aimed at self-governance and participation in the allocation of funds and assistance in the camp. UNHCR met the plan with 'some resistance,' as she paraphrases the opinion of a UNHCR officer:

> UNHCR is effectively the governing body of the three camps (of Dadaab). Refugee self-management is viewed by this staff member as dangerous because it poses the possibility of redirecting this power and reinstituting elder enclaves of supposedly autocratic power.
>
> (Hyndman 2000: 139)

Similarly, Sommers notes on the many training programs in refugee camps:

> Training is a form of empowerment. Targeting refugee elites – most of whom are male and educated – instead of the most vulnerable, may strengthen the existing power structure and contribute to the frustrations, and perhaps the violence, of the marginalized.
>
> (Sommers 2005: 204)

In reality, these elder enclaves were there anyway, backed by the power of violent threat and tribalism, as indicated in the previous section. Instead, refugee participations seemed to bridge these traditional structures, and UNHCRs desired order. The refugee administrations served as a liaison between UNHCR and the communities and groups in the camp and were part of a referral system between refugees and the agencies, and the Kenyan authorities and police. Refugee leaders could signal developments and needs in their communities and report them to the agencies, and the agencies used the refugee administrations to distribute goods and ideas, or to target the needy within communities.

The refugee administrations were organized according to nationality or ethnicity and location in the camp, depending on the size of the group. As such, refugee administrations existed at various levels and had various sub-divisions, roles and tasks. The Sudanese and the Somalis each had an overall community leadership structure, with different ethnic sub-administrations one tier lower in the administrative hierarchy. The overarching Sudanese leadership consisted of a chairman, a secretary, a vice chairman and a chairlady, and included the main ethnic representations – Dinka, Nuer and the combined Equatorian communities – and zonal leaders representing areas of residence in the camp. These were then followed by group leaders, then special committees and then youth leaders.

The top level of the Somali administration was organized in a similar manner with an overall chairman, secretary, vice chairman and chairlady. But one level below, it was subdivided into four different clan based administrations: Somali *Barawa* leadership, Somali *Bajuni* leadership, Somali *Bantu* leadership and Somali *Digle-Merifle* leadership. One level lower were the group leaders, the special committees and youth leaders. Here, the official organization did not represent place of residence in the camp. All the other nationalities had less elaborate structures for numerical reasons, although they still had their own chairman, secretary, vice chairman and a chairlady, followed by special committees and youth leaders.

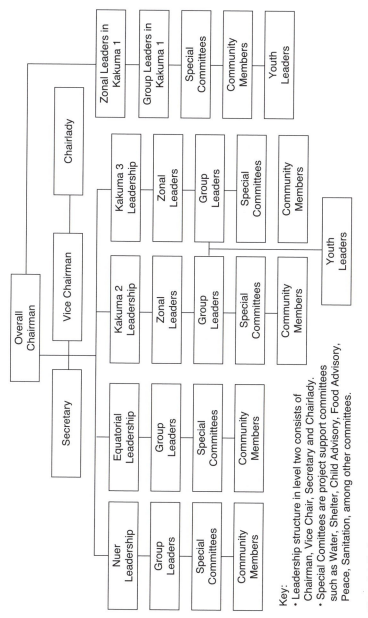

Key:
• Leadership structure in level two consists of Chairman, Vice Chair, Secretary and Chairlady.
• Special Comittees are project support committees such as Water, Shelter, Child Advisory, Food Advisory, Peace, Sanitation, among other committees.

Figure 7.1 Sudanese refugee leadership structure.

Source: UNHCR Kakuma.

The Ethiopian and Congolese communities were largely organized according to geographical location in the camp, but not exclusively. The newer 'New Area' and 'Multinational Area' in the third addition to the camp dating from the early 2000s were adaptations in grouping refugees together to accommodate what were multi-ethnic communities from the onset. This is an interesting development in the context of the camp. People from different backgrounds were grouped together in the new environment of the camp, and were forced to cooperate and interact with each other in an intimate way.

The aim of this form of participation was not only to smooth the running of the camp and to mitigate the negative aspects – from a perspective of humanitarian management – of tribal authority, but also simultaneously to train and expose people and leaders to the concept of democracy, aiming at possible positive impact upon repatriation. In theory, the administrations met with UNHCR on a weekly basis to discuss issues relating to their communities and to suggest or bring to the fore the needs and desires of their community members. Another part of the community leadership structure was a multitude of Community Support Committees dealing with specific aspects of camp governing, each of which liaised with an implementing agency. Over the years, the agencies contributed to the creation of pockets of authority that rest with one leg in the refugee project and the other in refugees' own, alternative adaptation of it.

Over time however, people with less traditional authority in tribal or ethnic groupings became part of the refugee participation environment. They were the minorities, women, youth and people with disabilities, which became targeted for courses, training and jobs as a result of the emancipation and empowerment goals of UNHCR. In the camp, some of these people became skillful in maneuvering the camp environment, understanding and bridging, or evading, because of understanding the different institutional arrangements. Turner refers to them as 'Small Big Men' (2006), indicating an alternative form of authority. This group of people was not so much ethnic or tribal in their role, but adhered to the categories of their empowerment and became advocates of that.

Interestingly, during a visit to the camp in 2012, the complete camp organization had been overhauled and changed. Not only was the spatial arrangement named differently, Kakuma One to Three, with 'zones' and 'blocks' instead of 'groups', organized in a more logical order which replaces the organic organization it had before. It can be read as an attempt to de-nationalize, de-ethnicize or de-tribalize the refugee leadership. Administrations were now organized according to location in the camp, regardless of who lived there; even though refugee communities are still somewhat organically ethnic, bureaucratically they are no longer. From an administrative perspective, the whole camp becomes a multinational community. This represents the ideological or social agenda of the agencies, sensitizing people to issues such as democracy, co-existence and peacebuilding – the bio-governmental adage that is mainstreamed into every aspect of the refugee-hosting program. But, it should also be understood as a response to the earlier strong ethnic leadership as counter authorities in the camp, and also to the earlier experiences of inter-ethnic conflict in the camp. In recent times this is especially relevant with regard to the new Somali majority, where there are fears of refugee warriors from Al Shabaab infiltrating the camp, as the SPLA once did, and becoming part of the authority structure. In this way, putting participation into practice is based on a form of progressive insight, or lessons learned.

The refugee camp economy

The third institutional field concerns the development of a refugee camp economy. The camp inhabitants gain room for maneuver and leverage in terms of resources. The economic landscape can be subdivided in three main sectors: refugees who are employed by UNHCR and the NGOs, refugees who receive remittances from relatives abroad, and refugees who are employed or have businesses in the camp economy. These three often co-exist, as refugees who receive remittances or a salary from the NGOs may invest these in businesses in the camp. The result, however, is that the total dependency on relief over time for many people has decreased and resources provide room for maneuver. Specifically, the everyday corruption in the camp, and its governance systems, mean that resources provide important and practical ways of circumventing the Kenya government's and the camp's restrictions to enable travel, business and other opportunities in the camp.

The first category of income is simultaneously a form of participation in the refugee-hosting structure. These are jobs, referred to as incentive work, with salaries and some secondary benefits. 'Counterpart managers', for instance, served as refugee chiefs of programs, as counterparts to the agencies' chiefs. There were counterpart managers for education, water, sanitation, and so on. Similarly, the directors of schools were refugees, and refugees were also hired as interpreters for the NGOs, and other roles such as cleaners, teachers, nurses, food distributors and clerks. Although expatriates and Kenyan staff, mainly from the south, hold all the managerial positions in the agencies, refugee staff constitute most of the employees of the refugee-hosting structure within the camp.

Incentive salaries reflect the fact that, officially, refugees are not allowed to work, and the 'incentive' is a way around this. Complaints about the limited salaries were widespread, but in the camp context, a salary of 3,000 Kenyan Shillings per month for a primary school teacher meant a lot for the livelihoods of refugees and their dependents. Moreover, by 2012 the salaries have grown considerably. Many incentive jobs included secondary benefits in the form of training or skills development. Additionally, access to the compounds and the refugee-hosting structure in general resulted in numerous other indirect benefits for refugees, ranging from additional sources of water to access to computers, internet, food and bicycles and, probably most important, to the humanitarian personnel and their offices (see also Sommers 2005, Verdirame and Harrell-Bond 2005).

The second category concerns remittance receivers. Since the start of the camp, many people have been resettled in the US, Australia, Canada and other western countries. Many resettled refugees who have their kin still in the camp – or whose kin arrived after their departure, drawn by a possible resettlement for themselves – send money for them to sustain themselves. In other cases, refugees who work elsewhere in Kenya provide cash for relatives.

The third category includes people who find ways to get employment or start some business in the camp itself, the latter often based on the above two categories of income generation as investment. The extent to which this economy operates is illustrative by the arrival of Somali Bantus from Tanzania as their first country of refuge. They were attracted by the prospect of resettlement, as 15,000 Somali Bantus had been screened and were in the process of relocating to the US during that time. Understandably, this was a powerful incentive. As 'irregular secondary movers,' they were screened out by UNHCR as legitimate refugees, and hence received no assistance. About 2,000 of them, however, decided to remain and were able to sustain themselves by finding work in the camp economy. Gradually, they developed a parallel community leadership that ran into problems with the regular Somali Bantu leadership.

Economic arguments have also been used to support claims. An example is what became known as the 'Ethiopian strike.' Ethiopians opted for alternative ways to try to influence policy by shutting down a very relevant economic sector in the camp. For two months they closed down the most elaborate market of Kakuma, and the leadership convinced almost every Ethiopian to join, including those with incentive jobs with the agencies. This shows how, with time, the camp economy came to be an important aspect of camp life and organization. Other initiatives did not so much challenge the refugee-hosting apparatus but instead linked up to them or surpassed them entirely, rooted in the benefits of the camp economy. In the Somali community, there were credit schemes for people who wanted to start businesses, modeled around earlier group micro-credit schemes that were now picked up by refugees themselves and organized independently of the NGOs. Similarly, schools were erected by communities, and madrassas and churches were built.

Over the years, several civic initiatives have challenged the non-political space that the camp is ideally meant to be. One of such initiatives was *KANERE* (the *Kakuma News Reflector*), an online newsletter/newspaper, another was a radio station; both were banned for reasons of civic disturbance. But *KANERE*, in the time of the Internet, still exists as a 'refugee free press.'[2] In a broader sense, refugee leaders who spoke out against the camp governors, UNHCR and the NGOs, have in the past been sanctioned, such as being fired from their jobs or released from their role in the refugee administration and, at least in one case, given a public beating by UN staff. On one of those occasions, economic capacity as a form of leverage was utilized by the Ethiopian community in a strike some years before my fieldwork. Later, in 2005, another strike, aimed at pushing UNHCR and the agencies to deal with troublesome Sudanese youth, not only made the market close its doors; also, the Ethiopian leadership successfully persuaded its constituency to refrain from performing their incentive jobs. This only worked until HCR proclaimed that everyone would be fired – but meanwhile the market had been closed for two months.

One of the most interesting initiatives that emerged in the course of 2005 was the creation of a workers' union. This also signified a social life beyond the paradigmatic bare life of refugees. They not only organized themselves on a political level, in the sense of the union, claiming a part in governing the camp, but also on the economic level, which indicated the emergence of a socio-economic stratum of people who had some money to spend. This stratification meant that another type of 'small big men' had emerged from the successful business people, although by now they became plain 'big men'. Their negotiating with the Kenyan authorities for the import of goods from elsewhere in Kenya meant they crossed boundaries of ethnic, national, bureaucratic, inter-NGO, and entrepreneurial networks of people.

Born out of this camp economy are ways in which refugees are able to support one another. I came across examples of foster parenting, micro credit schemes, school and educational initiatives such as English and literacy courses for elderly women, and churches and religious organizations,[3] health clinics and so on, that were part of how people shaped their own environment, independent of the humanitarian structure, or in cooperation with it. In some cases, UNHCR and the NGOs, or their individual employees, supported refugee initiatives with materials, housing, funding or facilitation. In one example, a refugee business was invited to open up a second restaurant inside the International Organization for Migration (IOM) compound deep inside the camp, to cater for staff and visitors, following the success of the original establishment in the Ethiopian community.

The development of a camp economy that gradually breaks away from the humanitarian system and becomes more autonomous, represents a field of parallel ordering. Humanitarian governance is maintained largely by the threat of withholding assistance, and 'durable solutions.' A refugee's autonomy in the camp environment, and his or her choice and ability to sustain him or herself in the camp economy, represents – freely following on Hyndman (2000) – a 'transfer point of power.' The irrelevance, circumvention or independence from aid is a moment of leverage for refugees. It remains to be seen, however, to what extent the economy can indeed be less dependent on humanitarian resources, and to what extent it would still be viable.

Analysis: twenty years of ordering refugees

The line of analytical reasoning in this chapter can be described in the following way. First, there is bare humanitarian governance in a refugee camp grid. The first emergence of a parallel order, or a competing form of governance, is based on tribal and ethnic affiliations. In the case of Kakuma, this was conflated with a rebel or military rationale, or threat, as many refugees came from rebel movements (such as the Sudanese) or from defeated military movements (such as the Ugandans, Ethiopians and Rwandans). This leadership was largely informal, customary and in competition with UNHCR, following the political limitations of the camp. An important form of leverage or legitimization is the threat or use of violence. Pockets of authority emerge or exist, led by elders, linked to political structures and governed by rationales of (past) conflict, comparable to what Nordstrom (2004) refers to as a 'warscape.'

A second step in the development of parallel authorities is a mediation between the first two forms. When the camp becomes protracted, the refugee regime increasingly adopts a participatory approach and emancipatory practices. Refugee leadership, built on the ethnic and tribal orders, becomes institutionalized in the main humanitarian framework, in part as a means to simultaneously pacify and control. But, also as a result of the more developmental approaches that become part of the protracted refugee-hosting apparatus, measures have been introduced such as gender and child rights education, training and capacity and peacebuilding programs, democracy awareness initiatives and programs for income generation. This is where interface agents emerge that are able to circum-navigate the old and the new. They are people who know the humanitarian system, work with or in it, but are also rooted in the primordial ethnic or tribal and religious orders.

Then, third, independent initiatives emerge, cross-cutting ethnicities and nationalities, that can be linked to the room for maneuver that refugees obtain as a result of the camp economy that has emerged over time. These then can be adopted or incorporated by the humanitarian regime. These are three fields of social organization in the camp that I want to comment upon in terms of process.

The three fields co-exist, are interrelated, and span the formal and the informal, the legitimate and the illegal. There is an official UN bureaucracy, and several separate refugee affiliations, tribal and clan-based. There are multiple linkages between the two, but they are also separate. Religion, politics and histories of violence feed into tribal, national and ethnic affiliations. These, in turn, translate into the spatial organization of the market areas, and entrepreneurial coopera-tion. There, processes also take place within and between humanitarian agencies, where tribalism and forms of everyday corruption shape practices of aid implementation.

In terms of governing refugee camps, the development of institutional multi-plicity is a phenomenon that agencies have to react to, but they also have a part in creating them. Institutional multiplicity in the camp means that refugees (but also NGOs) can go 'forum shopping' to address their issues or seek opportunity. One can try the tribal leadership, the camp administration, powerful brokers or business people, the Kenyan police, the NGOs or the UNHCR and all those individuals who work in these offices, or all of them together, in different ways.

The implication of this is that, out of a humanitarian construction, a new settle-ment takes shape with multiple institutions that approach the limits of the political and practical/aid restrictions to social organization. Protracted refugee camps do not exist in administrative vacuums. After 2008, the population of Kakuma decreased considerably to just over 60,000. During a visit in early 2010, the camp population was different also in cultural terms; many Sudanese had left, and now Somalis were coming in. The spatial organization of the camp had changed, complete communities had left, and one 'group' was made into a park. New arrivals were housed in a different manner, with new approaches to latrine placement for instance, but also taking into account flood-prone areas – all as a result of lessons learnt along the way. In 2012, the camp was growing again and bigger than ever.

Yet what does that mean? Is this a camp without end, becoming increasingly normal? Is it like humanitarian suburbs in the Middle East with the Palestinians; desert camps like those for the Sahrawi people in Algeria that have existed for more than 35 years; or the Burmese camps on the Thai border that have been there for 20 years? They are like accidental cities (Jansen 2011). In the Dadaab camps in Kenya, the population has reached more than 400,000 people. Here, children are being born from children who were themselves born in the camp. The question is what this means: does it slowly move away from being a humanitarian measure? And is the development of institutional multiplicity a sign of this? In Kakuma, as we have seen before, it may be that the way refugees interpret and reorder the UN-driven changes leads to yet another negotiated meeting between the various actors in the camp and then to the next step of Kakuma as a human settlement.

Conclusion

Kakuma refugee camp entered its twentieth year of existence in May 2012. From an anthropological and a policy perspective, it is important to recognize the development of institutional multiplicity in refugee camps, and the larger meaning or consequences of this for refugee hosting. Protracted refugee camps are social spaces, where people settle for a period of time and create, adapt or change systems of governance.

Protracted refugee camps like Kakuma are experiments in the meeting of humanitarian governance and the social organization of refugees that have no real precedent. Refugee camps are built to dissolve; camps that do not are perhaps not many, but they are significant in scale, expenses and humanitarian challenges. One of those challenges is how to plan the development of camps and, specifically, how to deal with that ambiguous space between restricting refugees and enabling their settlement in the restrictive architecture of refugee camps as places that are temporary, undesirable and artificial.

The notion of development indicates process. The development of institutional multiplicity is a contextualized process. Local history, identity and power relations feed into each section of refugee camp governance and permeate and create levels of formality and informality. The refugee-hosting organizations need to take into account the fact that groups of people seek ways to establish authority of their own, and that this authority may claim governance over issues that are of primary concern in terms of refugee protection.

Moreover, although the UNHCR and NGOs play a crucial and enabling role in refugee protection, they do not represent the only institutional arrangement in the camp. There are many, multiple and overlapping forms of social organization that seek to manage, restrict or enable actors and their behavior. The apolitical space is in practice a highly political one, in which all actors need to engage and compromise to find ways forward. It then needs to be replaced by a recognition of the refugees' capabilities to organize themselves and build on that.

Acknowledgements

Thanks to Jeroen Cuvelier, Hilde van Dijkhorst, Dennis Dijkzeul and Barbra Lukunka for their constructive comments on an earlier version of this chapter. All responsibility remains with the author.

Notes

1 During my fieldwork, the association between the rebel movement and the refugees/camp was a public secret. In my current research in South Sudan, I regularly come across the topic of Kakuma as an SPLA camp, and since the rebels turned legitimate government, these matters are now out in the open, and the Red Army is publicly saluted and honored.
2 http://kakuma.wordpress.com
3 There was a missionary training school in Kakuma that brought in foreign guest teachers, some from the US, and also one from the Netherlands.

References

Adelman, H. (2008) 'Protracted Displacement'. In: Adelman, H., *Protracted Displacement in Asia: No Place to Call Home*. Burlington: Ashgate Publishing Company. 1–28.

Agamben, G. (1998) *Homo Sacer: Sovereign Power and Bare Life*. Stanford: Stanford University Press.

Agier, M. (2002) 'Between War and City. Towards an Urban Anthropology of Refugee Camps'. *Ethnography* 3(3): 317–341.

Bauman, Z. (2004) *Wasted Lives, Modernity and its Outcasts*. Cambridge: Polity Press.

Beall, J., Mkhize, S., and Vawda, S. (2004) *Traditional Authority, Institutional Multiplicity and Political Transition in Kwazulu-Natal, South Africa*. Crisis States Programme working paper No. 48. London: LSE.

Boege, V., Brown, A., and Clements, K. (2009) 'Hybrid political order, not fragile states.' *Peace Review* 21(1): 13–21.

De Waal, A. (2010) 'The Humanitarians' Tragedy: Escapable and Inescapable Cruelties'. *Disasters* 34(S2): s130–s137.

Foucault, M. (1978) *The History of Sexuality. Volume 1*. New York: Pantheon Books.

Griek, I. (2007) 'Traditional Systems of Justice in Refugee Camps: Cause for Concern?' In: Mukherjee., D., *Refugee Rights and Issues: Concepts and Country Experiences*. Hyderabad: The Icfai University Press. 118–131.

Griffiths, J. (1986) 'What is Legal Pluralism?' *Journal of Legal Pluralism* 24: 1–55.

Harrell-Bond, B. (1986) *Imposing Aid: Emergency Assistance to Refugees*. Oxford: Oxford University Press.

Heijmans, A. (2012) *Risky Encounters. Institutions and Interventions in Response to Recurrent Disasters and Conflict*. PhD dissertation, Wageningen University.

Hilhorst, D. (2003) *The Real World of NGOs. Discourses, Diversity and Development*. London: Zed Books.

Horst, C. (2006) *Transnational Nomads: How Somalis Cope with Refugee Life in the Dadaab Camps of Kenya*. New York: Berghahn Books.

Hyndman, J. (2000) *Managing Displacement: Refugees and the Politics of Humanitarianism*. Mineapolis: University of Minnesota Press.

Jansen, B. J. (2011) *The Accidental City: Violence, Economy and Humanitarianism in Kakuma Refugee Camp, Kenya*. PhD thesis, Wageningen University.

Kaiser, T. (2006) 'Between a Camp and a Hard Place: Rights, Livelihoods and Experiences of the Local Settlement System for Long Term Refugees in Uganda'. *Journal of Modern African Studies* 44(4): 597–621.

Lischer, S. K. (2005) *Dangerous Sanctuaries. Refugee Camps, Civil War, and the Dilemmas of Humanitarian Aid*. Ithaca: Cornell University Press.

Long, N. (1989) *Encounters at the Interface: a Perspective on Social Discontinuities in Rural Development*. Wageningen: Wageningen University.

Long, N. (2001) *Development Sociology. Actor Perspectives*. London: Routledge.

Malkki, L. H. (1995) *Purity and Exile. Violence, Memory and National Cosmology among Hutu Refugees in Tanzania*. Chicago: University of Chicago Press.

Merry, S. E. (2003) 'Rights Talk and the Experience of Law: Implementing Women's Human Rights to Protection from Violence'. *Human Rights Quarterly* 25: 343–381.

Nordstrom, C. (2004) *Shadows of War: Violence, Power and International Profiteering in the Twenty-First Century*. Berkeley: University of California Press.

Schechter, J. A. (2004) *Governing 'Lost Boys': Sudanese Refugees in a UNHCR Camp*. PhD thesis, University of Colorado.

Sommers, M. (2005) *Islands of Education. Schooling, Civil War and the Southern Sudanese (1983–2004)*. Paris: UNESCO.

Terry, F., 2002. *Condemned to Repeat? The Paradox of Humanitarian Action*. Ithaca: Cornell University Press.

Turner, S. (2001) 'The Barriers of Innocence. Humanitarian intervention and political imagination in a refugee camp for Burundians in Tanzania'. PhD thesis, Roskilde University: 327.

Turner, S. (2005) 'Suspended Spaces? Contesting Sovereignties in a Refugee Camp'. In: Hansen, T.H. and Stepputat, F., *Sovereign Bodies. Citizens, Migrants, and States in the Postcolonial World*. Princeton: Princeton University Press. 312–332.

Turner, S. (2006) 'Negotiating Authority between UNHCR and "The People"'. *Development and Change* 37(4): 759–778.

UNHCR (2008) *Protracted Refugee Situations: a Discussion Paper Prepared for the High Commissioner's Dialogue on Protection Challenges*. Geneva: UNHCR.

Verdirame, G., and Harrell-Bond, B. (2005) *Rights in exile. Janus-faced humanitarianism*. New York: Berghahn Books.

8 Conflict minerals in Eastern Democratic Republic of Congo

Planned interventions and unexpected outcomes

Jeroen Cuvelier

Introduction

The international community, which played a prominent role in brokering peace agreements, restoring national unity and reshaping the political system of the Democratice Republic of Congo (DRC) after the official end of the war in July 2003, continues to have a significant influence on the way the Congolese government manages its affairs (Vircoulon 2007, Cuvelier 2011a, Trefon 2011, Reyntjens 2007). This is particularly evident in the mining sector, where international financial institutions, such as the World Bank, have urged the Congolese state to embark on a major reform of the mining business, consisting of the adoption of a new mining code and the introduction of a new set of standards for mining practices (Vlassenroot and Van Bockstael 2008, Mazalto 2009, Geenen 2011).

In addition to this, the Congolese authorities have been under enormous pressure to do something about the issue of 'conflict minerals', that is, minerals exploited in areas of violent conflict. The artisanal mining sector in eastern DRC has been under the scrutiny of UN sanctions committees, academics, non-governmental organisations (NGOs) and local and international media, all of whom are disturbed and concerned about the assumed links between natural resource exploitation and continuing armed conflict in the region. It has been argued that resource exploitation is the most important driver of conflict in eastern DRC, and that both state and non-state actors have derived benefit from the local mining business by levying taxes on mineral exports, selling minerals for their own profit, and trading mineral rights for financial and military support (Jackson 2002, Global Witness 2009, De Koning 2010, IPIS 2009, Enough Project 2009, UN 2011). In response to these concerns, the Congolese government has joined hands with a wide range of international institutions and companies operating in the region to design and implement measures aimed at making mineral commodity chains more transparent and preventing 'conflict minerals' such as tin, tantalum, tungsten and gold from entering international markets (IPIS 2011, Garrett *et al.* 2010).

The aim of this chapter is to show that the planned interventions in Congo's artisanal mining sector have generated unexpected outcomes. Contrary to what policy makers had hoped, the initiatives have failed to bring about a radical transformation of the mining business. In the provinces of North and South Kivu, the processes of extracting and trading mineral resources are still to a very large extent shaped by what Utas has described as the politics of 'bigmanity'. As a result of the persistent weakness of the Congolese state, and its incapacity to enforce official laws and regulations, local 'big men' have managed to retain the upper hand in the struggle for Kivu's mineral riches. Displaying a remarkable capacity to gather large groups of followers, through the provision of social security and protection in environments characterized by insecurity, volatility and social disruption, they have been able to 'transform social relations into strategic power and control' (Utas 2012: 8). Participants in Kivu's artisanal mining sector know that, in order to survive economically, they have to comply with the unofficial rules and regulations imposed by the aforementioned 'big men'.

Unlike De Koning (2012), who has also analysed eastern DRC's artisanal mining sector through the lens of Utas' theory on 'bigmanity', I will not focus my attention on military actors. Although I agree with De Koning that, over the years, 'military big men' have become highly influential in Congo's resource sector, and although I share his conviction that 'a superficial form of state consolidation' will not be able to put an end to 'the patterns of exploitation that emerged during the war' (De Koning 2012: 225), I also believe that a narrow focus on 'military commercialism' (Dietrich 2000) creates the risk of underestimating the enormous complexity of the political economy of artisanal mining in eastern DRC. By focusing exclusively on the looting strategies of military 'elite networks' (UN 2002), one creates the impression that the solution to all problems in the Kivutian mining sector lies in the dismantlement of these networks and the removal of the warlords orchestrating them. Yet, in reality, there is considerable variation in the way mines are governed and controlled (Geenen 2012). In an article on coltan mining in eastern DRC, Smith has noted that small mines are practically the only ones characterised by top-down divisions of labour and strict controls on mineral prices and access to mining sites by militarised local authorities, whereas large mines are organised in a more chaotic manner 'with multiple authorities, cooperatives, and buyers' (Smith 2011: 31). So, instead of simply underlining the pivotal role of 'military big men' and emphasising the militarisation of the mining sector in eastern DRC, it is probably more useful to pay attention to the complexity of different power structures in Kivu's mining areas and to be aware of the fact that, to a certain extent, every single mining site has its own unique characteristics in terms of resource governance dynamics. I intend to highlight the complexity of resource governance in eastern DRC by carrying out an in-depth case study analysis of how non-military strongmen at the local level develop multiple strategies and draw on multiple sources of power to stand their ground and secure their position; they do so in a hybrid and rapidly changing political landscape characterised by 'institutional multiplicity' (Hilhorst *et al.* 2010) and the presence of 'competing governance mechanisms and localised forms of authority, which might even be connected to the state through complex means' (Mallett 2010: 74). By examining closely how 'big men' operate, and how they collaborate and interact with members of other actor groups (artisanal miners, military officers, public servants and NGO workers), I want to shed more light on how individual players deal with the continuities and changes in Congo's resources game. My research confirms Putzel's observation that, although at times institutional multiplicity may put 'citizens and economic agents in complex, often unsolvable situations', it also has the potential of offering them the possibility of 'switching strategically from one institutional universe to another' (Putzel 2005: 8). Interventions by the international community, such as the initiatives to reform the resource sector in eastern DRC, do not automatically lead to the disappearance of this institutional multiplicity, but may 'simply add a new layer of rules, without overriding others' (ibid.).

It is important to bear in mind that the Congolese 'big men' controlling eastern DRC's mining business do not operate in isolation. They are very well connected to the global economy through their relations with so-called 'shadow networks' – transnational networks composed of private companies, brokers and entrepreneurs who prefer to operate in unstable environments where they can easily bend the law to their advantage (Taylor 2003, Nordstrom 2004). As will become evident in the course of this paper, it is thanks to their links with 'shadow networks' at the international level that Congolese strongmen have been able to circumvent many of the restrictions associated with the new mining reform initiatives.

The chapter is organized as follows. In the first part, I will give a brief description of the role of mineral resources in the armed conflict in eastern DRC. I will explain how and why decision-makers at the national and international levels have come to regard resource exploitation as one of the principle causes of the persistence of violence and insecurity in eastern DRC. The second part of the chapter will be dedicated to an overview of the various initiatives that have been taken to solve the issue of 'conflict minerals'. I will demonstrate that the initiatives – which for the most part have been taken after the official end of the Congolese war in 2003 – are inspired by the hope that the Congolese state will eventually strengthen its grip on the mining sector and will render it more transparent and less conflict-ridden. Finally, in the third part of the chapter, I will present a case study on the cassiterite mine of Kalimbi in the territory of Kalehe in South Kivu. The case study is partly based on fieldwork carried out by researchers of the Congolese NGO *Action pour la Paix et la Concorde* (ACP) and myself for a project funded by the European Union,[1] and partly on data derived from secondary sources such as UN reports, press articles and academic publications on the Kalehe area. It describes the power struggle between two rival 'big men', Placide Chirimwami and Tumaini Bagurinzira. Both of them draw on different sources of power, move back and forth between different 'institutional universes' (Putzel 2005) and establish links with networks in the global shadow economy, in order to remain the strongest players in the local resources game. The reform initiatives of national and international policy makers have done very little to change this dynamic.

Congo's resource curse: truth or fiction?

Autesserre has pointed out that people at the highest decision-making levels share the conviction that 'the illegal exploitation of mineral resources is the main source of violence in the Congo' (Autesserre 2012: 9). One explanation for the widespread nature of this belief is the influence of certain debates in the academic community. Since the end of the 1980s, academics from various disciplines have been debating the so-called 'resource curse', that is, the idea that 'natural resource abundance (or at least the abundance of particular types of natural resources) increases the likelihood that countries will experience negative economic, political and social outcomes' (Rosser 2006: 7). Research has been conducted on a wide range of topics associated with the phenomenon of the 'resource curse' such as the relationship between natural resource abundance and poor economic performance (Sachs and Warner 1995, Auty 2001, Neumayer 2004, Atkinson and Hamilton 2003), the relationship between natural resource abundance and low levels of democracy (Jensen and Wantchekon 2004, Ross 2001), and the relationship between oil wealth and rent-seeking behaviour (Karl 1997, Kaldor *et al.* 2007). Apart from discussions about the phenomenon of the 'resource curse', there have also been scholarly arguments about the motives of groups engaging in armed conflict. Several scholars have stressed armed actors' rapacity or greed for natural resources as a key factor in explaining the onset and continuation of armed conflict (Berdal and Malone 2000, Collier and Hoeffler 2005). Finally, the relationship between economic globalisation, organised crime, and the illicit trade in natural resources has also attracted a lot of attention. Some scholars have argued that, in resource-rich countries, characterised by political and economic misrule, poorly functioning governance structures, and endemic corruption, the exploitation and trade of natural resources are often controlled by criminalised transnational networks (Taylor 2003, Nordstrom 2004, Reyntjens 2005).

Another element that helps to account for the fact that the competition for mineral resources has come to be seen as the main driver of conflict in the DRC is the debate among civil society organisations and international institutions about the economic motives of the different belligerents. At the end of the 1990s and the beginning of the new millennium, European and North American advocacy groups, such as Global Witness, Partnership Africa Canada, Human Rights Watch and Amnesty International, started publishing reports about the looting of Congolese natural resources, expressing anger and indignation over the fact that the international community failed to prevent key players in the Congolese conflict from enriching themselves and financing their war efforts through the illegal sale of minerals and timber on the international market. As a result of growing pressure on the part of international NGOs and human rights organisations, which in 1999 had already successfully lobbied for the creation of the Kimberley Process (a mechanism aimed at solving the problem of 'conflict diamonds'), the UN Security Council decided to set up a panel of experts tasked with investigating 'the illegal exploitation of natural resources and other forms of wealth of the Democratic Republic of Congo'. Between 2001 and 2003, the panel released three reports that caused a great deal of controversy, not only because they contained detailed information about the shady business deals of a number of well-known multinationals, but also because they described the personal involvement in the looting operations of several prominent politicians and heads of state from all over Central Africa (UN 2001: §211). The UN Panel's revelations led to the creation of parliamentary commissions of inquiry in Belgium and Uganda, an investigation by the UK Department of Trade and Industry, and a series of talks with multinationals hosted by the national contact points of the Organisation for Economic Co-operation and Development (OECD). Moreover, the Panel's findings have served as important sources of inspiration for newly created and highly influential advocacy groups in the US such as the Enough Project and the Eastern Congo Initiative.

Although there is no conclusive evidence that resource abundance really increases a country's risk of performing poorly at the economic level as well as its risk of facing violent conflict (Brunnschweiler 2008, Brunnschweiler and Bulte 2009), the preceding account has shown that the belief in the existence of such a resource 'curse' in the DRC is widespread. The hegemonic discourse among the majority of policy makers, diplomats and decision-makers is that solving the problem of 'conflict minerals' is a condition *sine qua non* for bringing peace to the Kivu region. In the section below, I will give an overview of the various policy initiatives that have been taken with the intention of breaking the assumed link between mineral exploitation and armed conflict in the DRC. It will become evident that all initiatives are based on the assumption that transparency in the Congolese mining sector is the best guarantee for long-lasting peace in the region. There appears to be a general conviction among policy makers that, under transparent conditions, 'tainted' minerals will no longer be able to enter the commodity chain, so that armed groups will lose their principle source of revenue and therefore will no longer have sufficient financial means to continue their war effort. It is also believed that Congolese state institutions need to be strengthened so that they can obtain a firmer grip on the mining sector in eastern DRC and make it more governable (Geenen 2012). Unfortunately, little or no attention has been paid to the complex political-economic context in which the initiatives are to be implemented.

The road to the Kivus is paved with good intentions

In the years after the official end of the Congolese war in July 2003, several organisations and institutions took initiatives to tackle the problem of 'conflict minerals'. Roughly speaking, a distinction can be made between three groups of initiators: a first group composed of international organisations, a second group made up of governments, and a third group consisting of various bodies representing the interests of private actors in the international mineral trade and mining industry.

Initiatives by international organisations

In the first group of initiators, the UN has played a leading role. The Security Council has mandated a panel of experts to investigate and expose cases of illegal resource exploitation, while it has also urged member states to impose sanctions such as travel bans and asset-freezes on people and companies suspected of being involved in the illegal exploitation and trade of Congolese natural resources. In addition to this, MONUSCO – the UN mission in the DRC – has been working closely together with the Congolese government to set up so-called '*centres de négoce*' or trading centres, with the idea of allowing artisanal miners and mineral traders to do business in official and transparent conditions, under close supervision of the relevant government agencies and without interference from armed groups (De Koning 2011: 28, Verbruggen *et al.* 2011, Geenen 2012).

Another international organisation that is part of the first group of initiators is the OECD, an international discussion forum allowing governments to express their opinions, talk about shared experiences and reach agreements on various economic and development-related issues.[2] In order to encourage multinationals in the DRC to behave in a more ethical and responsible manner, the OECD has tried to make companies familiar with various tools and sets of guidelines such as the Risk Awareness Tool for Multinational Enterprises in Weak Governance Zones, the OECD Guidelines for Multinational Enterprises and, finally, the Due Diligence Guidance for Responsible Supply Chains of Minerals from Conflict-Affected and High-Risk Areas.

Apart from the UN and the OECD, the first group of initiators also includes an international organisation with a purely African identity, namely the International Conference for Peace, Security, Stability and Development in the Great Lakes Region (ICGLR), which works closely together with the OECD. The ICGLR came into existence in November 2004, when 11 heads of state and government of the Great Lakes region met in Dar-es-Salaam to talk about ways to put an end to the many wars and conflict in the area.[3] In September 2006, the organisation launched a 'regional initiative against illegal exploitation of natural resources', which is aimed at increasing the level of transparency in the management of natural resources in the Great Lakes region by setting up a framework for dialogue and consultation. The idea is that the establishment of this framework will make it easier for the different member states to exchange information and to harmonise their strategies and policies of cooperation.[4]

Finally, the World Bank can also be considered as part of the first group of initiators. The Bank has started a technical assistance project called PROMINES, which is supposed to be led and driven by the Congolese Ministry of Mines.[5] Co-funded by the UK Department for International Development (DFID), PROMINES is meant to support the Congolese government in its efforts to restructure the country's mining sector. The aim is to strengthen the capacity of Congolese state institutions involved in the mining sector so that they become capable of managing the mining business in a more responsible and transparent manner. Another key goal of PROMINES is to transform the Congolese mining sector in such a way that it turns into a resource for sustainable development.[6]

Initiatives by governments

In the second group of initiators, it is the US government that has taken the lead. This is evidenced by the Dodd-Frank Act, which was signed into law by President Obama on 21 July 2010.[7] The Act contains a provision on conflict minerals and requires companies involved in activities concerning colombo-tantalite, cassiterite and wolframite from the DRC and/or neighbouring countries to submit an annual report to the Securities and Exchange Commission. Furthermore, the Act asks the US State Department to support multilateral and US Government efforts with regard to the issue of conflict minerals. It stipulates that the American authorities should support further research by the UN Panel of Experts, that they should put together a series of maps with information on the location of armed groups and the mines controlled by them, that they should design a strategy to cope with the problem of conflict minerals, that they should insist on the inclusion of information about mining-related human rights violations in the annual human rights reports and, finally, that they should guide companies in the execution of their due diligence exercises.[8]

The German government has sought to contribute to the eradication of the phenomenon of 'conflict minerals' by creating a new system for the recording and certification of mineral substances. The system is called 'Certified Trading Chains' (CTC) and has been developed, on the one hand, by the Federal Bureau of Geo-Sciences and Natural Resources or BGR from Germany, and on the other hand, by several departments of the Congolese Ministry of Mines.

With its international credibility at stake as a result of the growing international concern over the issue of 'conflict minerals', the Congolese government has been eager to set up a number of initiatives of its own, though most – if not all – of them are carried out in close collaboration with foreign partners. In order to steer things in the right direction, the Congolese government has decided to create a so-called *Groupe Thématique*, which is led by the Congolese Ministry of Mines, which is charged with the coordination and harmonisation of the wide variety of measures aimed at 'cleaning up' the mining sector.[9] Moreover, the Kinshasa government has decided to set up a programme called STAREC, which is the acronym for the *Programme de Stabilisation et de Reconstruction des Zones Sortant des Conflits Armés*.[10] The STAREC plan, of which the total cost is estimated at US$ 1.204 million, has three components: a security component, a humanitarian and social component, and an economic component. The restoration of state authority over the timber and minerals sector is considered as an objective within the security component. The aim is to have the official Congolese security forces exercise permanent supervision over mining sites exploited by armed groups, to deploy a number of state agencies at the provincial level, and to set up checkpoints in the vicinity of airstrips and roads leading to mining areas.[11]

By far the most drastic measure of the Kinshasa government has been the introduction of a general mining ban. On 11 September 2010, the Congolese Ministry of Mines put out a statement in which it announced President Kabila's decision to suspend all exploitation and export of minerals from the provinces of North Kivu, South Kivu and Maniema until further notice. The statement explained that the ban was intended to put a stop to the illegal exploitation of natural resources in eastern DRC.[12] The ban was accompanied by a series of measures intended to make the mining and trading process more transparent; it was decided that the mining administration would make an inventory of all mineral stocks and operational mining sites, and that artisanal miners would sign up for registration and organize themselves into cooperatives (Geenen 2012). The ban remained in force for a period of six months and was only lifted in March 2011.

Initiatives by interest groups in the international mineral trade and mining industry

ITRI – previously known as the International Tin Research Institute – represents the tin industry in general, and tin miners and smelters in particular. Faced with criticism from a UN Panel of Experts and from several international NGOs working on natural resource issues, members of ITRI have come up with the idea of developing their own due diligence mechanism for tin minerals originating from the eastern part of the DRC. The mechanism has been created by an ITRI working group,[13] and has been labelled the ITRI Tin Supply Chain Initiative (iTSCi).

The Global e-Sustainability Initiative (GeSi) was created in 2001. It presents itself as 'an international strategic partnership of companies, industry associations, NGOs and inter-government organizations involved in the ICT industry'.[14] Generally speaking, its aim is to promote sustainable development. In June 2008, GeSi turned into an international non-profit association and decided to establish its main office in Brussels, Belgium.[15] As for the Electronic Industry Citizenship Coalition (EICC), this coalition came into being in 2004. At the time of writing, it includes more than forty electronics companies operating on a worldwide level. Members of the coalition have committed themselves to improving the social, economic and environmental conditions in the global electronic supply chain through the adoption of a standardised code of conduct.[16]

The important thing to remember from the preceding account is that all policy initiatives are aimed at making the artisanal mining sector more transparent and in line with official rules and regulations. Moreover, all efforts are geared towards strengthening the capacity of the Congolese state and enabling state institutions to monitor the mining and trading of minerals in a manner that is acceptable to foreign donors and investors. However, as the following sections will show, there is still a yawning gap between theory and practice. The reality of mining in eastern DRC is very different from what policy makers had in mind when they were working out plans for cleaning up the mining sector.

Old wine in new bottles

Box 8.1 The Nyabibwe case

The Kalimbi mine is situated near the town of Nyabibwe in the Buhavu chieftaincy of the territory of Kalehe in South Kivu (GTZ 2010: 54–55). Between 1980 and 1984, the *Société Minière de Goma (SMDG)* operated the Kalimbi mine in an industrial manner (Geodem Inc 2008: 12). After the departure of SMDG, all its mining assets were taken over by Jules Chirimwami, a member of the Havu ethnic group who held the position of *chef de groupement* of Mpinga and who was also related to the customary chief *(mwami)* of the Buhavu chieftaincy in Kalehe. When Jules Chirimwami died, his brother Placide – a big landowner who until then had been making a career for himself as a trader of coffee and cinchona – stepped forward and presented himself as the new owner of Kalimbi. Because he failed to evict the artisanal miners who had started working in the mine, he tried to win their sympathy by setting up an organisation called COOMBECKA (*Coopérative du Bien-être de Kalehe*), of which the majority of members were of Havu origin (Placide Chirimwami, *personal communication*). In 1993, the provincial authorities of South Kivu officially recognized COOMBECKA as a cooperative (GTZ 2010: 54–55). Taking advantage of his position as the president of COOMBECKA, Chirimwami imposed his own rules for the distribution of the mining revenues. Among other things, he ordered that, of each load of minerals dug up by a team of artisanal miners, 10 per cent would go to himself, while the remaining 90 per cent would be divided between the team leader and the ordinary team members (who had to sell their minerals at a fixed price to the team leader) (Ansoms *et al.* 2012).

In the second half of the 1990s and the first decade of the new millennium, the situation in the Kalimbi mine became increasingly complex, as the territory of Kalehe was confronted with the presence of several state and non-state armed groups, including the extremist Hutu militia *Forces Démocratiques de Libération du Rwanda* (FDLR), the Congolese national army (FARDC), the political armed militia *Congrès National pour la Défense du Peuple* (CNDP), the rebel group *Patriotes Résistants Congolais* (PARECO) and various Mayi Mayi militias (APC 2009). An additional complicating factor was the fact that, despite the unstable security situation, the Canadian mining company Shamika Resources took the risk of performing exploration activities in the area. In May 2007, Jean-Felix Mupande, the head of the national mining registry in Kinshasa (*CAMI/Cadastre Minier*) issued a research permit to Shamika Congo Kalehe Sprl (a subsidiary of Shamika Resources), which authorised the company to perform exploration work on deposits of cassiterite, niobium and tantalum in 51 *carrés miniers* (mining plots with officially designated boundaries) in the territory of Kalehe.[17] Although Placide

Chirimwami was initially on good terms with Shamika, he changed his attitude when he noticed that the mining population was afraid of being evicted as a result of the company's exploration activities.[18] Apart from Chirimwami and the artisanal miners, the provincial mining authorities were also unhappy with Shamika's plans for the Kalimbi mine. On 14 July 2007, South Kivu's Minister of Mines, Crispin Mutuedu, told reporters of Radio Okapi that Shamika's exploitation of cassiterite in the mine of Kalimbi was illegal. According to Mutuedu, Shamika did not have an exploitation permit and therefore it did not have the right to engage in any excavation activities. Rejecting Mutuedu's accusation as unfounded, Robert Muongo, the Director-General of Shamika Congo, argued that his company was only carrying out exploration activities in the area, which was perfectly in line with the exploration permit it had received from the Congolese mining authorities at the national level.[19]

In 2010, ITRI, the organization representing the interests of the tin industry, and BGR, the German Federal Institute for Geosciences and Natural Resources, selected Nyabibwe as a try-out site for a traceability and certification project, because, at that time, the mine was no longer under control of a non-state armed group. From the end of June 2010 onwards, employees of the iTSCi initiative started working together with agents of the technical state agency *Service d'Assistance et d'Encadrement du Small-scale Mining* (SAESSCAM), the Congolese Mining Division (*Division des Mines*), the Congolese NGO BEGEM and the American NGO Pact, in an attempt to make the export of minerals from the Kalimbi mine fully transparent and traceable.[20]

Meanwhile, the dominance of Placide Chirimwami's COOMBECKA was dealt a heavy blow by the emergence of the rival mining cooperative COMIKA (*Coopérative Minière de Kalimbi*). COMIKA was led by Tumaini Bagurinzira, a former PARECO officer, who had built up a business career by getting involved in the trade and transport of minerals. Apart from owning the main mining pit in the Kalimbi mine, he also owned a truck that transported minerals from Nyabibwe to Goma. On 28 July 2010, representatives of the government service SAESSCAM arrived from Bukavu in order to set up a meeting between representatives of the COOMBECKA and COMIKA cooperatives and representatives of several other interest groups in Nyabibwe. Opinions were divided on the meeting's goals. While some participants thought they were just going to discuss various pieces of legislation, others were convinced that the aim was to reinstate COOMBECKA, in accordance with a circular note from the former Provincial Minister of Mines. Eventually, it turned out that the aim of the meeting was to inform people in Nyabibwe that none of the parties claiming the right to manage the mine of Kalimbi fulfilled the conditions to do so (APC 2009: 13). Seriously disappointed about the message communicated during the SAESSCAM meeting, some artisanal miners went to Kalimbi on the following evening with the aim of occupying some of the most productive pits in the mine. When they were prevented from entering the mine by diggers from the rival cooperative COMIKA, this gave rise to an explosion of violence. On 30 July 2010, a violent confrontation between COOMBECKA and COMIKA left one person dead and 17 others wounded. Following instructions from the administrator of the territory of Kalehe, the police and the army intervened to put an end to the violence (Radio Okapi 2010). On 31 July 2010, the administrator of the territory of Kalehe arrived on the scene. He told the population of Nyabibwe that COMIKA would be given the right to manage Kalimbi on a temporary basis – in other words, until a neutral committee was ready to take over the mine's management (APC 2009).

With the rivalry between COOMBECKA and COMIKA left unresolved, the situation in the Kalimbi remained very tense in the second half of 2010 and the first half of 2011. Both Chirimwami and Bagurinzira made efforts to seek military support from influential officers in the Congolese army. When, in December 2010, Bagurinzira was arrested for murder[21] and transferred to the police station of Minova, powerful allies in the FARDC came to his rescue. On 25 December 2010, a team composed of Major Adoni, an intelligence officer of the 24th sector and 12 ordinary soldiers raided the police station in order to set him free. Bagurinzira also relied on his contacts in the FARDC to continue his mineral-buying operations during the period of the presidential mining ban. Between September 2010 and March 2011, he had a deal with Colonel Saddam Ringo, who offered him protection in exchange for money. Thanks to Ringo's protection, the COMIKA mining cooperative was able to continue selling minerals to the Hillside buying house in Goma. For his part, Chirimwami tried to win the sympathy of senior people in the Congolese army. In March 2011, he had two meetings with Bosco Ntaganda, with whom he discussed the possibility of a military intervention aimed at restoring COOMBECKA's dominance in Kalimbi. With the same goal in mind, he invited Colonel Nsabimana Mwendangabo to Kalimbi in June 2011 (UN 2011: §463–465).

This case study shows, first of all, that despite external interventions to make the mining business in Nyabibwe more transparent and to bring it more firmly under government control, two 'big men' have continued to dominate the scene, namely Placide Chirimwami and Tumaini Bagurinzira. Both of them have tried to achieve a position of absolute dominance by drawing on multiple sources of power and by concluding strategic alliances with state and non-state actors. By adopting this attitude, they have managed to adapt themselves to an environment characterised by a 'hybrid political order' and 'institutional multiplicity'.

Chirimwami is not only a successful businessman owning large stretches of land in eastern DRC, but he also has kinship ties with the head of the Buhavu chieftaincy, and he has good connections with politicians and administrators thanks to his longstanding involvement in local and regional politics (Cuvelier 2011b). Many farmers depend on the goodwill of large landowners like Placide Chirimwami to get access to a piece of land. The same thing holds true for artisanal miners. Since the latter do not own the land where they work, they run the risk of being chased off and losing their production as soon as the legal owner shows up to claim his property. In the Kalimbi mine, Chirimwami has tried to present himself as a responsible patron by offering protection to his followers in exchange for their loyalty. Not only has he tried to reassure members of the COOMBECKA cooperative when they were worried about the possibility of being evicted by the company Shamika Resources, but he has also made it possible for them to continue their mining operations during the period of the presidential mining ban.

For his part, Tumaini Bagurinzira has also combined several registers of power to consolidate his position in the Kalimbi mine. First, just like his rival Chirimwami, he has made skilful use of his success as a businessman to attract a large group of followers. Thanks to his ownership of a mine pit and a truck for the transport of minerals, Bagurinzira has been able to show that he is making enough money as a mineral trader to diversify his economic activities and to offer employment to some of his followers. Another power register that Bagurinzira has used to bolster his position in the Kalimbi mine is the ability to use physical violence against his enemies and competitors. The artisanal mining population is well aware of the fact that he used to occupy a high position in PARECO, an armed group with a sad track record in terms of human rights violations. Furthermore, Bagurinzira's escape from prison in Minova – made possible by friends in the Congolese army – has confirmed his status as a man to be feared.

The second observation that can be made with regard to the Nyabibwe case is that, despite the introduction of a wide range of mining reform initiatives, there are still 'competing sources of regulatory authority' (Roitman 2005). It is obvious that, apart from the official mining laws and regulations, there are also a large number of unofficial norms and rules that have a strong influence on the ways in which mining and trading activities are organised at the local level. Good examples of this are the rules for the distribution of mining revenues that were imposed on the members of COOMBECKA by Placide Chirimwami, and the deal between the COMIKA mining cooperative and Colonel Ringo during the period of the mining ban. Although between September 2010 and March 2011 the sale of minerals was officially prohibited, Bagurinzira and his workers still succeeded in selling their minerals to a buying house in Goma, thanks to protection from a corrupt officer in the Congolese army. Another indication of the existence of 'competing sources of regulatory authority' is the incident that occurred in Nyabibwe at the end of July 2010. While one would have expected a state institution such as SAESSCAM or the mining division to have immediately settled the dispute between the two mining cooperatives, it was only after long talks, a heavy battle, an intervention by the police and the army, and an intervention by the administrator of the territory of Kalehe, that things were finally sorted out.

The third observation that the Nyabibwe case allows us to make is that actors at the local level tend to give their own interpretations to measures and initiatives taken in the context of the reform of the mining sector in eastern DRC. The creation of mining cooperatives is a good case in point. While policy makers at the international level are convinced that the establishment of cooperatives is essential to strengthen the position of artisanal miners vis-à-vis other actor groups in the mining process, the case of Nyabibwe shows that 'big men', such as Chirimwami and Bagurinzira, tend to use these cooperatives for a completely different purpose, namely to gather a group of loyal supporters around them who accept their authority and who are prepared to defend their business interests in and around the mine.

Finally, the Nyabibwe case demonstrates that 'big men' at the grassroots level have managed to circumvent many of the restrictions on their activities (engendered by the mining reform initiatives) thanks to their connections with so-called 'shadow networks'. Over the years, Chirimwami and Bagurinzira have developed such a large number of contacts in different circles that it does not take them a lot of effort to violate a presidential mining embargo or to smuggle goods across the Congolese Rwandan border. Their contacts with high-placed officers in the Congolese army have proved to be very useful in this respect.

Conclusions

The aim of this chapter was to assess the local impact of the large number of policy initiatives that have been launched to solve the problem of 'conflict minerals' in eastern DRC. It has been shown that there are significant differences between, on the one hand, the theoretical plans of national and international policy makers for the reform of the mining sector in eastern DRC, and, on the other, the concrete implementation of these plans. At the local level, 'big men' connected to transnational 'shadow networks' have continued to run the show. Taking advantage of the weakness of state institutions in the war-torn eastern part of the country, they have developed their own rules and regulations for the exploitation and trade of mineral resources. As a result of this, a situation of hybrid political orders, institutional multiplicity and legal pluralism has come into existence. The artisanal mining population has had no other option but to adapt itself to the harsh reality of multiple state and non-state authorities continuously competing for superiority and forcing their subjects to comply with complex combinations of official and unofficial sets of rules. Rather than strengthening the capacity of the state and enabling state institutions to regulate and monitor the artisanal mining sector in a more transparent and rational manner than before, the measures taken in the context of the fight against 'conflict minerals' have only made the situation on the ground more complex than it already was. Policy makers should be well aware of the fact that the problem of 'conflict minerals' is not a purely technical issue that can be solved in a technical manner. The case study on Nyabibwe has underlined the importance of paying attention to local power dynamics. The exploitation and trade of minerals such as coltan, gold and cassiterite take place in a complex political and socio-cultural context, which needs to be thoroughly analysed, understood and monitored in order to increase the efficiency of policy interventions and to facilitate their implementation at the grassroots level.

Acknowledgements

I would like to thank Dorothea Hilhorst, Jeroen Warner, Gemma van der Haar, Koen Vlassenroot and Sara Geenen for their comments on an earlier draft of this chapter. Needless to say, I take full responsibility for all remaining errors and shortcomings. I would also like to express my gratitude to Franck Mushobekwa of the Congolese NGO APC, who played a vital role in the collection of primary data for this chapter.

Notes

1 The project was initiated and coordinated by the British NGO International Alert (IA), while staff members of the Belgian NGO International Peace Information Service (IPIS), my former employer, were commissioned by IA to do the research, in collaboration with a number of external consultants.
2 Information obtained from the OECD website: www.oecd.org, accessed on 28 February 2012.
3 'Great Lakes: Advocacy for the International Conference on the Great Lakes Region', EURAC press release, 31 March 2009.
4 ICGLR, *Regional Programme of Action for the Promotion of Democracy and Good Governance*, September 2006.
5 Personal communication with Rachel Perks (PACT), 21 June 2010.
6 Information obtained from the PACT website (http://pactworld.org), accessed on 8 June 2010.
7 'Obama signs Wall Street Bill affirming ongoing US Government support to ending violence in eastern DRC', press release Enough Project, 21 July 2010.
8 'NGOs welcome the Congo Conflict Minerals Act of 2009', Global Witness, press release 13 May 2009.
9 'Martin Kabwelulu évalue les travaux du Groupe Thématique', La Prospérité, 27 May 2010.
10 This can be translated as 'Programme for the Stabilization and Reconstruction of zones coming out of armed conflict'.
11 'Het STAREC-plan van de Congolese regering: een voorlopige analyse', Raf Custers (IPIS), August 2009.
12 'L'exploitation minière dans l'ancien Kivu suspendue jusqu'à nouvel ordre', *Radio Okapi*, 13 September 2010.
13 The working group included the Thailand Smelting & Refining Co Ltd and the Malaysia Smelting Corporation Berhad (MSC). It asked the Belgian company Traxys to serve as an expert adviser (source: 'DRC Tin Supply Chain Initiative, ITRI press release, 10 July 2009).
14 'Tracing a path forward: a study of the challenges of the supply chain for target metals used in electronics', *Resolve*, April 2010: ii.
15 Information from the GeSi website (www.gesi.org), accessed on 8 June 2010.
16 'EICC and GeSi Tracing Report Published', press release GeSi, 22 April 2010.
17 Documents seen by the author in the course of his research.
18 'Rebels cash in on Congo's riches', *The National*, 12 August 2008.
19 'Bukavu: exploitation illégale des minerais, le ministre provincial dénonce, *Radio Okapi*, 13 July 2007.

20 'DRC Ministry of Mines reconfirms official support for itSci mineral traceability project', ITRI press release, 11 June 2010.
21 He was accused of having killed someone during the clashes between COOMBECKA and COMIKA in July 2010.

Bibliography

Ansoms, A., Claessens, K. and Mudinga, E. (2012) 'L'Accaparement des Terres par des élites en Territoire de Kalehe, RDC', in F. Reyntjens (ed.), *L'Afrique des Grands Lacs: annuaire 2011–2012*. Paris: L'Harmattan.

APC/Life and Peace Institute (2009) *Analyse de Contexte du Territoire de Kalehe*, Bukavu: APC research report.

Atkinson, G. and Hamilton, K. (2003) 'Savings, Growth and the Resource Curse hypothesis', *World Development*, 31 (11): 1793–1807.

Autesserre, S. (2012) 'Dangerous Tales: Dominant Narratives on the Congo and their Unintended Consequences', *African Affairs* 111 (442): 1–21.

Auty, R. (ed.) (2001) *Resource Abundance and Economic Development*. Oxford: Oxford University Press.

Berdal, M. and Malone, D. (eds) (2000) *Greed And Grievance: Economic Agendas In Civil Wars*. Boulder, CO: Lynne Rienner.

Brunnschweiler, C. (2008) 'Cursing the Blessings? Natural Resource Abundance, Institutions and Economic Growth', *World Development*, 36 (3): 399–419.

Brunnschweiler, C. and Bulte, E. (2009) 'Natural Resources and Violent Conflict: Resource Abundance, Dependence and the onset of Civil Wars', *Oxford Economic Papers*, 61 (4): 651–674.

Collier, P. and Hoeffler, A. (2005) 'Resource Rents, Governance and Conflict', *Journal of Conflict Resolution*, 49 (4): 625–633.

Cuvelier, J. (2011a) 'Between Hammer and Anvil: The Predicament of Artisanal Miners in Katanga', in A. Ansoms and S. Marysse (eds), *Natural Resources and local livelihoods in the Great Lakes Region of Africa: A Political Economy Perspective*, Basingstoke: Palgrave MacMillan.

Cuvelier, J. (ed.) (2011b) *The Complexity of Resource Governance in a Context of State Fragility: The Case of Eastern DRC*. London: International Alert Publication.

De Koning, R. (2010) 'Controlling Conflict Resources in the Democratic Republic of Congo'. *SIPRI Conflict Brief*, available at http://books.sipri.org/product_info?c_product_id=407# (accessed on 7 February 2012).

De Koning, R. (2011) 'Conflict Minerals in the Democratic Republic of the Congo: Aligning Trade and Security Interventions', *SIPRI Policy Paper 27*, online publication: books.sipri.org/files/PP/SIPRIPP27.pdf, accessed on 28 February 2012.

De Koning, R. (2012) 'Big Men Commanding Conflict Resources: The Democratic Republic of Congo', in Utas, M. (ed.), *African Conflicts and Informal Power: Big Men and Networks*. London: Zed Books.

Dietrich, C. (2000) 'The Commercialisation of Military Deployment in Africa', *Africa Security Review*, 9 (1).

Enough Project (2009) *A Comprehensive Approach to Congo's Conflict Minerals – Strategy Paper*, available at www.enoughproject.org/publications/comprehensive-approach-conflict-minerals-strategy-paper (accessed on 7 February 2012).

Garrett, N., Mitchell, H. and Lintzer, M. (2010) 'Promoting Legal Mineral Trade in Africa's Great Lakes Region: A Policy Guide on Professionalization, Formalization and Increased Transparency', available at www.resourceglobal.co.uk, accessed on 7 February 2012.

Geenen, S. (2011) 'Local Livelihoods, Global Interests and the State in the Congolese Mining Sector', in A. Ansoms and S. Marysse (eds), *Natural Resources and Local Livelihoods in the Great Lakes Region of Africa: A Political Economy Perspective*. Basingstoke: Palgrave Macmillan.

Geenen, S. (2012) 'A Dangerous Bet. The Challenges of Formalizing Artisanal Mining in the Democratic Republic of Congo'. *Resources Policy*, 37 (3): 322–330.

Geodem Inc. (2008) *Preliminary Assessment and Technical Report for the Kalehe Project of Shamika Resources Inc*. Copy obtained from Robert Vivian, CEO of Shamika Resources.

Global Witness (2009) 'Faced with a Gun, What can you Do? War and the Militarisation of Mining in Eastern Congo'. Global Witness publication, available at www.global witness.org/library/faced-gun-what-can-you-do (accessed on 7 February 2012).

GTZ Burundi/OGP (2010) '*L'Economie des Groupes Armés au Sud-Kivu*'. Unpublished report.

Hilhorst, D., Christoplos, I. and van der Haar, G. (2010) 'Reconstruction "From Below": A New Magic Bullet or Shooting from the Hip?', *Third World Quarterly*, 31 (7): 1107–1124.

IPIS (2009) *Culprits or Scapegoats: Revisiting the Role of Belgian Mineral Traders in Eastern DRC*, available at www.ipisresearch.be, accessed on 7 February 2012.

IPIS (2011) *Guide to Current Mining Reform Initiatives in Eastern DRC*, available at www. ipisresearch.be, accessed on 7 February 2012.

Jackson, S. (2002) 'Making a Killing: Criminality and Coping in the Kivu War Economy', *Review of African Political Economy*, 93–94, 517–536.

Jensen, N. and Wantchekon, L. (2004) 'Resource Wealth and Political Regimes in Africa', *Comparative Political Studies*, 37 (7): 816–841.

Kaldor, M., Karl, T. and Said, Y. (eds) (2007) *Oil Wars*. London: Pluto Press.

Karl, T. (1997) *The Paradox Of Plenty: Oil Booms and Petro-states*. Berkeley, CA: University of California Press.

Mallett, R. (2010) 'Beyond Failed States and Ungoverned Spaces: Hybrid Political Orders in the Post-conflict Landscape', *eShape*, 15: 65–91.

Mazalto, M. (2009) 'Governance, Human Rights and Mining in the Democratic Republic of Congo', in B. Campbell (ed.), *Mining in Africa: Regulation and Development*, London: Pluto Press.

Neumayer, E. (2004) 'Does the "Resource Curse" hold for Growth in Genuine Income as well?', *World Development*, 32 (10): 1627–1640.

Nordstrom, C. (2004) *Shadows of War: Violence, Power and International Profiteering in the 21st Century*. Berkeley, CA: University of California Press.

Putzel, J. (2005) *War, State Collapse and Reconstruction: P2 of the Crisis States Programme*. London: LSE Working Paper.

Radio Okapi (2010)'Bukavu: un conflit meurtrier dans un carré minier à Nyabibwe'.

Reyntjens, F. (2005) 'The Privatization and Criminalization of Public Space in the Geopolitics of the Great Lakes Region', *Journal of Modern African Studies*, 43 (4): 587–607.

Reyntjens, F. (2007) 'Democratic Republic of Congo: Political Transition and Beyond', *African Affairs*, 106/423, 307–317.

Roitman, J. (2005) *Fiscal Disobedience: An Anthropology of Economic Regulation in Central Africa*. Princeton, NJ and Oxford: Princeton University Press.

Ross, M. (2001) 'Does Oil Hinder Democracy?', *World Politics*, 53: 325–361.

Rosser, A. (2006) *The Political Economy of the Resource Curse: A Literature Survey*. Brighton: IDS Working Paper 268.

Sachs, J. and Warner, A. (1995) *Natural Resource Abundance and Economic Growth*, NBR Working Paper Series 5398. Cambridge: National Bureau of Economic Research.

Smith, J. (2011) 'Tantalus in the Digital Age: Coltan Ore, Temporal Dispossession, and "Movement" in the Eastern Democratic Republic of the Congo', *American Ethnologist*, 38 (1): 17–35.

Taylor, I. (2003) 'Conflict in Central Africa: Clandestine Networks and Regional/Global Configurations', *Review of African Political Economy*, 30 (95): 45–55.

Trefon, T. (2011) *Congo Masquerade: The Political Culture of Aid Inefficiency and Reform Failure*. London: Zed Books.

UN (2001) Letter dated 12 April 2001 from the Secretary-General to the President of the Security Council (S/2001/1146).

UN (2002) *Final report of the Panel of Experts on the illegal exploitation of natural resources and other forms of wealth of the DRC* (S/2002/1146).

UN (2010) Letter dated 15 November 2010 from the Chair of the Security Council Committee established pursuant to resolution 1533 (2004) concerning the Democratic Republic of the Congo addressed to the President of the Security Council (S/2010/596).

UN (2011) Letter dated 18 October 2011 from the Group of Experts on the Democratic Republic of Congo addressed to the Chair of the Security Council Committee established pursuant to resolution 1533 (2004) (S/2011/738).

Utas, M. (ed.) (2012) *African Conflicts and Informal Power: Big Men and Networks*. London: Zed Books.

Verbruggen, D., Francq, E. and Cuvelier, J. (2011) 'Guide to Current Mining Reforms in eastern DRC', available on www.ipisresearch.be, accessed on 20 February 2013.

Vircoulon, T. (2007) 'L'état Internationalise: Nouvelle Figure de la Mondialisation en Afrique', *Etudes*, 1 (406), 9–20.

Vlassenroot, K. and Van Bockstael, S. (eds) (2008) *Artisanal Diamond Mining: Perspectives and Challenges*. Ghent: Academia Press.

9 Institutional multiplicity in post-conflict reconstruction

The case of a local church in Bunjei, Angola

Maliana Serrano

Introduction

State-building discourse assumes that local institutions collapse during conflict, leaving an institutional void that needs to be filled through external interventions. Alternative perspectives argue that, in conflict-affected contexts, where power is contested and legitimate state institutions may be absent, local actors find room for manoeuvre to pursue their interests in multiple institutional alternatives. Different institutional systems coexist and provide competing normative frameworks for action (Hesselbein *et al.* 2006). In addition to formal state institutions, several arrangements are involved in addressing the needs of local populations which range from conflict resolution to the provision of basic social services. These include citizen activities, traditional institutions, private initiatives and various aid actors.

This chapter examines the role of a local church in rural Angola as an example of the multiple actors that make up the post-conflict institutional landscape. It explores the case of the Evangelical Congregational Church in Angola (IECA) in Bunjei, Huíla province. This area was heavily affected by the war and remains significantly marginalised from broader recovery efforts. Since the end of the conflict in 2002, IECA has emerged as a prominent player in local reconstruction and development processes. It has become a *de facto* competitor of the state in service provision and local governance. This chapter explores why and how it developed such a position in local society.

State-building agendas have a limited perspective on how these processes operate in practice, because they tend to consider the state as the only legitimate service provider in post-conflict settings. At the same time, dominant writings on aid in conflict and post-conflict are centred on the international aid community, overlooking the role of local actors and institutions in assisting local populations. Faith-based organisations are important contributors to social transformation in fragile states, because they enjoy unique levels of trust and legitimacy among civil society actors (Hauck 2010). During the Angolan war, local churches performed an important function as providers of relief assistance and in peacebuilding efforts. However, literature on the role of the churches in post-conflict reconstruction processes has been limited. This chapter addresses this gap by analysing empirically the role of the protestant church IECA and its social work in Bunjei.

In fragile contexts where multiple institutional arrangements coexist and compete, the legitimacy of local actors and institutions is constantly being contested. 'Legitimacy' here is understood as a conferred quality rather than as a given trait and as involving legitimisation and de-legitimisation dynamics. Legitimacy-building is a negotiated and relational process affected by competing strategies of various actors (Douma and Van der Haar 2010). The chapter analyses how IECA crafts its legitimacy vis-à-vis local actors such as local communities, government and other social assistance providers. This means identifying IECA's main sources of legitimacy by examining various aspects of its organisational identity and culture, as well as its everyday social assistance practices. These are discussed in the broader context of local governance and service delivery, to show how they co-shape legitimisation processes. I focus particularly on the role of local state services and of other aid organisations. This, in turn, draws out post-conflict transition processes relating to the re-establishment of the civil service, and to the short-term involvement of international non-governmental organisations (NGOs). The chapter is based on fieldwork conducted in Huíla province between 2007 and 2009 to assess the interactions between aid interventions and local institutions.

Background

Since its independence from the Portuguese in 1975, Angola was immersed in a long civil war that lasted until 2002. Its main protagonists were the Popular Movement for the Liberation of Angola (MPLA), which has been in power since independence, and the National Union for the Independence of Angola (UNITA). The conflict involved various actors and motivations, including the Cold War superpowers. Its effects and manifestations varied according to local conditions, producing localised dynamics and multiple realities on the ground.

The Bunjei region, which belongs to Chipindo municipality in the north of Huíla province, is at the heart of the territory contested by the Government and UNITA. It was therefore severely affected by the war. It remained under UNITA control for long stretches of time. Contrary to its official propaganda discourse, UNITA did not provide welfare services to local people, except for a small minority working, often forcibly, for the regime, and their families. Civilians had to fend for themselves and were often forced to feed UNITA's troops through taxes on harvests and forced labour on collective plots (Serrano 2012). They experienced violent and frequent displacements during the war. According to official government estimates, 98 per cent of today's population was internally displaced (Gabinete do Plano 2009). Bunjei was described as a cemetery town because of its death rate in the later conflict years (Messiant 2004). The greater Chipindo area was estimated to have a lower than average family size in the post-war period (three members or less, instead of four) as a result of its conflict experience (Schot 2005: 5). Bunjei's formal services and state institutions collapsed, and it remained completely isolated from any form of external assistance throughout the war.

A significant humanitarian operation was launched in the immediate post-conflict phase, resulting in a typical case of institutional multiplicity. This involved major humanitarian actors, such as Médecins Sans Frontières and the World Food Programme, international NGOs such as Acción Contra el Hambre, ACORD and ZOA Refugee Care, national organisations such as IECA, and governmental relief. After 2005, the aid arena contracted significantly as most organisations withdrew. This followed a broader change in donor policy, whereby funding to Angola was reduced. In spite of continuing needs, by 2008 all international actors had left Bunjei. IECA became the only aid provider. Since 2004, it has been implementing a large intervention in 20 of the 28 local communities – the Integrated Programme for the Rural Development of Bunjei (PIDRB). PIDRB works across various social sectors to address low agricultural production and economic development, poor healthcare and education, and the lack of organisation within communities.

Angola is a predominantly Catholic country due to the Portuguese colonial influence. However, under the colonial system, different Christian missions were allocated different parts of the territory. IECA developed in the central part of Angola and became the dominant church in the Chipindo area. IECA was established under Portuguese colonial rule and originated from the work of two North American missions established in the 1880s. It is currently the most significant protestant church in the country, with around one million followers (IECA 2006, Jensen and Pestana 2010). Bunjei was one of its main missions, established in 1923 (Henderson 1990). With the eruption of the civil war, the mission was soon abandoned and its infrastructure shattered. The hospital for which it became well known was temporarily used as a military base for Government and Cuban troops. The mission was re-established in 2003 and its infrastructure is slowly being rehabilitated.

In the current reconstruction context, Bunjei and the wider municipality continue to be marginalised from broader recovery processes. Access to, and the quality of basic services remain remarkably low. Its isolation is both a result of and a reason for lack of investment by state and non-state actors. This is partly linked to its geographical and political distance from decision-making centres at provincial and national levels.

Institutional multiplicity in fragile states

The institutional multiplicity that characterises conflict and post-conflict societies, sometimes referred to as fragile states, is made up of various actors and arrangements, including state and non-state alternatives. Hesselbein *et al.* (2006: 1) classify this multiplicity into four competing institutional systems: rule systems adopted by the state (statutory law), the rule systems evolved over time by older communities (customary traditions), the rule systems that communities or groups have devised for survival, and the rule systems hatched by non-state centres of power (warlords, bosses, criminal gangs). In addition, new institutional arrangements for service provision often emerge, in the form of external aid agencies, churches, civil society organisations, private actors or citizen arrangements (Hilhorst 2005, 2007).

In post-conflict societies, institutional multiplicity is particularly relevant. Institutions are often more fluid and subject to change given the lack of legitimate state institutions, the contests between different sources of power and legitimacy, the challenges resulting from violence and displacement, and the presence of external interventions (Christoplos and Hilhorst 2009, Hilhorst *et al.* 2010). However, institutional multiplicity is characteristic of state formation processes in African societies, more broadly.

Aid organisations and their interventions are part of this multiplicity. They do not operate outside of societies but are embedded in local realities. They 'exist in an arena of social actors with competing interests and strategies' (Bakewell 2000: 104). My analysis builds on the notion of the aid *arena*, presented in the introduction of this volume. The *arena* paradigm challenges dominant perspectives on aid in conflict that centre on the role of international actors and the aid they provide (Hilhorst and Jansen 2010, Hilhorst and Serrano 2010). It opens up the scope of analysis to include multiple actors and motivations involved in service delivery in crisis, besides those conventionally labelled as humanitarian. It therefore recognises the role played by local actors in assisting local populations and in negotiating the outcome of external aid.

The role of IECA in Bunjei is analysed in this chapter as part of the aid arena in reconstruction. There are several aspects to IECA's role and identity. IECA functions as a prominent evangelical church in Angola (with links to an international network), as a religious mission in Bunjei during the colonial time, as well as a social assistance organisation. Given my interest in service delivery in post-conflict reconstruction, I focus the discussion on the social assistance function of IECA. The spiritual and social functions are intentionally separated within IECA's structure. In 1991 a department for social assistance, studies and projects – DASEP – was created as an operationally autonomous entity, separate from the spiritual branch. It operates much in the same way as other aid organisations.[1] It is within this structure that development interventions are implemented.

Local churches

Local churches, through their social work, have an important historical function in assisting local populations. Since their establishment during the colonial rule, Christian missions in Angola have been major providers of basic social services, such as healthcare and education. The colonial system delegated this function to the missions with the expectation that Christian values would strengthen colonial rule and strengthen its economic projects (Birmingham 2006). After independence, local churches were weakened by the civil conflict and by the repression by the post-independence Marxist state. Yet, they attempted to maintain this social assistance role. Several church organisations became implementing partners of international aid actors. They were also important actors in peacebuilding efforts

(Comerford 2005, 2009). However, these efforts were hampered somewhat by the historical links between the different churches and the various nationalist movements involved in the dynamics of war (Schubert 1999).

In post-conflict settings, faith-based organisations continue to be an important part of reconstruction efforts. A recent body of literature refers to their role in societal transformation in conflict-affected countries and its potential contribution to development. Ter Haar and Ellis (2006: 362) argue that the notions of religion and development have much in common, and that religion can contribute to development processes in four key areas: conflict prevention and peacebuilding, wealth creation and production, governance, and health and education. Religious institutions are seen as having the potential to mobilise social capital because they bring together resources and people with a shared vision and beliefs, and are thus more effective than individuals acting alone (Hays 2002: 250). Hauck (2010) reasons that, as a subset of civil society, they can contribute to governance and social capital in fragile states, particularly at the local level, because of the unique trust and legitimacy they leverage, their local networks and institutional links, and individual skills and capacities. In Angola, opinion surveys have shown the churches to have high levels of trust amongst the population (Republic of Angola National Opinion Poll in Shaxson *et al.* 2008: 22–23, BBC World Service Trust, 2008 in Jensen and Pestana 2010).

Writings about the churches in the Angolan context have centred on their social protection and assistance work during colonialism, on their influence on nationalism, on their role as peace advocates and providers of relief aid during the war, and almost exclusively on their peacebuilding function during the post-conflict phase. Yet, in reconstruction, local churches have remained important also in social assistance and service delivery. Although the core business of the churches continues to be the evangelisation mission, most have returned to their historical function as providers of education and healthcare (Jensen and Pestana 2010). This chapter aims to understand how these functions are negotiated and carried out in practice for the case of IECA and its integrated development intervention in Bunjei.

Seeking legitimacy

The legitimacy of aid organisations vis-à-vis other actors, and the processes by which they are accountable to the various stakeholders, are key elements associated with the quality of their work. Aid providers are expected to be accountable to various actors, crucially to their donors and beneficiaries. In the present discussion, I am less concerned with IECA's upwards accountability to its donors, and more with understanding how it crafts its legitimacy vis-à-vis local actors such as local communities, government and other social assistance providers.

Legitimacy is in the eye of the beholder. The legitimacy of a particular actor or institution is a quality conferred on it by others that gives it authority (Bellina *et al.* 2009). It is co-determined by people's perceptions, beliefs and expectations (Brinkerhoff 2005) and by people's behaviour in response to certain situations

(Van der Molen and Stel 2010). Different actors derive legitimacy from a combination of different sources. Brinkerhoff (2005) differentiates between three broad types of organisational legitimacy: normative (where an organisation reflects acceptable and desirable norms, standards and values), pragmatic (it fulfils needs and interests of its stakeholders and constituents), and cognitive legitimacy (it pursues goals and activities that fit with broad social understanding of what is appropriate, proper and desirable). He argues that churches, as a specific subset of organisations, tend to benefit from all three types of legitimacy, which in turn contribute to their performance capacity. In IECA's case, various factors impact its legitimisation and delegitimisation dynamics – its organisational identity and history, its organisational culture and practices, its local relations and social embeddedness, and the local institutional alternatives available. Each one is discussed below.

Organisational identity and history

IECA draws considerable normative or moral legitimacy from its Christian identity, mission and values, and theological obligations. In addition, it developed a strong social justice focus, and a tradition of social work. It is rooted in the American Missionary Society, whose primary commitment was the support and education of slaves liberated in the south of the US (Henderson 1990). A comparison between the main churches in Angola shows that, in IECA's vision, social action is specifically framed as part of its evangelisation mission (Jensen and Pestana 2010: 23). Moreover, it has 'an explicit and very strong focus on improving the social conditions of the society of which it forms part' (ibid.: 11).

IECA's historical service delivery function was key to the establishment of the mission at Bunjei. The three founding staff brought with them expertise in different fields, from agriculture to medicine (Henderson 1990). The mission hospital was crucial in assisting local populations and in training health workers, particularly during the colonial period. Additionally, IECA established a significant number of schools, as education was its primary evangelising instrument. Christian mission schools marked the social fabric of many generations in Angola. Besides political elites, many religious, military and social elites were educated in them (Santos 2008). This service delivery function of IECA was interrupted in Bunjei because the mission was destroyed.

The education function of IECA became problematic for its legitimacy, as it contributed to the association of IECA with UNITA. This resulted from the fact that Savimbi and other prominent UNITA figures attended evangelical mission schools. In addition, several UNITA leaders took on responsibilities within congregational communities (Schubert 1999: 407). The other main nationalist movements were likewise associated with different religious missions. These perceived links with UNITA may have legitimised IECA amongst the movement's regime and its militants, but had the opposite effect vis-à-vis government institutions. I return to this politicisation aspect of IECA in later sections of the chapter.

In the post-war context, service provision has re-emerged as a key source of cognitive and pragmatic legitimacy for IECA, through the implementation of its integrated rural development programme – PIDRB.

Organisational culture and practices

IECA's organisational culture and practices have been important in defining its performance and how it is perceived. During Angola's emergency period which was dominated by relief interventions, IECA underwent a series of internal reforms. These aimed to improve its social assistance work and its organisational capacity to respond to growing needs and to access donor funding. The creation of its social assistance department (DASEP) resulted from these changes. Over the years, IECA also sought to strengthen its democratic character through reforms intended to increase consultation and participation by different staff and members in decision-making processes.

IECA has been able to leverage considerable legitimacy internally through certain organisational practices that influence the motivation and morale of its staff. As I shall explain, staff are a key determinant of local perceptions and expectations. Training opportunities, personnel coaching and internal accounta-bility procedures contribute to building ownership, trust and legitimacy within the organisation. At the project quarters in Bunjei, the question of internal accountability is taken very seriously. Management staff go to great lengths to uphold transparency and fairness amongst the project team. In one instance, when a member of staff took unauthorised leave, details of the consequent salary deduction were posted publicly on the office noticeboard.

Programme staff stressed the importance of having access to training courses and teaching material on various themes and methodologies. Examples include IECA's internal meetings for reflection and sharing of experiences, DASEP's established training programme for Community Development Agents, and the daily coaching of field staff by PIDRB's own programme coordinator.

Organisational practices also have a de-legitimising effect internally and vis-à-vis other actors. For instance, the separation of the spiritual and social branches ended up creating tension within the church. IECA's implementation model of social assistance through DASEP meant that it had to compete with other organisations for donor funds. As a result, the spiritual branch accused its social counterpart of neglecting its spiritual basis, thereby losing support internally.

Social embeddedness

The way in which IECA relates to local populations, or the degree of its social embeddedness is a key aspect of its legitimacy. Relevant to this is its religious iden-tity. 'Religious beliefs, and religious institutions, play a central role in defining what is considered morally right, appropriate, sinful, wrong etc. in a society and in shaping people's political expectations and conceptions of authority' (Bellina *et al.*

2009: 19). Well-established faith-based organisations thus enjoy a significant degree of taken-for-granted legitimacy amongst certain groups, because their structures, procedures and activities are understood and accepted by society (Brinkerhoff 2005: 5).

As one of the longest established churches, IECA has developed a close relationship with people at the local level. As explained by DASEP's Programme Director, 'We always have a home to start from and a strong base and link to the community.' IECA has deep-seated knowledge of local realities and personal and institutional relations from which it draws support. Other major churches were present in Chipindo, namely the Catholic Church and IESA[2] (the other large evangelical church), but they each developed a stronghold in different areas. IECA thus developed a unique relationship with local people in Bunjei.

Local staff

The most striking aspect from the observation of IECA's local relations and legitimacy relates to its local staff. Programme staff displayed a remarkable sense of commitment to fulfilling the objectives of the intervention and to helping the local population. They often go beyond the call of duty to help members of the communities where they work. 'Sometimes I take some of my old clothes to give to the "mais velhos". I feel bad seeing them living in such poverty.'[3] The behaviour of individuals is important in understanding their organisations' practices and relationships with other actors, including local government and populations. Such behaviour is influenced by organisational cultures (shared assumptions and beliefs) and other institutions (written and unwritten rules, codes of conduct, patterns of interaction, procedures, rituals and myths) (Walkup 1997: 38, Hilhorst and Schmiemann 2002). The profile, reputation and motivation of local staff, as the representatives of an organisation, are central to the perception and relationships with other actors. It is thus essential to examine how they make sense of the local situation and build the trust of local actors through their everyday practices and decisions.

Such close relationships with community members are not exceptional to IECA, for aid workers are most often deeply committed and respectful of beneficiary populations. What sets IECA apart from other aid organisations in post-conflict Bunjei is the *de facto* proximity of staff to the local population. Although the mission was abandoned during the war, IECA has had a long-term presence on the ground compared to other aid providers, who left after the post-conflict resettlement phase.

PIDRB's members of staff are rarely isolated from the people with whom they work. In their everyday lives there is no clear division between personal and professional relations and time. They expect and accept that local people show up at the mission unannounced to discuss all kinds of issues. The technical personnel were recruited from the provincial office in Lubango, as they require specialised training and skills. However, support staff were largely selected locally in Bunjei. In both cases, individuals are not recruited as short-term field workers, temporarily assigned to the project. They are all expected to be part of local society. They teach or study in the local school, experience the same everyday problems as the local population, are part of collective events such as local weddings and sports events, and also actively promote social activities. During the 2010 football African Cup of Nations hosted by Angola, PIDRB staff arranged for local people to go and watch Angola's games at the mission offices where an electricity generator and television were available. This type of interaction with the local population has significant meaning for the building of trust and accountability.

Staff motivation

Particularly relevant for the relationship between IECA and local actors, is the drive and motivation of its staff for working in the isolated context of Bunjei. For a long time, a job with a local organisation like IECA represented a valuable opportunity for income security and prestige. Recently, the financial appeal was considerably reduced because of large-scale recruitment for the civil service in rural areas, offering attractive working conditions. Other considerations beyond economic ones thus drive local staff in their jobs. These include a moral dimension, associated with notions of solidarity and altruism that attract people to social work and charitable organisations across the world. For many of IECA's staff, religious values play an important role. Work with local communities is looked upon as part of the Christian mission to help others. Within the PIDRB team itself, a sense of camaraderie is fostered as people share their living space and domestic chores, meals and social time. As Hays (2002) observes:

> Religious institutions provide a community of like-minded persons who help the individual overcome his or her sense of isolation and powerlessness, both through shared ritual and through interpersonal relationships.

One of PIDRB's team explained how important being part of the IECA community was for him:

> I don't earn a lot of money and I work long and irregular hours. I cannot take evening classes as my colleagues do, so that one day I have a chance at finding another job. But I really like my work. I get so much comfort from my colleagues and the church community. I lost a child to illness not long ago. I was in Namibia at the time and had to travel back for the funeral. When I arrived here, they had taken care of all the arrangements. It was all done. My brothers and sisters of IECA helped me so much.[4]

Institutional alternatives: contesting legitimacy

The legitimacy of a particular actor or institution is affected by the availability, performance and perception by local people of other alternatives for addressing needs and resolving problems. Legitimacy is relational and constantly negotiated. Where institutional multiplicity is particularly intense, as in fragile contexts, actors find room for manoeuvre to pursue their interests and realise projects, by engaging with different institutions or playing them out against each other. However, competition between institutional alternatives may be problematic if it becomes a source of conflict (Christoplos and Hilhorst 2009). In IECA's case, when PIDRB was established, institutional alternatives were limited as the aid arena had already contracted. Nonetheless, IECA's legitimacy was shaped by the role of the other two categories of social service providers – non-governmental aid organisations and state institutions.

Impact of aid interventions on IECA's legitimacy

The presence of other aid actors directly affected IECA's legitimisation and de-legitimisation dynamics. The interaction with their interventions had a bearing on how IECA's programme (PIDRB) was received on the ground. This was linked to differences in organisational identities, approaches and practices.

The case of ZOA Refugee Care illustrates how such differences affected competition with IECA. The two organisations coincided for approximately one-and-a-half years during 2003/2004. They started off as implementing partners, whereby IECA was supposed to give continuity to ZOA's programme after its withdrawal. A disagreement resulted in the splitting of interventions and coverage into separate projects, both intended to assist the resettlement of local people in their communities. When ZOA withdrew, PIDRB took over 10 of its 18 intervention communities.

The identities of ZOA and IECA were important in defining their mission and intervention rationales. Both are Christian-based organisations. However, their profiles are quite distinct. ZOA is an international NGO focused on relief aid to refugee and displaced communities during crisis and transition periods. Its intervention in Bunjei was, therefore, conceived as an emergency project to assist the displaced population with immediate needs and with resettlement. The social work of the local church IECA, on the other hand, has been traditionally focused on the longer-term needs of local communities, including the provision of social services such as education and health care, skills training and livelihood support. PIDRB was the first intervention in Bunjei specifically aiming to go beyond relief activities. It was conceptualised as a longer-term integrated development programme, aspiring to innovate. It included, for example, an adult literacy component.

The implementation strategies of the organisations were significantly different. ZOA's aid was targeted at all members of each beneficiary community and was distributed for free. IECA mostly worked through credit systems that required beneficiaries to partly reimburse the cost of inputs, either in kind or in cash. During a hunger spell in 2004, ZOA provided 20 kg of maize per family. IECA, in an attempt to maintain a development approach, decided to only give 5 kg, plus training in agricultural techniques:

The communities were angry and rejected this. Some even threatened to use the 5 kg of maize as food instead of seed. But eventually attitudes changed. This approach takes time. Development takes a constant re-negotiation within communities.[5]

Both organisations also implemented an animal component involving the distribution of oxen and ploughs to small groups, to work the families' land on a rotation system. ZOA gave the animals for free whilst PIDRB's used a credit system. The idea was to ensure continuity and expansion of the animal credit and to create a sense of ownership amongst beneficiaries. Not surprisingly, members of PIDRB's intervention villages often resisted having to reimburse inputs when neighbouring villages did not have to do so. Moreover, this strategy was undermined by claims that the credit system excluded the poorest community members, due to their inability to pay.

The distinct ways in which the organisations established community-based groups in their intervention villages also illustrate how people's perceptions were affected. ZOA established Management Committees that based themselves on existing traditional institutions, and therefore tended to mirror the hierarchy of the traditional authorities[6] (ZOA and ADESPOV 2002). PIDRB's Community Development Nuclei (NDC), in contrast, intentionally excluded the traditional leaders from specific group functions, in an attempt to extend decision-making power to other community members. They therefore faced more resistance. ZOA's Committees were primarily intended to support project-related activities, such as the distribution of aid. They were therefore either discontinued, or replaced by PIDRB's groups, when ZOA withdrew. PIDRB's NDCs were conceptualised as more sustainable and independent from the project (IECA 2006). They were intended to manage their own projects, but had modest achievements.

The distinct approaches and practices of IECA and ZOA highlight some of the issues that determine the way interventions unfolded and were received on the ground. On the one hand, ZOA set the scene for aid interventions and contributed to IECA's capacity by initially working with/through it. The broader approach of PIDRB's NDC groups and their achievements, albeit modest, appear to have benefited from ZOA's previous experience with Community Management Committees. On the other hand, ZOA also set a precedent of expectations with local people that discredited PIDRB's approach and position. Notably, IECA struggled to challenge ZOA's free distribution approach, which it could not keep up. This was summed up by members of PIDRB's staff as follows:

> PIDRB had many difficulties in establishing itself here because those villages that belonged to ZOA would receive free seeds and food whereas the IECA PIDRB villages would only get seeds on a reimbursement basis. Our only way out of this situation in the end, was the withdrawal of ZOA. Then the communities started valuing our capacity-building activities and the project won its ground.[7]

IECA's position thus appears to have been consolidated more by the departure of ZOA as a competitor in social assistance than from the perceived value of PIDRB's developmental approach.

Competing with the state

The relative absence of the state and its services from the lives of local people has also contributed to IECA's prominent role in social assistance. 'PIDRB is doing everything in Bunjei, from bridge building to vaccinations.'[8] Moreover, the breadth of its intervention in terms of geographical coverage and thematic focus was a response to the continued absence and dysfunction of local state institutions. IECA's local legitimacy was largely derived from filling this institutional void and providing tangible assistance to the local population.

PIDRB and its staff in Bunjei have become an alternative structure to the state for the provision of services. This represents what van der Haar (in Nuijten *et al.* 2004) terms an alternative 'claim to governance', which involves an assertion of acting for, and on behalf of, the common interests of the public. 'To a certain extent these claims exist in parallel fashion, but they may enter into contradiction in specific domains or at specific critical junctures' (ibid.: 108). This claim to governance is observable in the expectations formulated by local people and local government. Communities expect more of PIDRB than just the standard distribution of aid. Programme staff are often called upon to help resolve individual or collective conflicts. The human rights advisor, for instance, is frequently approached to mediate community and family disputes, because he is perceived as a neutral party.[9]

The coexistence of the state and PIDRB results in some dynamics of accommodation and complementarity, but is mostly dominated by competition and confrontation. This underscores the tense relationship that has developed between the two. The local administration finds itself in competition with IECA's staff for people's recognition and authority. IECA's conflict mediation and resolution role is telling. One instance entailed a land dispute involving a community near the forest belt of Gove, which was established by the colonial administration in 1971 for the production of eucalyptus as raw material for a paper factory. The factory was never built, and the local population has since then been collecting firewood from the area. Recently, the forest belt was bought, allegedly by three military generals, and access by local populations has been blocked. Small but violent incidents between local security guards and community members have occurred. PIDRB's staff was asked by the community to intervene. It became their negotiator for controlled access to the area.[10] Local residents perceive staff as having important negotiating power and being trustworthy in representing their interests vis-à-vis external actors. These expectations not only reflect and consolidate IECA's legitimacy with local populations, but also highlight its competition with other relevant local institutions – in this case the traditional authorities and the state. The traditional authorities were considered to have little power or influence outside their communities, whilst it was feared that the local state administration would side with the military men. A senior member of DASEP summed this up as follows:

> We work with human rights issues in our communities. This is basically about civic education and may be perceived as challenging the government. Community members in Bunjei will more easily go to our human rights adviser to resolve conflicts than to the local government or even the traditional authorities. People will turn to those that are close to them, and that is us. But when they express gratitude or appreciation for IECA or NGOs, the government gets angry.[11]

Modest dynamics of accommodation and complementarity developed in areas where the state's lack of capacity and IECA's added value was promptly recognised by government representatives. The local administration frequently turns to IECA to address local problems, rather than to the state's administrative hierarchy. When asked about the government priorities for the development of Bunjei, the local administrator stressed the importance of agricultural support, but promptly identified this to be something for NGOs, and PIDRB in particular, given the lack of government capacity.[12] Examples of complementarity include one-off collaboration initiatives with state services, resulting from the commitment of specific individuals, rather than of formal institutional links. For instance, the government's water brigade has recently taken over from PIDRB the task of treating a number of boreholes.

Politicisation of the Bunjei arena

The role of IECA as a *de facto* competitor of the state in the governance of local services is strongly linked to politicisation processes in the aid arena. Such politicisation mostly has a weakening effect on IECA's position. The underlying mistrust between the local government and IECA relates to the role of partisan politics. On the one hand, IECA is suspicious that governing practices and decisions of the local administration are dictated by MPLA party interests. In Angola, a strong interconnection remains between the government and the ruling MPLA party. An overwhelming majority of local state administrative posts are filled by MPLA party members, as in the case of Bunjei. On the other hand, because of IECA's perceived links to UNITA, it is seen as promoting anti-government sentiment.

Such politicisation processes are expressed in the dynamics of the co-option of social assistance interventions. This co-option has been blatantly directed at PIDRB:

> Many people will talk of the aid they received in the past as being Government aid or aid by the [MPLA] party and this is the fault of the leaders who say that it was the party that sent organisation x or y to come and help the people. We give a lot of information about the funding sources of PIDRB, so that people know where it's really coming from.

PIDRB staff recount that, after the 2008 legislative elections, when they went to congratulate the administrator for the victory of his party, he simply responded that it was thanks to PIDRB's work that the population voted for MPLA – they were helping to implement the government's development agenda.[13]

Tensions arising from politicisation processes have important repercussions for IECA's claims to governance. When the government launched a competition for teachers to be incorporated into the education system, only two of PIDRB's pool of 35 government-trained teachers were selected. The explanation amongst IECA staff was that priority had been given to MPLA supporters, given that the only two selected candidates from PIDRB were also the two that were MPLA party secretaries in their communities. This episode highlights the limited capacity of IECA to exercise certain rule-making or enforcement aspects of governance, in spite of its considerable legitimacy vis-à-vis local people.

IECA's future role

The examination of IECA's role relative to those of other aid organisations, such as ZOA and state institutions, has shown how the daily practices and performance of other actors co-shape people's perceptions and expectations of IECA. It substantiates the perspective that legitimacy is a constant process of negotiation rather than a given quality, and that it is therefore problematic to engineer. This has implications for IECA's future role in Bunjei. Although it has carved out an important function in social assistance, its legitimacy is contingent upon its ability to manage and adapt to ongoing challenges to its legitimacy, such as politicisation dynamics and state competition.

How the remaining institutional landscape develops in the coming years is crucial in this respect. Although there appears to be little interest by other aid actors in the region, the growing importance of the civil service as a livelihood option for the local population is transforming the local context. Large-scale recruitment of civil servants has changed the job market considerably. Several workers of PIDRB have moved over to government institutions. Many have taken up part-time jobs as school teachers or have enrolled in night classes to obtain the education level required for teaching, with the aim of joining the state education services full time. In addition, the emergence of private sector jobs, albeit modest, is encouraging locals to leave their communities. Many are key activists involved in PIDRB's activities and their departure affects implementation efforts. Although IECA's management recognises the positive impact these developments represent for the region, in discussions about the organisation's future and its role in reconstruction efforts, the loss of qualified personnel to the civil service was framed as a threat to its survival. Given that local staff have been a key source of IECA's legitimacy and relationships with local actors, it is likely that these changes will affect legitimisation processes and its future position.

In addition to increased competition from the state, IECA is also faced with a changing strategy of its donors, including a shift in focus towards community development and a reduction in funds. This will probably affect IECA's ability to sustain its tangible sources of legitimacy and require that it reassess its focus and role in the local context.

Conclusion

In conflict-affected societies, it is important for the analytical understanding of service delivery to map institutional landscapes because they tend to be particularly fragmented in such contexts. This chapter has looked at the role of a local church – IECA – as a subset of the multiple institutional arrangements for social assistance that prevail in post-war settings. I have focused on the social assistance work of IECA, and specifically on its integrated development programme in Bunjei – PIDRB.

From an analysis of the reconstruction arena in Bunjei, IECA has emerged as especially prominent in service delivery, with considerable recognition by local people. Following a typical case of institutional multiplicity in the immediate post-conflict period, it was the only aid provider that remained during the ensuing reconstruction phase. This stands in contrast with dominant discourses on aid in conflict and post-conflict that centre on the work of international agencies and that reduce the role of the churches in Angola's reconstruction to peacebuilding. IECA's historical role in social assistance and rural development remained essential in the post-war period and in the context of Bunjei's continued marginalisation. This chapter has sought to understand how this position evolved.

The analysis has shown that this position has involved important legitimisation and de-legitimisation processes. Overall, IECA's case in Bunjei supports the argument that church organisations have close links to local societies from which they leverage significant recognition and trust from local people. Such legitimacy comes from a variety of sources. Some are inherent in its identity and history, including its religious basis and evangelical mission. Others are linked to its organisational culture, involving a long tradition and historical performance in social work, as well as to its internal organisational practices, such as investment in staff capacity, accountability mechanisms and support networks. The behaviour and motivation of IECA's staff came out as a defining element in determining the ways in which the organisation is perceived by local actors, and the kinds of expectations it generates.

The influence of the actions and performance of other actors in the local arena of governance of social services also emerged as central to IECA's legitimacy building. The perceived quality of PIDRB's assistance evolved against a backdrop of inadequate and slack state services, and the absence of significant and lasting alternative service providers. In the initial post-war phase, IECA's position was challenged by the presence of other aid agencies. Different organisational identities and missions translated into distinct implementation strategies which had a bearing on local perceptions on the ground. As the case of ZOA Refugee Care illustrated, its approach set standards that IECA could not maintain, such as the free distribution of assistance. It was the removal of this competition that eventually consolidated IECA's legitimacy, rather than its development-oriented approach.

I have also shown that legitimacy is differentiated – it is in the eye of the beholder. While IECA enjoys significant legitimacy amongst local communities, its relationship with local government is dominated by strong competition. IECA has come to represent an alternative 'claim to governance' to the local government in Bunjei. Such competition is intertwined with politicisation dynamics of the local aid arena, and has a strong de-legitimising effect for IECA vis-à-vis the state. IECA is fiercely opposed by local government for its alleged links to UNITA. This affects its capacity to exercise certain enforcement aspects of governance, as seen from the exclusion of its qualified teachers from the recruitment for the state education system.

The dynamics of competition mean that IECA's position is under constant negotiation and is thus likely to change considerably in the future. Perhaps the most relevant question for the development of Bunjei is how IECA and local state services will affect each other's legitimacy in the future. Until recently, IECA's replacement of the social assistance function of local government may have undermined the legitimacy of the state. Currently, the government is attracting IECA's qualified staff by providing competitive employment conditions. While this may weaken IECA's capacity and position, it has the potential to improve the quality and legitimacy of state service institutions, for instance by making services more efficient.

Acknowledgements

The author wishes to thank Bram J. Jansen, Gerrit-Jan van Uffelen, Ian Christoplos and Didier Péclard for their constructive comments on an earlier version of this chapter. All responsibility remains with the author. Further thanks to the staff of PIDRB and IECA in Bunjei, and to all the interviewees from the local communities in Bunjei.

Notes

1 In 2008, DASEP's portfolio included 40 projects in 15 of Angola's 18 provinces.
2 Evangelical Sinodal Angolan Church.
3 The term 'mais velhos' means elderly and is used as a sign of respect. Informal communication with human rights advisor, 9 October 2008, Bunjei.
4 Interview, 10 October 2008, Bunjei.
5 Interview with head of DASEP – IECA, 10 February 2008, Luanda.
6 These are usually made up of the community leader (the *soba*) and his advisors (the *sekulus*).
7 Interview on 20 May 2008, Bunjei.
8 See Endnote 5.
9 Interview with human rights advisor of PIDRB, 29 May 2008, Bunjei.
10 Interview with PIDRB staff member, 20 and 30 May 2008, Bunjei.
11 See Endnote 5.
12 Interview, 9 October 2008, Bunjei.
13 Informal communication with PIDRB staff, 6 and 7 October 2008, Bunjei.

References

Bakewell, O. (2000) 'Uncovering Local Perspectives on Humanitarian Assistance and Its Outcomes'. *Disasters*, 24: 103–116.

Bellina, S., Darbon, D., Eriksen, S. S. and Sending, O. J. (2009) *The Legitimacy of the State in Fragile Situations. Report for the OECD DAC International Network on Conflict and Fragility*, Oslo: NORAD. 1–44.

Birmingham, D. (2006) *Empire in Africa: Angola and its neighbours*, Ohio, Ohio University.

Brinkerhoff, D. (2005) *Organisational Legitimacy, Capacity and Capacity Development*, Discussion Paper No 58A, Maastricht: European Centre for Development Policy Management. 1–16.

Christoplos, I. and Hilhorst, D. (2009) *Human Security and Capacity in Fragile States*, Occasional paper 01, Disaster Studies, Wageningen University. 1–52.

Comerford, M. G. (2005) *The Peaceful Face of Angola: Biography of a Peace Process (1991–2002)*, Luanda, Angola: Michael G. Comerford.

Comerford, M. G. (2009) 'Building Peace and Advocating for Human Rights: Angolan Churches'. In Vidal, N. and Chabal, P. (eds) *Southern Africa: Civil Society, Politics and Donor Strategies. Angola and its neighbours – South Africa, Namibia, Mozambique, Democratic Republic of Congo and Zimbabwe*. Luanda, Lisbon: Media XXI, Firmamento. 161–184.

Douma, N. and Van Der Haar, G. (2010) 'Service Delivery in Post-conflict Settings'. In Noor, M. and Al, E. (eds) *Multi-Stakeholder Processes, Service Delivery and State Institutions. Theoretical Framework and Methodologies Working Paper*. http://www.psdnetwork.nl/index. php Peace Security and Development Network.

Gabinete Do Plano, G. (2009) *Informação sobre o Município do Chipindo, Governo da Província da Huíla*. http://www.huilaweb.org/HuilaWeb/displayconteudo.do2?numero=19656.

Hauck, V. A. (2010) 'The Role of Churches in Creating Social Capital and Improving Governance in Papua New Guinea: Lessons for Working in Fragile Situations'. *Public Administration and Development*, 30: 49–65.

Hays, R. A. (2002) 'Habitat for Humanity: Building Social Capital Through Faith Based Service'. *Journal of Urban Affairs*, 24: 247–269.

Henderson, L. W. (1990) *A igreja em Angola. Um rio com várias correntes*. Luanda: Além-Mar. O Barquinho.

Hesselbein, G., Golooba-Mutebi, F. and Putzel, J. (2006) *Economic and Political Foundations of State Making in Africa: Understanding State Reconstruction*. Working Paper 3, Working Paper Series 2, London: Crisis States Research Centre, LSE. 1–40.

Hilhorst, D. (2005) *Aid under Fire: People, Principles and Practices of Humanitarian Aid in Angola. Vidi Research Proposal*. Wageningen: Wageningen University.

Hilhorst, D. (2007) *Saving Lives or Saving Societies? Realities of Relief and Reconstruction. Innaugural Lecture*. Wageningen: Wageningen University.

Hilhorst, D. and Jansen, B. J. (2010) 'Humanitarian Space as Arena: A Perspective on the Everyday Politics of Aid'. *Development and Change*, 41: 1117–1139.

Hilhorst, D. and Schmiemann, N. (2002) 'Humanitarian Principles and Organisational Culture: Everyday Practice in Médecins Sans Frontieres-Holland'. *Development in Practice*, 12: 490–500.

Hilhorst, D. and Serrano, M. (2010) 'The Humanitarian Arena in Angola, 1975–2008'. *Disasters*, 34: S183–201.

Hilhorst, D., Christoplos, I. and Van Der Haar, G. (2010) 'Reconstruction "From Below": A New Magic Bullet or Shooting from the Hip?' *Third World Quarterly*, 31: 1107–1124.

IECA (2006) *Proposta do Projecto. Programa Integrado de Desenvolvimento do Bunjei*. IECA. Lubango: DASEP.

Jensen, S. K. and Pestana, N. (2010) *The Role of the Churches in Poverty Reduction in Angola*. Bergen: Chr. Michelsen Institute.

Messiant, C. (2004) 'Angola: Woe to the Vanquished'. In Weissman, F. (ed.) *In the Shadow of 'Just Wars'. Violence, Politics and Humanitarian Action*, pp. 109–136. Ithaca, New York: Cornell University Press.

Nuijten, M., Anders, G., Van Gastel, J., Van Der Haar, G., Van Nijnatten, C. and Warner, J. (2004) 'Governance in Action. Some Theoretical and Practical Reflections on a ey Concept'. In Kalb, D., Pansters, W. and Siebers, H. (eds) *Globalization and Development. Themes and Concepts in Current Research*. Dordrecht: Kluwer Academic Publishers. 103–127.

Santos, G. (2008) *Mapeamento dos actores da educação: relatório*. Rede Educação Para Todos da Sociedade Civil.

Schot, S. (2005) *Evaluation Report of ZOA's Programme for the Resettlement and Reintegration of IDP's and Returnees in Caconda and Chipindo*. Lubango: ZOA Refugee Care.

Schubert, B. (1999) 'Os Protestantes na Guerra Angolana depois da Independência'. *Lusotopie*, 405–413.

Serrano, M. (2012) *Strengthening Institutions or Institutionalising Weaknesses? Interactions Between Aid and Local Institutions in Huíla Province, Angola*. Doctorate, Wageningen University.

Shaxson, N., Neves, J. and Pacheco, F. (2008) *Drivers of Change, Angola*. London: DFID.

Ter Haar, G. and Ellis, S. (2006) 'The Role of Religion in Development: Towards a New Relationship between the European Union and Africa'. *The European Journal of Development Research*, 18: 351–367.

Van Der Molen, I. and Stel, N. (2010) 'The Changing Role of the State and State-society Relations. Multi-stakeholder Processes, Service Delivery and State Institutions'. Theoretical Framework and Methodologies Working Paper. *Peace Security and Development Network* 00030. Clingendael: Clingendael Institute.

Walkup, M. (1997) 'Policy Dysfunction in Humanitarian Organizations: The Role of Coping Strategies, Institutions, and Organizational Culture'. *Journal of Refugee Studies*, 10: 37–60.

ZOA and ADESPOV (2002) *Projecto de Emergência com Deslocados e Reassentados em Bunjei: Relatório de Progresso, Setembro a Novembro 2002'*, Lubango: ZOA Refugee Care, ADESPOV.

10 Flying below the Radar

Inter-ethnic marriages in Sri Lanka's war zone

Timmo Gaasbeek

Introduction

For more than a quarter of a century, Sri Lanka was plagued by violent conflict between militants fighting for a separate Tamil state in the country's north and east and forces loyal to the (Sinhala-majority) Sri Lankan state.[1] While factors such as skewed development, state repression and violence, and socio-political marginalization of the country's peripheries have played important roles in shaping the conflict (Goodhand and Klem 2005), it is undeniable that ethnicity dominates interpretations and representations of the Sri Lankan conflict (Frerks, Chapter 2 this volume).

As is widely the case in research on conflict and disaster, the focus of most research on the Sri Lankan conflict has been either on agony, suffering and survival, or on wider political, economic and social causes, implications and discourses. In the process, people are reduced to pitiful victims, skilful survivors or mere pawns on the chessboard of larger actors – their lives determined by the conflict. However, there are many aspects of normalcy that continue during crisis and that need to be accounted for (Hilhorst 2007, Ring 2006). Although conditions may be severely constraining, people still get married, babies are still born, and children still play cricket. In order to understand how people shape their everyday lives in such a context – and in order to understand grassroot-level possibilities for (ethnic) peace – there is a need to look at the smaller spaces of relationships and interactions which both link to, and depart from, the wider context of ethnicized conflict.[2] While there is a wealth of documentation on such things as peacebuilding, conflict resolution, the role of non-governmental organisations (NGOs) in Sri Lanka, there is very little that connects these with everyday interactions.

This chapter looks at specific kinds of relationships and interactions in Kottiyar Pattu, a part of Sri Lanka's war zone: inter-ethnic marriages. Though mixed marriages are not very common, there are enough for almost everyone in Kottiyar Pattu to personally know a mixed couple. By their very nature, such couples bridge the ethnic boundaries associated with Sri Lanka's conflict. This forces them (and the people around them) to deal with ethnicity and its complications. While intermarriage is 'expected to promote the social cohesion of societies in which different ethnic groups live together' (Gündüz-HoÐsgör and Smits 2002: 419), things may be very different in a context of violent ethnicized conflict. It is worth asking (1) how the conflict influences intermarriage trends; (2) who gets involved in mixed marriages; (3) what happens to those who step into such a marriage; and (4) how mixed couples deal with being between two communities.

The chapter is based on in-depth ethnographic research that was conducted between 2003 and 2008 and focused on everyday inter-ethnic interaction in Sri Lanka's war zone (Gaasbeek 2010). Also relevant to note is that the author himself is married to a Sri Lankan wife from a very multi-ethnic family.

I will first review existing literature on intermarriage, followed by a brief description of the research area. This is followed by a description of empirical findings, which aims to answer the first three questions above. The chapter concludes with a reflection on the fourth question, and on what inter-ethnic marriages teach us about ethnicity.

Previous research on intermarriage

Throughout the twentieth century, the attention given to the topic of inter-group marriage in the social sciences has been limited in focus and in methodology. It has largely stayed within the domains of western sociology and demography. This often involved statistical analysis requiring sufficiently large and reliable data sets, and thus the bulk of research on intermarriage has been conducted in developed countries, particularly the United States. Anthropological research has for a long time tended to focus on bounded groups, rather than on people on the definitional margins of such groups, and while ethnicity is an increasingly important element in the study of development interventions and in the larger fields of economic and political science, intermarried people are largely irrelevant to these debates.

It is striking to note how little research on intermarriage has involved actually asking mixed couples themselves how they deal with being in a mixed marriage: among just more than 80 articles that I found about intermarriage, fewer than fifteen are based on interviews with mixed couples. Of these, three use qualitative information only anecdotally. Another four articles deal with a single research project (Golden 1953, 1954, 1958, 1959).

While intermarriage has been observed to occur in conflict-prone countries, such as Rwanda (Magnarella 2005) and the former Yugoslavia (Botev 1994, Oberschall 2000, Pickering 2006), I have been unable to find any research on how mixed couples cope in a context of violent conflict. On the other hand, Golden's research on fifty interracial couples in the city of Philadelphia and the (sometimes severe) hostility that they encountered proved valuable.

With respect to content, research on intermarriage has largely focused on three elements. The first element deals with explaining why intermarriage occurs in a given marriage market. Explanatory factors are arranged along two axes: opportunity and preferences (Gray 1987). Opportunity is related to the relative share of a group in the total marriage market: if the proportion of in-group potential spouses is small, the chances of meeting a suitable in-group spouse are reduced, and opportunities for chance encounters with otherwise suitable out-group spouses are increased. Preference is related to 'the combination of social barriers and social distance between groups' (ibid.: 368). Kalmijn (1998) further refined the preference axis by distinguishing between individual preferences and preferences of third parties: the family, the surrounding community (religious, ethnic, caste) and the state. Gray's model is useful in understanding how many people inter-marry, but it focuses on in-marriage: both opportunity and preference rates dictate to what extent people marry *within* their own group, and intermarriage forms the leftover component comprising those unable or unwilling to marry within their own group. Blau *et al.* (1982) highlighted that heterogeneity within the (sub-) ethnic category leads to an increase in intermarriage, because the in-group is comparatively small. Based on Simmel's insight that 'the social structure of complex societies and communities entails multiple group affiliations with inter-secting boundaries', Blau *et al.* (1984: 585) further stressed that intersecting group affiliations (of, for example, education and social status) contribute to intermar-riage. Ethnicity is not the only factor that people look at when selecting a spouse: if there are many people in the same ethnic group but few of the same educational level or social status, the likelihood of someone looking for a spouse of the same educational or social status but a different ethnic group increases. Kalmijn turns the argument around: '[p]eople have a tendency to marry within their social group or to marry a person who is close to them in status' (1998: 395). If people have intersecting group affiliations, homogamy along the lines of one group affili-ation automatically causes intermarriage along the lines of other group affiliations. For some, ethnicity is the overriding identifier, for others religion, for others education, and for yet others it is social status.

The second element of research into intermarriage focuses on broader patterns of societal integration between groups. Results are varied: in some cases, inter-marrying minority groups were found to assimilate into the majority group. In cases where there is no really dominant group, one may find one or several 'melting pots', in which differences are mitigated and a joint new identity is built. Thus, among white immigrants of highly varied ethno-national origin in the United States, three overarching groups formed: one Protestant, one Catholic, and one Jewish (Kennedy 1944, 1952). In yet other cases, intermarriage does not fundamentally alter pre-existing group identities, because the group of inter-married people is not significant enough to pose a challenge to group identities (Okun 2004: 185, Dart 1985: 139–147). The impact of intermarriage on society at large thus depends to a very large extent on the nature of society itself.

The third element of research into intermarriage is in a sense somewhat patho-logical in focus, asking to what extent mixed couples and their children are more prone to trouble (divorce, marital unhappiness, marginalization) than other couples (Roer-Strier and Ben Ezra 2006).

I am only aware of two locations where inter-ethnic marriage has been studied in Sri Lanka: the mixed-ethnic village of Panama, in the far south of the Eastern Province, and a cluster of 'Coastal Vedda' villages near Vakarai, directly south of

Kottiyar Pattu. When Yalman visited Panama in 1955, he found an ethnically hybrid community: 'a halfway mark had been reached in kinship terms; in terms of caste the two systems had been merged without difficulty; and even in worship an excellent solution had been found' (1967: 319). However, an externally induced process of ethnic separation was already visible, for example, through the setting up of separate Tamil and Sinhala schools by the government. Yalman expected this process to be accelerated by the Sinhala Only law of 1956, the riots of 1956 (which saw violence not far from Panama) and 1958, and the gathering momentum of Tamil protest in the early 1960s (ibid.: 324, n.8). Almost half a century later, ethnic separation was virtually complete, especially for the younger generation. To all intents and purposes, Panama is now a Sinhala-Buddhist village with some Tamil families living on the margins (Abeyrathne 2003).

In the Vedda villages studied by Dart, he came across a limited number of marriages between Veddas and Tamils (of generally higher status) that were generally accepted, but did very little to pull the Veddas out of their situation of marginalization and poverty (1985: 139–147). Importantly, Dart found that poverty allowed Sri Lankans of all ethnic backgrounds to more or less dispense with the prescribed norms of status and separation, thus making inter-ethnic and inter-caste marriage among the marginalized easier than among better-off households.

Kottiyar Pattu

The area known as Kottiyar Pattu (see Figure 10.1) covers three administrative divisions in Trincomalee District, on Sri Lanka's east coast.

It covers an area of about 650 km^2 and is inhabited by approximately 90,000 people: almost 44,000 Tamils, a little over 37,000 Muslims and almost 9,000 Sinhalese. The Muslims are concentrated in the towns of Muthur and Thoppur and a small cluster of villages in between, the Sinhalese are concentrated in a string of settlements in the south-western quarter, and the Tamils inhabit villages in the rest of Kottiyar Pattu. Tamils and Muslims have lived in the area for centuries; Sinhalese only moved into the area in the 1950s when the Allai Extension Scheme was developed. This irrigation-cum-settlement scheme was mostly settled with landless Sinhala farmers from the south and centre of Sri Lanka.

Until 2006, Kottiyar Pattu was a sideshow in the larger conflict between the Sri Lankan armed forces and Tamil militants: an insurgent logistics trail ran through the area, some coastal villages saw smuggling of supplies, and several hundred people were recruited into the ranks of the militants over the years. Although there had been a few small incidents of violence in preceding years, the watershed riots of 1983 largely passed unnoticed in Kottiyar Pattu. Things really got bad after the Liberation Tigers of Tamil (LTTE) massacred over a hundred worshippers at Sri Lanka's holiest Buddhist shrine in Anuradhapura in May 1985. Two weeks later, a wave of violence was orchestrated that resulted in the destruction of every single Tamil village within walking distance of the Sinhala villages in Kottiyar Pattu. A few months later, the remaining Tamil villages in the area were

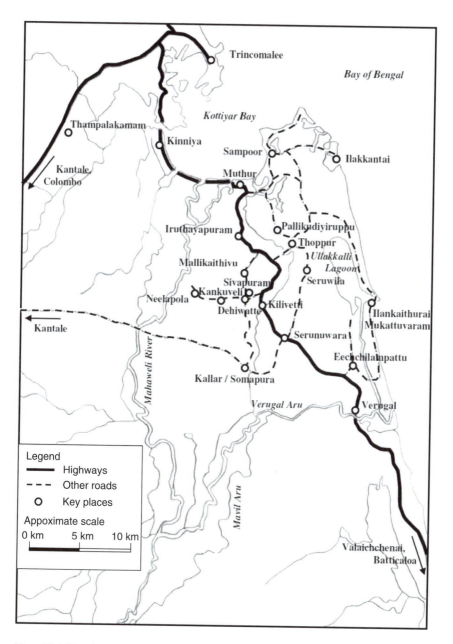

Figure 10.1 Sketch map of Kottiyar Pattu.

destroyed by the Sri Lankan armed forces.[3] In the process, about 200 people died, almost all of them Tamil civilians. The entire Tamil population was displaced and – significantly – many found refuge with Muslim acquaintances in the towns of Muthur and Thoppur. Over the next two years, there was a string of massacres of Tamil civilians and landmine attacks against Sinhalese civilians. In 1987, the Indian Peace Keeping Force arrived to monitor a ceasefire. This changed the balance of power, and one result was that half of the Sinhalese population was chased away by Tamil militant attacks; 1987 also saw the first bout of Tamil-Muslim violence. The next period of severe violence was in 1990, when several hundred people were killed, and almost the entire population of the area was displaced for several months up to several years. From this moment onwards, a stalemate developed. Gradually, the landscape became increasingly militarized. Ever more army camps, bunkers and checkpoints were put up, and boundaries between areas controlled by the government and areas controlled by the LTTE were increasingly demarcated. A ceasefire between 2002 and 2006 caused a substantial improvement in relations between Tamils and Sinhalese, but because the LTTE tried to exercise increasing control over the Muslim population, relations between Muslims and Tamils soured. In 2003 there were Muslim-Tamil riots, followed by further periods of tension in 2005 and 2006.

The final phase of Sri Lanka's war began in Kottiyar Pattu. From late 2005, tensions had gradually built up and both sides had started preparing for war. The blockage of the main irrigation channel in Kottiyar Pattu by the LTTE in June 2006 finally became the pretext for open warfare. By the end of the year, the entire area was under the control of the government. While the war raged on for another two years in the north of the country, normalcy slowly returned to most of Kottiyar Pattu, although several thousand Tamils have been permanently denied access to their original villages.

The occurrence of inter-ethnic marriages in Kottiyar Pattu

Inter-ethnic marriages were not common in Sri Lanka even before violent conflict broke out. Fernando (1980: 434) estimated that about 3 per cent of all couples registered between 1960 and 1975 were of mixed ethnicity, with a heavy bias towards urban areas. It is unlikely that ideals of ethnic homogeneity were the sole or even the primary reason for this low percentage. The vast majority of Sri Lankans grow up in ethnically homogenous social groups. They find their spouses within their own community as defined by language, religion, caste, class and, to a lesser extent, even blood ties. Especially in rural areas, many Sri Lankans will not even consider ethnicity as a factor in spouse choice, as generally they have very few potential spouses of other ethnicities in their social milieu.

Where marriage was concerned, Kottiyar Pattu was a very conservative rural area until at least the 1980s, and the intermarriage rate was well below the national average. Currently, there are an estimated 120 mixed couples in Kottiyar Pattu, which gives an intermarriage rate of about 0.5 per cent. This pattern seems consistent with most other parts of Sri Lanka's Eastern Province. In the (Muslim-Tamil) mixed-ethnic region around Akkaraipattu (about 130 km south of Kottiyar Pattu), Dennis McGilvray rarely encountered mixed marriages during ethnographic fieldwork that spanned four decades: he met some Roman Catholic couples of Sinhala-Tamil background, and a very few Tamil women who had married Muslims and converted to Islam (McGilvray 2008).[4] However, one of my research assistants, who himself comes from Akkaraipattu, pointed out one noteworthy difference: in Akkaraipattu, intermarriage is generally considered an embarrassing topic that should not be discussed in public while in Kottiyar Pattu many people spoke freely, and neutrally, about it. During the years that I lived in the east of Sri Lanka, I met only a handful of mixed couples in the towns of Batticaloa, Trincomalee and Kalmunai, and found one enclave of Sinhala-Tamil mixed families near the town of Valaichchenai which had developed when Sinhalese labourers working in the Valaichchenai paper factory married local wives.

The number of mixed couples may be small, but their geographical spread means that, with exception of the Tamil villages in former LTTE territory, every village in Kottiyar Pattu has one or more mixed couples. This means that almost everybody in the area knows at least one mixed couple. Table 10.1 presents the estimated breakdown of mixed couples living in Kottiyar Pattu by the classificatory ethnicity[5] of the spouses.

Apart from the mixed couples living in Kottiyar Pattu, about forty mixed couples with one or both spouses originating from Kottiyar Pattu live elsewhere. About 25 of these couples are Roman Catholics with one Tamil and one Sinhala spouse; they left during the war. The rest married an 'outsider' spouse (mostly Sinhala, in some cases Muslim) and either moved to his or her home town or to a new location altogether. These couples are excluded from the analysis because I was unable to gather enough information about them.

Historically, intermarriage seems to have been even rarer than it is now. People to whom I spoke could only tell me of three inter-ethnic marriages that took place in the first half of the twentieth century. One involved an English officer based in Trincomalee who married a Vedda woman from the area; the second involved a son from this marriage who married a Tamil woman; and the third

Table 10.1 Estimated breakdown of mixed couples in Kottiyar Pattu by classificatory ethnicity of spouses

Ethnicity of husband	Ethnicity of wife	Number of couples
Muslim	Sinhala	< 5
Sinhala	Muslim	< 5
Muslim	Tamil	50–65
Tamil	Muslim	< 5
Sinhala	Tamil	50–65
Tamil	Sinhala	< 5
Total: approximately 110–140		

involved a Sinhala-Tamil intermarriage. From about 1930, a group of migrant Catholic fishermen from Negombo on Sri Lanka's west coast started returning annually to the mouth of the Mahaweli River, near Muthur. As the Catholics of Muthur and this group actively participated in each other's church festivals, it is not unthinkable that some of the fishermen married local women (who were of the same caste and religion).[6] It must be remembered, though, that there were very few Sinhalese in Kottiyar Pattu at this time. There were hardly any intermarriages between Muslims and Tamils either. This had nothing to do with Muslim-Tamil enmity, which did not exist. Until at least the mid–1980s, almost all marriages were arranged, and candidates were generally only considered suitable if they were of the same caste and religion. Several elderly people told me that close inter-ethnic, inter-religious and sometimes even inter-caste friendships were not uncommon before the war, but few people would ever consider marrying their child outside their own community. So-called 'love marriages' (even between spouses of the same ethnicity) were very rare, and nearly always resulted in elopement. In order to make sure that adolescent women did not get up to any mischief, they were closely guarded from the time that they attained age until their wedding day. The women were generally kept inside the cluster of compounds where the extended family lived. If they left this area, they were virtually always chaperoned and if a girl happened to walk alone, she would do so cautiously. An elderly lady once told me that 'earlier, when a Muslim girl walked on the road and a man came her way, she would go into the nearest house so that she would not be seen. Now they go on motorbikes.' It was thus almost impossible for a girl to strike up a conversation with a stranger, let alone start a romantic relationship, *unless the stranger was so familiar that he could casually come to the compound.* The only strangers who could do so were members of migrant harvesting gangs, who often kept coming back to the same families at harvest time, and itinerant traders.

The only times when adolescents could really mingle without too much social control was during religious festivals and weddings. Wedding ceremonies in particular were often used to plan future weddings. Weddings brought suitable people together who would normally not meet each other very often. Particularly among some of the Tamil service castes, spouses were sourced from same-caste villages that could be up to 200 km away, including Pottuvil on the south-east coast and Jaffna in the north of the country. Several Muslim families also had long-lasting marriage links with Muslim communities along the entire east coast. First-generation Sinhala settlers often sourced spouses for their children from their home areas that could be over 250 km away from Kottiyar Pattu. Itinerant traders or labourers played a vital role in spreading information about available potential brides or grooms. Regional Hindu, Buddhist, Roman Catholic and (Sufi) Muslim religious festivals brought comparatively large groups of people together who were not necessarily suitable marriage partners for reasons of caste, class or even religion. The festivals thus provided virtually the only opportunity for subversion of the mores about choosing a spouse.

Although the settlement of several thousand Sinhalese in the early 1950s increased inter-ethnic interaction, not many marriages resulted because all the settlers were married couples with children. With the settlers, however, came some itinerant traders and shopkeepers, of whom several found Tamil wives.

In the late 1970s and early 1980s, several second-generation Sinhalese settlers intermarried. Some people in these marriages were themselves children of mixed couples. Among these were about two dozen Roman Catholic couples from farming families, who all left the area after the war broke out.

After the ceasefire of 2002, inter-ethnic interaction became a lot easier. A small surge in mixed marriages followed, especially between third-generation Sinhalese settlers and Tamils, but also between soldiers posted in Tamil villages and local girls.

While there may have been earlier marriages on the periphery of Muthur town (I was told of Muslim-Tamil couples living there, but have never met any of them), Muslim-Tamil intermarriages started becoming more common only from the late 1980s onwards, *after* Muslim-Tamil relations had become seriously strained following periods of Muslim-Tamil violence.

An intuitive assumption would be that ethnicized conflict and the accompanying hardening of ethnic boundaries will lead to a significant decrease in inter-marriage rates. This happened in places like Rwanda and the former Yugoslavia, where pre-conflict intermarriage was fairly common and accepted. The same thing happened in the village of Panama, particularly after an army camp was placed in the village in the late 1980s (Abeyrathne 2003). In Kottiyar Pattu, however, the ethnic conflict paradoxically was a *direct contributing factor* to an increase in intermarriage rates, together with the general development of the area involving an influx of traders, labourers and settlers, and the development of education and infrastructure.

The emancipating role played by the war (both with regard to inter-ethnic and inter-caste marriages) should not be underestimated. The experience of displacement (for Tamils), as well as the experience of being posted in Tamil areas (for Sinhala soldiers), tore people away from norms that traditionally bound them (Golden 1959: 273) and brought people into touch with others whom they would otherwise not have met. Most of the time, this had devastating consequences, but for some people, it proved to be an opportunity.

Besides, the high risk for Tamil men of getting arrested at checkpoints or in Muslim or Sinhala settlements substantially increased the mobility of Tamil women who suddenly became responsible for doing purchasing outside their own village. The gender differentiation in risks involved with this form of segregation (Golden 1958: 267) is the main factor to which the difference in intermarriage rates between Tamil women and Tamil men can be attributed.

Nine love stories: who intermarries, and how they cope

This section looks at the personal stories of nine mixed couples in Kottiyar Pattu whom I interviewed in detail: four Tamil-Sinhala, four Muslim-Tamil, and one Sinhala-Muslim. Based on their stories, I analyse what characterizes those engaged in mixed marriages, and how mixed couples shape their marriages.[7]

Meeting each other

The ways in which couples met each other are summarized in Table 10.2. As can be seen, the main factor that enabled the nine couples whom I interviewed to meet each other was geographical mobility. This enabled them to move outside their normal social environment and meet people they would otherwise not meet.

This pattern was the same among other mixed couples whom I heard about: either the husband had a mobile job (quite often as home guard or soldier) and worked in his future wife's village, or the wife met her future husband while she was in secondary school or while she went to town to do grocery shopping. The 2002 ceasefire meant that movement restrictions were lifted. This substantially increased opportunities for youth of different ethnic backgrounds to meet each other. Further, a number of inter-ethnic peacebuilding projects actively brought people together. In a few cases, this led to mixed marriages. Note the similarity with the list of facilitating factors identified by Golden: shared employment, interaction between customer/client and staff, meeting in schools, shared use of recreation facilities, meeting through mutual friends, and shared membership of an organisation (1959: 274).

Getting married, and the reactions of others

Eight of the nine mixed couples whom I interviewed were in so-called 'love marriages'; the ninth marriage was 'semi-arranged' – they fell in love and then suggested to their relatives to arrange the marriage (Corwin 1977: 827 n.6, De Munck 1996). This pattern was the same for all the other mixed marriages that

Table 10.2 Ways in which interviewed mixed couples met each other

Way in which the couple met	Frequency of occurrence	Husband mobile?	Wife mobile?
Husband itinerant labourer or itinerant trader, regular (work-related) visits to wife's family	3	Yes	No
Wife going to school, met husband in nearby shop during school breaks	2	No	Yes
Husband policeman, met wife on the road when she was going to secondary school	1	Yes	Yes
Wife regularly going grocery shopping in town, met husband in shop	1	No	Yes
Wife teacher, met husband (colleague's wife's brother) in colleague's house	1	No	Yes
Husband and wife both working in the same government institution	1	Yes	Yes
Total	9	5	6

people told me about. In a context where arranged marriages are still the norm, this is significant.

With exception of this last couple, all the couples whom I spoke to were married against the wishes of immediate relatives on at least one side. This disapproval may not always have been caused by mere prejudice; relatives may well have been genuinely concerned about the couple's welfare (see also Golden 1958: 268–269).

In order to get married without the approval of the immediate family, most couples eloped and were married elsewhere. Courtships were typically brief, between two and six months. This follows common practice in rural Sri Lanka, where being (young and) single and being married are auspicious states, but where being in a relationship without being married puts people at risk of serious damage to their reputation due to gossip and character assassination. It is not for nothing that Sri Lankans use the English term 'affair' (with all its negative connotations) to describe romantic relationships between people who are not married to each other, even those that are perfectly honourable. A number of the mixed couples had an extra reason to marry quickly. Some wanted to be married before their family found out, in order to prevent relatives who would object from physically ending the relationship. In one case where the courtship lasted longer, the girl's family sent her to the Middle East for a year as soon as they found out about the relationship. When she returned, her future husband picked her up from the airport and ran away with her.

The disapproval by immediate relatives is often so strong that they disown their son, daughter or sibling, at least temporarily. Sometimes this goes very far. One lady to whom I spoke was not only denied dowry and inheritance, but was even barred from attending her mother's funeral. In another case, a young mixed couple was widely accepted in both the husband's and the wife's village. Their wedding had been a very festive and very inter-ethnic celebration. The boy's mother, however, disapproved so strongly that he ended up committing suicide because he could not handle the pressure. A third couple attributed the chronic illness of the wife and other misfortunes to spells that relatives had arranged for a sorcerer to put on them.

Intermarriage in the face of opposition from the family is a clear act of defiance, and points to another important enabling factor for inter-ethnic marriages. In the interviews with mixed couples in Kottiyar Pattu, but also in conversations with intermarried friends and in-laws, I was often struck by the strong-willed and independent character of the wives in particular. The inter-ethnic relationships that I encountered were triggered by romantic love, not by deliberate reasoning. This fundamentally undermines claims for the causal explanatory value of demographic models: factors such as proximity or similarity in status or education make it easier for people to bump into each other, but do not explain why people fall in love and decide to go against a strong prevailing cultural norm.

In the case of Muslim men marrying non-Muslim women, the conversion of the wife to Islam is generally a precondition for acceptance in the wider Muslim community. Muslims whom I spoke to knew of two cases where the wife was suspected not to have converted, and of one or two cases where a Muslim girl had married a non-Muslim and given up her religion; the reaction was unanimously negative. Between Buddhists and Hindus, this is not such a big issue (most Sri Lankan Buddhists worship Hindu gods, and many Hindus have at least some respect for the Buddha). Among Catholics, marrying someone of another religion used to be as big an issue as it is for Muslims, until at least the 1980s.

While opposition by relatives has caused a lot of suffering for the mixed couples, it was – to some extent – to be expected. What is more interesting is the fact that, in the case of at least five of the nine couples to whom I spoke, one side of the family either did not enforce their disapproval of the marriage, or openly approved of it. This lack of disapproval (or rather, the quick acceptance of the marriage as a *fait accompli*) may have had to do with another factor: in seven of the nine cases, at least one of the parents of at least one of the spouses had passed away before the mixed marriage took place. In an eighth case, the wife's father was so conspicuously absent from the narrative that I suspect that he had either died or run away before the marriage of his daughter. Since the authority of the remaining parent (if there was one) over the son or daughter was weakened, the eldest male sibling or a maternal uncle had to take over part of this responsibility. These relatives, being in a less direct position of authority, generally disapproved, but were not able to exert as much negative pressure as a parent could have done. At the same time, an elopement relieved the uncle or brother of the responsibility of finding a good spouse, and – in cases where the woman was orphaned – of the responsibility of providing a dowry.

Being married

After marriage, eight of the nine couples whom I spoke to lived neolocally, that is, not with either the family of the husband or the family of the wife. One, a teacher, moved in with her husband, whose family had no problem with her. After a while, five of the neolocal couples ended up living in the husband's original village. Neolocal residence or residence in the husband's village is the general pattern among mixed couples in Kottiyar Pattu. The only exceptions I came across were about five to ten Sinhala youths who married Tamil girls from adjoining villages between about 2005 and 2007, and who settled in their wives' villages. Apart from the presence or absence of links with relatives, the place of residence of the couple was important for another reason: most villages in Kottiyar Pattu are largely mono-ethnic, and in many cases the choice of residence implies a choice of dominant ethnic self-representation of the couple.

The habitation patterns of mixed couples are interesting. Among Muslims and Tamils in the east of Sri Lanka, it is customary for couples to live in the wife's native village, often with or next door to the wife's parents. Land is generally divided among the daughters as dowry, and, when possible, the parents will try to build a dowry house for their daughters as well (McGilvray and Lawrence 2010).[8] Not moving into the wife's village means that the couple will have to do without land and/or a house, and thus will have no resources to fall back on in case of emergencies. Also, when children are born, it means that the wife will be dependent on her mother-in-law rather than on her mother (and sisters) to help her with the baby.

While from this perspective, the settlement pattern of mixed couples is unfavourable, it does give them better chances of becoming accepted (or at least tolerated) in the wider ethnic community in which they live. Rather than presenting themselves as mixed couples, most wives ended up *taking on the ethnicity of their husbands*. Where there was a language difference, the wives took on their husband's language. I had an interview with a Tamil woman in Sinhala,[9] and three interviews with Sinhala women in Tamil. Most non-Muslim wives of Muslim men converted to Islam; two men told me that their converted wife was a better Muslim than they were. The women's choice of clothes also changed; one Tamil lady wore distinctly Sinhala dress, a Sinhala lady wore distinctly Tamil dress, and others (both Sinhala and Tamil) wore distinctly Muslim dress. Most dramatic of all, some of the women who converted to Islam formally changed their ethnicity by adopting a new name, and obtaining a new identity card. For the husbands, changing ethnicity does not seem to be an option; the only thing that some of the husbands who married across the Sinhala-Tamil language divide did was to learn their wife's language.

In the cases where couples ended up in the original village of either spouse, the defining element that brought about rapprochement with disapproving relatives was the birth of the first child. This is a standard pattern following elopement in Sri Lanka. The birth of the first child brings about child-rearing responsibilities, and shows that the 'affair' has become a relationship with long-term commitments. Since breaking up the relationship no longer makes sense (a daughter or sister with a child is very hard to marry off), the alternative is to make the best of it all. A similar pattern was observed by Baber (1937).

Raising children

The arrival of children brings family acknowledgement to an inter-ethnic marriage, but it also creates a new problem: children need to be raised, and parents need to decide how much of both cultures they want to pass on.

The way in which mixed parents raise their children, and the extent to which they are willing to let their children marry someone of another ethnicity, are strong indicators of the extent to which the parents perceive themselves to be a multicultural couple. With the exception of three Sinhala-Tamil couples, all couples indicated that they raise(d) their children according to the ethnicity of the village where the children grow/grew up – and thus according to the ethnicity of the father. Where the spouses have different mother tongues, the children are generally raised bilingually, but as the wife generally takes on the religion of the husband and (with the exception of Christianity) religious affiliation is pretty much divided along ethnic lines, most children are taught one religion. The mono-ethnic child rearing practices go further: with exception of some of the Sinhala (Buddhist)–Tamil (Hindu) couples, the wives by and large refrain from teaching their children songs, customs, games, stories and so on that are considered unique to their own culture.

With regard to the spouse choice of the children, the answers were again nearly uniform: with one exception, the fathers strongly preferred their children to marry someone of their own ethnicity. Some fathers did not want their children to have to go through the hardships that they themselves had gone through, and some insisted that their children maintain their father's religion. Sometimes, I got the impression that there was a more fundamental ambiguity: even though they themselves had entered into a mixed marriage, that did not make it the preferred option. Only one man, who identified himself as Tamil, had a Malayali father and Sinhala mother, and a 'Sinhala' wife with a Sinhalese father and Tamil mother, was very willing to accept that his children would marry whoever they chose.

The mothers were not as rigid. One woman who married a Muslim and adopted the Muslim faith gave a slightly embarrassed smile when I asked her, and then answered 'as long as he or she is a Muslim'. The smile betrayed more ambiguity than she could express verbally. As soon as she said this, an elderly relative of her husband who evidently had been listening in, popped her head around the door of the back room. A Tamil lady who had married a Sinhalese and who had become very Sinhala in her demeanour said that her first child had married a Tamil against the father's wishes, but she accepted it. Her other children all married Sinhalese.

Conclusion

While the context of ethnicized conflict contributed to an increase in inter-ethnic marriages, it also meant that individual boundary crossing by mixed couples rarely led to a broader spreading of inter-ethnic understanding or interaction. The couples were no different from other couples who eloped in that, once they were established as 'normal' couples (often after the birth of their first child), the couples were generally accepted in the village where they settled.

In periods of relative peace, some non-confrontational forms of bridging do take place. Two ladies whom I spoke to were, or had been, teaching Sinhala to children in their husbands' Tamil-speaking villages. A few people in Hindu (Tamil)–Buddhist (Sinhala) households spoke of taking Hindu friends to Buddhist festivals, and of taking Buddhist friends to Hindu festivals. Finally, some mixed families living in the towns of Serunuwara and Muthur had a reputation for helping Tamils from outside gain access to public services in these places.

While mixed-ethnic families can thus contribute to broader inter-ethnic understanding in times of relative peace, the gun-enforced policing of ethnic boundaries by soldiers, home guards, rebels, ethno-nationalist politicians and local thugs forced the mixed couples to keep their multiculturalism 'below the radar', and remain irrelevant to macro-level concerns about ethnic purity by making sure that they were not identified as a distinct group (Golden 1958: 269, Okun 2004: 185). Rather than acting as a bridge between their communities, mixed couples (and their children) were faced with suspicion from both sides during most of the war. Borrowing from Thiranagama (2010: 134), I suggest that by bridging the ethnic boundary, mixed couples are 'neither/nor' to the people around them, and thus potentially traitors. Being 'above the radar' was very risky: most of the mixed households whom I spoke to had been threatened, and at least two households had suffered from targeted violence (one couple was severely injured in a targeted shooting attack). The couples interpreted these threats and violence as almost a form of exorcism, aimed at driving out the elements that subverted claims to ethnic purity. What was exorcized here was a perceived (multicultural) subversive attitude of the targeted couples, and not the mixed marriage per se: even some ethnonationalist hardliners have spouses of another ethnicity, without this being seen as a problem.

In practice, this situation almost always meant that the wives 'jumped the boundary' and, to all intents and purposes, took on the ethnicity of their husbands, while all but cutting off interaction with their own communities.[10] This 'ethnicity swapping' is the ultimate denial of ethnicity as an in-born identity. Paradoxically, however, this very denial is made necessary precisely because ethnicity is such a powerful social force in Sri Lanka. Where couples marrying between castes can simply stop talking about their castes and become more or less 'caste-less', inter-ethnic couples in Kottiyar Pattu are forced to choose an ethnicity, generally the one of the village in which they settle. Together with other stories on, for example, sharing of resources and local defusing of tensions (Gaasbeek 2010), the mixed couples in Kottiyar Pattu thus teach us that, though difficult, it is possible for people to work around ethnic discourses in a context of violent ethnicized conflict. It is this hidden pragmatism that makes a form of everyday normalcy possible in crisis situations.

Acknowledgements

The author wishes to thank Dr Becky Walker and Professor Dennis McGilvray for their constructive comments on an earlier version of this chapter. All responsibility remains with the author.

Notes

1 There are three main ethnic groups in Sri Lanka: Sinhalese, Tamils and Muslims. Sinhalese form about three-quarters of the population, speak the Sinhala language, and are largely Buddhist (about 7 per cent are Christian). Tamils form slightly less than a fifth of the population, speak the Tamil language, and are largely Hindu (about 20 per cent are Christian). Among Tamils, a distinction is made between Sri Lankan Tamils, who have lived in the island for millennia, and Indian Tamils, who arrived in the late-nineteenth and early-twentieth centuries to work on the British coffee, tea, and rubber plantations. Muslims are about 7 per cent of the population, speak Tamil and often also Sinhala, and are Muslim by religion. Apart from these, there are several tiny ethnic groups: Veddas (the stereotypical aboriginal population of Sri Lanka), Burghers, Malays, and a number of South Asian trading communities. Since independence, the main ethnic conflict line has been between Sinhalese and Tamils. In addition, intermittent violence between Muslims and Tamils became prominent in Sri Lanka's north and east after 1985.
2 Thanks to Rebecca Walker for pointing this out.

3 This was part of a larger campaign of destruction waged in Trincomalee District from 1984 until 1986. After September 1986, there was a substantial drop in attacks against Tamil property, simply because there were hardly any undamaged Tamil houses left in the district.

4 Do note, however, that the myths of origin of several Muslim communities in the province begin with intermarriage: Muslim traders helped one Tamil caste to defeat another caste, and were rewarded with wives (and thus with matrilocal dowry land) in return (McGilvray 2008: 75–77).

5 'Classificatory ethnicity' refers to people's emic categorization of ethnicity before marriage. Where someone comes from a mixed-ethnic family, this is obviously problematic. In most cases, a person's classificatory ethnicity is his/her father's ethnicity. Thus a child of a Sinhala father and a Tamil mother will be considered Sinhalese. If he/she marries a Sinhalese, the marriage will generally be seen as mono-ethnic, but if he/she marries a Tamil, the marriage will be seen as mixed-ethnic.

6 In terms of ethnicity, this is however problematic. Many of the Sinhala Catholics on Sri Lanka's west coast are descended from Paravar and Mukkuvar fishing communities along the southern coast of present-day Kerala and Tamil Nadu and spoke Tamil until the mid-twentieth century. A process of Sinhalization only gathered serious momentum after Sinhala became the language of education at many Catholic schools in the 1960s. Many of the Tamil Catholics in Muthur also belong to the Paravar caste.

7 Two interviews were with both husband and wife; four were only with the husband (in one case the wife was not at home but a daughter joined in the conversation, in the other cases, it was considered inappropriate for the wife to speak with my male research assistant and me); three interviews were with only the wife (once because the husband had already passed away, once – with prior permission from the [Muslim] husband – because the husband was out of town, and once because we met the wife in her work-place and she just started talking to us).

8 Among Sinhalese settlers in Kottiyar Pattu, land is generally passed on to the youngest son as inheritance, and dowry is given more in terms of gold, cash or other movables than in the form of a house. Neolocal residence is therefore the norm.

9 This lady's television gave her away: when we entered the house, she was watching a Tamil television programme.

10 Only in one case outside Kottiyar Pattu, I have come across a Tamil man who adopted the ethnicity of his Sinhala wife. He changed his name, language and culture to avoid harassment by the Sri Lankan security forces.

References

Abeyrathne, U. (2003) 'War and ethnic identity in an ethnically mixed village community: Panama a village in the Ampara District of Sri Lanka'. In Sri Lanka Studies Network, *9th International Conference on Sri Lanka Studies*. Matara, Sri Lanka 28–30 November 2003. Matara: University of Ruhuna.

Baber, R. (1937) 'A Study of 325 Mixed Marriages'. *American Sociological Review*, 2(5): 705–716.

Blau, P.M., T.C. Blum and J.E. Schwartz (1982) 'Heterogeneity and Intermarriage'. *American Sociological Review*, 47(1): 45–62.

Blau, P.M., C. Beeker and K.M. Fitzpatrick (1984) 'Intersecting Social Affiliations and Intermarriage'. *Social Forces*, 62(3): 585–606.

Botev, N. (1994) 'Where East meets West: Ethnic Intermarriage in the Former Yugoslavia, 1962 to 1989'. *American Sociological Review*, 59(3): 461–480.

Corwin, L.A. (1977) 'Caste, Class and the Love-marriage: Social Change in India'. *Journal of Marriage and the Family*, 39(4): 823–831.

Dart, J.A. (1985) *Ethnic Identity and Marginality among the Coast Veddas of Sri Lanka*. PhD. University of California, San Diego.

De Munck, V.C. (1996) 'Love and Marriage in a Sri Lankan Muslim Community: Toward a Reevaluation of Dravidian Marriage Practices'. *American Ethnologist*, 23(4): 698–716.

Fernando, D.F.S. (1980) 'Ethnic and Religious Factors in Marriage in Sri Lanka'. *Journal of Biosocial Science*, 12(4): 429–436.

Gaasbeek, T.J. (2010) *Bridging Troubled Waters? Everyday Inter-ethnic Interaction in a Context of Violent Conflict in Kottiyar Pattu, Trincomalee, Sri Lanka*. PhD. Wageningen University and Research Centre.

Golden, J. (1953) 'Characteristics of the Negro-White Intermarried in Philadelphia'. *American Sociological Review*, 18(2): 177–183.

Golden, J. (1954) 'Patterns of Negro-White Intermarriage'. *American Sociological Review*, 19(2): 144–147.

Golden, J. (1958) 'Social Control of Negro-White Intermarriage'. *Social Forces*, 36(3): 267–269.

Golden, J. (1959). 'Facilitating Factors in Negro-White Intermarriage'. *The Phylon Quarterly*, 20(3): 273–284.

Goodhand, J. and B. Klem (2005) *Aid, Conflict and Peacebuilding in Sri Lanka 2000–2005*. Colombo: The Asia Foundation.

Gray, A. (1987) 'Intermarriage: Opportunity and Preference'. *Population Studies*, 41(3): 365–379.

Gündüz-Hoðsgör, A. and J. Smits (2002) 'Intermarriage between Turks and Kurds in Contemporary Turkey. Inter-ethnic Relations in an Urbanizing Environment'. *European Sociological Review*, 18(4): 417–432.

Hilhorst, D. (2007) *Saving Lives or Saving Societies? Realities of Relief and Reconstruction*. Inaugural address, Wageningen University.

Kalmijn, M. (1998) 'Intermarriage and Homogamy: Causes, Patterns, Trends'. *Annual Review of Sociology*, 24: 395–421.

Kennedy, R.J.R. (1944) 'Single or Triple Melting-pot? Intermarriage Trends in New Haven, 1870–1940'. *The Amerian Journal of Sociology*, 49(4): 331–339.

Kennedy, R.J.R. (1952) 'Single or Triple Melting-pot? Intermarriage in New Haven, 1870–1950'. *The American Journal of Sociology*, 58(1): 56–59.

McGilvray, D.B. (2008) *Crucible of Conflict. Tamil and Muslim Society on the East Coast of Sri Lanka*. Durham and London: Duke University Press.

McGilvray, D.B. and P. Lawrence (2010) 'Dreaming of Dowry: Post-tsunami Housing Strategies in Eastern Sri Lanka'. In D.B. McGilvray and M.R. Gamburd (eds) *Tsunami recovery in Sri Lanka: ethnic and regional dimensions*. London and New York: Routledge. 106–124.

Magnarella, P.J. (2005) 'The Background and Causes of the Genocide in Rwanda'. *Journal of International Criminal Justice*, 3: 801–822.

Oberschall, A. (2000) 'The Manipulation of Ethnicity: From Ethnic Cooperation to Violence and War in Yugoslavia'. *Ethnic and Racial Studies*, 23(6): 982–1000.

Okun, B.S. (2004) 'Insight into Ethnic Flux: Marriage Patterns among Jews of Mixed Ancestry in Israel'. *Demography*, 41(1): 173–187.

Pickering, P.M. (2006) 'Generating Social Capital for Bridging Ethnic Divisions in the Balkans: Case Studies of Two Bosniak Cities'. *Ethnic and Racial Studies*, 29(1): 79–103.

Ring, L.A. (2006) *Zenana. Everyday Peace in a Karachi Apartment Building*. Bloomington and Indianapolis: Indiana University Press.

Roer-Strier, D. and Ben Ezra, D. (2006) 'Intermarriages between Western Women and Palestinian Men: Multidirectional Adaptation Processes'. *Journal of Marriage and Family*, 68: 41–55.

Thiranagama, S. (2010) 'In Praise of Traitors: Intimacy, Betrayal, and the Sri Lankan Tamil Community'. In S. Thiranagama and T. Kelly (eds) *Traitors. Suspicion, Intimacy and the Ethics of State-building*. Philadelphia: University of Pennsylvania Press. 127–149.

Yalman, N. (1967) *Under the Bo Tree. Studies in Caste, Kinship, and Marriage in the Interior of Ceylon*. Berkeley, Los Angeles, London: University of California Press.

Part III
Arenas of interventions

11 Humanitarian space as arena

A perspective on the everyday politics of aid[1]

Dorothea Hilhorst and Bram J. Jansen

Introduction

Humanitarian action is ideal – typically associated with service delivery in temporary conflict situations, according to principles of impartiality, neutrality and independence. The phenomenon is epitomized by the concept of humanitarian space. Humanitarian space is defined as 'an environment where humanitarians can work without hindrance and follow the humanitarian principles of neutrality, impartiality and humanity' (Spearin 2001: 22). Like any type of space, humanitarian space has physical and metaphorical dimensions. It refers to physical environments: refugee camps, humanitarian corridors during ceasefires or safe havens where peacekeepers and humanitarians provide physical protection and basic services. It also refers to the manoeuvring space for humanitarians to work without fear of attack in dangerous situations and alongside other actors.[2] This notion of humanitarian space is rooted in the work of Henri Dunant who founded the Red Cross in 1862. He believed that the organization, in order to gain access to war victims, would have to remain *neutral* and maintain *independence* from sponsoring governments (Dunant 1986).

The effectiveness of humanitarian spaces is very limited in practice. Many safe havens and refugee camps become militarized, and the abuse of humanitarian aid often makes a mockery of the principals involved (Keen 1994, Le Billon 2000, Rieff 2002, Magone *et al.* 2011). Nonetheless, the notion of humanitarian space as the site of principled aid remains widely accepted as the expression and aspiration of humanitarian assistance. The Red Cross/Red Crescent movement, the UN bodies, the non-governmental organization (NGO) Code of Conduct and the Good Humanitarian Donorship Initiative all adopt similar wording to embrace the basic humanitarian principles of impartiality, neutrality and independence. Research in 12 humanitarian crisis situations has shown that actors and aid recipients worldwide acknowledge and appreciate its universal character (Donini *et al.* 2008). Interestingly, much of the academic criticism of the politicization of humanitarian space is, 'undergirded by the taken-for-granted assumption that humanitarian spaces and relations can and must be separated from politics' (Kleinfeld 2007: 174).

This chapter addresses a question that follows from the contradiction that, despite the criticism of the notion of humanitarian space, it continues nonetheless to be a core concept in humanitarian assistance. Hugo Slim observes of this aspirational dimension, 'If those who hold economic, social, political and military power in a war can be persuaded to "buy" the humanitarian norms and principles of international humanitarian law then civilians are more likely be protected than killed' (Slim 2003: 3).

In addition, we are interested in the *idea* of humanitarian space in practice. The language and principles of humanitarian space are strategically or tacitly used by different actors to advance or legitimize their respective interests, projects or beliefs. This is not a new development. Fiona Terry (2002) and Alex De Waal (1997) have analysed how humanitarian assistance contributes to the legitimization of political actors by allowing authorities to fulfil their social and material obligations or by lending recognition to territorial authorities through cooperation and negotiation. In the case of Angola, for example, it has been suggested that UNITA could only survive in its final years because of the credibility and resources it could generate as a result of the humanitarian operations (Hilhorst and Serrano 2010). As such, '[H]umanitarian aid, viewed through this lens, can be imagined as a conduit between places and people, facilitating relief and reconstruction assistance as well as political legitimacy and, hence, the political and economic stability of a place' (Kleinfeld 2007: 170).

Political legitimacy is also sought by humanitarian agencies themselves. DeChaine analysed how by ' "humanitarianizing" space – representing it as a space for ethical and humane interaction – humanitarian agencies present themselves to donors as actors void of the territorial or political context in which they operate' (2002: 363). Agencies thus use this language and the image of the humanitarian space to hide their self-interest in humanitarian action and their intended or unintended political roles.

The language of humanitarian space is thus used for what we may call its official purpose – humanitarian diplomacy to be able to access people in need – as well as legitimization processes. This raises the question of how the idea of humanitarian space is rooted in the socio-political dynamics of crisis situations. How is humanitarian space constructed in practice? Which actors get access to the space, which legitimization processes take place, how are humanitarian beneficiaries selected, and how is the distribution of resources contested and organized in practice?

This chapter offers an analytical framework of the humanitarian arena that enables us to examine these questions. It is actor-oriented and grounded in the study of humanitarian practice. The questions will be addressed with reference to two cases: ongoing assistance to the Kakuma refugee camp in Kenya, that has been in existence since 1992, and the response to the 2004 tsunami in Sri Lanka. The discussion of the tsunami is based on fieldwork carried out by Dorothea Hilhorst.[3] The discussion of Kakuma is based on extensive fieldwork carried out by Bram J. Jansen.[4]

Both case studies are different from the theatres of war that have inspired the Dunantian body of thought. Nonetheless, the idea of humanitarian space remains equally relevant for both cases. Their humanitarian character is uncontested, and they are incorporated into humanitarian budgets and coordination. Humanitarian agencies equally refer to the humanitarian principles and employ the concomitant language to explain their presence and activities in the relative peace of refugee camps, in the aftermath of natural disasters, and in post-conflict settings, as in classic conflict situations. The principles are a central tenet of their identity and cover all types of operations. This is partly justified because natural disaster and refugee situations are often intertwined with conflict.

Humanitarian space as arena

We view humanitarian action as an arena where actors negotiate the outcomes of aid. Social negotiation encompasses any kind of strategy, including coercive violence, written statements, formal interactions, schemes deployed in the shadows of the official process and the banalities of everyday gossiping. The realities and outcomes of aid depend on how actors along and around the aid chain – donor representatives, headquarters, field staff, aid recipients and surrounding actors – interpret the context, the needs, their own role and one another. The idea of an arena is founded in an actor-oriented approach which departs from the assumption that social actors reflect upon their experiences and what happens around them and use their knowledge and capabilities to interpret and respond to their environment (Long 1992, 2001).

Actors do not display the same, predictable, behaviour in every situation. Their practices are driven by different motives, and decisions are taken in response to actors' interpretation of the needs of the situation and in interaction with others. Language plays an important role in this, and the actor-oriented approach therefore pays much attention to the analysis of the different discourses that actors draw on to advance their ideas or activities. Foucault has paved the way for studying discourse as a close interweaving of knowledge and power (Foucault 1978). The effect of discourse is that certain ways of understanding society, including its organization and the distribution of power, become excluded whereas others attain authority. However, as Long (1992) points out, there are always multiple discourses at work.

> Since social life is never so unitary as to be built upon one single type of discourse, it follows that, however restricted their choice, actors always face some alternative ways of formulating their objectives, deploying modes of action and giving reasons for their behaviour.
>
> (Long 1992: 25)

In an arena approach, the kinds of actions or actors considered to be humanitarian are not predetermined nor are the principles that qualify as humanitarian established in advance; instead, we ask ourselves how the conditions of service delivery in crisis situations are shaped in practice, and how aid gets shaped through the interactions between multiple actors. Service delivery during crises is, in reality, not only delivered by humanitarian agencies, but encompasses many more actors. These include UN agencies, multiple mandate NGOs, the private sector, churches and the military. In this sense, humanitarian space is open to a range of actors. However, 'the ICRC [International Committee of the Red Cross], by virtue of its mandate, claims a specific "sub-part" of this "space"' (Grombach Wagner 2005: 4).

From the arena perspective, humanitarian principles are seen as socially negotiated and acquiring meaning in practice. Despite their universal semblance, different actors interpret the humanitarian principles differently (Leader 2002). They are contextual and imbued with different meanings, even within the ICRC itself (Minear 1999). The way the principles work out in practice is even more diverse. They only become real through the ways in which service providers interpret them and use them in their everyday practice (Hilhorst and Schmiemann 2002). Principles are partly negotiated with reference to other principles that are important to service delivery. These could be the other (operational) principles of the Code of Conduct,[5] such as accountability, participation, partnership, vulnerability reduction and respect for culture, or professional standards of other service providers, such as corporate social responsibility or military integrity standards.

Another important feature of the arena approach is that it recognizes that humanitarian action is based on a range of driving forces besides a humanitarian ethic. Political motivations may partly inspire humanitarian action, as well as organizational politics, showing the public that an agency is doing good work. The multiple driving forces of humanitarian action are well known, but the way they interact with each other in practice is less examined. It is, for example, often assumed that geopolitics overwhelmingly determine humanitarian allocations, but research shows that these come about through an amalgam of geopolitics, media and public sentiments, and humanitarian diplomacy (Olsen *et al.* 2003). How the different drivers of aid delivery interact and influence each other can be explored through research into its everyday practices. This requires attention to what can be referred to as the frontline workers, the life worlds of the humanitarians. How they define and organize their work makes a difference. This is as much mediated by the mandates of their organizations, their assessments of needs and their context analysis as by their expectations and motivations or frustrations, and the organizational culture they develop accordingly (Walkup 1997).

Last but not least, we pay much attention to the strategizing and constructive roles of aid *recipients* in shaping humanitarian aid. The notion of humanitarian space conveys an image of agencies seeking access to people in need. However, we see the humanitarian encounter as an interface where aid providers and aid-seekers meet each other. Aid recipients do not passively hang about until aid arrives, but strategize to reach agencies and become eligible for their services. While agencies derive their legitimacy from their image of being moral actors, recipients derive their legitimacy from the fact that they are in need, which is, in part, negotiable.

Our focus on everyday practices emphasizes that phenomena acquire meaning in their everyday realities. By studying the way actors shape the reality of aid in a given context, the working of principles and policies in practice can be explored. The following sections take up the case of the Kakuma refugee camp and the 2004 tsunami. The cases are very different: unlike the tsunami response, which involved civil society at large, the refugee camp of Kakuma is a relatively closed arena. While the tsunami response was geared towards restoring people's lives, the camp is meant to be temporary until people are able to return home. However, despite the very different arenas presented, we will also see important similarities. These appear to be rooted in the global, yet local, character of the political arena of humanitarianism. In both cases, we can follow the dynamics of inclusion and exclusion from the humanitarian arena.

The humanitarian arena: Kakuma refugee camp

Refugee camps are intended as temporary facilities for the protection of refugees. Many camps, however, exist for many years and undergo processes of develop-ment and change, resulting in substantial changes in the working of the humani-tarian arena and the terms of service delivery. Kakuma refugee camp was established in 1992 in the marginalized northwest of Kenya, bordering South Sudan, Uganda and Ethiopia. By 2006 it hosted approximately 95,000 refugees, mainly from Sudan and Somalia, but also from Ethiopia, Eritrea, Uganda, Rwanda, Burundi and DR Congo (UNHCR 2007). Wilde refers to camp situa-tions like Kakuma as 'development camps': 'sophisticated polities, with market-places, schools, hospitals, mosques, churches, running water, and decision making fora' (1998: 108), while Agier labelled them 'naked cities' (2002). The presence of international agencies with their material, social and political resources elevates these camps above the level of facilities and infrastructure in surrounding areas. In this section, we will analyse the relations between the different agencies and authority in the camp, and the ways in which refugees themselves play a part in shaping the aid relations. We will focus on one particular aspect, the possibility of resettlement, to demonstrate how categories of vulnerability are negotiated in the practice of aid services.

Interface between host state and UNHCR: delegation of authority

In many refugee camps, the responsibilities and executive power of the host state are largely delegated to the United Nations High Commissioner for Refugees (UNHCR) (Wilde 1998, Pallis 2006), and it resembles a sovereign handing out something comparable to citizenship. The normative framework that orders the social contract between the quasi 'state-citizens' is derived from humanitarian standards, such as those provided by the Sphere project. The Sphere standards set minimum standards in humanitarian aid, and form, together with international conventions, human rights, international refugee law and humanitarian princi-ples, the framework of service delivery. As Turner observed, the result is 'the crea-tion of a new kind of citizen' (2004) governed by what Agier and Bouchet-Saulnier (2004) call 'regimes of exception'. Indeed, Kakuma camp has gradually grown into an 'island of entitlements' in the semi-desert of northern Kenya.

UNHCR acts like a government in the camp, with NGOs as implementing partners providing services and protection to refugees. Although many of the NGOs have their own mandates, they act as little more than line agencies for UNHCR. However, this situation where UNHCR has become the main authority in the camp is not uncontested, as social negotiation by refugees around resettlement shapes much of the resettlement practice. This leads to a situation where UNHCR's authority is challenged and its identity as protector of people changed into one where it also breaches people's rights.

Negotiating resettlement

The basic basket of protection by humanitarian agencies consists of food, basic education, shelter, health, water and sanitation. Beyond these, there are other services and opportunities, such as refugee jobs with the agencies, secondary, vocational and special education, and special protection measures for the vulnerable. Many refugees view these additional services as entitlements, and obtaining access to them has become a key driver in refugee strategies.

One area of additional services consists of resettlement to a third country. While UNHCR maintains that resettlement is exceptional, a large number of refugees from Kakuma have been resettled in practice. At the end of 2000, the United States Refugee Program (USRP) started with 3,800 Sudanese 'unaccompanied minors'. They were part of the 20,000 so-called 'Lost Boys': young Sudanese who came to Kakuma in 1992 after their expulsion from refugee camps in Ethiopia. In 2003, 15,000 Somali Bantus – a Somali minority experiencing discrimination in Somalia – constituted the single largest group ever to be resettled from Africa (UNHCR 2004: 10). In total, 27,450 refugees were resettled from Kenya from 2001 to 2005, mostly from Kakuma (UNHCR 2007).

Resettlement was very visible in Kakuma, through the lists of resettlement interviews displayed on information boards, planes taking off a few times a week, and a steady flow of visitors to the camp engaged in screening and selecting refugees. This visibility enhanced refugees' belief that resettlement was something they could organize themselves. Resettlement thus became subject to strategizing and social negotiation. It could be achieved on account of group insecurity, or on an individual basis.

Group resettlement from Kakuma started in the US with a lobby for a solution for the Lost Boys (Bixler 2005: 13). After the resettlement of the Somali Bantus, refugees came to see clan affiliations as a 'gateway to resettlement'. In order to become eligible for resettlement, groups began to organize themselves as discriminated minorities. In 2004, a headcount was conducted in the camp. This presented an opportunity for Somalis to change their ethnicity. Many refugees re-registered to be members of the Somali *Madiban*, *Asharaf* or *Barawa* clans, who were at the time under consideration for group resettlement. The screening also attracted new people from Somalia, informed by friends and relatives from the camp, who registered and returned to Somalia to wait for the resettlement interview. In Nairobi, courses were offered for training and preparation for resettlement interviews. In the camp, different Somali groups established their own (sub)community buildings and leadership structures within the overall Somali community. They started to write letters to embassies, the UN and human rights groups about their alleged minority status and discrimination in the country of origin. Refugees, in other words, learned to employ a rights language to claim vulnerability on the basis of ethnic identity.

Several visitors came to the camp who promised to facilitate resettlement of a particular group, responding to attempts by refugees to alert the outside world to their plight. One NGO that came to the camp invited the entire Somali community to forward the reasons and details for their wish to resettle in the US, without coordinating with UNHCR. It wanted to find out how many people of the Somali-Bantu target group were still in the camp. For three days, refugee representatives came running with letters and copies of ration cards, also from other Somali communities. When the NGO representative realized the frenzy she had created, she prepared to leave the camp, but not before she was picked up and asked to leave by the police and UNHCR. UNHCR does not organize large-scale resettlement by itself. Instead, governments and NGOs now lean on the International Organization for Migration (IOM) to organize resettlement. IOM offers governments the possibility to enter and work in refugee camps, thus bypassing some of UNHCR's authority.

Negotiating individual vulnerability for resettlement

Refugees could also opt for individual resettlement. This would often be followed by resettlement of relatives in the context of 'family reunification'. Individual resettlement could be achieved on the basis of vulnerability, or on the grounds of merit. Refugees have ample room to manoeuvre to play a significant role in these decisions.

The vulnerabilities on the basis of which refugees apply for resettlement are partly produced by 'empowerment programming' of the refugee regime. Turner wrote: 'These power structures are productive in the sense that we may expect that the governing of the refugee camp produces certain categories and hence certain subjectivities' (2001: 43). The empowerment and rights agendas have labelled certain social phenomena as problematic, such as gender-based violence and discriminatory practices. Education contributes to changes in traditional and cultural norms. Billboards and T-shirts in the camp read: *Women's rights are human rights too; Stop stigmatization against people living with HIV/AIDS; Stop domestic violence,* and so on. These norms have been incorporated into the protection repertoire of refugees. By sensitizing refugees that domestic violence is against women's rights, women come to recognize that their rights are being infringed. UNHCR and its implementing partners are then compelled to act on their behalf. Sexual abuse has become one of the grounds for resettlement.

Individual resettlement cases are usually referred by refugee committees. Refugees participate in their own governance through refugee administrations, making the community leadership a powerful gatekeeper that can forward or dismiss cases for resettlement. Cases are referred through a chain. The refugee case worker and the chairman or woman present cases for consideration to an NGO, who can intervene or forward the case to the UNHCR offices that deal with protection, gender, social services and resettlement. This process renders the refugee leadership quite powerful and results in the creation of sub-authorities. Becoming eligible for resettlement usually involves these authorities, who act as middlemen. To be considered for resettlement involves a tedious play with chairmen, (refugee) agency personnel and security guards. In many cases, personal relationships or pre-established modes of access determine a refugee's entry into the system. Being able to play the game was more decisive than the actual vulnerability and misrepresentations were common. People would claim various forms of insecurity, including fake violent attacks and rape (Jansen 2008).

Individual resettlement on the basis of merit

Another way to obtain resettlement is through scholarships. Many refugees collected certificates, diplomas and references of courses, training and jobs done in the camp. They knew that proactive behaviour, knowledge of English and education significantly enhanced their chances to be resettled. Dutch resettlement guidelines specifically state a preference for refugees with qualifications in order to smooth the integration process in the Netherlands. Sommers (2005) indicated that this leads to brain drain, because refugees who have a contribution to make in the running of the camp keep being resettled. In a community-based rehabilitation centre in the camp run by the International Rescue Committee (IRC), four of the five refugee staff that had been recruited and trained were resettled.

Who becomes eligible for scholarship grants is determined in the interaction between refugees and the implementing agencies. The Jesuit Refugee Service (JRS) can decide who is granted scholarships elsewhere in Kenya. The Windle Charitable Trust selects approximately 25 candidates every year for a four-year sponsored university degree in Canada. The interfaces between refugees and the agencies are thus important, as they largely determine access to services. The power to facilitate access to services creates certain forms of authority. Businessmen, the refugee leadership, those with incentive jobs and young creative refugees who 'speak the language' of the agencies can negotiate a new social order in the camp and become examples of these multiple forms of authority in Kakuma. In the confines of the camp, access is power.

The practices surrounding resettlement eroded the authority of UNHCR in the camp. IOM and other NGOs were mobilized by external actors to facilitate resettlement. Refugee committees, meant to function as counterparts to UNHCR, in effect became competing authority structures. Refugees moulded their identity around social profiles that favour resettlement. By focusing on the everyday practices of resettlement, the case study thus reveals some of the mechanisms through which power is transformed and aid relations change. UNHCR and its implementing agencies, and sometimes governments, are assigned the power to declare who is vulnerable and who is not, and thus who receives special protection and who is eligible for resettlement. In practice, this power of inclusion or exclusion is largely seized by refugees, which is made possible because refugees form part of the governance system. It is mainly performed through negotiating the language and diagnostics of vulnerability. Refugees acquire the language of rights and proceed to build their identity around the requirements to qualify for resettlement. This contributed to changing the relations amongst aid providers. It eroded the authority of UNHCR and the agency felt obliged to take measures that conflict with the basic rights of refugees and the mandate of protection that the agency and its staff embody.

The humanitarian arena: after the 2004 Indian Ocean tsunami

The Indian Ocean tsunami of December 2004 claimed 225,000 lives and displaced 1.8 million people. The international resources available for relief and reconstruction were US\$ 14 billion, 6 billion of which came from private donations, excluding the contributions of local governments, residents and diaspora communities (Telford and Cosgrave 2005). In financial terms, the humanitarian operation was the largest ever, and more than 20 times bigger than the second-largest that preceded it, namely US\$ 680 million raised after Hurricane Mitch (Guha-Sapir *et al.* 2004: 51). While the potential benefits of the tsunami response were staggering, the downside was immediately visible, too. The hundreds of agencies that came to Sri Lanka all needed to allocate money rapidly. The competition for humanitarian space, and the allocation of resources, was 'negotiated' at different interfaces: between agencies and the government and within the humanitarian community. Aid recipients were partly disavowed as agents in the response by aid givers, yet turned out to have an important role in setting the terms of the allocation of aid. Issues of legitimization were important at these different levels of negotiation and found expression in contests for humanitarian space and the language of rights.

The interface between humanitarians and authorities

The response to the tsunami in Sri Lanka was severely affected by the conflict in the country at the time. The government and the rebels of the Liberation Tigers of Tamil Eelam (LTTE) used the language of humanitarian space to stake their claims on peoples and territories (Kleinfeld 2007). This was apparent, among others, in the contested buffer zone that the government declared unsafe for building (Hyndman 2009). The government and its opponents were not only using the response to advance their political projects, they also wanted to claim control over the resources that were made available internationally. Efforts by the international response community to maintain a distance from both the government and the LTTE resulted in a strong reaction, particularly from the government. On 27 March 2005, *Silumina*, a government-owned newspaper, carried an extra-large headline: 'NGOs Have Taken Nine Out of the Ten Billion Foreign Aid'. The message was that NGOs were using the money which should have come to the government. The Sri Lankan state, under different governments, has often claimed in the past that NGOs appropriate resources which should have been made available to the government, and they ascribe a conspiratorial role to NGOs as promoting western interests (Fernando 2003).

Underlying these criticisms, however, was the government's sense of marginalization from the humanitarian arena. As a result, political lobbying against International NGOs (INGOs) continued and became one of the drivers of people's discontent. It became common practice to complain that the INGOs 'did nothing for us', which severely restricted the potential of the INGOs to interact with local authorities and people.

Among humanitarian agencies, severe competition erupted (Stirrat 2006). Whereas agencies normally compete over funds, this time they had to compete over territory, programmes, people and staff. Headquarters pressured local staff to ensure space for their organization. One representative received a phone call from his manager that he had to draw up a proposal for US$ 6 million within a week. Many INGOs already had a presence in Sri Lanka due to the ongoing conflict. What should have been an advantage often turned out instead to be problematic: NGO staff members with experience of the country clashed with headquarters over decisions that were imposed on them, and the pressure under which they had to work. Gaasbeek (2005) recorded a case where an aid worker was confronted with a television crew that came with a plane-load of high-energy biscuits. When he refused to distribute the biscuits, since there was no malnourishment, a conflict ensued that led to his resignation. In other instances, resident staff who were very familiar with the context, were pushed aside by strangers to Sri Lanka, on account of the latter being specialists in humanitarian emergencies.

Sri Lankan NGOs were another group of service providers vulnerable to displacement from the humanitarian space. Sri Lanka has many development NGOs who were well placed to take on rehabilitation programmes, but international actors developed a tendency to brush local actors aside. Immediately after the tsunami, IT companies started developing software for coordination, and within a week the Coalition of Humanitarian Agencies (CHA) had a coordination system up and running. When the UN sent a coordination team five weeks later, the CHA staff perceived the UN to be abrasive: 'It was as if they were saying "all right you amateurs, move over, the professionals have arrived" '.[6] In this case, the problems were set aside and a fruitful partnership evolved between the two. Many other agencies fared worse, and local NGOs complained that the humanitarians who came were totally unaware of operating in functioning societies, 'behaving as if they were in Darfur or Somalia' (Ville de Goyet and Morinière 2006: 59).

Local organizations found it hard to enter into the humanitarian arena. When one local agency presented a proposal for rehabilitation work to one of their European core funders, they received the reply that they best 'leave the tsunami work to the international agencies and concentrate instead on the continuation of their work in the non-affected areas'. Fortunately, they found their other core funder responsive to their initiative and were awarded the tender to construct temporary shelters in two villages. During the preparation phase, the NGO found out that the government had also given an international agency permission to construct shelters in one of the villages. After a few weeks they wrote to the funding agency that it was 'pressured by the government to withdraw from both villages'.

Another interesting aspect to the dynamics concerned the large number of private humanitarian initiatives in the tsunami response. The widely televised tsunami appeared to be 'everybody's disaster'. All over the world, individuals assessed the damage, identified needs and evaluated the progress of aid. As Stirrat (2006) observed, this had as a consequence that agencies became more conscious of their accountability towards the public and had to prioritize photogenic projects in order to legitimize their efforts back home. It also meant that many individuals came to offer assistance. Many came from the diaspora to Sri Lanka to help their people. But many others, with no other relation to the island than as tourists, got on a plane with relief supplies and money collected through their personal, neighbourhood, professional or church networks. We call this new category of humanitarian actors the Non-Governmental Individuals (NGIs). The NGIs constitute a diverse group, yet many share a growing dissatisfaction with the established agencies. In their view, official agencies spend too much money on maintaining their expensive offices and bureaucracies. The humanitarian agencies, on the other hand, tend to dislike the NGIs, regarding them as amateurs who get in the way of professional help. The question is whether this was justified.

One NGI travelled to where he used to spend his winter holidays with 130 kg of relief items and some cash with which he reconstructed four houses (Fernando and Hilhorst 2006). Although he had never heard of the Code of Conduct, his own (implicit) set of principles was very similar and he made sure to be accountable to his constituencies via email. Just like the NGOs, NGIs represent a variety of good and not-so-good humanitarians and cannot be lumped together into one category. Moreover, the difference between the professional and amateur humanitarian workers is not as clear-cut as presumed. The debate over legitimacy, cast in the language of humanitarian professionalism versus the humanitarian spirit, must be understood as a competition over access to the humanitarian arena.

Interface between agencies and tsunami-affected people

Surveys revealed a declining level of satisfaction with the aid that was received. Many people complained about the discrepancy they perceived between the vast resources available and what they received.

> Across the board, people pointed to the highly centralised government machinery, inadequate needs assessments and consultation, corruption and a lack of transparency and accountability. [. . .] In many communities people observed how the competition between INGOs and NGOs appeared to take precedence over delivering assistance to the affected.
>
> (Fernando 2005: 3)

International agencies disregarded community-based organizations. Humanitarian agencies, in order to fulfil their function, need vulnerable people to assist. The language of vulnerability is thus the vital twin of the humanitarian discourse. By 'vulnerabilizing' people, agencies can legitimize their own intervention and claim the need for their expertise. Women in particular tend to be 'vulnerabi-lized', and the efforts of women's organizations were not 'seen' by the inter-nationals (Fulu 2007, Scharffscher 2011). While agencies tend to ignore or oversee existing organizations, they are instead keen to form new ones that can become their counterpart in the area of implementation. In the atmosphere of competi-tion, one way in which agencies claimed legitimacy was by responding to the humanitarian ideal of beneficiary participation. It was not uncommon to come across agency representatives who claimed to be an exception to general aid implementation because *they* took beneficiaries seriously. Actually, there was much engagement, and often of the wrong kind. Numerous agencies carried out partici-patory needs assessments which raised expectations that often were not followed up. Towards the end of 2005, every agency we interviewed based its programme on collaboration with local civil society groups. Tsunami-affected people were overwhelmed by requests for their participation, often by multiple agencies working in the same community. Some villages carried the burden of forming five beneficiary organizations – all with overlapping membership – to cater to different agencies that had come to their area.[7]

In the meantime, locals devised their own strategies to obtain humanitarian resources. Stories were told of people who successfully claimed a boat even though they had never been to sea, of fishermen who claimed a number of boats, and of families with seven sewing machines. A notorious example was a group of families that refused to leave their tents for more robust shelter because they wanted to continue their profitable business of telling media representatives and other visi-tors how 'they had never received aid'.[8] Local authorities and village leaders were often asked to make beneficiary lists and they either connived by adding ineligible people to the list, or were unable to resist the pressure of local power holders. Hence, in several complicated ways, the 'humanitarian gift' became commodi-tized as part of cultural symbolism and exchange relations between patrons and clients (Korf *et al.* 2010).

Participation practices are often based on a discourse of rights. A current trend is to view aid recipients as clients with consumer rights. An example at international level is the initiative by the US-based Fritz Institute that asked tsunami survivors about their consumer satisfaction with the goods and services received (Berger 2006). An unintended consequence of such approaches is that they reward the individualization of aid recipients and encourage local rivalry over aid. Local aid providers related how individuals equipped with a rights discourse undermined community-based attempts to respond to the tsunami.

Analysis: The global yet local character of humanitarianism

Kakuma is a long-term refugee camp, a geographically bounded safe area under the tight control of UNHCR management. UNHCR acts as gatekeeper for other aid providers. Post-tsunami Sri Lanka constituted its opposite: a sudden-onset, open-ended humanitarian arena everybody could seek access to, including large numbers of NGIs. Notwithstanding these differences, we found important similarities in the use of the *idea* of humanitarian space and its accompanying language of principles, vulnerability and services, although these processes altered and gained specific meaning in the different cases.

Inclusion and exclusion from the humanitarian arena

The humanitarian arena is not 'out there'. It is discursively created by agencies, media and other stakeholders. Even in the crowded arena of the tsunami response, agencies cherished the idea that they were the only ones caring about a neglected community or target group, and agency websites rarely mentioned other agencies working in the same area. In reality, as the cases show, humanitarian situations are not blank slates to be occupied by lone agencies, but are shaped by social negotiations over inclusion and exclusion.

Gaining access to targeted aid recipients was a struggle in the case of the tsunami response. Agencies were in fierce competition, and the outcome of their struggle was informed by their command over power and money, with international agencies gaining the upper hand over local authorities and local NGOs. Part of this struggle was over the question of who constitutes a real humanitarian. The government and the humanitarians ascribed political motives to each other, in attempts to exclude the other from the humanitarian arena. International humanitarian actors used their expertise in dealing with humanitarian crises to disempower resident staff, local NGOs, non-governmental individuals and community organizations. Although questions over 'humanitarianship' can concern real matters of expertise and experience, it is important to note that they are also part of competition over access to humanitarian budgets, programmes and target groups. This turns the debates over who is a legitimate humanitarian into a political rather than a principled one.

Compared to the tsunami response, the Kakuma refugee camp appeared well managed under the supervision of UNHCR. Yet, closer scrutiny reveals that UNHCR's position was contested. When national governments, ignited by lobbying on the part of their constituency, sought to augment the number of resettlements, they found ways to by-pass UNHCR through IOM and other self-appointed agencies who have considerable scope for this.

Defining beneficiaries or target groups

Aid recipients have certain pre-described roles in humanitarian aid, ranging from expressing their needs to recipient participation in the selection of beneficiaries for programmes. It is the prerogative of the humanitarian agency to define its beneficiaries. On the basis of vulnerability categories and needs analyses, those eligible for aid are selected. Our cases illustrate that the role of recipients in these processes may be greater than appears to be the case at first sight.

Aid recipients have a huge influence on the allocation of aid and other benefits provided by the international humanitarian community. International relief after the tsunami was so abundant, and the coordination among the aid providers so dismal, that many local people had no moral reservations at all in grabbing as much aid as they could. In the case of Kakuma, refugees rather than agencies sometimes appeared to determine who was eligible for services and entitlements. Much of the allocation dynamics of entitlements remained invisible to agencies whose staff live in a closed compound some distance from the camp and are not intimately familiar with everyday life in the camp. There is no incentive for agencies to know these realities, as this might jeopardize their programmes. While retaining their innocence to some of these realities, they can report to their back-donors that everything is under control.

Humanitarian agencies have been famously accused of *creating* a dependency attitude among people through the built-in anti-participatory ideology of the givers (Harrell-Bond, 1986). We showed that this is a mutual process. People likewise shape the objects of intervention. This was most clearly demonstrated in the case of Kakuma. The many instances of refugees drawn to the camp by the facilities that were made available eventually led to UNHCR restricting the provision of services. This gradually transformed UNHCR from a protection agency into a double-faced agent that protected, as well as infringed upon, the rights of war-affected refugees. Another example is offered by those refugees who follow NGO courses and whose only objective is to become eligible for resettlement, thereby effectively turning NGOs into vehicles of the brain drain from the camp to the West.

It is important to note that the capacity of refugees and disaster survivors to determine the allocation of aid does not mean that aid never reaches the really vulnerable. The many community leaders involved in Sri Lanka ensured that aid was distributed according to need. In Kakuma, refugee strongmen are usually part of intricate patron-client relationships and have adopted a number of orphans or otherwise vulnerable people. In exchange for their loyalty and jobs, they are protected and can share in the entitlements of their patrons. However, in these cases, accessing the most vulnerable people almost becomes collateral. It certainly does not follow the procedures of distributing aid on the basis of needs, as agencies claim.

The language of rights

Both cases illustrate the striking impact of a new language of rights on humanitarian realities. While the body of humanitarian principles and the language of humanitarian space have gradually developed since 1864, it has only recently been supplemented with the notion of rights. The Sphere standards, which were introduced in 2000 to enhance agency accountability to aid recipients, have brought about the notion that aid recipients are rights holders. This has resulted in a new vocabulary in which beneficiaries of aid are recast as rights holders who are entitled to basic services and protection against violence and disaster risks. In both cases, the new language of rights is used by agencies to constitute their subjects. In Kakuma, agencies have defined a new domain of intervention in educating people to take responsibility for security in their community, for instance by combatting domestic violence. While the moral elevation of people has been used to legitimize interventions since before colonization, we now see a new variation on this theme in the attempts of agencies to forge standards derived from human rights on people's personal life choices. It is important to consider how this shapes interventions and the kinds of resentment it engenders. Rights education has had the unintended effect of creating a permanent sense of dissatisfaction among refugees. While they are being taught their rights, they are at the same time confined to the camp, leading to advanced and frustrated aspirations at the same time. In Sri Lanka, the use of a rights discourse, where beneficiaries are framed in a manner that is reminiscent of consumers, has advanced individualization to the detriment of community solidarity. It is important to conduct more systematic research on the manner in which the new rights languages are being employed in practice, and its impact on the delivery of impartial aid to people in need.

Conclusion

In this chapter we have approached humanitarian space as a socially negotiated arena and explored the way in which actors employ the *concept* of humanitarian space to further their projects and ambitions. It is partly in the struggle over language (the 'real' humanitarian, the 'proper' rights-framework, the 'suitable' narrative of insecurity) that humanitarian arenas are being shaped.

Our cases highlight the significant impact of the response of aid receivers, as well as other actors in the humanitarian arena. These responses determine to a great extent how agencies can access the humanitarian arena and realize their programmes, and how certain people become eligible to receive aid and others not. The dissemination of ideas, allocation of humanitarian resources and implementation of relief projects take place through subtle power processes that transcend preconceived notions about humanitarian agents and aid recipients. Processes by which actors define one another do not follow definitions or principles as such; they constitute political struggles in which discourses of humanitarianism and human rights act as major devices. For instance, the use of the concepts 'participation' and 'ownership' has the effect of transforming beneficiaries into humanitarian agents (local staff). The creation or maintenance of local power configurations are part of the fabric of contemporary humanitarian action.

In studying humanitarian spaces as arenas, our understanding of the dynamics of aid should focus on the manner in which actors engage with, and respond to, their surroundings. It requires grasping the formal dimensions of aid, as much as what is happening between the lines and in informal daily interaction. By focusing on the everyday practices of aid, it becomes clear how humanitarian headquarter-claims to political neutrality and the application of universal normative values are negotiated through the micro-physics of power in humanitarian arenas.

Notes

1 This chapter is a revised version of an earlier publication that appeared in *Development and Change* 41(6): 1117–1139, in 2010.

2 For a review of recent definitions of humanitarian space, see Sida (2005: 26).
3 The author made five field visits between 2005 and 2006 as a consultant for the Sri Lankan Coalition of Humanitarian Agencies (CHA).
4 This fieldwork took place over a period of 18 months between 2004 and 2010, as part of the author's PhD research.
5 See the Code of Conduct for the Red Cross and Red Crescent Movement and NGOs in disaster relief: http://www.icrc.org/web/eng/siteeng0.nsf/htmlall/57JMNB#a8
6 Interview with CHA director, March 2005.
7 Workshop by Consortium of Humanitarian Agencies, Hambantota, August 2006.
8 Interview Galle representative Consortium of Humanitarian Agencies, August 2006.

References

Agier, M. (2002) 'Between War and City. Towards an Urban Anthropology of Refugee Camps', *Ethnography* 3(3): 317–341.
Agier, M. and Bouchet-Saulnier, F. (2004) 'Humanitarian Spaces: Spaces of Exception', in F. Weissman, *In the Shadows of 'Just Wars': Violence, Politics and Humanitarian Action*. New York: Cornell University Press. 297–313.
Berger, L. (2006) 'Listening to Tsunami Survivors. Treating Aid Recipients like Valued Customers Gives Insights into Disaster Relief', *Stanford Social Innovation Review*. Stanford University.
Bixler, M. (2005) *The Lost Boys of Sudan: An American Story of the Refugee Experience*. London: The University of Georgia Press.
De Waal, A. (1997) *Famine Crimes: Politics and the Disaster Relief Industry in Africa*. Oxford: James Currey.
DeChaine, R. (2002) 'Humanitarian Space and the Social Imagery: Médecins Sans Frontières/Doctors Without Borders and the Rhetoric of Global Community', *Journal of Communication Inquiry*, 26(4): 354–69.
Donini, A., Fast, L., Hansen, G., Harris, S., Minear, L., Mowjee, T. and Wilder, A. (2008) *Humanitarian Agenda 2015. The State of the Humanitarian Enterprise*. Medford: Feinstein International Center, Tufts University.
Dunant, H. (1986) *A Memory of Solferino*. Geneva: International Committee of the Red Cross.
Fernando, L. (2005) *Post Tsunami People's Consultations Project Report*. Colombo: Disaster Relief Monitoring Unit, Human Rights Commission of Sri Lanka.
Fernando, U. (2003) *NGOs in Sri Lanka: Past and Present Trends*. Colombo: Wasala Publications.
Fernando, U. and Hilhorst, D. (2006) 'Everyday Practices of Humanitarian Aid: Tsunami Response in Sri Lanka', *Development in Practice* 16(3–4): 292–302.
Foucault, M. (1978) *The History of Sexuality. Volume I*. New York: Pantheon Books.
Fulu, E. (2007) 'Gender, Vulnerability and the Experts: Responding to the Maldives Tsunami', *Development and Change* 39(5): 843–64.
Gaasbeek, T. (2005) 'What Remains is Sadness – Narratives of Humanitarian Aid Workers Who Left their Organisations after the Tsunami. The Globalisation of Disaster Response: Tsunami Aid from Donor and Recipient Perspectives', Wageningen: Wageningen University.
Grombach Wagner, J. (2005) 'An IHL/ICRC perspective on "humanitarian space"'. http://www.odihpn.org/report.asp?ID=2765#comments. Retrieved on 12/07, 2007.
Guha-Sapir, D., Hargitt, D. and Hoyois, P. (2004) *Thirty Years of Natural Disasters. 1974–2003: The Numbers*. Louvain: Presses Universitaires de Louvain.

Harrell-Bond, B. (1986) *Imposing Aid. Emergency Assistance to Refugees*. Oxford: Oxford University Press.

Hilhorst, D. and Schmiemann, N. (2002) 'Humanitarian Principles and Organizational Culture: Everyday Practice in Médicins Sans Frontières-Holland', *Development in Practice* 12(3/4): 490–500.

Hilhorst, D. and Serrano, M. (2010) 'The Humanitarian Arena in Angola, 1975–2008', *Disasters* 35(S2): s183–s201.

Hyndman, J. (2009) 'Siting Conflict and Peace in Post-tsunami Sri Lanka and Aceh, Indonesia', *Norwegian Journal of Geography* 63: 89–96.

Jansen, B.J. (2008) 'Between Vulnerability and Assertiveness: Negotiating Resettlement in Kakuma Refugee Camp, Kenya', *African Affairs* 107: 569–87.

Keen, D. (1994) *The Benefits of Famine: A Political Economy of Famine and Relief in South Western Sudan, 1983–1989*. Princeton: Princeton University Press.

Kleinfeld, M. (2007) 'Misreading the Post-tsunami Political Landscape in Sri Lanka: The Myth of Humanitarian Space', *Space and Polity* 11(2): 169–184.

Korf, B., Habullah, S., Hollenbach, P. and Klem, B. (2010) 'The Gift of Disaster: The Commodification of Good Intentions in Post-tsunami Sri Lanka', *Disasters* 34(S1): s60–s77.

Le Billon, P. (2000) *The Political Economy of War. What Relief Agencies Need to Know*. London: Humanitarian Practice Network.

Leader, N. (2002) *The Politics of Principle: the Principles of Humanitarian Action in Practice*. London: Humanitarian Practice Network.

Long, N. (1992) 'From Paradigm Lost to Paradigm Regained? The Case for an Actor-oriented Sociology of Development', in N. Long and A. Long, *Battlefields of Knowledge: The Interlocking of Theory and Practice in Social Research and Development*. London: Routledge: 16–43.

Long, N. (2001) *Development Sociology. Actor Perspectives*. London: Routledge.

Magone, C., Neuman, M., and Weissman, F. (2011) *Humanitarian Negotiations Revealed: the MSF Experience*. London: C. Hirst & Co Publishers Ltd.

Minear, L. (1999) 'The Theory and Practice of Neutrality: Some Thoughts on the Tensions', *International Review of the Red Cross* 833: 63–71.

Olsen, G.R., Carstensen, N. and Høyen, K. (2003) 'Humanitarian Crises: What Determines the Level of Emergency Assistance? Media Coverage, Donor Interests and the Aid Business', *Disasters* 27(2): 109–26.

Pallis, M. (2006) 'The Operation of UNHCR's Accountability Mechanisms', *Journal of International Law and Politics* 37(4): 869–915.

Rieff, D. (2002) *A Bed for the Night: Humanitarianism in Crisis*. London: Vintage.

Scharffscher, K. (2011) 'Disempowerment Through Disconnection: Local Women's Disaster Response and International Relief in Post Tsunami Batticaloa', *Disaster Prevention and Management* 20(1): 83–81.

Sida, L. (2005) *Challenges to Humanitarian Space: A Review of Humanitarian Issues related tot the UN Integrated Mission in Liberia and to the Relationship Between Humanitarian and Military Actors in Liberia*. Liberia: Humanitarian Information Center.

Slim, H. (2003) 'Marketing Humanitarian Space. Argument and Method in Humanitarian Persuasion'. http://www.hdcentre.org/files/Marketing.pdf. Retrieved on 23/07/2010.

Sommers, M. (2005) *Islands of Education. Schooling, Civil War and the Southern Sudanese (1983–2004)*. Paris: UNESCO.

Spearin, C. (2001) 'Private Security Companies and Humanitarians: A Corporate Solution to Securing Humanitarian Spaces?', *International Peacekeeping* 8(1): 20–43.

Stirrat, J. (2006) 'Competitive Humanitarianism. Relief and the Tsunami in Sri Lanka', *Anthropology Today* 22(5): 11–16.

Telford, J. and Cosgrave, J. (2005) *Joint Evaluation of the International Response to the Indian Ocean Tsunami: Synthesis Report*. London: Tsunami Evaluation Coalition.

Terry, F. (2002) *Condemned to Repeat? The Paradox of Humanitarian Action*. Ithaca, NY: Cornell University Press.

Turner, S. (2001) *The Barriers of Innocence. Humanitarian Intervention and Political Imagination in a Refugee camp for Burundians in Tanzania*. PhD dissertation, Roskilde University.

Turner, S. (2004) 'Under the Gaze of the "Big Nations": Refugees, Rumours and the International Community in Tanzania', *African Affairs* 103: 227–47.

UNHCR (2004) *Resettlement Handbook 2004*. Geneva: UNHCR.

UNHCR (2007) *Statistical Yearbook 2005*. Geneva: UNHCR.

Ville de Goyet, C. and Morinière, L. (2006) *The Role of Needs Assessment in the Tsunami Response*. London: Tsunami Evaluation Commitee.

Walkup, M. (1997) 'Policy Dysfunction in Humanitarian Organisations: The Role of Coping Strategies, Institutions and Organisational Culture', *Journal of Refugee Studies* 10(1): 36–60.

Wilde, R. (1998) '*Quis Custodiet Ipsos Custodes?*: Why and How UNHCR Governance of "Development" Refugee Camps Should be Subject to International Human Rights Law', *Yale Human Rights and Development Law Journal* 1: 107–28.

12 The politics of peacebuilding through strengthening civil society

Mathijs van Leeuwen

An important critique of contemporary peacebuilding interventions that focus on the strengthening of local civil society is that they fail to take proper account of the politics involved; they shy away from taking positions on whose interests to support and what societal transformation to envision, yet implicitly promote particular (e.g. neo-liberal) development agendas, or unwittingly take sides in conflict. This chapter underscores the fact that peacebuilding through civil society strengthening is indeed a highly political exercise. Yet, rather than blaming the organizations concerned for being blind about the politics involved in their interventions, it seeks to explore how peacebuilding interventions actually come about and *become* political in everyday organizing practices, and in practices of ordering and framing conflict and defining interventions. Insofar as this (de-)politicization is intentional, it not only relates to the conflicts in which organizations operate, but is also part of the organizational politics of legitimization. The findings underscore the fact that, despite increasing attention to the politics involved in peacebuilding, intervening agencies indeed lack analytical capacities. Yet, rather than falling short in analysing social and political processes, they fail to analyse their own practices of interpreting conflict and peace and the simplifications involved in this, as well as the role played by their own organizational dynamics and politics.

To make this argument, the chapter first introduces the notion of peacebuilding, international development actors' concern with local civil society building from this perspective, and the critique that those practices fail to take account of the political choices implicit in their conflict analyses and in the interventions they design. The second part outlines an analytical perspective on the de-politicization of peacebuilding and related support to civil society. The third part discusses three case studies of peacebuilding through strengthening civil society – in Burundi, the African Great Lakes region, and Guatemala. In each of those, the organizations involved implicitly – and often unwittingly – make highly political choices. The analysis of everyday organizing practices of peacebuilding organizations underscores the importance of framing and simplifying conflict situations and the role of internal organizational dynamics in this, notably the politics of legitimization.

The politics of civil society peacebuilding

Peacebuilding has become a major area of development intervention since the early 1990s. In the post-Cold War era, international peacebuilding ambitions shifted from only negotiating agreements to preventing future conflicts through the transformation of societies. From this new, ambitious aim of conflict transformation, substantial attention was given to civil society. The term 'civil society' refers to the sphere of organized society that exists outside of government and the private sector (Biekart 1999). It may cover a wide variety of actors, ranging from internationally operating development organizations to national and local initiatives (non-governmental organizations [NGOs], churches, labour unions, media) and traditional forms of association (customary authorities). In peacebuilding, civil society actors were considered to represent those that had been marginalized in conflict or that had not taken up arms, and thus were a necessary party to include in formal peace processes. Strengthening civil society would contribute to the cultivation of alternative political processes and institutions to authoritatively and legitimately manage group conflicts (Cousens *et al.* 2001). Civil society could build bridges between polarized groups, promoting dialogue and reconciling people.

This predilection for civil society in peacebuilding reflected its popularity in development cooperation in general. Civil society was often seen as the 'imagined agent of development' (Pearce 2005), being more effective than governments in fulfilling development needs (Crowther 2001). This counted even more for post-conflict settings, where state institutions had failed to provide security, accountability, and basic services. Here, civil society was considered more representative and closer to the grassroots than government institutions (Van Rooy 1998: 6). Moreover, civil society would reinvigorate the state by contributing to good governance and democracy (Biekart 1999). Civil society organizations would enable citizens to hold government officials accountable for their actions, and articulate public interests (Paffenholz and Spurk 2006). Even more, they would be key players in renegotiating the social contract between state and society, which had been broken or compromised by civil war (van Leeuwen and Verkoren 2012).

Consequently, the creation and consolidation of civil society organizations became an indispensable part of, and a popular strategy for, peacebuilding. Enthusiasm for building peace through strengthening civil society remains pertinent. Even if, since 9/11, there has been a renewed emphasis on the role of the state as a key player in accomplishing societal transformation (Macrae and Harmer 2003), more recent conceptualizations of statebuilding by European donors again emphasize the contributions civil society building could make to reshaping state-society relations (OECD-DAC 2008, DFID 2010).

However, from the moment civil society peacebuilding became a core concern for development practitioners, they have been critiqued for failing to take account of the politics involved (e.g. Uvin 1998, Crowther 2001, Duffield 2001, Bebbington *et al.* 2008, Fisher and Zimina 2009). Interpreting conflict and defining peacebuilding interventions is a highly political exercise, in that it always implies choices about which conflicts to address and which to ignore, what societal transformation and development to promote, what actors to empower or support, and whose vision of peace to favour. Development interventions are never 'neutral', because advancing the interests of particular stakeholders implies leaving out or even curtailing others (Gready and Ensor 2005). This counts all the more in conflict situations, where intervention may interfere with the very interests at stake in the conflict.

Over the years, the claim that civil society peacebuilding fails to take proper account of the 'politics of conflict and peace' has appeared in different forms. Early on, critics warned that supporting civil society often implies taking sides in conflict. They have pointed out that many of those assumed to be 'neutral' civil society organizations share the despised characteristics of state institutions (such as corruption and clientelism) or are controlled by state actors (e.g. Ellis 1995). They have argued that the image of civil society as a peaceful force neglects the internal conflicts and ethnic biases of civil society, and their different visions of political options (Crowther 2001, Cardoso 2003). In this connection, (historical) linkages between state and civil society, and the origins of civil movements in political parties or violent resistance movements have been highlighted (Uvin 1998, Hilhorst 2003). It has been argued that ignoring the political character of civil society depoliticizes peacebuilding work (Duffield 2001). Strategic intervention opportunities are missed, while uncritical support to civil society may come down to taking sides in conflict or promoting particular agendas.

More recent discussions concern the failure of contemporary peacebuilding and civil society building practices to contribute to real societal transformation. Critiques point to the failure to engage with the 'real' issues at stake, such as economic injustices, denial of rights and participation, and (inter)national power imbalances (Fisher and Zimina 2009), or see the enthusiasm for civil society building conveniently obscuring lack of commitment to more substantial intervention (Duffield 2001). Moreover, while civil society building may aim to strengthen state–society relations, to change power balances, or to foster institutions, interventions are criticized for creating and strengthening local NGOs and their roles in 'apolitical' service delivery, not civil society at large and its more political roles vis-à-vis the state (Biekart 1999, Bebbington *et al.* 2008). And even if various donors fund local civil society in highly political ways, for instance through supporting advocacy work, this is the exception rather than the rule. Donors are reproached for being reluctant to support more politically-oriented activities which may jeopardise their 'neutrality' or relations with host governments. In this way, civil society building is de-politicized: it becomes uncritical of structural issues and power imbalances. Increasingly, NGOs come to act as 'tamed' social movements (Kaldor 2003: 86). At the same time, such strategic choices are highly political – by choosing to work through the existing *status quo* rather than radically reforming the political set-up of a country (Howell and Pearce 2001, Bebbington *et al.* 2008).

Various authors point out that many such practices of apolitical civil society building actually neatly fit within what is called the 'liberal peace agenda' – the specific mix of democratic governance reform, rule of law, and free market-oriented economic policy that is promoted under the headings of peacebuilding and statebuilding. 'Liberal peace' critics conclude that peace-building policies and practices in post-conflict countries aim to transform societies in the image of Western market-oriented democracies in which universal values are promoted as a remedy for local problems (Richmond 2006, Paris and Sisk 2009). It is claimed that much of contemporary civil society building is aligned to such an agenda. For instance, Dagnino (2008) points out how movements that used to campaign for more social governmental policies are now co-opted into the neo-liberal system by carrying out social services that were previously considered the responsibility of the state.

Finally, in addition to critiques on the ideological choices implicitly made in civil society strengthening, reviewers point out that intervention is a contentious strategy in itself. By definition, intervention is one-directional, promoting agendas that do not necessarily correspond to the interests of the communities concerned (Chigas and Woodrow 2009). While interveners themselves may see intervention as more politically correct than not intervening, those affected by it may see it as interference or imposition.

In diverse ways, civil society strengthening is thus a political exercise, implying choices about whether and how to intervene, and what and whom to support. The question is then: why do international development organizations fail to take account of this adequately? Why is civil society strengthening so often depoliti-cized and seen as 'neutral'? Why is it that interveners fail to see that their interven-tions imply political choices regarding conflict and peace? Some have argued that the answer is to be found in the fact that the 'neo-liberal peace' discourse has become so dominant that it does not occur to international development organi-zations to question it (Duffield 2001). For instance, staff members of development organizations are not aware of being co-opted in a project of promoting Western bureaucratic rationality when trying to live up to expectations of measurability and tangible results (Pearce 2010). This chapter seeks the answer in the ways in which international and local organizations operate: (de-)politicization processes are contingent upon the practices of organizing and interpreting conflict, and the organizational politics involved in this.

Analysing the politics and de-politicization of civil society peacebuilding

This chapter conforms to the idea of seeing aid interventions as an arena where aid is renegotiated and its outcomes shaped by the interactions of a multiplicity of actors (see Hilhorst and Jansen, Chapter 11 this volume). Policies and interven-tions of an organization can only be understood by looking at how they come about as a result of the everyday practices of their staff, not only at headquarters but also in the field, and the everyday practices of members of the communities where they implement their programmes as well as those of surrounding actors. From such a perspective, policy is not so much a technical response to a given problem. Rather, it is an ongoing process of interpretation of a problem, which is shaped and negotiated along the way by different stakeholders in the policy issue (Long 2001, Hilhorst 2003, Mosse 2004).

What peacebuilding interventions look like is thus not only defined in the head offices of organizations, but also results from the daily practices of organizing (Hilhorst and van Leeuwen 2005). Within an organization, organizational cultures, bureaucratic rationales, and intervention routines have an impact on the way in which programmes are conceived. The notion of peacebuilding is adopted by different people to advance their own understandings of reality and projects. In the implementation of peacebuilding, not only personal visions and experience of staff members may play a role but also the interpretations and choices by community members and local authorities that redefine peacebuilding to fit it to their life worlds, perceptions, priorities, and interests. As a consequence, peacebuilding may come to promote particular agendas, including political ones, in unplanned and decentralized ways.

Then, when trying to understand conflict and defining objectives and interventions, development practitioners are actually defining and interpreting the reality in which they operate. Such processes are political in their consequences. To explore how this works, the notion of 'discourse' is useful, or the collective practices of ordering and 'framing' in the minds of actors, who try to organize and make sense of their experiences through coherent schemes. In the tradition of Foucault, discourses are often seen as implying power – as dominant traditions of looking at the world which eliminate alternative visions, or as affecting social relations. In that sense, discourse might be a vehicle for advancing particular political interests. Yet, while acknowledging the 'power' of discourse, we should be aware that discourse is also a cognitive process to simplify reality, a necessary response to the complexity in which peacebuilding organizations operate.

In situations of conflict and violence, accurate information is difficult to obtain, causes and factors underlying violence constantly change, and the outcomes of interventions are unpredictable. To be able to operate in such a context requires organizations to reduce conflict to a manageable and predictable situation. Here, 'framing' comes in. Framing is an ordering practice that helps to understand and simplify the world, by creating coherence out of fragmented ideas, experiences, and practices (cf. Law 1994). It helps to conceptualize reality in such a way that we can not only better understand it, but also respond to it. As such, it facilitates policy making. However, as framing always simplifies, it may result in important parts of reality being lost (see Mol and Law 2002). Nonetheless, those parts of reality that are ignored affect the ways in which interventions work out. A major casualty of 'framing' in peacebuilding practice is awareness of the political choices implied by particular understandings of reality.

It would, however, be short-sighted to interpret simplification only as a cognitive process, and its political implications only as an unfortunate side effect. Certainly, peacebuilding organizations, their staff, and their constituents tend to be deeply involved in the politics of conflict and peace and to make deliberate ideological and political choices. However, many of their choices are not so much related to the conflict in which they operate but are the consequence of daily organizational practices, as outlined above. Here, another type of politics plays an important role. Peacebuilding organizations are involved in what we may call the 'everyday politics of organizations' (Hilhorst 2003), including efforts to legitimize their organization vis-à-vis other stakeholders. Organizations are in constant competition with one another for legitimacy, funding, or support in the communities where they work. To find clients and supporters for their peacebuilding interventions, they have to convince others of their appropriateness and trustworthiness (cf. Mosse 2004). Such organizational dynamics interfere with the ways in which organizations understand conflict and define peacebuilding interventions.

The major tenets of this chapter are, therefore, first, that – unintentionally – peacebuilding through civil society often has political implications as a result of everyday organizational practices and processes of interpreting conflict and defining interventions. Second, insofar as this politicization is intentional, it not only originates from political and ideological choices vis-à-vis the context of conflict in which organizations operate, but also has a lot to do with the organizational politics of legitimization.

De-politicizing civil society and peacebuilding in practice

To explore the dynamics of de-politicization in practice, the above framework is applied to three case studies of interventions to strengthen civil society in the African Great Lakes Region, Burundi, and Guatemala. After brief introductions of the cases, presenting the strategic political choices implicitly made in assessing the conflict and defining the interventions, the section analyses the everyday practices of organizing, the tendencies of ordering at play, and the organizational politics involved.

The case studies were conducted as part of a PhD project in Wageningen Disaster Studies, in collaboration with several NGOs. Fieldwork stretched over the period from 2004 to 2007, including 14 months in Burundi and the Great Lakes Region, and 10 months in Guatemala (van Leeuwen 2009). The case studies were not designed for comparison. The countries were selected collaboratively with the Dutch NGO Cordaid which at that time was elaborating its peacebuilding programme. All the cases were grounded in a similar conceptual framework and methodology, and all explored the question of how civil society organizations analyse conflict and define their interventions. In the case of the Great Lakes Region, I conducted interviews and participated in regional events. In Burundi and Guatemala, I did assignments for several local organizations, and so acquired insights from within as to how peacebuilding policies and interventions take shape. In those two cases, findings on the politics of interpreting conflict and defining peacebuilding have been discussed with the local organizations involved.

Regional peacebuilding in the African Great Lakes Region

This first case concerns efforts by international development organizations to promote regional peacebuilding in the African Great Lakes Region in 2004/2005 (van Leeuwen 2008). At that time, there was increasing awareness that if insecurity trespasses national borders, causes of conflict may need to be addressed in a regional way. Various international development organizations thus encouraged their partners from civil society from different countries to become involved in regional networks and to share and coordinate peacebuilding efforts. In practice, however, the actual scale of regional peacebuilding remained limited and focused on regional meetings rather than programmatic collaboration. In most of these regional encounters, the politics of regional conflict and peacebuilding – how insecurity in one country was caused by problems and interference from neighbouring countries – were hardly addressed.

Within local civil society, these regional politics were lost in the daily practices of implementation. While underwriting the regional discourse, in practice, local civil society organizations primarily focused on local issues: support to local peace committees, community development, and basic infrastructure. They found it difficult to deal with national issues, while regional affairs were completely beyond their scope of intervention.

At the same time, the politics of regional conflict were hardly addressed because of the highly political nature of civil society organizations. Donors had good experiences with the local peacebuilding roles of their partners from civil society, and the assumption was that regional exchange between civil society organizations would thus contribute to peace at regional level as well. Such a perspective did not recognize the fact that civil society organizations were deeply embedded in the politics of regional conflict. Their individual regional analyses were strongly shaped by the political space in their home countries. This resulted in a strong reluctance to talk about regional politics during regional meetings. Regional peacebuilding was thus reduced to a shared notion of suffering, without attribution to political causes.

Resolving post-conflict land disputes in Burundi

In 2005, many local and international organizations in Burundi worried that land disputes accompanying the massive return of refugees after the civil war would cause a serious security threat and re-ignite the preceding violence. Organizations interpreted land disputes in ethnic terms due to Hutu returnees finding their land occupied by Tutsi. Hence they started programmes to enhance the capacities of local and traditional institutions to deal with the disputes of returnees.

This focus on the returnee crisis by Burundese and international organizations refuted the view that most land disputes did not result from the return of refugees and had no relation to ethnicity. In the four communities where we conducted fieldwork, the most serious conflicts involved members of the same family. Various conflicts were the result of the policies of the (past) government and corrupt authorities rather than local disagreement. The existing conflicts thus had a long-term character. Rather than strengthening mediation and dispute-resolving capacities at the local level, they required structural, but contested, solutions at the national level to facilitate agrarian reform and off-farm employment. Further, framing the situation as a returnee problem determined what institutions to support, whose capacities to develop (traditional or state institutions), and whose suffering to relieve. Yet, at the local level, focusing on returning refugees only, rather than on all victims of land disputes, was perceived as unfair, and even fuelling division, or supporting the new Hutu government (van Leeuwen 2010b).

Agrarian conflict after the Guatemala Peace Accords

This final case is based on research in Guatemala in 2007, for and with Pastoral de la Tierra of the Catholic Diocese of San Marcos (PTSM) (van Leeuwen 2010a). At that time, ten years after the peace agreements, Guatemalan civil society organizations found it difficult to define how the societal changes envisaged in the peace accords could be realised and how they could contribute.

Guatemalan organizations viewed their development work primarily as obstructed by the slow pace of post-conflict societal transformation. This created a serious dilemma. To realize agrarian reform, should they opt for radical change by confronting the state? Or should they try to make the best of the limited possibilities that the Peace Agreement provided through the reformed judicial system and newly-established state institutions, even though this had only modest results in terms of changing rural power relations? And certainly, the government's violent responses to activism on land in the past also made them cautious.

In contrast, such realities received little acknowledgement from supporting donors and international NGOs, who failed to perceive this dilemma. International organizations had become reluctant to support local civil society organizations who, in their perspective, had failed to make a transition 'from protest to proposal' and to redefine their relation to the state. After the peace agreements, civil society organizations became divided by external funding, the politics of legitimization and survival, and internal organizational problems (own interviews, Pearce and Howell 2001, Sieder *et al.* 2002).

In the case of PTSM, their strategy to support peasants with land conflicts was – intentionally as well as unintentionally – highly political. To maintain legitimacy among the influential landlords in the Diocese, and to guarantee funding from donors willing to support legal work but not activism, the organization adopted a conformist approach. This resulted in a legalistic approach towards land disputes, involving collaboration with the government institutions. An unintentional downside of the approach was the reduction of conflict to its legal aspects, thereby neglecting perceptions of justice and demands for redress of historic harm amongst the intended beneficiaries. PTSM's conformism to the existing institutions of the state affirmed the existing legal and political order and sidetracked its agenda of reforming state institutions and criticizing the belief in market-mechanisms for agrarian reform.

Politics in the everyday practices of organizing

When analysing the politics involved in the above case studies, the aforementioned critique on the political naivety of civil society strengthening seems applicable. The case of regional peacebuilding illustrates how idealized images of civil society among donors and international NGOs result in inadequate assessments of how civil society might contribute to peace at a regional level. In practice, the interventions of local civil society reflected little attention to the regional dynamics of conflict. The case of Guatemala is in line with critiques that donors refrain from supporting more politically-oriented activities, and in their intervention practices unwittingly conform to a liberal peacebuilding agenda. The case of Burundi, finally, seems to underscore the incapacity of both local and international organizations to understand the political implications of their analyses of conflict situations.

Yet, such analyses seem to be at odds with all the efforts put into conflict analysis, and the commitments of donor and NGO staff alike to take account of the politics of peacebuilding interventions and the political engagement of some. Apparently, the problem is not so much a lack of analysis or awareness of the unintended political consequences peacebuilding might have. The problem is rather in the ways that peacebuilding interventions actually come about.

To start with, peacebuilding policies are not only defined at head offices of organizations. Staff members at all levels reflect on the meaning of the organization, the context in which they work, and the events that happen around them. Defining peacebuilding is an ongoing process, in which visions and experience of staff members play a role and also the interpretations and choices by community members and local authorities. In the dialogues between civil society organizations from the Great Lakes Region, for instance, international discourses of regional peacebuilding translated into an emphasis on shared suffering which was far removed from the international discourse on regional politics. In a similar way, though PTSM initially had the intention to advocate agrarian reform, their profound research into particular disputes and interaction with affected people resulted in an approach that involved assisting individual cases.

As a consequence of those practices of organizing, peacebuilding may become political or may be de-politicized in unplanned and decentralized ways. For instance, peacebuilding strategies become political because they always come to serve an amalgam of interests of different people inside and outside organizations. People participating in a peacebuilding organization may be committed peace activists, but may also acquire an income from their work with an organization. For instance, peacebuilding organizations in the Great Lakes Region were simultaneously vehicles for the political ambitions of their leaders who were excluded from the political process. In Guatemala, the choice for more conformist approaches was not surprising, considering that in the recent past land activists had been murdered.

Then, organizations are indeed fundamentally political in nature. For example, in the Great Lakes Region, civil society organizations strongly identified with the regional politics of their respective governments. But organizations are not just involved in the politics of peace and conflict, but as much in everyday organizational politics to produce meaning, reallocate resources, and legitimize themselves. In Guatemala, organizations were deeply involved in politics of survival, competing heavily for constituents, and being reluctant to work collaboratively out of fear of becoming superfluous. In assisting local peasants in land disputes, PTSM continuously needed to convince those peasants of the legal strategies and definitions of justice they applied. In a similar way, international NGOs need to convince their donors of their continuing relevance (cf. Guttal 2005, Barnett *et al.* 2007) and, therefore, might get involved in peacebuilding, or continue their business as usual, while relabelling their activities as peacebuilding (cf. Denskus 2007).

Framing conflict, defining peacebuilding and its political implications

The case studies illustrate that awareness of the political implications of intervention was lost in the practices of ordering and framing. Framing conflict in the Great Lakes Region in regional terms, and assuming that regional cooperation and exchange between civil society organizations would contribute to peace, diverted international interveners' attention away from the need to address the highly politicized character of civil society. Framing land disputes in Burundi as a returnee crisis implied choices about on which people and whose suffering to focus, what institutions to support, and whose capacities to develop. This was locally perceived as unfair. The intervention strategy of PTSM highlighted the legal aspects of land conflict to the neglect of the feelings of injustice of their local beneficiaries. Donors' framing of the problems of Guatemalan civil society in terms of institutional capacity neglected the actual political context and let donors conveniently forget about the failure of the government to fulfil promises made in the peace agreements.

What processes play a role in how donors and NGOs simplify the reality in which they operate and in how they define interventions? The case studies point to some common tendencies in the practices of ordering and framing of international and local peacebuilding organizations.

In the first place, while over the last few years academics have emphasized the continuities between 'conflict' and 'normal' situations of development, in practice 'conflict' and 'peace' tend to be approached as entirely different situations, requiring different modalities of interventions (see Cramer 2006, Richards 2005). This makes interveners forget about long-term continuities between war and peace, and the need to take those into account when addressing violence. In Guatemala, assuming that a new order had emerged since the peace agreements led international organizations to forget about continuities in inequality and limited political representation.

Furthermore, organizations working in (post-) conflict settings tend to interpret conflict situations in terms of an emergency, where problems are conflict-related, urgent, and require immediate intervention. In Burundi, policies to address returnee-related land disputes developed at the height of humanitarian activities and on the threshold of the massive return of refugees. Framing land disputes as a returnee problem was in line with the sense of urgency felt by many interveners at that time. However, by focusing on land disputes from a crisis perspective, as a pressing and abnormal situation requiring urgent intervention, organizations forgot about the long-term structural character of land conflict and underplayed more development-like interventions.

At the same time, development practitioners find it difficult to deal with *discon*tinuities in conflict settings. Although dynamics of conflict at national level may strongly relate to what happens at the local level, local experiences and manifestations of violence and conflict seldom run parallel to conflict at national level (see e.g. Kalyvas 2003). Peacebuilding is thus a process taking place at different paces for different people and at different levels. In the case of Burundi, local land disputes were indeed related to national issues such as the massive return of refugees, but also had many local dimensions. The way ethnicity manifests itself in the national political process does not necessarily correspond to how it plays a role in local community relations and disputes about land. Yet, interventions focusing on the local dimensions of conflict started from the assumption that communities would be torn apart by (ethnic) conflict, forgetting about the involvement of the state in such conflicts.

Then, organizations tend to interpret conflict situations in terms of technical or organizational deficiencies, rather than as stemming from different political visions. In the Great Lakes Region, international interventions to promote regional peacebuilding through civil society basically interpreted the coming together of civil society as a process of exchange and collaboration. Little attention was given to the problem of reconciling those organizations. In Burundi, many organizations interpreted land disputes mainly as originating from contradictions in, or the absence of, proper legislation, and the failure of juridical institutions. Such an analysis legitimized working on the development of new legislation, re-establishing formal institutions, and promoting the legal expertise of local institutions. Thereby they forgot about the accessibility and fairness of all those institutions, both state and local ones. In both Guatemala and Burundi, many civil society organizations applied legal approaches to deal with conflict at the local level, neglecting mediation and political reform at national level. This 'legal reflex' – the belief that law is the most effective form of protection against conflict (Gready and Ensor 2005: 9) – is widespread among organizations involved in peacebuilding.

Frequently, interpreting conflict and imagining peacebuilding responses closely reflects the – ideological, religious, urban, or occupational – background of the organization and the particular experiences of their staff. In the Great Lakes Region, regional analyses strongly reflected the expertise of organizations, with human rights organizations highlighting the regional character of human rights violations. This tendency was also clear in the case of Burundi, where the framing of land problems as a returnee issue corresponded to the focus on and experience of many humanitarian organizations with resettling returning refugees, strengthening community reconciliation processes, and enhancing local capacities for conflict resolution. The occurrence of the above-mentioned 'legal reflex' in peacebuilding is no surprise, if one considers that staff members with a legal background tend to be overrepresented in civil society organizations. Clearly, PTSM's affiliation with the Catholic Church and liberation theology, as well as the participation of staff members in earlier efforts of the Church to unearth human rights violations during the civil war, shaped the emphasis in the programme on truth and justice.

Experiential and ideological background also plays an important role in the peacebuilding policies of international development organizations, in the activities and partners they prioritize, and the extent to which they consider civil society strengthening as a technical exercise of strengthening organizational capacities of civil society, or as enhancing local organizations' capacities to contribute to societal transformation. The activist past of an organization such as Norwegian People's Aid (NPA) comes about in emphasizing social justice, attributing civil society roles in countering political oppression and economic marginalization. An organization like the UN Development Programme (UNDP), with governments as its 'natural' partner, on the other hand, would not press for political change, and depicts civil society as representative of local communities that can inform and complement state programmes (van Leeuwen 2009).

Finally, an important tendency is that of resorting to preconceived ideas about conflict situations. In the Great Lakes Region, discussion was ongoing on how to analyse the interrelatedness of crises across borders, but there was consensus that there were a lot of similarities between countries in the region. Nonetheless, limited attention in the analyses was being given to the existing differences in the strength and capacities of the states, the role of civil society in different countries, and the significance of ethnicity in the political process and at the local level. In the case of Burundi, anxiety within international NGOs about the role of ethnicity in the crises in the Great Lakes probably played a role in their emphasis on ethnicity in depicting local community relations and disputes about land. In the absence of accurate knowledge of local conflict situations, NGOs assume correspondence with other situations they have experienced. In addition, assumed comparability influences observation when local conflict situations are interpreted.

Framing as part of organizational politics of legitimization

Simultaneously, the cases illustrate how interpreting conflict situations and defining peacebuilding interventions is not only a rational exercise, but may be political at the same time. Here, while the politics of conflict and peace and ideological choices play a role, organizational politics are very important. Framing is contingent upon organizations' concerns for legitimizing themselves, protecting organizational interests, and positioning themselves vis-à-vis donors, stakeholders, and other organizations (see also Serrano, Chapter 9 this volume).

For instance, the tendency described above to interpret context and possible interventions in terms of the type of interventions an organization is capable of implementing may relate to a concern to be relevant and create opportunities for intervention. In the Great Lakes Region, difficulties in arriving at shared interpretations of regional conflict not only resulted from the lack of analytical capacity, but also from deep political cleavages and unwillingness to arrive at interpretations that highlighted regional inter-linkages between problems. In framing regional conflict, local civil society organizations focused on the consequences of conflict rather than on causes, thereby limiting the need for collaboration.

Framing land disputes in Burundi as a returnee issue created opportunities for and legitimized intervention. Framing land disputes as resulting from failing institutions and improper laws enabled legally-oriented organizations in Burundi to legitimize work in legal training, civic education, and advocacy for legal reform, and to present themselves as useful. Consequently, they urged the development of new legislation, re-establishing juridical institutions, and enhancing legal knowledge of local conflict-resolving institutions. In their analysis, they gave little attention to the accessibility and fairness of state and local institutions, or locally prevailing perceptions of fair solutions. More generally, framing conflict in terms of intra-state conflict legitimizes limited international diplomatic involvement and places responsibilities for peacebuilding on local actors (Duffield 2001). Various ordering practices thus legitimize organizations to intervene but also not to intervene.

Framing practices also help organizations to conceive reality in such a way that intervention is possible. In the Great Lakes Region, international development actors' concern with regional approaches for peacebuilding effectively represented conflict in such a way that it could be addressed, and that conflict situations could be compared. Such a framing decreased the importance of specific and local knowledge, enabling the use of general models and strategies. In practice, however, the regional framing failed to provide the necessary details at national level. Regional approaches thus lost their significance when applied in practice in the different countries. More generally, framing conflict situations in terms of complexity may have advantages. Complexity in itself may legitimize intervention – 'we do not know how it will work, but we simply have to do something' – as well as inaction – 'as we do not know how it works, we cannot take a decision yet'.

The importance of organizational politics in interpreting conflict and defining appropriate responses was also clear in the work of PTSM in Guatemala, where limited political space reduced the kind of strategies the organization could apply. Its 'neutral' legalistic approach ensured that the organization could address the highly political issue of agrarian conflict. However, the framing of agrarian conflict in legalistic terms resulted in land disputes being reduced to the legal conflicts they included, thereby ignoring dimensions of conflict that could not be solved by law or the state institutions established to deal with land disputes. Hence, the interventions did not achieve the comprehensive justice expected by local actors, and as a result the intention of PTSM to contribute to 'justice' and peace was only realized to a certain extent. In the latter case, it was clear that the politics of framing are not just about opportunistic actors promoting their own organizational or private interests. Framing also results from the need of agency staff to assist their constituents while at the same time they need to assure the survival of their organization.

Finally, a tendency in ordering is to interpret interventions in apolitical terms. Authors such as Duffield (2001) and Dagnino (2008) point out that the failure of development organizations to take account of the politics of conflict and peacebuilding unwittingly feeds into particular (neo-liberal) development agendas. Yet, the above cases point out that de-politicization also feeds into organizational needs, and thus that organizations may prefer de-politicization. For instance, we may understand in this way the 'legal reflex' of international development organizations working in Guatemala and Burundi to prioritize organizations involved in legal assistance rather than their political activist colleagues. In Guatemala, despite the fact that international organizations knew better, they supported civil society organizations as if it was a time of peace. It was easier for international organizations to frame the Guatemalan situation as a 'normal' situation of development, focus on capacity building of local civil society organizations and leave them the responsibilities for change, rather than to confront the government and demand implementation of the peace agreements. Similarly, the regional framing of conflict and peacebuilding in the Great Lakes Region helped international development organizations to see their interventions as apolitical. By focusing on the region, there was no more need to deal with individual capricious governments, thus leaving responsibilities for political transformation to civil society. At the same time, to local civil society organizations, regional approaches legitimized a focus on the effects of regional dynamics rather than on causes and the prevention of regional conflict dynamics. In Burundi, framing land disputes as a local problem, to be addressed by local reconciliation activities, enabled NGOs to work in a 'neutral' way, without burning their fingers on the politically sensitive issue of agrarian reform. Those examples make clear that de-politicization may be both a political strategy – neutrality may be advantageous in realizing peacebuilding aims – and an organizational one.

Conclusion

This chapter concurs with the critique on contemporary practices of peacebuilding through civil society strengthening that too little attention is given to the fact that peacebuilding always implies political choices on what social transformation and whose development to promote, what actors to empower to realize this, and whose vision of peacebuilding to favour, let alone the question whether outside intervention should take place at all. However, this does not imply that organizations do not think through their interventions. On the contrary: there is a lot of discussion going on within development organizations on how best to address local conflict, and, indeed, take care of the politics of intervention. To understand why de-politicization takes place, or why the political implications of intervention are overlooked in organizations, this chapter has underscored the importance of exploring how peacebuilding interventions actually come about, and become political or (de-)politicized. The chapter highlights two important processes in how this happens.

First, defining peacebuilding is an ongoing process that is shaped along the way by actors within and outside the organization, all with their own political agendas or ideas about what the problem actually is and what needs to be done. As a consequence, peacebuilding may become political in unforeseen and decentralized ways. Further, organizational politics play an important role in defining interventions. Second, defining peacebuilding interventions always involves a cognitive process of ordering and framing the context in which one operates. In this process, organizations tend to split reality into parts, to focus on techniques of interventions, or to perceive contexts and peacebuilding interventions from the perspective of their particular expertise. This framing necessarily implies simplification, and losing sight of the politics involved. At the same time, intentionally and unintentionally, organizational politics of legitimization play important roles in this ordering. NGOs tend to promote representations of reality that are in line with their possibilities for intervention, or that legitimate them to intervene. Particular framings may both open up possibilities for intervention and restrict them, and may underscore the politics of interventions or instead de-politicize them.

Such findings underline how the de-politicization of civil society strengthening may be not so much the result of grand geo-political agendas implicitly underlying international peacebuilding discourses, but rather of the everyday practices and politics of peacebuilding organizations and the processes of ordering involved in the identification of strategies. Further, de-politicization is not so much the result of improper analysis and a lack of political strategy. It may be a strategy in itself, which benefits organizational needs. An apparent neglect of the politics of intervention or deliberate choice for apolitical technical work may be politically and organizationally strategic.

Then, the practices of framing, and the influence of organizational practices and politics described, can be observed among both international donors and development organizations, and local organizations. For this reason, we should not assume that local organizations, by definition, are more capable of dealing with the politics involved in peacebuilding. Indeed, they might be more knowledgeable about the intricacies of local conflict politics. Yet, in their intervention strategies the tendencies of ordering and organizational politics described in this chapter probably play an equally important role as in those of their international counterparts.

Finally, for development organizations working in complex situations of violence and conflict, the message is thus not so much to do a better job in analysing conflict situations and defining politically aware interventions. Rather, they need to become more aware of their own practices and predispositions in framing, as well as of the dynamics within their own organizations. Only then may they be able to unearth, and better account for, the political choices they now wittingly and unwittingly make.

Acknowledgements

The research on which this chapter is based was funded by WOTRO Science for Global Development (part of the Netherlands Organisation for Scientific Research). I wish to thank Cordaid, CED-Caritas Burundi and the Pastoral de la Tierra de San Marcos for the opportunity of conducting research with them, as well as all those women and men in rural Burundi and Guatemala who were willing to share their lives and stories with me. I am grateful for helpful comments on this chapter by Kees Biekart, Jenny Pearce, Dorothea Hilhorst, Gemma van der Haar, Timmo Gaasbeek, and Maliana Serrano.

References

Barnett, M., Kim, H., O'Donnell, H. and Sitea, L. (2007) 'Peace-building; What is in a Name?', *Global Governance*, 13(1): 35–58.

Bebbington, A.J., Hickey, S. and Mitlin, D.C. (2008) *Can NGOs make a difference? The Challenge of Development Alternatives.* London, New York: Zed Books.

Biekart, K. (1999) *The Politics of Civil Society Building; European Private Aid Agencies and Democratic Transitions in Central America.* Utrecht, Amsterdam: International Books, Transnational Institute.

Cardoso, F.H. (2003) *High Level Panel on UN-CS; Civil Society and Global Governance.* Contextual paper prepared by the Panel's Chairman. New York: United Nations.

Chigas, D. and Woodrow, P. (2009) 'Envisioning and Pursuing Peace Writ Large', in Schmelzle, B. and Fischer, M. (eds.) *Peacebuilding at a Crossroads? Dilemmas and Paths for another Generation.* Berlin: Berghof Research.

Cousens, E.M., Kumar, C. and Wermester, K. (2001) *Peacebuilding as Politics; Cultivating Peace in Fragile Societies.* Boulder/London: Lynne Rienner Publishers.

Cramer, C. (2006) *Civil War is not a Stupid Thing; Accounting for Violence in Developing Countries.* London: Hurst and Company.

Crowther, S. (2001) 'The Role of NGOs, Local and International, in Post-war Peacebuilding', *CTTS Newsletter*, 15.

Dagnino, E. (2008) 'Challenges to Participation, Citizenship and Democracy: Perverse Confluence and Displacement of Meaning', in Bebbington, A.J., Hickey, S. and Mitlin, D.C. (eds) *Can NGOs make a Difference? The Challenge of Development Alternatives.* London, New York: Zed Books.

Denskus, T. (2007) 'Peacebuilding Does Not Build Peace', *Development in Practice*, 17(4–5): 656–662.

DFID (2010) *Building Peaceful States and Societies: A DFID Practice Paper.* London: Department for International Development.

Duffield, M. (2001) *Global Governance and the New Wars; The Merging of Development and Security.* London, New York: Zed Books.

Ellis, S. (1995) *Democracy in Sub-Saharan Africa: Where did it come from? Can it be Supported?* Paper presented at the study day by the Foundation for a New South Africa, The Hague.

Fisher, S. and Zimina, L. (2009) 'Just Wasting our Time? Provocative Thoughts for Peacebuilders', in Schmelzle, B. and Fischer, M. (eds) *Peacebuilding at a Crossroads? Dilemmas and Paths for another Generation.* Berlin: Berghof Research.

Gready, P. and Ensor, J. (2005) 'Introduction', in Gready, P. and Ensor, J. (eds) *Reinventing*

Development? Translating Rights-based Approaches from Theory into Practice. London/New York: Zed Books.

Guttal, S. (2005) 'The Politics of Post-war/Post-conflict Reconstruction', *Development*, 48(3): 73–81.

Hilhorst, D. (2003) *The Real World of NGOs; Discourses, Diversity, and Development*. London: Zed Books.

Hilhorst, D. and van Leeuwen, M. (2005) 'Grounding Local Peace Organizations; A Case Study of Southern Sudan', *Journal of Modern Africa Studies*, 43(4): 537–563.

Howell, J. and Pearce, J. (2001) 'CS, Democracy, and the State: the Americanization of the Debate', in Howell, J. and Pearce, J. (eds) *Civil Society and Development: A Critical Exploration*. Boulder/London: Lynne Rienner Publishers.

Kaldor, M. (2003) 'The Idea of Global Civil Society'. *International Affairs*, 79(3): 583–593.

Kalyvas, S.N. (2003) 'The Ontology of Political Violence: Action and Identity in Civil Wars', *Perspectives on Politics*, 1(3): 475–494.

Law, J. (1994) *Organizing Modernity*. Oxford/Cambridge MA: Blackwell Publishers.

Long, N. (2001) *Development Sociology; Actor Perspectives*. London/New York: Routledge.

Macrae, J. and Harmer, A. (2003) *Humanitarian Action and the 'Global War on Terror': A Review of Trends and Issues*. London: Overseas Development Institute.

Mol, A. and Law, J. (2002) 'Complexities; An Introduction', in Law, J. and Mol, A. (eds) *Complexities: Social Studies of Knowledge Practices*. Durham/London: Duke University Press.

Mosse, D. (2004) 'Is Good Policy Unimplementable? Reflections on the Ethnography of Aid Policy and Practice', *Development and Change*, 35(4): 39–71.

OECD-DAC (2008) *State-building in Situations of Fragility: Initial Findings*. Paris: OECD.

Paffenholz, T. and Spurk, C. (2006) *Civil Society, Civic Engagement, and Peacebuilding*. Washington: The World Bank.

Paris, R. and Sisk, T. (2009) 'Conclusion: Confronting the Contradictions', in Paris, R. and Sisk, T. (eds) *The Dilemmas of Statebuilding: Confronting the Contradictions of Postwar Peace Operations*. London/New York: Routledge.

Pearce, J. (2005) 'The International Community and Peacebuilding', *Development*, 48(3): 41–49.

Pearce, J. (2010) 'Is Social Change Fundable? NGOs and Theories and Practices of Social Change', *Development in Practice*, 20(6): 621–635.

Pearce, J. and Howell, J. (2001) 'Civil Society Discourses and the Guatemalan Peace Process', in Howell, J. and Pearce, J. (eds) *Civil Society and Development: A Critical Exploration*. Boulder/London: Lynne Rienner Publishers.

Richards, P. (2005) 'New War: An Ethnographic Approach', in Richards, P. (ed.) *No Peace No War: An Anthropology of Contemporary Armed Conflict*. Athens/Oxford: Ohio University Press, James Currey.

Richmond, O. (2006) 'The Problem of Peace: Understanding the "Liberal Peace"', *Conflict, Security and Development*, 6(3): 291–314.

Sieder, R., Thomas, M., Vickers, G. and Spence, J. (2002) *Who Governs? Guatemala Five Years after the Peace Accords*. Cambridge: Hemisphere Initiatives.

Uvin, P. (1998) *Aiding Violence: The Development Enterprise in Rwanda*. West Hartford: Kumarian Press.

Van Leeuwen, M. (2008) 'Imagining the Great Lakes Region; Discourses and Practices of Civil Society Regional Approaches for Peacebuilding in Rwanda, Burundi, and DR Congo', *Journal of Modern African Studies*, 46(3): 393–426.

Van Leeuwen, M. (2009) *Partners in Peace; Discourses and Practices of Civil Society Peacebuilding*. Aldershot: Ashgate Publishing Ltd.

Van Leeuwen, M. (2010a) 'To Conform or to Confront? Civil Society and Agrarian Conflict in Post-conflict Guatemala', *Journal of Latin American Studies*, 42: 91–119.

Van Leeuwen, M. (2010b) 'Crisis or Continuity? Framing Land Disputes and Local Conflict Resolution in Burundi', *Land Use Policy*, 27: 753–762.

Van Leeuwen, M. and Verkoren, W. (2012) 'Complexities and Challenges for Civil Society Building in Post-conflict Settings', *Journal of Peacebuilding and Development*, 7(1): 81–94.

Van Rooy, A. (1998) 'Civil Society as Idea; An Analytical Hat Stand?', in Van Rooy, A. (ed.) *Civil Society and the Aid Industry; The Politics and Promise*. London: Earthscan Publications Ltd.

13 The everyday politics of disaster risk reduction in Central Java, Indonesia

Annelies Heijmans

The frequency and intensity of disaster events has increased alarmingly over the past few decades, affecting the livelihoods of poor people. In response, policy makers and aid practitioners adopted community-based approaches to disaster risk reduction (CBDRR) as an alternative to top-down disaster management. Many aid organizations operationalize CBDRR by addressing the immediate unsafe conditions as direct manifestations of risk, rather than tackling the underlying risk factors and root causes. Although the social, economic and political origins of disasters that make populations vulnerable are beginning to be recognized, they still are largely ignored in practice (Wilkinson 2012, Bender 1999, Blaikie *et al.* 1994). This chapter analyses the spatial, institutional and political dimensions of CBDRR in Central Java, Indonesia, and argues that interpreting disasters and identifying risk reduction measures are negotiated and political processes. This requires CBDRR interventions to think ahead of objectives to be achieved at institutional and spatial levels beyond the village.

Origins of community-based approaches in response to failing development strategies

The origins of CBDRR-traditions are closely related to the different ways of 'seeing' disasters (Bankoff and Hilhorst 2009). For a long time, experts such as meteorologists, seismologists and vulcanologists have been 'seeing' disasters as sudden external events caused by nature. Loss of life and the extent of damages are regarded as a function of the magnitude, frequency and intensity of the natural hazard. This view still prevails and has been called the dominant hazard-focused viewpoint (Hewitt 1983). Since the 1970s, this view has received critiques challenging the argument that disasters are natural. Researchers and practitioners started to view disasters as a matter of vulnerability related to processes of underdevelopment (O'Keefe *et al.* 1976, Cuny 1983, Wijkman and Timberlake 1984, Blaikie *et al.* 1994, Twigg and Bhatt 1998). Maskrey's publication *Disaster Mitigation: a Community-based Approach* (1989) highlights the efforts of people at the grassroots in reducing disaster risk from a local perspective. The principal message of his book is that disaster mitigation is not strictly the domain of scientific and technical disciplines, but that grassroots inhabitants and local governments have a voice too in reducing disaster risks and demanding politically safety and security.

During the 1990s, the development policy of governments, the UN and the World Bank started to promote community-based approaches in various fields, including CBDRR (IDNDR 1994, 1999). The rise of community-based approaches is actually a response to the errors and failures of top-down development approaches which have capital, science and technology as key ingredients (Escobar 1995, Chambers 2010). Involving local people is assumed to make interventions more efficient and to 'empower' people, mainly in terms of forming community organi-zations, a type and level of empowerment that poses no serious threat to prevailing power relations (Bebbington *et al.* 2007: 598). 'People's participation' is here not meant to question or confront power inequalities, but what is meant is that people act as volunteers to do the work on behalf of government to save resources (White 1996). In practice, 'participation' is not something people will 'do' when asked, since people always participate in ongoing events, and influence and respond to these events even if they are *not* asked to participate (Long 1992). The Hyogo Framework for Action (HFA) constructs an image of disaster-affected people as underdeveloped, ignorant, uninformed, unprepared and unplanned – detaching people and their vulnerability from the broader social and institutional context (Heijmans 2012). It ignores the social, economic and political origins of disaster vulnerability, still 'seeing' disasters as external events. Concluding, CBDRR approaches hide the different ways of 'seeing' disasters and proposed interventions for the same risk problem. This chapter shows how local people, civil society organ-izations and government agencies 'see' floods differently, and why they propose different risk reduction measures for the same event. The chapter argues that we should view CBDRR interventions as political arenas where different actors pursue, negotiate and debate about risk solutions, resources and values (Long 2001), looking beyond the top-down and bottom-up approaches to reduce risks.

The political arena of disaster risk reduction

Disasters are events to which political systems must respond, and therefore 'within minutes after any major impact, disasters start to become political' (Olson 2000: 266). The way governments explain disasters, and manage disaster risk, influences their interaction and relationships with their citizens. This chapter shows how local villagers struggle to put their risk-problem on the government's agenda, and how government officials try to get support for *their* proposed solution. Disaster risk reduction (DRR) is not a sectoral issue, but requires the involvement of a range of government departments at different levels. The 'political arena of DRR' refers here to the broader institutional context in which district governors, line departments, civil society organizations, citizens and international non-governmental organizations – (I)NGOs – interpret and frame disaster events, and how everybody tries to get support for their specific risk solution.

There are many conceptualizations of what constitutes 'politics', ranging from state politics to the everyday politics of all human interaction (Kerkvliet 2009).

Conventional studies on politics usually limit the analysis of disaster politics to what government authorities, states, political parties, their supporters and lobbyists do, putting politics in a realm far removed from most citizens (Kerkvliet 2009). Kerkvliet refers to government authorities, states, political parties, labour unions and so on as actors involved in 'official politics' (2009: 231). They hold authoritative positions and are authorized to take decisions on policies, regulations and laws. Such a restricted view of politics, however, misses a great deal of what is politically significant when one tries to understand what affected populations do to survive or cope with disaster events, when (I)NGOs, corporations, religious organizations, media, universities, unions, and other institutions also distribute aid resources and create space for their own legitimacy (ibid.). Kerkvliet (2009) refers to the latter as 'everyday politics', a form of politics beyond the 'official politics'. 'Everyday politics' refers to how people comply with, adjust and contest norms and rules regarding authority, and to social ordering and re-ordering after disasters occur. Everyday politics can take various forms – support, compliance, modifications, evasions and resistance – involving little or no organization. An example is people refusing to obey government's evacuation orders, or practices of self-organized evacuation evading the formal government's sites. These everyday forms of resistance and modification may eventually feed into more organized and confrontational forms of what Kerkvliet refers to as 'advocacy politics', which contributes to authorities rethinking programmes and policies. Everyday politics is therefore as equally significant as other forms of politics.

To analyse 'disaster politics', I use the framework of Olson (2000) who uses 'disaster politics' to describe ways in which actors frame and explain disaster events, questioning who can be held responsible and how resources are allocated to whom, where and for what purpose after disasters hit. The author offers a framework which, in my view, brings the different forms of politics together to deepen the understanding of the political arena of disaster risk reduction. The framework poses three fundamental questions after a disaster event:

1   'What happened?' This question starts the process of defining the event and the social construction of meaning, 'which is political at least as much as it is scientific or technical' (ibid.: 266). This question refers to how actors frame and interpret disaster events using their discursive power. The way disasters are framed has implications for ways in which disaster responses' goals are formulated.

2   'Why were the losses high/low?' This question is political since it refers to the fundamental pre-event and post-event public policy decisions associated with accountability and responsibility issues. What are the existing policies, laws and regulations to reduce disaster risks, and are these implemented by the responsible authorities? Who can be held accountable for the losses? These questions relate to understanding *why* people affected by the disaster are affected in the way they are, referring to their vulnerable conditions. Institutions, policies, and laws regulate people's behaviour and create power relations.

3   'What will happen now?' After the immediate emergency period, people engage in recovery efforts which involve resources, and decisions on how to use and distribute these resources. This involves politics referring to the '*who, how, and what*' of policy making and interventions.

Olson's focus is, however, limited to state-actors, whereas I propose to ask these questions also of disaster-affected people, NGOs and other actors involved in disaster risk reduction. These various actors interpret disaster events, their circumstances and what is happening around them differently. Therefore local people, NGOs and state-actors will reply to Olson's questions in different ways considering their social position. They will use their agency to convince the others of *their* explanation of events, their risk definitions, whom to blame and how to allocate resources when they debate, confront each other, negotiate about issues, resources, and values. Local people are not victims but are regarded as capable actors in affecting change through negotiation, innovation or experimentation, even if their social space to manoeuvre is restricted (Long 2001).

The key actors in DRR in Pati Central Java, are *Serikat Petani Pati* (SPP), the Pati's Farmers' Organisation which supports flood-affected farmers; *Jaringan Masyarakat Peduli Sungai Juwana* (Jampi Sawan for short), meaning *People's Network That Cares for the Juwana River*, created in 2009; and the Society for Health, Education, Environment and Peace (SHEEP), a local NGO involved in CBDRR. All villagers living along the Juwana River and affected by floods – like farmers, fishermen and labourers – can become a member of Jampi Sawan, which has become an influential actor in negotiations with the government. Key actors within the government are the village heads, the district governor/(vice-)governor and the various line departments that are responsible for spatial planning, watershed and river management, and environmental protection.

This chapter uncovers some of the complexities and the political nature of DRR. The implication for aid agencies is that they should invest time and effort to find out who cooperates and who opposes particular risk reduction measures and why, and to deal with these power plays in such a way that marginal groups could succeed in their demands for protection and safety. This resonates with a political economy approach which is gaining recognition in the field of DRR and focuses on institutions through which policies are developed and implemented, on an understanding of power relations and incentives, and on exploiting room for manoeuvre (Wilkinson 2012). Those involved with CBDRR interventions have to think ahead about the objectives to be achieved at institutional levels beyond the village. Rather than simply aiming for isolated village-level project objectives, the case from Central Java shows that CBDRR results have to be achieved at provincial and even national level.

I visited Central Java once or twice a year over a period of six years from 2006 to 2012. It was one of the localities included in my PhD project; this involved interactive research with Dutch aid agencies and several local partners in Afghanistan and Indonesia which wished to pilot CBDRR taking a political and institutional approach (Heijmans 2012). During the six years, I followed the interactions amongst the different actors to discover certain patterns and contradictions between them. To enrich the research, two MSc students of Disaster Studies spent four months in Pati District during 2010 conducting in-depth research into negotiation processes concerning CBDRR interventions involving state and non-state-actors. I used Olson's three questions to study and reflect on these interactions, and this forms the structure of this chapter.

'What happened?' Explaining and framing flood events

Pati District is located in the north of Central Java province and situated between two mountains: the Muria Mountain in the north-west and the Kendeng mountain range in the south. Most of Pati area is lowland, and used for rice production. The Juwana River, a 60 km-long river with a large watershed covering five districts, flows from the mountains towards the Java sea in the east (see Figure 13.1). The Juwana River forms the lower part of a large irrigation system constructed in 1918 during the Dutch colonial period. At that time, Juwana was not yet a river, but a swamp. A large dam upstream, which is part of the irrigation system, intentionally released water into the low lands of Pati District to raise the soil level through sedimentation, making the land suitable for agriculture. The Indonesian government closed the gates of the dam in 1982 to stop flooding and to allow permanent settlement in the area. In cases of extreme rainfall, the gates are opened to release excessive water – without prior warning. 'Floods are part of our normal life' according to local people.

They developed coping strategies to deal with floods, combining farming with fishing. In the lower parts of the area, where houses are flooded, people lift their belongings, make a floating kitchen of banana stems or move to the first floor if possible. When water levels rise further, they practice family-based evacuation strategies using boats, and stay with relatives on higher ground. Since 2003, people who could afford it started to elevate their houses, and also mosques or community halls began to be designated as evacuation centres when need arises. In February 2006, the Juwana River overflowed and inundated 36 villages in 7 sub-districts in Pati District, including 5,657 hectares of ready-to-harvest paddy fields. The harvest failed as the rice was submerged for several months. Since then, people observed increasing occurrence of floods and started to alter their explanations of the flooding.

Farmers increasingly face difficulties adhering to their seasonal cropping calendar because floods occur earlier – during harvest time – and stay longer, thus hampering planting a second crop. They began explaining floods as a combination of extreme rainfall, the sedimentation of the Juwana River due to deforestation on the mountains, and of new infrastructure that obstructs proper drainage to the sea. Fishermen, who live closer to the sea and experience negative effects from flooding as well, frame their risk problem differently from farmers; it is not sedimentation that they view as the main problem, but the big waves from the sea entering fish ponds, and the chaotic parking of boats in the harbour near the river

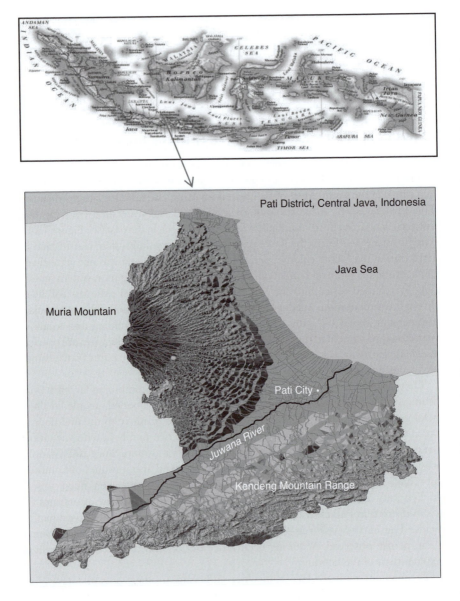

Figure 13.1 Rivers and mountains in Pati district, Central Java.

Source: Bakorsurtanal, Coordinating Agency for National Survey and Mapping, digitized by SHEEP.

mouth that obstruct water flowing to the sea. Local villagers increasingly realised that their own measures fell short because they lack the means to tackle the underlying risk factors.

The reasons to alter local narratives could be attributed to the factual increase in flood events, but also to SHEEP's engagement with these villagers through its CBDRR interventions, because SHEEP regards the 'floods are part of normal life' narrative as problematic. SHEEP and the other NGOs in Central Java construct a disaster narrative that aims to convince both grassroots people and government authorities that disasters are not natural, but a matter of vulnerability for which the Indonesian government can be held responsible. Although the government is held most responsible, the NGOs advocate a multi-actor approach to DRR involving communities, media, civil society organizations (CSOs), and business and government institutions. The NGO-CSO networks in Pati District use disasters as an entry point for making people more conscious about the reasons that contribute to flooding. Their proposed solution is lobbying government officials to make the Juwana river wider and deeper – locally referred to as 'river normalization'. In two sequential CBDRR-interventions,[1] lobbying, advocacy, community alliance building and media campaigns were the main strategies implemented to pressure government to take action on river normalization, environmental protection and appropriate land use planning particularly in the uplands of the Juwana watershed.

Asking government officials why floods happen in Pati District, the majority respond that 'disaster is an act of God' or due to climate extremes (SHEEP 2010). Only a few attribute flooding to the sedimentation of the Juwana River and to deforestation. The government tends to view disasters as external events for which they cannot be held responsible. Asked about DRR, they start talking about relief operations. Government officials in Pati seem to evade discussions about river normalization by saying that flooding is not an urgent issue and the situation is not getting worse (Hauwere and van der Zouwen 2010).

Nonetheless, politicians discovered the political perspective that floods offer, especially during election time. Politicians promise to build evacuation centres, while they escape discussions about river normalization. An evacuation centre is easy to implement, it is a small project, very visible in the village, and shows benefits before the next elections. This is not the case with river normalization, which is costly and involves a complex long-term process involving government institutions beyond the district level, and without immediate benefit for the district government. However, local people do not need evacuation centres, since they stay with relatives nearby when their properties are flooded.

To legitimize the government's resistance to normalization, district officials further argue that they do not always implement what citizens demand, because they have incorrect ideas and views, portraying local people as ignorant and under-developed. A district government official explained this:

> For instance on the radio, when the topic is about river normalization, there are many phone calls from people who urge that river normalization should

start immediately. However, river normalization requires calculations, how deep it should be, as the depth can differ for different areas. If they dig too deep, it is will result in intrusion of salty water, the water would not be able to flow back to the sea and the people cannot irrigate their fields. So people's needs can differ from wants. If people's needs are not fulfilled, it will trouble them. But if they want something, it does not mean that the government has to fulfil it.

(Hauwere and van der Zouwen 2010: 149)

It is true that citizens are not always aware of the technical implications of interventions and that the government cannot fulfil all suggestions of its citizens. Nevertheless, diverse opinions are always subject to competing discourses, and what counts as 'correct' or 'incorrect' depends on the actor's interests. While the flooding in Pati is real, there is room for the DRR actors to socially construct its urgency and the extent to which the flooding is worth an intervention (Slovic 2003). Further, framing the villagers' demands either as 'needs' or 'wants', the risk involved in flooding is subsequently prioritized or minimized.

Concluding, the various actors explain and frame floods differently, and consequently they propose different risk reduction measures (see Table 13.1). Their views also differ in terms of the urgency of response, and consequently negotiations, debates and protests will take place related to *who* has the discursive power to frame the flood-risk problem and the related solution, and *who* decides *whose* risk reduction measures are taken seriously and *whose* ideas and proposals are left out.

Table 13.1 Differing views on floods and risk reduction measures

Framing and explaining floods	Risk reduction measures	Actors
Floods are part of normal life	Coping and adaptation of livelihoods	Local farmers
Floods happen due to big waves from sea, and the chaotic parking of huge commercial fishing boats in the harbour obstructing water to flow to the sea	Coping and adaptation of livelihoods, law enforcement regarding parking of boats in harbour and Juwana river	Local fishermen and fishpond owners
Floods occur due to a combination of extreme rainfall, sedimentation, deforestation and poor drainage due to new infrastructure	Lobby, advocacy, media campaigns and community-alliance building aimed at pressuring government to take action for river normalization and environmental protection	NGOs and CSOs
Floods are external events, an act of God, or happen due to extreme climate events	Relief, and construction of evacuation centres	Government

'Why are losses so high/low?' Policy decisions and accountability for DRR

The second question posed by Olson (2000) refers to pre-event policy decisions and to the question of who can be held accountable for disaster losses and safety. In January 2005, the Government of Indonesia signed the Hyogo Declaration shortly after the December 2004 tsunami. The Hyogo Framework for Action provided a push for reform, which coincided with lobby efforts of the United Nations Development Programme (UNDP) and the Indonesian Society for Disaster Management, known as MPBI (Lassa 2011). MPBI is an association and comprises UN staff, government officials, NGO activists and academics. It successfully lobbied for a more proactive disaster management (DM) law to reduce the immense losses such as those experienced during recent major disasters in the country, and stresses the need to look into causes of disasters and not only into impact. This new DM Law 24, enacted in July 2007, is integrated into the decentralization policies, meaning that power to formulate DRR policies for its respective territory is delegated to the district and village government levels. The law prescribes that DRR policies should be in line with development policies and should include disaster management cooperation policies with other districts, provinces or cities.

In practice, it turns out to be difficult for flood-affected communities in Pati District to address the underlying risk factors, such as inappropriate land use causing landslides and floods, by taking a watershed perspective. In the case of the Juwana River, five districts would be involved, and the authority of government institutions that are supposed to play a crucial role in disaster risk reduction does not operate at district level. Provinces still have autonomy in spatial planning, public works, and environmental issues, among others, and the national level retains responsibility for natural resources. Whereas Pati district has had a DRR plan and policy since July 2010, the adjacent districts lack any DRR policy or structure, making cooperation almost impossible. Aside from the lack of knowledge and understanding of the new responsibilities at the various government levels and departments concerning DRR, the decentralization did not result in the decentralization of revenues. This implies that districts can set their priorities but are not sure whether they will have the budget for implementation. This is another constraint preventing the district government from investing in big projects like river normalization. In the end, it remains unclear what exactly has been decentralized (Schulte-Nordholt 2003). Short-term interventions such as relief and the construction of evacuation centres remain the dominant response to floods by Pati's District government.

The institutional context of ill-defined responsibilities between administrative levels and departments regarding DRR, together with the democratization process, offers opportunities for civil society groups to find space to manoeuvre to lobby for structural DRR measures. During Suharto's time, civil society organizations had to operate under heavy regulations and repression, preventing labourers, farmers and fishermen from organizing themselves to oppose government policies

(Antlöv 2003), whereas nowadays they are less afraid to speak out about their concerns or dissatisfaction. Flood-affected farmers supported by SPP and SHEEP increasingly complained to village and district authorities that relief should not be the only answer, and that government should keep its promises including implementing river normalization and halting deforestation on the surrounding mountains. These CSOs were instrumental in the conscientization of farmers by challenging their conventional thinking on hierarchy in Indonesian society. They further facilitated the interaction between farmers' groups and fishermen's associations. The first had frequent inter-village farmers' group meetings where the idea was born to form a broader network of people concerned about the flooding in Pati District, with the aim of being more influential during negotiations with the district government. To mobilize the fishermen's groups and other concerned citizens into such a broad network, the risk problem should be framed in such a way as to mobilize a larger constituency and to create effective agency (Long 1992). After lengthy discussions, farmers and fishermen agreed to frame the problem in this way: 'Juwana river is in bad condition' referring to the problems of sedimentation and boat parking. On 20 May 2009, they officially established their network *Jampi Sawan – Jaringan Masyarakat Peduli Sungai Juwana*, meaning *People's Network That Cares for the Juwana River*. All villagers living along Juwana river or who are affected by floods indirectly – such as labourers – can become a member of Jampi Sawan. In this way, people's everyday politics to deal with floods became mobilized and organized into a network, creating leverage and legitimacy as it aims to negotiate and lobby with the district government.

Despite the relatively little financial means that SHEEP and Jampi Sawan have to foster the government's accountability, they brought in multiple creative CBDRR strategies to engage both with government and concerned citizens. They engaged with village authorities, the district governors and line departments, politicians and provincial level authorities to understand policies and responsibilities better and to find potential support for flood mitigation efforts. To bring the political debate into the village, one example is when members of Jampi Sawan took their camera and boat to map all kinds of issues and problems encountered along the Juwana River, and they discussed their observations with villagers living there. Through civic education, SHEEP–Jampi Sawan made villagers aware of public policies, spatial land use planning and citizens' rights. In particular, they intended to mobilize the village heads to raise their voices, since this group still tends to await instructions from district level and is not yet used to the possibility of deviating from the district's plans, or they simply refuse to cooperate. Through media like local newspapers and radio, SHEEP and Jampi Sawan raised the issue of river normalization and proper land use planning as frequently as possible, bringing the political debate both into the village and the district government. Getting stories published is not always easy, as the media has an interest in highlighting the issues of the day and not necessarily in background articles on why floods happen or about unfulfilled promises of politicians. But since the media in Indonesia are sensitive to the occurrence of disasters, SHEEP and Jampi Sawan constantly strategize about how they can best use these opportunities to bring out the structural shortcomings in governmental policy and to pressure government to take its responsibilities. At the same time, politicians use *their* media to create an image of goodwill and taking responsibility.

Aside from confrontational strategies, SHEEP and CSOs applied simultaneously more diplomatic and formal strategies, portraying themselves as bridge-builders. They organized meetings to bring various actors together, such as district government, village officials and community-based organisations (CBOs) to discuss DRR. During these meetings, all actors manoeuvre to frame their concerns in culturally accepted ways and avoid direct political confrontations. Village officials attend these meetings in their professional capacity, and since respect for people higher in the hierarchy is still considered important, directly blaming government officials for their failures will jeopardize their participation in such meetings in the long run. Besides, to be able to influence the government, it is for the NGOs important to have some government officials on board. In the end, these meetings rather serve the purpose of staying on speaking terms and maintaining relationships, rather than actually negotiating policies and plans. SHEEP, Jampi Sawan and village officials need to know what happens behind the façade of 'official politics', to make their lobbying for river normalization and pressure on the district governor effective. So, social investigation and research into the institutional relationships is an important activity of their CBDRR work.

Exploring the institutional context implies investigating what the relevant (new) laws are, which agency or department is responsible, what the trends are in spatial planning processes within the government in order to anticipate new risks and to understand institutional bureaucracies. It is important to discover who in the bureaucracy is supporting the people's agenda, and who is opposing it. When civil society organizations are aware of the institutional context, they are more conscious of how the various government agencies perform their powers in the arena where the various actors negotiate, debate and struggle for safety, protection and secure livelihoods. In this way, SHEEP and Jampi Sawan discovered internal contradictions between local and national agendas regarding DRR in general, and river normalization in particular. These contradictions are embedded in risk reduction measures like river normalization itself: river normalization refers to a technical process of increasing the capacity of a river by making it deeper and wider. It is part of a broader package of planned river management, such as diversion channels, floodways and dam reparations. River widening has social and political consequences for people whose land is situated within 20 metres of the river and will have to move and are entitled to receive compensation.

The government department responsible for the technical part of normalization is *Balai Besar Wilayah Sungai Pemali Juana*, the head office in charge of the management of Juwana River, authorized by the Ministry of Public Works at national level. It will request tenders from several contractors to take care of the implementation. *Balai Besar* reserved a budget just enough for widening and deepening 10 km of the river, according to a local contractor digging in one of the villages. This amount included 900 million Indonesian Rupiah (IDR) for the district government which is responsible for informing and paying the people who are entitled to receive compensation for the land that they will lose when the river normalization is implemented.[2] *Balai Besar* is not entitled to buy land. *Balai Besar* informed SHEEP and Jampi Sawan that the funds were available but that the District Government was still not willing to invest. It was opposing the idea of river normalization. Why?

A regulation exists preventing people owning land or building houses within a range of 20 meters from the river, but this regulation has never been enforced. Jampi Sawan mapped the land ownership along the river to make people aware that they are entitled to receive compensation and started to link the opposition of the District Governor to the buildings and factories along the river and the financial interests behind them. The Governor seemed to protect Chinese factory owners, to the disadvantage of the farmers and fishermen who struggle to secure their livelihoods in a flood-prone area. In one village along the river, where several parliament members live, a wealthy family built a dike to protect the village against floods, directing the water to flood the opposite river banks. If the normalization succeeded, it would mean that this whole village would need to be relocated. Aside from the technical and social dimension of the intervention, a political debate exists about who should be protected by whom, at whose expense (Warner 2008). The flood risk problems of the farmers and fishermen were subordinated to the flood risk problems and solutions of wealthier groups who not only obtained physical protection through a dike but also the District Governor's political support as protection. This explained the opposition of the District Governor towards river normalization.

Once it became common knowledge that the Governor was blocking the project, tensions between departments at different levels escalated into a conflict. In a meeting of the District Parliament in the first week of March 2010, SHEEP and Jampi Sawan took another opportunity to advocate river normalization by emphasizing that the budget was already made available and that *Balai Besar* was looking for ways to start normalization. In preparation for this meeting, Jampi Sawan and SHEEP had gone to *Balai Besar* to inquire about the proper procedures to realize river normalization and asked to see the correspondence between them and the district governor. *Balai Besar* provided all the letters. These letters were presented during the District Parliament meeting. The District Governor was shocked and surprised by the fact that ordinary citizens could possess this information. By uncovering the internal conflicts within the governmental institutions in a public meeting, the CSOs and village officials leveraged their position as negotiators. From all the actors present in the meeting at the District Parliament, no one wanted to be blamed for not taking action, and the District Governor gave in and agreed to make a start with widening and deepening the Juwana river where the least number of families had to be removed.

In sum, the different ways of 'seeing' and 'explaining' disasters lead to negotiations and debates about *which* risk reduction measures will be implemented, and *where*. At village level, SHEEP and Jampi Sawan supported village authorities to integrate DRR into village regulations, but the majority of village heads were not interested or were reluctant to engage with CSOs. Further, village institutions do not operate at the appropriate scale to address flood mitigation, watershed management or spatial planning. Therefore, CBDRR strategies focused on how to rework relationships with various government agencies beyond village level, so that they were pressured to provide safety and protection to their citizens, to take up their responsibility and implement past policy decisions. This implied that CBDRR in Central Java focused on alliance-building among citizens facing similar risk problems, and in finding allies within government and beyond who shared an interest in the same outcomes, independent of their individual motivations. The successful cooperation between *Balai Besar* and CSOs was, however, temporary, aimed at leveraging their own bargaining position.

It has to be added here that, while SHEEP focused its efforts on flood mitigation in the lowlands of Pati, it formed a coalition with NGOs in the adjacent districts of Jepara and Kudus, called the Muria Coalition. This Coalition aims to address the underlying risk factors that cause flooding in the lowlands including environmental degradation on Muria Mountain due to deforestation, illegal mining, inappropriate land use planning and the lack of law enforcement.

'What will happen now?' Negotiations on how to use and allocate resources

While negotiations, debates and conflicts concerning the proposed river normalization were played out, the District Government approved the construction of five evacuation centres. An evacuation centre is a perceived need by the District Government, but not one that is recognized by local people. People usually stay in their houses or evacuate to relatives close by. Those villagers who were aware of the plan for the evacuation centres expressed their disapproval, and felt as if the District Government was forcing this plan upon them. Neither SHEEP nor Jampi Sawan were involved in the idea of the five evacuation centres, since they prioritized lobbying and advocacy for river normalization – which turned out to be an effective strategy. Nevertheless, the villagers realized that it would be impossible to convince government officials to spend its budget on more urgent matters in the village and suggested an alternative purpose for the building once it was built, such as drying rice, community meetings and stockpiling relief goods. It is not clear how government officials will react to this reinterpretation of its project and whether the alternative usage will still provide them with political benefits. This particular example illustrates the top-down nature of CBDRR practice by local government.

Meanwhile, the negotiation processes regarding the river normalization did not stop. It was expected that the 'first phase' of normalizing 10 km would last till September 2011. Jampi Sawan was aware that the available budget was insufficient to normalize the whole river, and was afraid that the project would not result in reducing flood risks. On the other hand, if Jampi Sawan refused further cooperation with the government, it feared that the government would never look for additional funding. And this was not the only dilemma. The District

Government requested Jampi Sawan to take on the 'socialization' process, that is, disseminating information about the widening of the river and its consequences such as re-allocation of houses and land, probably to legitimize the whole activity and because it has little capacity itself. On the other hand, it rejected all kinds of ideas and inputs from Jampi Sawan. For instance, Jampi Sawan used art, theatre, and religion to inform people about what would happen with the river and the consequences. The Government did not like this and was not willing to provide financial resources to Jampi Sawan, although there was 150 million Rupiah available for 'socialization' purposes. However, when there were problems with land issues, the government immediately asked for the help of Jampi Sawan to mediate. People who had to move their house or had to sell their land, claimed land elsewhere and this caused frictions between villagers and the government. Hauwere and van der Zouwen (2010) found that in the negotiations concerning compensation, for instance, villagers influenced one another not to settle for the proposed price offered by the government. Although refusing to sell the land is not an option, people tried to find out how far they could go. Another problem was that many people have land but not an official land certificate. No certificate meant no compensation. Jampi Sawan anticipated problems and advised each village to form a lobby committee to support such cases.

It is expected that river normalization in Pati District will still face many dilemmas, opposing interests and agendas. Besides difficulties in getting the necessary funding, internal government politics are likely to cause further delays or to prove an obstacle to complete the normalization for the whole river. The actors involved all use their agency and their powers to create room to manoeuvre and to change or defend institutional arrangements to their own advantage. So far, the everyday politics of citizens has led to more concerted 'advocacy politics', and to district authorities implementing a comprehensive DRR policy beyond their short-term top-down CBDRR practice.

Discussion and conclusions

Unfortunately, the impact of this CBDRR intervention and river normalization cannot yet be fully assessed. The normalization of the 60 km long Juwana River started in September 2010 and was still going on at the time of writing. There are, however, some tangible outcomes: through local-level lobbying and advocacy, civil society organizations could access national level financial resources for disaster risk reduction. Considering that 90 per cent of the financial resources for DRR are being kept by the government at the national level,[3] it is quite an achievement that civil society organizations at district level could access these resources for a structural risk reduction measure. A second important outcome is the change in the civil society-government relationship from antagonistic towards agonic, meaning that the District Government no longer regarded Jampi Sawan as its opponent but as a legitimate actor in the political arena. They do not share the same views on disaster risk reduction but they realize that they need to engage with one another to address floods. To reduce people's vulnerability to disasters locally, CBDRR should focus on re-working social relationships and institutions at multiple levels, and think ahead about the objectives to be achieved at institutional levels beyond the village.

(I)NGOs and civil society organizations tend to romanticize CBDRR approaches, assuming that CBDRR is inherently 'good' because of its 'participatory' and 'empowering' features. But the experiences from Central Java reveal that local people, local NGOs, and government officials attach different meanings and objectives to CBDRR, and that comprehensive risk reduction measures require protests, negotiations, and debates with a variety of actors from other communities and with government. The District Government interpreted CBDRR as a village-level intervention to reduce immediate suffering and people's exposure to floods through relief and the construction of evacuation centres – measures that are redundant in the view of flood-affected people. People's risk perspectives were not recognized, and the proposed measures were regarded as a waste of scarce resources. This CBDRR practice was not participatory at all, but was top-down.

Local people, NGOs and CSOs, on the other hand, viewed floods as a matter of vulnerability, and of policy decisions that were not implemented due to internal contradictions between government agencies and administrative levels. They prioritized river normalization and viewed 'community-based' not as an isolated village-level project, but as a multi-actor and multi-scale intervention, involving flood-affected people living along the 60 km long Juwana river organized into *Jampi Sawan* and *Balai Besar*, the responsible government authority for Juwana River management at national level. So, behind a shared CBDRR language, actors attach radically different meanings and strategies to CBDRR. These different meanings and strategies imply that there is no such thing as *the* CBDRR approach.

SHEEP was instrumental in changing local people's views of the reasons for floods happening and their 'frames of reality' that legitimized previous relationships and arrangements between village government, CBOs, NGOs and the national government. This altered people's options for dealing with floods in Pati, from their everyday politics of coping and adapting livelihoods towards mobilizing effective agency for 'advocacy politics' and entering the political arena with authorities and government, to become a legitimate actor in 'official politics' with the objective of obtaining safety and protection. NGOs and CSOs played a facilitating role in this process, particularly using their ability to bring opposing parties together, while understanding the actors' needs within their full social and political context. The transformative nature of CBDRR is linked to strategies and options that arise from a local institutional context which expands relationships outside people's innate social networks, building on people's social, organizational, motivational and political resources to create effective agency and to change antagonistic relationships (Heijmans 2012: 260). The significance of this case is that it shows the need to look beyond the top-down and bottom-up approaches to reducing risks and to understand how, in the political arena of disaster risk reduction, the adherents of the different CBDRR practices negotiate the principles and features of their specific approach.

The case reveals that CBDRR has very different meanings and therefore policy makers and practitioners have to be aware of how CBDRR interventions are based on various assumptions, perceptions, ideologies and experiences when they engage with other actors in the political arena of disaster risk reduction. Actors have different values and norms for people's participation, varying risk constructs and understandings about what constitutes a community. They attach different meanings to the concepts that make up CBDRR, such as disasters, risk, community, vulnerability, participation and empowerment. The meaning of these concepts and the actor's CBDRR policy are being negotiated and transformed through the interactions with multi-level institutions, from the conceptual policy design stage up to the arena where decisions on risk solutions and resource allocations are made.

Politics is omnipresent in our everyday CBDRR practice. Policy makers, donors and practitioners should start to accept that CBDRR is not a series of short-term local interventions, but a long-term political process. This means that we make the social, institutional and political context visible in the risk analysis. Each actor produces a 'risk construct' according to their interests, interpretations and values that may be hidden for others involved in the process. Although these underlying values and views are in themselves political in nature, it will be a challenge to bring them into the open from the start. If not, they will probably become evident during the process of shaping, implementing and evaluating risk reduction measures together, as the case of normalization shows. Practice-based research into CBDRR interventions, where power dynamics, different values, worldviews, negotiation outcomes, skills and knowledge play a role, could hopefully contribute to the shift mentioned by Christoplos (2001) – a shift from a focus on which technical solution works, towards a concentration on the political process through which these choices are made, and their impact.

Acknowledgements

The author wishes to thank J.C. Gaillard and Bruno Haghebaert for their constructive comments on an earlier version of this chapter. Further thanks go to the staff of SHEEP for their involvement during the data collection and analysis for the case study. All responsibility remains with the author.

Notes

1   The first CBDRR intervention lasted from Jan 2007 till the end of 2008, and the second from December 2008 till December 2010.
2   The district government – department of public works – had a budget of 900 million Rupiah (€77.799,000): 150 million Rupiah to inform the people, and 750 million Rupiah for compensation.
3   Statement made by several members of the Global Network of Civil Society Organizations for Disaster Reduction during the Global Conference in London, January 2010.

References

Antlöv, H. (2003) *Civic Engagement in Local Government Renewal in Indonesia*. Retrieved from http://ipdprojects.org/logolink-sea/resources/pdf/SEA%20Regional%20Paper4.pdf

Bankoff, G. and D. Hilhorst (2009) 'The Politics of Risk in the Philippines: Differing Perceptions of Disaster Preparedness and Management', *Disasters* 33(4:) 686–704.

Bebbington, A., D. Lewis, S. Batterbury, E. Olson and M.S. Siddiqi (2007) 'Of Texts and Practices: Empowerment and Organizational Cultures in World Bank-funded Rural Development Programmes', *Journal of Development Studies* 43(4): 597–621.

Bender, S.O. (1999) *The Vulnerability Context of Disasters*. Contribution to the UN-IDNDR and QUIPUNET Internet Conference, 14–25 June 1999, The International Decade for Natural Disaster Reduction, www.quipu.net:1999/

Blaikie P., T. Cannon, I. Davis and B. Wisner (1994) *At Risk: Natural Hazards, People's Vulnerability and Disasters*. London/New York: Routledge.

Chambers, R. (2010) 'Paradigms, Poverty and Adaptive Pluralism', Institute of Development Studies Working Paper 344.

Christoplos, I., A. Liljelund and J. Mitchell (2001) 'Re-framing Risk: The Changing Context of Disaster Mitigation and Preparedness', *Disasters* 25(3): 185–198.

Cuny, F. (1983) *Disasters and Development*. Oxford: Oxford University Press.

Escobar, A. (1995) *Encountering Development, the Making and Unmaking of the Third World*. Princeton, NJ: Princeton University Press.

Hauwere, K. de and L. van der Zouwen (2010) *Disaster Risk Reduction in Perspective(s): Actor Perspectives and Interaction in a Flood Prone Area in Central Java, Indonesia*. MSc Thesis Disaster Studies, Wageningen University.

Heijmans, A. (2012) *Risky Encounters: Institutions and Interventions in Response to Recurrent Disasters and Conflict*. PhD, Wageningen University.

Hewitt, K. (1983) 'The Idea of Calamity in a Technocratic Age', in K. Hewitt (ed.) *Interpretations of Calamity from the Viewpoint of Human Ecology*. The Risks & Hazards Series 1, Allen & Unwin Inc. 3–32.

IDNDR (1994) http://www.unisdr.org/eng/about_isdr/bd-yokohama-strat-eng.htm

IDNDR (1999) http://web.archive.org/web/19991217192322/idndr.org/idndr/about.htm

Kerkvliet, B.J.T. (2009) 'Everyday Politics in Peasant Societies (and ours)', *Journal of Peasant Studies* 36(1): 227–243.

Lassa, J. (2011) *Contribution from Indonesia to the Review of the Draft GAR 2011*. Chapters 5, 6 & 7, retrieved through http://www.radixonline.org/latest.htm

Long, N. (1992) 'From Paradigm Lost to Paradigm Regained? The Case for an Actor-oriented Sociology of Development', in N. Long and A. Long (eds), *Battlefields of Knowledge, The Interlocking of Theory and Practice in Social Research and Development*. London: Routledge. 16–43.

Long, N. (2001) *Development Sociology: Actor Perspectives*. London: Routledge.

Maskrey, A. (1989) *Disaster Mitigation: A Community-based Approach*. Development Guidelines No. 3, Oxford: Oxfam.

O'Keefe, P., K. Westgate and B. Wisner (1976) 'Taking the Naturalness out of Natural Disasters', *Nature* 260: 566–567.

Olson, R.S. (2000) 'Toward a Politics of Disaster: Losses, Values, Agendas, and Blame', *International Journal of Mass Emergencies and Disasters* 18(2): 265–288.

Schulte-Nordholt, N. (2003) 'Renegotiating Boundaries: Access, Agency and Identity in Post-Suharto Indonesia'. *Bijdragen tot de Taal-, Land-, en Volkenkunde*, 159(4): 550–589.

SHEEP (2010) 'Presentation of Preliminary Findings of the Institutional Context Concerning DRR issues in Muria Region'. PowerPoint presentation in Bahasa Indonesia, Yogyakarta, 4 October.

Slovic, P. (2003) 'Going Beyond the Red Book: The Sociopolitics of Risk', *Human and Ecological Risk Assessment* 9: 1–10.

Twigg, J. and M.R. Bhatt (1998) *Understanding vulnerability: South Asian Perspectives*. London: Intermediate Technology Publications.

Warner, J. (2008) *The Politics of Flood Insecurity: Framing Contested River Management Projects*. PhD, Wageningen University.

White, S.C. (1996) 'Depoliticising Development: The Uses and Abuses of Participation', *Development in Practice* 6(1): 6–15.

Wijkman, A. and L. Timberlake (1984) *Natural Disasters: Acts of God or Acts of Man?* London/Washington, DC: Earthscan.

Wilkinson, E. (2012) 'Transforming Disaster Risk Management: A Political Economy Approach', *Background Note*, London: Overseas Development Institute.

14 Post-conflict recovery and linking relief, rehabilitation and development in Angola

From crisis to normality?

Hilde van Dijkhorst

Introduction[1]

This chapter investigates post-conflict recovery processes and Linking Relief, Rehabilitation and Development (LRRD) approaches in Angola, by presenting case study material from research in two municipalities in Huíla province. It shows that there are multiple ways of envisioning and pursuing post-conflict recovery which do not necessarily build on what is there and sometimes even run counter to it. In this chapter, I argue that whereas LRRD approaches are based on the notion that post-conflict recovery processes follow a linear route from crisis to normality, in Angola this linear route is not present. LRRD in Angola has overwhelmingly and uncritically been approached through 'seeds and tools' interventions by aid agencies, revealing a narrow understanding of rural livelihood dynamics. The chapter analyses the roles of local people, aid agencies, and the Angolan state in the re-shaping of rural society as part of post-conflict recovery processes.

Policy and practice of LRRD

During the African food crises of the 1980s, the aid community increasingly realized that the complex emergencies they were faced with were not just temporary disruptions of 'normality', and as such required a different aid response from before (Buchanan-Smith and Fabbri 2005, Duffield 1994, White and Cliffe 2000). What followed were approaches called 'linking relief and development', 'relief to development continuum' and 'relief to development contiguum', the latter as a testament to the debates that acknowledged that moving from relief to development was anything but a linear process in complex emergencies (Russo *et al.* 2008, Duffield 2000, Christoplos 2006). What these approaches had in common was the notion that relief and development could become more intertwined in addressing both humanitarian needs and deeply rooted socio-economic and political issues simultaneously. Acknowledging a big gap between relief and development approaches and the grey space between them, the concept of rehabilitation was added, leading to the Linking Relief, Rehabilitation and Development (LRRD) approach.

The term rehabilitation here, or reconstruction, conjures up an image of a rather technocratic move towards building back what was there, but has increasingly come to be understood as a transformation of society and, as such, to 'build back better' (Hilhorst *et al.* 2010: 1108). LRRD implies that a process is started which will lead to development, or 'normality'. This requires some considerable reorganizing of aims, objectives, processes and the nature of interventions. For instance, instead of focusing on individual and/or households as beneficiaries of aid programmes (relief), villages or even societies become the object of interventions. Intervention characteristics move from being short-term and top-down (relief) to aiming for long-term impact on underlying poverty processes in a participatory way. Table 14.1 illustrates the differences in interventions' objectives and styles which characterize LRRD approaches, but should not be interpreted as the way things work in reality. Rather, it guides the ideal-typical intervention styles of many organizations working in post-conflict and post-disaster contexts.

It is clear that these different domains of relief, rehabilitation and development would require a substantially different way of working and focus from aid agencies. LRRD requires a different mindset among aid staff and policy makers,

Table 14.1 Ideal-typical dimensions of relief, rehabilitation and development phases and interventions

	Relief	*Rehabilitation*	*Development*
What people do	– (Forced) migration – Sell assets – Deploy further survival/coping strategies	– Resettle to areas of origin – Reconnect to physical and social environment – Recover assets and activities	– Obtain employment – Sustain future and durable livelihood strategies
Intervention characteristics	– Short–term – Top-down – Distribution of material and logistics	– Introducing participatory elements – Physical reconstruction	– Long-term impact and socio-economic change – Underlying processes
Objectives of interventions	Survival	Rebuilding livelihoods	Economic growth
Beneficiary focus	Individuals/households	Households/villages/society	Villages/society
Engagement with state	Taking over basic service delivery	Integrating services with government institutions	Long-term integration with state plans
Underlying assumptions	– No local capacity – Undesirability of coping strategies – People have no assets left – Markets have stopped functioning	– Dependency syndrome – Assets base is restricted – Agricultural production as key to livelihood recovery and development	– Need for socio-economic and institutional reforms – Strong state engagement

Source: van Dijkhorst (2011: 27). This figure partly builds on the dimensions of relief and sustainable development, as presented by Frerks *et al.* (1999: 32).

and requires a long-term commitment on the part of the aid agencies, for instance, in the shift towards long-term and intensive state engagement to ensure the sustainability of the interventions. As indicated above, relief, rehabilitation and development phases are rarely linear, although LRRD approaches do carry this assumption. Local realities change, they can shift from rehabilitation to relief and then to development through the opportunities and constraints that arise in people's daily lives. Aid agencies often lack the flexibility to respond to these changes quickly, and they are also constrained themselves by strict donor formats that require definitions of aid according to these fixed phases. Often, programmes are defined during the immediate post-war period and are rarely fundamentally revised to fit the changing local needs. Furthermore, engaging with the state in these programmes is highly dependent on the willingness and capacity of state institutions which, in post-conflict states, have often been severely weakened.

The next section will present post-conflict recovery processes in Huíla province, Angola, and the role of LRRD practices and assumptions underlying them. The empirical data were gathered during fieldwork in 2007 and 2008 in the municipalities of Caluquembe and Chibia, Huíla province. Caluquembe, located in the northwest of the province, was heavily affected by conflict, saw many NGO interventions take place, and mostly relies on rain-fed agriculture. Chibia, in the south of the province, was not at the centre of fighting during the war, was in the state's focus for its national reconstruction programme, and is a semi-arid region. In these two municipalities, three villages each were selected and compared in relation to conflict, aid, livelihoods and post-conflict recovery processes. The research was an ethnography of recovery, in which use was made of both qualitative and quantitative methods.

Crisis and normality in Angola

Although the recent history of Angola would read like a storybook case of a move from crisis to normality by overcoming a long and violent history of war to currently being the fastest-growing economy in Africa, crisis and normality for the majority of the Angolan population has not necessarily followed this seemingly linear process.

In 1961, the armed struggle for independence from the Portuguese intensified when increasing calls for self-determination and the emergence of nationalist movements merged with violent resistance against the forced labour practices on white settler-owned cotton plantations (in the north of the country) and an attack on a prison in the capital Luanda in order to release political prisoners. In 1975, Angola became independent, yet this did not bring 'normality'. Rather, independence was the starting point for an increasingly internationalized power struggle between the two main liberation movements, with the Movimento Popular de Libertação de Angola (MPLA) and the União Nacional para a Independência Total de Angola (UNITA) fighting each other over control of the country. The ensuing Angolan civil war was severely influenced by Cold War parties during the first 15 years. Cuba and the Soviet Union supported the MPLA (which incorporated a Marxist ideology until the 1990s), whereas UNITA drew support from South Africa and the United States (Vines 2000). The end of the

Cold War signalled the first attempt to reach a peace accord between MPLA and UNITA. The Bicesse accord, signed in 1991, only proved durable for one year when, in 1992, MPLA won the first parliamentary elections in Angola with a slight majority of votes, an outcome which was contested by UNITA and which led to violent reprisals. This was the start of one of the most violent periods in the Angolan civil war, with the UN at one point estimating a thousand deaths per day as a result of the conflict (Lanzer 1996: 19). Another attempt at peace in 1994 came with the Lusaka accords, which lasted until 1998. After this, four more years of conflict culminated in the killing of UNITA leader Savimbi in 2002. This immediately led to the end of the civil war.

Although the history of conflict has left an enormous mark on Angolan society, one cannot speak of one shared experience of war, nor can one say that local experiences of crisis and normality amongst the population followed the overall course and dynamics of the war. For instance, waves of displacement did not necessarily coincide with times of conflict, as illustrated in the history of the three villages in Caluquembe municipality. Most of the population from the villages of Camucuio and Cue 1 fled during the 1980s when UNITA troops were closing in on the municipal centre and living in the surrounding 'bush' where these villages were located. Catala, on the other hand, located close to Caluquembe town, was completely deserted only after the MPLA reoccupied it in 1994. During 1995–1997, the entire population of Catala fled, together with UNITA, the party supported by the village chief. This period, 1994–1998, coincided with the cease-fire and the Lusaka peace accords. Whereas the inhabitants of Catala were never displaced during the war, they fled during peacetime.

Even though the 'big politics' of the war played out locally to some extent in the way people connected themselves, or were forcibly connected, to the main political parties, other dynamics were also at play. In the case of people in Chibia municipality, hunger and suffering during war was not a direct consequence of political violence, but rather from recurring droughts in the area. On the other hand, people in Caluquembe were still producing food, yet had to do this at great personal risk, as troops would carry out attacks on farmers, place landmines in agricultural fields, or steal harvests in order to feed their own troops.

During the war, oil production and export had been expanding, whereas agricultural industry and trade fell, creating a clear division in the country, with the capital Luanda as an oil enclave where business was carrying on, but leaving the rural area and economy neglected (Hodges 2004, Le Billon 2007). Angola's countryside was left littered with landmines, its infrastructure destroyed, massive displacement of its population mostly from rural to urban areas, and a collapse of social service delivery. When peace was declared, most aid policies focused on resettlement of the displaced from urban centres back to their rural areas of origin, and less on what shape development could take. As aid agencies and the Angolan state started designing and planning the official resettlement programmes, many of the displaced people did not wait for them, but found their own ways to return. By May 2003, 1.8 million Internally Displaced Persons (IDPs) had already reset-tled in their areas of origin, of which 70 per cent had done so without making use of a formal resettlement plan (United Nations 2003). Many displaced people did not participate in these resettlement programmes, sometimes out of fear of a recurrence of conflict, or because they had found other opportunities, and were therefore reluctant to go back to an uncertain situation.

Six years after peace was declared, the situation on the ground did not necessarily signal stability or 'normality' in terms of people's livelihoods. People's experiences and opportunities were much more fluid, and recent natural hazards had uncovered the vulnerable state of agricultural development in some places. Attempts to reach post-war 'normality' had been mostly approached through people's own recovery efforts and the national reconstruction programmes of the Angolan state, as well as through the LRRD approaches by non-governmental organizations (NGOs) that had been present. The next section shows how these recovery processes took shape.

Local recovery and LRRD in practice: the case of Huíla province

Although Chibia had not been at the centre of fighting, the municipality experienced the consequences of war, such as the large number of IDPs settling there, and the lack of goods and basic services. Trade and local alcohol production formed important income generating activities throughout the war and after, often performed by female household members:

> Sometimes we make *macau*,[2] when we have sugar. We only sell it from the house, not in the marketplace. Sometimes we also sell maize flour and other items from the house, like meat. If we need to buy shoes for the children we sell some *macau* for income. In August and September there might be some maize again, but your husband will beat you when you go out to sell maize, you need his permission to sell items from the household.[3]

Looking at livelihoods in Chibia today, one can see a diversity of options, from small trade, agricultural production and livestock rearing, day jobs, formal employment, and trade with the markets in the provincial capital, Lubango.

During the conflict period, people in Caluquembe struggled to maintain the resources that made up their livelihoods and, due to the fighting, they lost the opportunities to continue their jobs, trade and agricultural production. People that had been forced to take refuge in, and close to, Caluquembe town, saw their options for making a living diminish. Some would try to continue working on their plots during the day, and return to the town area at night to avoid being caught by troops. Another option was to seek day jobs at the few large commercial farms that were still operational. Collecting firewood around town, and then selling it as charcoal, occurred on a large scale. Other inhabitants of Caluquembe indicated they collected wild foods, practiced beekeeping and were involved in petty trade activities. Most of these activities have continued after the war, although much less time is dedicated to them. These activities are often referred to as coping or survival strategies. Coping strategies are perceived as a sequence of steps that households take to deal with crises (Ellis 2000, Corbett 1988). A coping strategy is characterized by risky short-term behaviour, whereas a livelihood strategy, in contrast, is considered to be sustainable in nature, consisting of multiple assets which can be used to deal with future shocks without compromising the household's ability to recuperate (Ellis 2000).

Migration is one of the important livelihood strategies that was pursued by people during conflict, but often considered to be a coping strategy. Studies on migration in Africa have for a long time focused on the potentially negative effects of migration and, although family, traditional leadership and social bonds can be weakened, it does not lead to a breakdown of rural societies as a whole, as has been argued (McDowell and De Haan 1997). Migration and remittances can have very positive outcomes on rural livelihoods through the cash and goods flows stemming from it, as well as the economic, social and political transformations that migration can bring (De Haan 2000, Horst 2002, Savage and Harvey 2007). The research in the three villages in Caluquembe uncovered some of these effects of migration: of the 48 households in the three villages, 17 had one or more children that had migrated out of Caluquembe municipality. Often they resided in Lubango, Luanda, or in other Angolan provinces, and all of them had found formal employment or had become commercial traders. Many young people from the villages chose to stay in Lubango or other urban centres after the war. They indicated that they either had lost their agricultural skills, or found life in rural villages without health and education facilities too harsh. In Camucuio, people felt this lack of a younger generation but also saw the positive sides of this type of migration, especially possible remittances generated from employment. The young people in urban areas sometimes sent parts of their salaries or goods to their family members in Camucuio. Of the 17 households in the villages that had children who had migrated and found employment, 7 of them received remittances in the form of cash and/or goods. Also, use was made of the trading networks that people had established in the urban areas. For instance, one young man who during the war had settled in Lubango, had found work at the Joao de Almeida market, one of the biggest informal markets in Lubango. Having resettled again in Camucuio, he now made regular trips by taxi to Lubango, taking with him local produce which he sold at Joao de Almeida market through his former network of vendors.[4]

Due to migration processes, the population of Angola's capital city Luanda had grown explosively during the war; from an estimated population of 738,000 in 1978 to 3.28 million in 2000 (Cain 2003: 9). This enormous growth of Luanda's population cannot be attributed to the war alone, but was also said to be due to the lack of basic services and the limited projects that were available, especially to youths in the rural areas (Pacheco 2002). Cain (2003: 8–9) notes that people who decided to stay in post-conflict Luanda were often reluctant to give up their stakes in the urban informal economy. New economic linkages and networks were formed this way, enabling trade and benefits to households and villages, as shown above in the example of Camucuio. However, the Government of Angola (GoA) made it an official post-conflict priority in their 2003 Poverty Reduction Strategy Paper (PRSP) that pressure should be taken off the urban centres by pursuing rural development strategies (GoA 2003). This has also often fed into the post-conflict aid response of resettlement to areas of origin.

From the beginning of the 1990s, political space had opened in Angola for the emergence of local NGOs as well as the entrance of more international aid agencies into the country. Most of the aid response was geared towards providing relief to the population. With the end of the war in 2002, the challenges that the rural areas of Angola were facing were enormous: demining of agricultural land, recapitalization of peasant households, recovery of rural-urban trade, land rights, and reviving the agricultural extension system (Hodges 2002: 31). Aid agencies were deemed to have essential roles to play in addressing these challenges and had to rethink their relief policies and practices to adapt to the changing circumstance. Instead of food aid distributions, attention soon turned towards resettlement programmes combined with food security and livelihood support approaches. Food security approaches are popular in immediate post-conflict contexts, following the logic that supporting small-scale agriculture leads to household food production, diminishes reliance on food aid, and will eventually also lead to income from any surplus harvest that is produced (Levine and Chastre 2004).

In Huíla province, most organizations focused on assisting people in the rural areas with their resettlement and re-starting agricultural production. Few needs assessments were carried out amongst the rural and returning population. Rather, the rationale for the ensuing aid response seemed to be born out of the idea that people's agricultural resources and productivity needed to be supported in order to decrease dependency on food aid and counter further urbanization. Moreover, information on livelihoods conditions and needs were extrapolated from the relief operation, or based on perceptions by local staff that the most common livelihood strategy was assumed to be subsistence level farming. This assumption leaves little space for the diversity of local responses that people tend to develop. The actions and ideas in the immediate post-conflict period in Angola have put a significant stamp on the LRRD policies and practices that were developed in the 5–6 years after the war finished.

The intended and unintended effects of seeds and tools

In the 33 interviews with staff of aid agencies and government institutions in Huíla province, 22 interviewees indicated that their agencies were pursuing direct seeds and tools distribution programmes as their main aid response in rural areas. The other interviewees were often representatives of organizations that specialized in health care, and in de-mining. Rural livelihood recovery programmes have been dominated by direct seeds and tools distribution almost continuously from 2002 until 2008. They were often similar in nature and approach, crop types, and often even in the same locations. Usually, 250 households would be selected by the village chiefs, after which NGOs distributed seeds – mainly for maize and beans, occasionally some sorghum, millet or horticultural seeds if water was available nearby. Hoes, machetes and ploughs were made available to assist with main-taining the plots of land, and in some instances oxen were distributed amongst the households to be used on a rotational basis. Commercialization options or local transformation of products to add value were not included in the aid response. One organization had stated the creation of market access for commercialization purposes as a specific objective, but was unable to deliver because, according to them, households were not producing sufficient quantities by the time that the funding for the programme had stopped in 2007. The idea that these households were not yet prepared for the next step towards commercialization was disproven during this research. Some of the households that had received seeds and tools during the post-conflict period had already been selling parts of their produce even during the war. Seeds that they were using were procured from different sources: their own reserves, from aid agencies, and from the local markets. House-holds had been scrutinizing the seed distributions by the various aid agencies on the basis of the most commercially interesting seed varieties that they handed out, knowing the exact prices that produce would fetch on local markets for each variety, and producing them accordingly. Mere household survival was no longer the main driver for production, but how to get access to markets and increase profits.

The practical implications and effects of these interventions were well illustrated in Caluquembe, where many of these agencies had operated their seeds and tools programmes. The rural landscape in this region nowadays is dominated by maize and bean crops. From 48 households that were surveyed in three villages in Calu-quembe, it emerged that all households were involved in maize production, and 40 in bean production as well. Other livelihood activities deployed by these house-holds centred on some small-scale fruit and horticulture production, beekeeping, picking wild foods, fishing, occasional day labour, semi-skilled labour, formal employment as teacher and nurses, and trade. Maize and beans were the crops traded on the local markets most often, although for a very low value.[5] Seeing the enormous quantity of maize being produced, but with little access to more distant markets, local farmers are in direct competition with one another and see very little return on their crops, which at the same time are very labour intensive. At the time of the fieldwork, village inhabitants indicated that they wanted to start producing more lucrative crops, such as coffee, as the market value for maize was too low to bring in cash, but could only be exchanged for other items such as salt or soap.[6] Also, some of the seeds that NGOs had distributed required more exten-sive use of fertilizers, which made additional financial investments necessary by the involved households.[7] Coincidentally, when the region was hit by a drought in 2008, it showed the vulnerable position of livelihoods through the overreliance on maize and bean production. The crops did not survive the drought, and people reported they did not have any alternatives or savings to fall back on.

During the war, so much attention and resources had been turned towards the war machine that the rural areas had suffered tremendous lack of investment. Agricultural production had become more one-sided because certain crops were abandoned as they were considered too risky, markets were not fully functioning any more, and necessary inputs were increasingly scarce. Yet, people continued producing foods for their households' survival, and were sometimes even able to sell part of the produce on the local markets. During the time of the surveys in the three villages, more than two-thirds of the households were selling excess produce of maize and beans on the local markets. Coffee, on the other hand, a crop that prior to 1975 had been produced quite extensively in the region, had disappeared. As coffee plants take 2–3 years to start producing, and markets had become inaccessible during the war, people had directed their attention to producing crops with which they knew they could quickly feed their households. However, the fact that maize and beans were used during the war to ensure household survival did not necessarily make them the best crops of choice for aid agencies, if the desired end objective for LRRD was poverty alleviation or even sustainable economic growth.

Underlying assumptions in post-conflict recovery aid interventions

Rural post-conflict recovery aid responses are often characterized by agricultural rehabilitation programmes, because donors prefer it as a sustainable and effective way of spending their resources, and farmers (but often not traders) are unlikely to complain about receiving free inputs, even if they chose to sell or eat them rather than plant them (Longley *et al.* 2006: 5). Seeds and tools are considered neutral aid interventions, and assumed to 'do no harm'. Sperling and McGuire (2010) have, however, made quite some compelling arguments to the contrary. On the basis of their extensive research into seed systems and seed relief, they have made several observations on how seed relief can actually do harm, and why assumptions on seeds and tools as effective and neutral interventions are not necessarily true. First, they argue that although seed distribution is considered an effective link between relief and development, interventions are rarely evaluated to understand their long-term effects. Needs assessments, on which these interventions are designed, also rarely take place, with needs being extrapolated from the relief period. Second, the assumption that during conflict, local markets and seed systems stop functioning is often a driving factor for seed relief. The assumption is that local seeds are no longer available, and therefore farmers need to have a supply sufficient to plant but also to act as household reserves. However, markets often continue functioning to a certain extent, and seed is also often procured during crisis through alternative institutions and networks. Neighbours and kinship structures are crucial for households' access to seeds (Sperling and McGuire 2010: 197). By supplying farmers with seeds, these markets and informal institutions that people rely on can actually be undermined. Third, improved seed varieties are often made available that should increase the yield. However, these improved seed varieties are not necessarily better than the varieties farmers rely on during crisis. Sperling and McGuire (2010: 198) note that these improved varieties do not always lead to better yields, as they don't respond well to the low-input conditions in which they are used. In these circumstances, local varieties in comparison actually give better results.

These examples show that seeds and tools distributions are not necessarily a 'do no harm' intervention. Rather, a better understanding is necessary of the effects on the informal arrangements through which people procure their seeds and on which they rely, especially when the formal institutional environment is not sufficiently prepared to address seed needs once aid agencies leave.

Aid programming is often not informed by an empirical analysis of labour markets and the impact that aid has on these (Hilhorst *et al.* 2010: 1114). Seeds and tools programmes operate under the assumption that household labour is sufficiently present among beneficiaries. Research done in Northern Uganda by Wairimu (2012) revealed that seeds and tools interventions can actually entrench vulnerabilities for non-able-bodied people in communities unable to contribute labour to household production. Also, aid agencies' preference for handing out seeds and tools, as opposed to oxen and ploughs, for instance, (which could potentially assist households in enlarging their area of land under cultivation and increase their production and thus revenues) were also laid bare in this research. Next to the higher costs of providing oxen as compared to seeds and tools, the aid agencies stated that they would have to report a lower amount of beneficiaries to their donors, making investment in oxen less popular than seeds and tools, although the impact on household productivity could have been significant (Wairimu 2012: 8). Maize is an especially labour-intensive crop requiring high field maintenance but also processing time and energy. Grinding the maize into flour that can be used to make maize porridge requires hours of labour, twice a day, which is a task that is part of women's household responsibilities. Next to the fact that sowing the maize plots is also often considered the work of the household females, this makes maize-based seeds and tools interventions quite a gender-insensitive aid response.

In the case of Angola, off-farm livelihoods were largely ignored in recovery projects, which is a common oversight in rural aid programming (Longley *et al.* 2006, Ellis 2000, Ellis and Biggs 2001). The image of rural society persists in which everyone is assumed to engage in smallholder farming (Cramer 2006). This ignores social differentiation and the existence of alternative livelihoods, especially those developed during conflict. Working the fields of others, migration, firewood collection, hunting or other off-farm activities are often interpreted as unsustainable coping strategies. This narrow conceptualization of rural society perpetuates the 'yeoman farmer fallacy', the myth that all rural people rely on farming alone for their livelihood (Farrington 1998). This image often shapes the one-size-fits-all response towards recovery and development in rural areas, and fails to take into account people's differentiated needs, desires and capabilities. By paying more attention to people's own recovery processes and off-farm activities that are pursued, aid interventions can more adequately deal with people's varying needs during and after conflict. This lack of attention for the variety of needs has especially affected the younger generations in the rural areas who often felt disconnected from a rural or farming lifestyle. Their decision against resettlement, has, however, had some positive effect in the form of remittances, new networks and increased rural-urban linkages. More attention in the aid response could have been given to alternative pathways to recovery and development of rural livelihoods, by including off-farm livelihoods, but also by including access to markets, value adding of products, and other ways in which farming systems could have been supported in addressing the vulnerable state of rural livelihoods today.

State reconstruction processes

The Angolan state's post-conflict reconstruction policies and practices were very visible and far-reaching in some parts of the country, but less present in other parts. Conceptualizing reconstruction as a return to pre-war 'normality' in Angola's case would mean a return to the Portuguese colonial history, which in fact is the way that the Angolan's state recovery plans can be characterized (Pacheco 2002). The state's reconstruction focus mostly centred on urban and coastal areas with the rehabilitation of roads, rails and bridges, and neglect of the interior and rural areas – a perpetuation of colonial policies (Ruigrok 2010: 641–642). Examples of state reconstruction projects in Chibia also show a reinvention of the centralized planning strategies which guided the rural policies of the MPLA-led government until the 1990s.

In 2003, the GoA launched its PRSP in which the objectives for food security and rural development were to minimize the risk of hunger and starvation, to satisfy the internal food needs and to re-launch the rural economy as a vital sector for sustainable development especially by focusing on the 'traditional sector' (GoA 2003: 52–53). The main obstacles for reviving the rural economy were thought to be the damaged infrastructure which blocked the arrival of agricultural inputs (seeds, fertilizers and tools) and also limited people's options for transporting their produce, a lack of credit opportunities, and poor local markets (GoA 2003: 52). Although the traditional sector was considered a priority area, attention soon turned towards infrastructural development and large-scale farming instead.

Road rehabilitation was considered essential for rural producers to gain physical market access and thus move beyond subsistence level (Kyle 2005). The effects of these policies were very noticeable in the municipality of Chibia, which lies in closest proximity to the provincial capital Lubango. But it also draws more personal interest from government officials, as several members of the provincial political elites own cattle ranches in the area. Although the road rehabilitation has enhanced people's access to markets, trade and employment in Lubango, it has also led to some negative side-effects – as one Chibian farmer noted. He complained that, with the road works nearing completion, connecting Lubango with the border of Namibia, he had hundreds of kilos of onions rotting away on his field. He was unable to sell them to the supermarkets in Lubango, as nowadays Namibian trucks filled with onions passed him by on the rehabilitated highway. Another example of the negative effects of the infrastructural elements of the national reconstruction programmes was noted by Orre (2010) in the case of the rehabilitation of the Moçamedes railway. This railway was built in 1961, and connected the provinces of Huíla and Namibe, but was abandoned during the civil war. In 2009, the rehabilitation of the railway started in Lubango with massive forced evictions (mostly IDPs) by the provincial government, and the demolition of their homes without notice or provision of alternative housing (Orre 2010: 2). The GoA's attitude towards prioritizing infrastructural rehabilitation over the socio-economic wellbeing of the more vulnerable population does not stand alone. As Orre notes,

> The event thus illustrates the government's reconstruction strategy centred on the fast development of large-scale infrastructure in a process which seemingly shows little concern for the more immediate needs of the vast masses of the urban and rural poor.
>
> (Orre 2010: 3)

In the post-conflict period, conflicts over land have erupted in the south of Huíla province, where grazing land for pastoralists is said to be diminishing due to the fencing practices of new large commercial landowners. The potential for new conflicts over land is ongoing as long as no real solutions are found to the problem of land grabbing and the lack of standardized political agreements over compensation to affected communities. Further illustration of the unintended effects of a national reconstruction projects is given in Box 14.1, with an example of a state reconstruction project in Chibia.

Box 14.1 The Sogangelas project in Chibia

The Sogangelas agricultural project in Chibia is presented by the Angolan Government as a prime example of modern agricultural development, and a means to combat unemployment and poverty by creating at least 300 jobs in the sectors of agriculture, industry and commerce (Jornal de Angola 2010). A plot of land of around 6,000 hectares was prepared for large-scale production of cereals, horticulture and fruits, and 24 kilometres of irrigation canals were installed. The local agricultural extension office in Chibia carried out a market study and advised a production of wheat instead of maize, because of its potential for bigger profits, and to avoid competition with smallholders in the area who are selling their surplus maize on markets as well. Small plots of irrigated land would be distributed to interested big and small farmers in the area. Pilot production started in 2008 using some smaller-sized plots of land, focusing mostly on maize, beans and some vegetable crops. The harvest during the agricultural season of 2009/2010 was only half of what had been expected, due to severe rains and lack of funds for fuel to keep the generators of the irrigation system running (Angop 2010). In 2010, 74 small and big farmers had been employed by the project to cultivate the pilot plots. Sogangelas indicated in the same year that they would need a further investment of US$ 300,000 in order to supply the farmers with seeds, fertilizers, as well as fuel for the generators of the irrigation system (Angop 2011).

All people who had been living and working on the Sogangelas premises were relocated by the state. But not everyone has received compensation for their lost land and houses, its disbursement often depending on whether or not they had left their lands and houses within the allowed time limits. For a group of displaced people living opposite the Sogangelas terrain, the start of the project meant the end of their agricultural activities. The land and water they had been using until that time had been assigned to Sogangelas. Furthermore, due to the reconstruction of the existing irrigation channels in the entire Chibia area, access to water had been cut off for many other households.

The Sogangelas project has actually led to a part of the population becoming disconnected from their livelihoods and has reversed some of the results of earlier assistance programmes where seeds and tools programmes have become useless due to a sudden lack of land and water. Sogangelas highlights the Angolan state's preference for large-scale, high-tech and commercial agriculture, as a strategy for rural development in the country. These reconstruction projects are reminiscent of the centralized planning strategies of the 1970s and 1980s, which were characterized by a drive towards nationalizing large farms and mechanization as a way to deal with the collapse of the rural economy after the withdrawal of colonial structures (Bhagavan 1980). In order to deal with the food shortages that occurred thereafter, the MPLA-led government turned its attention to stimulating productivity of the abandoned large farms and supporting further mechanization (Kofi 1981). Although large state farms were also considered to have a positive effect on peasant ways of production, which were considered backward, in reality little effort was made to connect the two ways of production or to stimulate the peasant production especially (Young 1988). A reinvention of historical rural policies can be distinguished in the manner in which the GoA overall prioritizes an urban focus for post-conflict reconstruction of the country, as well as displaying a preference for a high-tech, large-scale and infrastructural push for the rural economy. This shows a discrepancy between the GoA's policy and practice in its rural development strategies. Whereas the PRSP states that priority is given to the traditional rural sector, priorities in practice show that large commercial projects and large landowners are allowed to accumulate land to the detriment of the traditional rural sector: namely, small-holders and pastoralists.

Conclusions

There is much continuity and normality to be found during crisis. Crisis does not affect all regions of a conflict-affected country equally, there always remain areas and situations in which people are able to maintain their daily routines and pursue their livelihoods. At the same time, there can be crises in post-conflict situations, revealing the vulnerable state of people's post-conflict livelihoods. Through a better understanding of recovery processes at play, aid interventions can more adequately respond to people's varying needs during and after conflict.

Post-conflict recovery processes often reflect conflicting interests from various actors and different assumptions about what is needed. This chapter on post-conflict recovery processes and LRRD in Angola has shown that there are multiple pathways to recovery, and these pathways interact and intertwine with varying results. People's own recovery processes in Huíla province have been character-ized by a diversity of activities that were developed during the war, and which continued to a certain extent afterwards. Day labour, labour migration, trade and agricultural production have provided people with means to deal with the destruc-tive effects of conflict. After the signing of the peace agreement in 2002, state and aid agencies had to rethink their policies and strategies towards the rural areas, and development thinking became increasingly relevant. Although attempts had been made to incorporate and coordinate aid strategies with local governance structures, such as the agricultural extension office, issues such as commercializa-tion, value adding, access to markets and diversification were hardly implemented. Most donor funding for Angola dried up in 2007, and many international aid agencies had to withdraw. Local NGOs are struggling to secure funding to continue their aid programmes.

Case study evidence from Huíla has shown that LRRD approaches have made several assumptions about livelihood responses to crisis and the best ways to achieve development and a change from crisis to normality. Development as an end-objective is about improving the socio-economic wellbeing of populations, which includes reducing people's vulnerability to shocks. The uncritical and repeated delivery of seeds and tools, however, neglects the reality of rural liveli-hoods and the diversified activities that people undertake. Seeds and tools programmes do not automatically lead to development. There is a need to criti-cally assess the assumptions about desirable livelihoods in these contexts. Who defines what 'normal livelihoods' are in post-conflict recovery processes, which transitions take place along the way, and how do these underlying assumptions inform the shape and directions that interventions and people's future activities take? As this chapter shows, LRRD approaches have done little to strengthen people's economic base, which in turn has weakened people's ability to cope with sudden shocks such as natural hazards because they are left with few alternative sources of income. All their time, labour and assets have been focused on the production of crops that can, in case of a successful harvest, feed the household and earn a little bit of cash or be traded for other necessities. Therefore, seeds and tools distributions are not neutral and are not a 'do no harm' intervention. More attention is needed in understanding the long-term effects of these interventions on, for instance, informal seed markets, labour pressures, and the overall sustain-ability of these interventions.

Aid and state recovery processes have, in some instances, run counter to the post-conflict recovery processes that people themselves established. They have led to a uniform rural society with few opportunities for diversification, in which most available household labour is absorbed by subsistence agriculture alone. Combined with the lack of institutional and industrial developments, this leaves the inhabit-ants vulnerable to new shocks.

Acknowledgements

The author wishes to thank Jeroen Cuvelier, Annelies Heijmans, Inge Ruigrok and Shawn McGuire for their constructive comments on an earlier version of this chapter. All responsibility remains with the author.

Notes

1 This chapter builds on PhD research carried out on the intended and unintended outcomes of post-conflict recovery processes on rural livelihoods in the province of Huíla, Angola (van Dijkhorst 2011).
2 *Macau* is a local beer or liquor made of sorghum, and is considered important as a form of local currency.
3 Interview with inhabitant *kimbo* in Nolata, 22 July 2008.
4 Interview with inhabitant Camucuio, 5 February 2008.
5 1 kilo of maize fetches an average of 15 kwanza (0.15 Euro) on the local Caluquembe market. On the urban markets, a kilo of maize would fetch 50 kwanza, but access to these markets is difficult due to lack of means of transportation. Most maize flour that is sold in the Angolan supermarkets actually originates from Namibia and South Africa.
6 Interview with inhabitant Cue 1, 30 January 2008.
7 Interview with inhabitant Catala, 1 February 2008.

References

Angop (2010) *Produção Agrícola no Perímetro das Gangelas Abaixo da Capacidade Instalada*. Source consulted on 1 February 2011: http://www.portalangop.co.ao/motix/pt_pt/noticias/economia/2010/9/41/Producao-agricola-perimetro-das-Gangelas-abaixo-capacidade-instalada,127a46a6-d0ca-47da-af20-f9ebb2c35637.html
Angop (2011) *Perímetro Irrigado das Gangelas Necessita de Mais de AKZ 28 Milhões para Fomentar Produção*. Source consulted on 1 February 2011: http://www.portalangop.co.ao/motix/pt_pt/noticias/economia/2011/0/2/Perimetro-irrigado-das-Gangelas-necessita-mais-AKZ-milhoes-para-fomentar-producao,5b16ef2a-dc94-427b-80e3-2ea599206b6e.html
Bhagavan, M.R. (1980) *Angola: Prospects for Socialist Industrialisation*, Research Report No 57, Uppsala: Scandinavian Institute for African Studies.
Buchanan-Smith, M. and P. Fabbri (2005) *Linking Relief, Rehabilitation and Development: A Review of the Debate*, London: Tsunami Evaluation Coalition.
Cain, A. (2003) *Civil Society and Community Reconstruction in Post-War Angola*. Paper presented to the Roundtable Discussion on International Donors and Civil Society Implications for Angola's Recovery and the Displaced, Luanda 16–17 July 2003.
Christoplos, I. (2006) *Links Between Relief Rehabilitation and Development in the Tsunami Response*, London: Tsunami Evaluation Coalition.
Corbett, J. (1988) 'Famine and Household Coping Strategies', *World Development*, Vol. 16, No. 9: 1099–1112.
Cramer, C. (2006) *Civil War is not a Stupid Thing. Accounting for Violence in Developing Countries*, London: Hurst & Company.
De Haan, A. (2000) *Migrants, Livelihoods, and Rights: The Relevance of Migration in Development Policies*, Social Development Working Paper No. 4, London: Department of International Development.

256   *Hilde van Dijkhorst*

Duffield, M. (1994) 'Complex Emergencies and the Crisis of Developmentalism', *IDS Bulletin* 25, No. 4: 37–45.

Duffield, M. (2000) 'Humanitarian Conditionality: Origins, Consequences and Implications of the Pursuit of Development and Conflict', in G. Loane and T. Schumer (eds) *The Wider Impact of Humanitarian Assistance; The Case of Sudan and the Implications for a European Union Policy*, Nomos Verlagsgesellschaft Baden-Baden: Conflict Prevention Network (SWP-CPN) 60/6.

Ellis, F. (2000) *Rural Livelihoods and Diversity in Developing Countries*, Oxford: Oxford University Press.

Ellis, F. and S. Biggs (2001) 'Evolving Themes in Rural Development 1950s–2000s', *Development Policy Review*, Vol. 19, No. 4: 437–448.

Farrington, J. (1998) 'Organizational Roles in Farmer Participatory Research and Extension: Lessons from the Past Decade', *Natural Resource Perspectives*, London: Overseas Development Institute.

Frerks, G., D. Hilhorst and A. Moreyra (1999) *Natural Disasters: A Framework for Analysis and Action*, paper produced for MSF Holland, Wageningen: Wageningen University.

GoA (Government of Angola) (2003) *Strategy to Combat Poverty: Social Reinsertion, Rehabilitation and Reconstruction and Economic Stabilisation*, Luanda: GoA.

Hilhorst, D., I. Christoplos and G. van der Haar (2010) 'Reconstruction "From Below": a New Magic Bullet or Shooting from the Hip?' *Third World Quarterly*, Vol. 31, No. 7: 1107–1124.

Hodges, T. (2002) 'Angola's Economy: Perspectives for Aid Partners', in I. Tvedten (ed.) *Angola 2001/2002: Key Development Issues and Aid in a Context of Peace*, CMI Report R 2002:8, Bergen: CMI.

Hodges, T. (2004) *Angola: Anatomy of an Oil State*, Oxford: James Currey.

Horst, C. (2002) *Xawilaad: The Importance of Overseas Connections in the Livelihoods of Somali Refugees in the Dadaab Camps of Kenya*, Working Paper No. 14, Oxford: Transnational Communities Programme.

Jornal de Angola (2010) *Produção Agrícola Aumenta na Chibia*. Source consulted on 7 July 2011: http://jornaldeangola.sapo.ao/14/16/producao_agricola_aumenta_na_chibia

Kofi, T.A. (1981) 'Prospects and Problems of the Transition from Agrarianism to Socialism: The Case of Angola, Guinea-Bissau and Mozambique', *World Development*, Vol. 9, No. 9/10: 851–870.

Kyle, S. (2005) *A Strategy for Agricultural Development in Angola*, Department of Applied Economics and Management, Working Paper 2005–25, New York: Cornell University.

Lanzer, T. (1996) 'The UN Department of Humanitarian Affairs in Angola: A Model for the Coordination of Humanitarian Assistance?' *Studies on Emergencies and Disaster Relief*, Uppsala: Nordiska Afrikainstitutet.

Le Billon, P. (2007) 'Drilling in Deep Water: Oil, Business and War in Angola', in M. Kaldor, T.L. Karl and Y. Said (eds) *Oil Wars*, London: Pluto Press.

Levine, S. and C. Chastre (2004) *Missing the Point: an Analysis of Food Security Interventions in the Great Lakes*, London: Humanitarian Policy Group.

Longley, C., I. Christoplos and T. Slaymaker (2006) 'Agricultural Rehabilitation: Mapping the Linkages between Humanitarian Relief, Social Protection and Development', *Humanitarian Policy Group Research Briefing*, No. 22, London: ODI.

McDowell, C. and A. de Haan (1997) 'Migration and Sustainable Livelihoods: A Critical Review of the Literature', *IDS Working Paper*, No. 65. Sussex: Institute of Development Studies.

Orre, A. (2010) *Who's to Challenge the Party-State in Angola? Politicial Space and the Opposition in Parties and Civil Society*, Bergen: Chr. Michelsen Institute.

Pacheco, F. (2002) 'The Role of Civil Society in the Social Reconstruction of Angola', in I. Tvedten *Angola 2001/2002: Key Development Issues and Aid in a Context of Peace*, CMI Report R 2002:8, Bergen: CMI.

Ruigrok, I. (2010) 'Facing Up to the Centre: The Emergence of Regional Elite Associations in Angola's Political Transition Process', *Development and Change*, Vol. 41, No. 4: 637–658.

Russo, L., G. Hemrich, L. Alinovi and D. Melvin (2008) 'Food Security in Protracted Crisis Situations: Issues and Challenges', in L. Alinova, G. Hemrich and L. Russo (eds) *Beyond Relief: Food Security in Protracted Crisis*, Rugby: Practical Action Publishing.

Savage, K. and P. Harvey (2007) 'Remittances During Crises: Implications for Humanitarian Response', *HPG report* 25, London: Humanitarian Policy Group.

Sperling, L. and S. McGuire (2010) 'Persistent Myths about Emergency Seed Aid', *Food Policy*, Vol. 35: 195–201.

United Nations (2003) *Angola: Mid-Year Review, May 2003*, New York and Geneva: UN.

Van Dijkhorst, H. (2011) *Rural Realities between Crisis and Normality: Livelihood Strategies in Angola, 1975–2008*, PhD Thesis, Wageningen University: Wageningen.

Vines, A. (2000) *Angola: Forty Years of War. Conference of Demilitarisation and Peace-Building in Southern Africa*, Pretoria: Centre for Conflict Resolution and Bonn International Centre for Convention.

Wairimu, W. (2012) *Labour Questions in Post-Conflict Northern Uganda*, Research brief for the IS Academy 'Human Security in Fragile States', Wageningen: Wageningen University.

White, P. and L. Cliffe (2000) 'Matching Response to Context in Complex Political Emergencies: "Relief", "Development", "Peace-building" or Something In-Between?', *Disasters*, Vol. 24, No. 4: 314–342.

Young, T. (1988) 'The Politics of Development in Angola and Mozambique', *African Affairs*, Vol. 87, No. 347: 165–184.

15 Doing good/being nice?

Aid legitimacy and mutual imaging of aid workers and aid recipients

Dorothea Hilhorst, Gemma Andriessen, Lotte Kemkens and Loes Weijers

This chapter explores interfaces between aid workers and aid recipients in contexts of crises and post-crises where much aid is given under the label of humanitarian assistance. It builds on three field researches among formerly displaced people in Northern Uganda, Bhutanese refugees in Nepal, and post-conflict communities of South Sudan. The central question of these researches was: 'What images do humanitarian aid workers and aid recipients have of themselves and of each other and how are these images related to the legitimacy of aid in the field?' A major claim we make is that the level of appreciation actors have of one another is an important determinant of aid legitimacy. To put it simply: aid workers that are nice, are more likely to be perceived as doing good.

The chapter is placed in a literature tradition that recognises the importance of actor images for the organisation, effectiveness and legitimacy of aid. The ways in which aid workers perceive their clients, and the other way around, affects aid relations and outcomes. Most of the literature, however, addresses only one side of the relationship, and focuses either on labelling by aid workers or on perceptions of the recipients.

Since the 1980s, considerable attention has been paid to the processes of labelling of refugees by aid agencies. 'Labelling refers to the process by which policy agendas are established, and more particularly the way in which people, conceived as objects of policy, are defined in convenient images' (Wood 1985). More than an innocent categorising of people, labelling is intertwined with power and has far-reaching consequences for the organisation, services, implementation and legitimisation of aid (Christoplos 1998, Bakewell 2000). Labelling is used to define boundaries between aid-eligible and non-aid-eligible people. Once eligible categories are labelled, boundary protection leads to strict measures to exclude people undeserving of aid, including night raids and other de-humanising measures (Zetter 1991, Hyndman 2000).

Labelling practices also have an effect on the aid packages that are offered. Services offered by agencies may not be based on a needs analysis but on unfounded assumptions about what particular categories of people require. Van Dijkhorst, in Chapter 14 of this volume, shows how agencies assumed that survivors of war in Angola were self-sufficient in agriculture. This idea was translated into programmes for the distribution of seeds for staple foods. This in turn led to a negative price spiral for staple foods in an oversupplied market while marginalising more commercial crops that farmers in Angola could rely on for their income. There has also been attention in the literature to the effects of stereotyping aid recipients as suffering from a dependency syndrome. This inhibits humanitarian agencies embracing participatory approaches to aid (Clark 1985, Harrell-Bond 1986, Hilhorst *et al.* 2011). It also distorts accountability because it allows aid agencies to dismiss complaints from their 'beneficiaries' by using references to their 'dependency attitude'. Labels ascribing psychological features to refugees may thus be used to put the blame for aid failures on the recipients (Malkki 1995).

We also see attention to the reverse relationship, namely how aid recipients perceive aid agencies, and how this affects aid. In an early contribution to the debate, Jok Madut Jok (1996) wrote about the issue of how loose Western lifestyles and the age and gender profile of Western aid workers had a negative effect on the working relations with local authorities in Sudan. It was simply unacceptable for the elder men in authority positions to take 'orders' from predominantly female aid managers who, in their eyes, were too young, of a subordinate gender, and inappropriately dressed. Kibreab (2004) describes how aid recipients have no qualms about cheating the aid agencies: 'Outmanoeuvring the rich and powerful organisations, as well as their cohorts, the *kwajas* (white people), was seen as a valiant act.' It is increasingly acknowledged that aid agencies should invest in knowing how recipients perceive them, in order to improve their programmes. Dijkzeul and Wakenge (2010) argue that aid organisations should invest more in understanding the perceptions of aid recipients, since they lack the consumer feedback provided to commercial organisations (Péchayre 2011: 13).

Our chapter argues for a symmetrical analysis that takes into account imaging of both aid workers and recipients, of themselves and each other. While most of the literature referred to above either focuses on aid recipients' perspectives or on aid agencies' labelling practices, this chapter aims to analyse their mutual imaging. Ethnographic research into aid relations brings out how both aid givers and recipients respond to the stereotyped ways in which they are treated, and that this interaction shapes the relations and content of aid. Hilhorst found that the roles and activities of a non-governmental organisation (NGO) differed substantially in different areas of intervention, due to differences in views and responses of villagers that 'boxed' the NGO into particular behaviour (Hilhorst 2003, Hilhorst and van Leeuwen 2005, 1999).

Most literature assumes that aid workers and aid recipients are two clearly distinguished groups that have little in common. In this chapter, we step away from this idea. By asking similar questions to both groups of respondents, and analysing these with a Q-methodology (elaborated from page 261), we identify perspectives that contain shared elements and that may cut across these different categories. We therefore have an open-ended research frame that allows us to find similarities and contradictions within and between these two groups of actors.

After a theoretical and methodological introduction, we will present findings from Northern Uganda, Nepal and South Sudan.[1] Our research reveals that aid workers and recipients are not separate categories and that there is a large diversity in the images they have of themselves and each other. Factors such as ethnicity, social distance, type of aid and history with aid played a role, and accounted for much more commonalities between these categories, as well as diversity within them. We also find that the specific ways in which imaging and legitimacy are linked differs per case, yet it is clear that these images affect legitimacy. Our findings particularly call for attention to the importance of local aid providers from among the communities of refugees in mediating and brokering aid relations.

Fieldwork was conducted over three months in each country in 2011/2012. In Northern Uganda, fieldwork was done in Pader District among the aid recipients and aid workers of 15 agencies. In Nepal, research was done in the Beldangi-1 camp near Damak, where around 12,000 Bhutanese refugees resided at the time. The research concerned recipients and workers of the Lutheran World Federation Nepal (LWF Nepal) which is in large part responsible for the management of the camp and the care and maintenance of the refugees. Fieldwork in South Sudan was done with seven NGOs in the water and sanitation sector in Eastern Equatoria State. LWF Nepal, LWF Uganda and SNV in South Sudan kindly hosted our research, provided introductions to agencies and recipients, and generously allowed us to interview their staff.

Theoretical approach

We view humanitarian action as an 'arena' where actors negotiate the outcomes of aid (Hilhorst and Jansen 2010, Hilhorst and Serrano 2010). The realities and outcomes of aid depend on how actors along and around the aid chain – donor representatives, headquarters, field staff, aid recipients and surrounding actors – interpret the context, the needs, their own role and each other. The idea of an arena is founded in an actor-oriented approach, which departs from the assumption that social actors reflect upon their experiences and what happens around them and use their knowledge and capabilities to interpret and respond to their environment (Long 2001).

In our perspective, we pay much attention to the strategising and constructive roles of aid *recipients* in shaping humanitarian aid, which can be exemplified by revisiting the notion of labelling. The literature we refer to above focuses on aid workers as labelling agents. They portray their clients as vulnerable, a label that renders people helpless and deprives them of their agency. Without denying the powerful workings of agencies' labels, we want to draw attention to the role of aid recipients in these processes. While agencies derive their legitimacy from their image as moral actors, recipients derive their legitimacy from the fact that they are in need. They will therefore endeavour to present their most vulnerable face to aid workers. The representation of the self as passive and suffering can be seen as an expression of agency, which Utas (2005) aptly refers to as 'victimcy'. Sandvik (2008) likewise refers to this as a 'choreography of suffering and empathy'. While humanitarian workers 'vulnerabilise' their clients in order to legitimise their presence and their command over resources that are available for the victims of crises, we recognise that clients are complicit in their own vulnerabilisation. This makes vulnerability less of a labelling practice by the aid-provider than the emerging property of the interaction of aid-providers and their clients.

We prefer the concept of *imaging* over that of *perceptions or labelling*. *Images* are the mental entities that are used by people to create social representations of themselves, one another and the world around them (Potter and Wetherall 1987). We are aware that many scholars, including those referred to above, have a similar meaning in mind when using the concept of *perceptions*. As Dijkzeul and Wakenge (2010: 1140) observe: 'in almost all research on perceptions [. . .] the concept is used synonymously with view, and sometimes with the related terms interpretation, belief or critical opinion'. The term 'perception' originates from psychology where it refers to the process through which sensations are interpreted with the use of knowledge and an understanding of the world, in order that they become meaningful experiences (Bernstein 2008: 153). Perceptions, in their psychological meaning, are properties of agents, and tend to become frozen. In studying interaction, we emphasise the social character of images that evolve interactively and are not just personal and cultural, but also contextual and multiple. Imaging processes have elements of internalisation, where images are products of past experiences, culture or aid discourse. Yet, they also contain elements of strategising. Actors create representations by playing with their self- and othering images, partly in response to how they imagine to be imaged by others.

We are interested in the question how the mutual imaging of aid workers and recipients affects the legitimacy of aid. Building on works by Lister (2003) and Slim (2002), we can distinguish several sources from which agencies can derive their legitimacy, including their accountability, performance, experience and reputation. However, as noted by Lister (2003: 178), legitimacy is not the sum of these elements but rests in the eye of the beholder. 'Legitimacy is often regarded as something which is socially constructed and given meaning by the normative framework within which it exists'. One intriguing question that arises from this constructivist approach is whether the legitimacy of aid will be equal to the legitimacy of aid agencies with which aid recipients interact and build relations?

Methodology

Our focus on everyday practices emphasises the fact that phenomena acquire meaning in their everyday realities. Ethnographic inquiry, in which we study the everyday interactions of relevant actors, is particularly appropriate in unravelling these dynamics. Fieldwork in all three countries was based on participant observation, in order to learn about day-to-day life and the interaction between aid workers and aid recipients. Apart from this, we have sought to investigate systematically the mutual images by using the so-called Q-methodology. This was designed in the 1930s by William Stephenson to research viewpoints, opinions, beliefs and attitudes (Brown 1993). The process started with the development and selection of statements on aid giver and aid recipient relations. The statements we developed were partly theory-driven. This initial set of statements was adjusted for each of the countries on the basis of a first qualitative exploration of the field and interviews that led to additions to statements. Statements covered the potential range of viewpoints on four themes: power relations (e.g. 'If refugees want to improve their situation they need connections with staff'); the quality of the relations between aid providers and recipients (e.g. 'Refugees and staff are equal'); communication (e.g. 'Refugees tell the staff what they need'); and personal characteristics of staff and refugees (e.g. 'Refugees tend to criticise').

In Q-methodology, the selection of the participants consists of a structured sample of respondents who are theoretically relevant to the problem under consideration. In our case, the Q-methodology was done with a total of 28 to 39 participants per country which included beneficiaries, volunteers and incentive workers, and staff from different NGOs. Contrary to many other quantitative analyses, a Q-methodological study requires only a limited number of respondents. The number of respondents required is that needed to establish the existence of a factor, for purposes of comparing one factor with another (Brown 1980). 'The aim is to have four or five persons defining each anticipated viewpoint, which are often two to four, and rarely more than six' (Van Exel and de Graaf 2005: 6). The respondents were asked to value the statements (from 'strongly disagree' to 'strongly agree'). Subsequently, individual scores were subjected to factor analysis to define clusters of statements that constitute social perspectives on the issue at hand. For this, we used the software programme 'PQ method', a statistical programme that uses 'statistical techniques of correlation and factor analysis to reveal patterns in the way people associate opinions' (Webler *et al.* 2009: 6). The content of the perspectives is determined by which statements most strongly, positively or negatively, connect to the perspective. The different respondents can then be coupled to these narratives on the basis of their scores on the statements. As illustration, Box 15.1 below presents an example of a narrative composed from the Nepal research. It concerns the narrative that was mainly given scores by passive beneficiaries of aid.

Box 15.1 Example of a Q-methodology narrative derived from the Nepal fieldwork

Those respondents that scored highly on this narrative (mainly beneficiaries) believe that the aid organisations are there to help the beneficiaries, although they do not know which organisations are helping and what these organisations do exactly. They do not necessarily do a good job, but in general they do. The unknown staff of these unknown organisations is not really ignorant about what is important for the beneficiaries, but still the beneficiaries need to work in order to survive. The relation between beneficiaries and aid workers is not one of equality though; they could not be friends, and they do not know each other well. The respondents that used this narrative think positively about the (sub) sector head. Beneficiaries need good relations with the staff otherwise their lives would be even more difficult. Bribing is not necessary though.

Case 1: Pader District in Northern Uganda

Pader District is located in Northern Uganda and forms part of the Acholi region. Ninety per cent of the local population consists of subsistence farmers. Since the mid-1980s, Pader District has experienced insecurity and this has exacerbated poverty levels in all its forms. Of particular relevance for Northern Uganda is the Ugandan Lord's Resistance Army (LRA). The insecurity caused by this conflict led to the displacement of between one and two million people in Northern Uganda. Since 1996, these people were placed in Internally Displaced Person (IDP) camps in Northern Uganda. In these camps, freedom of movement was severely restricted. In 2006, the security situation in Northern Uganda improved, and IDPs started to return home. The vast majority of former IDPs have now returned home to rebuild their livelihoods after having lost relatives, houses, cattle, crops and land entitlements.

Slowly but surely, aid in Pader District has become less humanitarian and more developmental in character. In recent years, a number of humanitarian NGOs have left Pader District. Still, there are quite a number of aid organisations present in the area. These include international NGOs (such as Caritas, Concern, International Aid Services, Lutheran World Federation, War Child and World Vision) as well as a number of national NGOs and Community-Based Organisations (CBOs). Almost all of these organisations have their offices in Pader Town. They are active in a number of areas such as supplementary feeding programmes, seed handouts, the construction of huts, the construction of bore-holes, agricultural training, savings groups, and hygiene and sanitation training. In order for an aid organisation to be active in Pader District, it needs the consent of the Ugandan central and local governments, and it must operate in line with national and local development plans.

A total of 42 interviews and 39 Q-sort sessions were conducted. Respondents consisted mainly of aid recipients and aid workers. The aid recipients included in the research are mainly female farmers with children. Almost all of the aid recipients have spent time in IDP camps. The aid workers included in the research represent 15 different aid organisations, including international NGOs, national NGOs and CBOs. These aid workers represent a wide range of job functions such as field extension workers, programme managers, a nutritionist and a social worker. A number of incentive workers, local governmental and non-governmental leaders, and community members who did not receive aid during the fieldwork period, were included in the research as well. An important characteristic for the aid landscape in Pader District is that these different research population groups predominantly share the same (cultural) background. They predominantly share the Ugandan nationality, the Acholi ethnicity and language, and a Christian religion.

From the interview data, six different narratives were extracted which are used by aid recipients and aid workers to describe themselves, each other and the aid provided in Pader District. They are relevant because each of these narratives is connected to aid legitimacy. The first four narratives are connected to perceived problems with the quality of aid. Two of these narratives, which are mainly used by aid workers, blame aid recipients for such problems, with the catch phrases 'dependency syndrome' and 'bad attitudes'. The third of these narratives can be summarised with the phrase 'beggars can't be choosers' and is used by aid recipients who feel that they are not in a position to be critical of the aid provided. The fourth of these narratives states that 'government and donors are to blame' for perceived problems with the quality of aid. An additional fifth narrative evokes the history of 'war and camp-life'. It stresses the hardships people have encountered and is broadly used to legitimise the continued provision of aid. Finally, there is a positive narrative on aid, where both aid workers and recipients generally believe that NGOs in Pader District do a good job helping the local population.

The Q-sort method was used to analyse the distribution of the narratives among respondents. Using the criteria set by Webler *et al.* (2009) of simplicity, clarity, distinctness and stability, three groups were defined. The first group comprises mostly aid recipients, and the second, mostly aid workers. The third is a mixed group comprising four aid workers, four aid recipients and one community member. Ten respondents did not score significantly on any of the narratives.

Similarities and differences

In Pader District a number of narratives are used by both aid workers and aid recipients. Both groups use the 'war and camps' narrative and the 'positive' narrative. Both groups use the 'government and donors are to blame' narrative, albeit in slightly different manners. The data from the Q-sort methodology also show that there are some images that are shared by the different factor-groups. For example, respondents (who are included in factor-groups) share the opinions that NGOs should work closely together with local leaders, that it is not so easy for community members to complain to an NGO, that the contact between aid workers and recipients is good, and that NGOs are generally not involved in corruption. The fact that one factor-group comprises both aid workers and aid recipients indicates, as well, that it is possible within aid arenas for different aid actors to share opinions.

The large proportion of respondents that was either scored in a mixed group or did not score in a single group further testifies to the large diversity of opinions among aid workers and recipients. These differences were tested for patterns around a number of possible explanatory variables, such as age, gender, profession, length of time spent in Pader District and type of aid given or received, but none of these provided valid results. This leads us to conclude that, in a case like Pader, where cultural differences between aid givers and recipients are relatively small, elements at the individual and personal level, such as variances in personal experiences, preferences and character, play a larger role.

This being said, there are also differences between the narratives used by aid workers and recipients in Pader District. The 'beggars can't be choosers' narrative is used by half of aid recipients, but not by any aid worker. The 'bad attitude' narrative and the 'aid-dependency' narrative are regularly used by aid workers but rarely by aid recipients. The results from the Q-sort method further indicate that aid workers and recipients use different images. For example, the 'aid recipients' group predominantly shares favourable images of aid recipients while the 'aid workers' group shares a number of negative images of aid recipients. Also, the 'aid recipients' group strongly agrees with the statement that NGOs should provide more handouts while the 'aid workers' factor-group totally disagrees with that statement. Surprisingly, the 'aid workers' group attaches more importance to local participation than the 'aid recipients' group. As the cultural and social characteristics of the aid workers and recipients are highly similar, the differences between these two groups can be explained by the different roles that these groups assume within the aid arena, namely, that of the providers of aid and the receivers of aid.

Case 2: Bhutanese refugees in Nepal[2]

This case is based on research in the refugee camps around Damak, Nepal, where, since the early 1990s, more than 80,000 Bhutanese refugees have resided (Hutt 2003). They concern refugees that originate from Nepal and have been moving eastwards since the nineteenth century, in response to undue taxation and violence. In the 1970s, several decades after Bhutan's independence, these people became increasingly marginalised and forced to assimilate, leading to protest and escalating oppression. In the early 1990s, the first refugee camps were established in Eastern Nepal, and the refugee numbers grew to 100,000 in 1996. For fifteen years, these refugees lived in camps without knowing what the future would bring: Bhutan would not take them back but Nepal did not want them either. Only in 2008 did it become clear that the refugees would become eligible for resettlement in a third country (US, Canada, Australia, New Zealand, Netherlands, Denmark, Norway).

The refugee camps in eastern Nepal are considered by the United Nation High Commissioner for Refugees (UNHCR) as models of good practice, and the high level of participation led to a highly effective infrastructure. Education and general living conditions in the camp are considered one of the best for refugee camps around the world. The different camps are organised per sector: each sector has a sector head and several sub sector heads, who together form a voluntarily commission in charge of the daily matters such as food distribution and other services. Next to these volunteer functions, refugees can also work as incentive worker for one of the organisations active in the camp. As incentive workers, refugees receive a small incentive from the organisation for their job. With this incentive, refugees can buy meat, vegetables, clothes and other items that are not provided by the organisations. The refugees have a bamboo hut, children receive education, there are clinics in the camps, and every two weeks food rations are distributed (rice, lentils, vegetable oil, sugar, salt, wheat soya blend). Officially refugees are not allowed to have a job outside the camp, hold animals or have electricity.

Several aid organisations are active in camp Beldangi-1 where our fieldwork was concentrated. Lutheran World Federation Nepal is in charge of the camp management (housing, distribution of food, infrastructure), the Association of Medical Doctors of Asia Nepal is in charge of medical services, Caritas-Nepal is in charge of education, the World Food Program provides the food, mental health-care is provided by Transcultural Psychosocial Organisation, Happy Nepal helps people with addictions, while the Nepal Bar Association provides the refugees with legal advice.

Aid legitimacy and relations in Nepal

The Q-methodology was done with 28 respondents. It produced four different narratives that were scored by sections of the respondents. In these, we could clearly recognise the four categories of actors we interviewed: beneficiaries, active beneficiaries (volunteers and incentive workers), staff in the NGO camp office of LWF Nepal, and staff of their office in town. The correspondence was not complete, and could be read more as a scale than as a set of different categories; the majority of passive beneficiaries (e.g. beneficiaries not working in the camp as incentive worker or volunteer) scored on the first narrative, while none of these beneficiaries scored on the narrative predominantly held by staff from the town office. The narratives showed differences, but, interestingly, they also overlapped to a large extent. All narratives were, for example, positive about relations between aid workers and refugees. An important factor explaining the positive mutual images and relationship between aid workers and refugees may be the fact that they share the same culture. The refugees were Bhutanese of Nepali descent, and all staff were Nepali nationals. In interviews, aid workers would say things like: 'In my view, I find them like other Nepali people, but their lifestyle is a little different.' Several of the staff related that their appreciation of the refugees grew over time. 'Before I came to the camp, I thought they had an unmanaged life, but now I know that they are OK.'

Another striking similarity across the categories, brought out by the Q-methodology and interviews, was that aid is regarded as too little, both in terms of quantity and scope. The food provided is too little to sustain the refugees, who have to find other ways to supplement their diets, and aid does not cover other refugees' needs such as clothes, meat and vegetables. Interestingly, this points to a remarkable discrepancy in legitimacies. Whereas the legitimacy of aid as right and effective is not high, we do not see this translated into a negative image of aid workers, as we would expect when legitimacy of aid was defined by performance. Interestingly, this balance shifted for two other types of assistance: the provision of bamboo and thatch for repairing the refugee huts, and the resettlement to a third country. Mutual understandings of practices and their legitimacy, built over time, were much less prevalent when it came to these issues, illustrating how complex on-the-ground social dynamics shape the legitimacy of aid.

Huts in the camp are made of bamboo and thatched roofs that require regular maintenance. The distribution of bamboo is irregular; only once every two years can a family obtain bamboo, and distribution is far less regulated than that of food items. Here, refugees have the opinion that staff do not always do a good job. 'In case of bamboo and thatch we have given official complaints. But the staff just writes a letter about it, they don't address the problem.' Complaints regarding the aid workers were even stronger in the case of third country resettlement. The resettlement of the refugees to third countries started in 2008, and is one of the most daunting resettlement programmes in the history of refugee care. The US alone intends to absorb half of all the Bhutanese refugees. The programme is implemented by the International Organisation of Migration (IOM) and the UNHCR. At the time of research, quite a large number of families had already departed and the remaining refugees were being concentrated in what are going to be two camps. The resettlement led to much confusion among the refugees and was surrounded by many rumours. A particular source of anxiety is the fear of being separated from close relatives, as the registration concerns only the nuclear family. There are also quite a lot of people who are keen to resettle and concerned they might not get a chance to go.

There were different myths going around the camp about resettlement. One often repeated story was that the resettlement programme was going to stop within six months, leaving out all those that had not moved by then. There was also the story that the camp would close altogether. These stories were obviously not true, but other stories were harder to invalidate. A number of refugees who were interviewed spoke of bribing practices, indicating that the aid workers requested bribes before they would deal with the beneficiaries' issues.

Pulling these threads together, one of the intriguing aspects of our findings is that refugees rarely complain about the food aid that is distributed, even though every category of actor agrees that there is a shortage of such aid. Yet, bamboo and thatch and the resettlement programme lead to a lot of anxiety. Bamboo and thatch distribution was fraught with irregularity. Also, resettlement is not organised in the regularised refugee-managed aid scheme. For resettlement, refugees interact directly with the staff of IOM and UNHCR. Another difference seems to be that, whereas the distribution of food and other items had become routinised in 20 years, resettlement was still new and people were not familiar with the procedures, thus leading to a lot of confusion and suspicion. More than the performance of aid *per se*, the legitimacy of aid seemed to depend on the ways it was embedded in the organisation and regulations of the camp and whether the programme was routinised. Legitimacy resulted from the mutual understandings that had developed over time through interaction between aid recipients and aid givers.

Case 3: Post-conflict communities in South Sudan

The research in South Sudan took place in two counties of Eastern Equatoria State, located close to the Kenyan and Ugandan border: Kapoeta North County and Magwi County. Kapoeta North County is a semi-desert area where inhabitants are mainly pastoralist. Magwi County is a mountainous area where the inhabitants mainly depend on subsistence agriculture. From 1956 to 2005, there were two civil wars between the North and the South of Sudan, which also highly affected Eastern Equatoria State. A big part of the population fled to neighbouring countries, or hid deep in the bush. Since the peace agreement in 2005, people have returned and the state is slowly rebuilding itself, with international support. A start was made to recover basic services (education, health care, water and sanitation) and improve infrastructure. This is mainly done by international NGOs, who support the local government and provide the majority of basic services.

This research focuses on six NGOs that are active in the Water and Sanitation sector of Eastern Equatoria State: Association of Aid and Relief (AAR) Japan; Save the Children; Carter Centre; Catholic Relief Services (CRS); Norwegian Church Aid (NCA); and Catholic Dioces of Torit (DOT). All of them run several projects in the area that focus on drilling boreholes, constructing latrines, training pump mechanics, training 'Water Management Committees' (community members who are responsible for maintaining the boreholes) and educating the communities about sanitation and hygiene. The seven NGOs have different backgrounds, but they have in common that they all started working in South Sudan as humanitarian organisations during the civil war. Since the signing of the peace agreement, activities have changed from humanitarian assistance to development work.

The research was done with workers of the seven studied NGOs, community members and leaders from eight villages in Kapoeta North County and five villages in Magwi county, and community volunteers of three studied NGOs. The research methods were Q-methodology (36 respondents), interviews (49 individual interviews and 18 group interviews) and observations during a fieldwork period of 3 months in the area.

Imaging each other

Aid beneficiaries in South-Sudan have a general notion that NGO workers are skilled professionals, who come to assist the community, yet cannot be relied on and do not keep their promises. Underneath this general idea hides a diversity of opinions and interpretations. There were differences, for example, between people in Kapoeta North and Magwi, men and women, community leaders and community members, direct beneficiaries (people who participate in projects) and indirect beneficiaries (people who do not participate, but benefit indirectly), and between people who live in the centre and the periphery of the county. A significant finding was that people who have more contact with NGO workers because they are community leader, direct beneficiary or live in the centre of the county, have a more positive image of NGO workers than others. These people underlined the importance of NGO assistance, and scored negatively on statements indicating that NGO workers are arrogant or that NGO workers are stealing money or favour their own tribe. Apparently, a more proximate relationship with NGO workers, based on real experience, leads to a more positive image than the image based on (negative) stereotypes.

We also found major differences among NGO workers. Although most NGOs had similar mandates and objectives, in practice there were two groups. The first group could be said to have a 'relief mentality'. It focuses more on the material side of development, on drilling boreholes and constructing latrines. Quick results and good planning are seen as very important, and success is measured against the yardstick of the donor. With this group of NGOs, follow-up is low, and NGO workers usually have a different ethnic background than community members. They see community members more as dishonest, ungrateful and resistant to change. There was a strong focus by this group of NGOs on reaching targeted results, and this resulted in a frustration about the non-cooperativeness of community members.

A second group of NGOs can be considered more 'development oriented' and focused more on awareness raising and behavioural change. Having a connection with the community is seen as very important, and a measurement for success. Follow-up is high, and the majority of NGO workers have a similar ethnic background as the community members. Aid workers of this second group see community members as lacking knowledge, but eager to learn. According to this second group, change can happen and is happening, step by step. A main difference between the two groups is that aid workers of the second group spend more time in the communities and hence have more direct interaction with the aid recipients than the staff of the first group.

Community volunteers

Half of the NGOs in the study worked with so-called 'community volunteers'. These are community members who are trained by the NGO to do unpaid work in their own community. Usually this includes transferring information, when the volunteers of different villages are trained together at the NGO office, and are then expected to organise education sessions in their village to pass on their knowledge. But it can also be more practical, such as vaccinating children or detecting cases of guinea worm disease.

When studying the data of these community volunteers, it becomes clear that the images of community volunteers are a mixture of the images of NGO workers and community members. Their position is in between these two groups. They work for the NGO, but belong to the community, and this is also shown in the images that they have of community members and NGO workers. They have some of the same critique of community members about NGO workers. They find NGO workers important for the community, yet some NGO workers cannot be trusted. Another problem is that some NGO workers do not spend enough time in the community. Interestingly, the community volunteers also share some of the critique of NGO workers on community members. Community volunteers think of their community as open to change and eager to learn from NGOs. However, they also see community members as passive and not actively improving their own situation.

Interestingly, community volunteers found it difficult to make generalising statements on aid workers as part of the Q-methodology. Several of them underlined that every NGO worker and every community member is different.

Since community volunteers are in direct contact with NGO workers and community members, their images of both NGO workers and community members were more based on experiences than on stereotypes, and therefore, in general, more colourful and diverse than the images NGO workers and community members had about each other.

Legitimacy and trust

How did the images of NGO workers, community members and community volunteers affect the legitimacy of water and sanitation projects in Eastern Equatoria State? Using Lister's (2003) framework for legitimacy, it became clear that NGO workers and community members had different criteria for establishing the legitimacy of aid. According to NGO workers, legitimacy is created by a combination of reaching results, and applying the appropriate approaches. Their focus is on planning, models and methods, like using theatre and music, or more theory-based approaches, like Community-Led Total Sanitation. NGO workers judge their own organisation as legitimate when results are reached and the right approach used. However, all other actors – community members, leaders, and volunteers – put a much higher value on trust and connection. When community members feel a lack of trust and connection with staff of a specific NGO, they judge the legitimacy of the NGO as low. With each using their own tacit criteria, aid workers judged their organisations as legitimate, while community members were more negative. In the eyes of community actors, the legitimacy of the first group of NGO workers, who have a more 'relief-mentality', was found to be quite low. For those NGOs that have a more proximate relation with the community members, because their staff have the same ethnic background as the population and regularly visit the community, and because they actively use community volunteers, legitimacy was found to be higher. The appreciation of this latter group of NGOs thus led to a higher legitimacy of their programmes.

Conclusion

Recent decades have seen growing attention to the importance of the ways in which aid workers and recipients see each other. Our chapter aimed to contribute to this literature in three ways. We have offered a theoretical perspective of aid as a socially negotiated arena where the construction of images is the outcome of interaction between different actors. Rather than speaking of *labelling* (which is done to people), or *perceptions* (resting in one actor's head), we emphasise the agency people deploy in manipulating their own images in other people's eyes and actively and contextually forging images of 'others'. Second, we look into mutual imaging of aid workers and recipients (rather than focusing on one side of the relationship), as we are interested in the ways mutual imaging affects the legitimacy of the different actors and the aid operation as such. Third, we wanted to break through the duality of aid workers and recipients often presented as two different categories of actors with incompatible life worlds. We approached this by using a Q-methodology that symmetrically researches different groups of actors (by posing the same questions). With this methodology, we were able to distil different narratives on which we could score respondents.

Our data from three countries are consistent in pointing out that aid workers and recipients may have different images of themselves and each other, yet there is also a high level of overlap between them and there is also much diversity within these categories. Aid workers and recipients are certainly not worlds apart. They are not actors with incommensurate views on aid relations, as assumed in much of the literature. One aspect of this is the common cultural background of aid workers and recipients in all three cases. The only exception was a sub-group of agencies working in Kapoeta North County in South Sudan, and this translated in a more negative image of aid among the aid recipients. Cultural likeness is actually a normal characteristic of international aid, where the vast majority of staff is recruited locally. This renders the aid relation not very different from other aid relations outside of humanitarian encounters, such as clients of welfare or medical care anywhere in the world. One outstanding difference is, perhaps, that recipients of humanitarian aid often consist of large populations, rather than individual clients. Notwithstanding, we maintain that the aid relation within humanitarian situations merits being analysed primarily as a 'normal' aid relation, and that such analysis could therefore draw more on theory and literature from these fields.

Given the differences in imaging between general recipients and active recipients or incentive workers, particularly in Nepal and South Sudan, we find that our research points to the importance of the interaction between frontline (implementing) staff and active beneficiaries. The use of beneficiaries as incentive workers or volunteers is common in aid programming, but these people rarely receive analytical attention in organisational studies (they do figure in studies on power relations among refugees: see Jansen 2011, Agier and Bouchet-Saulnier 2004). Perhaps this is not surprising, as this category of actors challenges the duality of aid workers and recipients that is maintained in much of the literature. *Ni l'un, ni l'autre*, they cannot be easily categorised as either aid worker or recipient because they have a dual identity of being both at the same time.

Our findings suggest that the role of these active volunteers and incentive workers is ambiguous. On the one hand, their presence and dual identification (with the aid regime and their fellow refugees) puts them in a position as brokers that may smooth the divide between aid agencies and their clients. On the other hand, their proximity to the aid regime may also lead to tensions. Their close observation of aid makes them particularly informed about the details of possible misgivings, and the closeness of relations could easily lead to irritation or a sense of deprivation when it is not clear why recipients would not be fully salaried for their work. While this chapter points to the importance of the specific roles of volunteers and incentive workers, the way they play out these roles and the effect this has on imaging processes and the legitimacy of aid is context-specific and a domain of further research.

This research aimed to delve into the relation between imaging and aid legitimacy. Accountability, performance, experience and reputation are important factors in the legitimacy of aid. As legitimacy is socially constructed, we maintain that mutual imaging plays an important role in the ways these factors translate into legitimacy. In Uganda, aid workers blame other actors, including aid recipents, the government and donors, for problems with the quality of aid, and fail as a result to reflect on the question of how they can improve aid legitimacy and effectiveness. In Nepal, criticism of aid did not always translate into lower legitimacy of the agencies, depending on the type of aid. Moreover, it was shown that legitimacy is a process that depends on the way the aid relations evolve through the years. In Sudan, legitimacy was differentiated according to the frameworks within which aid workers and recipients understood legitimacy. Across the three countries, we find that aid workers tend to expect their legitimacy to depend on their activities and working methods, whereas recipients judge agencies to a large extent for the frequency and quality of interaction they have with their staff. In the eyes of aid recipients, 'being nice' is important for aid workers and partly determines whether recipients feel that they are 'doing good'. A focus on mutual imaging processes of aid workers and recipients thus brings out a more differentiated, context-sensitive and process-oriented understanding of aid legitimacy.

Acknowledgements

The authors wish to thank Margit van Wessel and Anne-Meike Fechter for their constructive comments on an earlier version of this chapter, as well as many other people who provided feedback during various stages of the research. Their gratitude also goes out to the staff from the Lutheran World Federation in Pader District, Uganda, and in Nepal, for their facilitation of the research, and to all the participants in the research. All responsibility remains with the authors.

Notes

1 The fieldwork was conducted by Lotte Kemkens in Northern Uganda, Loes Weijers in Nepal, Gemma Andriessen in South Sudan. It lasted three months in each country, and was part of the MSc degrees of the researchers.
2 The case of Nepal was analysed in more detail in Hilhorst *et al.* (2012).

References

Agier, M. and F. Bouchet-Saulnier (2004) 'Humanitarian Spaces: Spaces of Exception', in F. Weissman *In the Shadows of 'just wars': Violence, Politics and Humanitarian Action*, New York: Cornell University Press. 297–313.
Bakewell, O. (2000) 'Uncovering Local Perspectives on Humanitarian Assistance and its Outcomes', *Disasters*, 24(2): 103–116.
Bernstein, D.A., L.A. Penner, A. Clarke-Stewart, and E.J. Roy (2008) *Psychology (8th edition)*, Boston, MA: Houghton Mifflin Company.
Brown, S. (1980) *Political Subjectivity: Applications of Q Methodology in Political Science*, New Haven, CT: Yale University Press.
Brown, S. (1993) 'A Primer on Q methodology', *Operant Subjectivity*, 16(3/4): 91–138.

Christoplos, I. (1998) 'Humanitarianism and Local Service Institutions in Angola', *Disasters*, 22(1): 1–20.

Clark, L. (1985) *The Refugee Dependency Syndrome: Physician, Heal Thyself*, Washington, DC: Refugee Policy Group.

Dijkzeul, D. and C. Wakenge (2010) 'Doing Good, But Looking Bad? Local Perceptions of Two Humanitarian Agencies in the Eastern DRC', *Disasters*, 34(4): 1139–1170.

Harrell-Bond, B. (1986) *Imposing Aid. Emergency Assistance to Refugees*, Oxford: Oxford University Press.

Hilhorst, D. (2003) *The Real World of NGOs: Discourse, Diversity and Development*, London: Zedbooks.

Hilhorst, D. and B. Jansen (2010) 'Humanitarian Space as Arena: a Perspective on the Everyday Politics of Aid', *Development and Change*, 41(6): 1117–1139.

Hilhorst, D. and M. van Leeuwen (1999) 'Villagisation in Rwanda: A case of Emergency Development?', *Disaster Sites*, no. 2, Wageningen University, Disaster Studies.

Hilhorst, D. and M. van Leeuwen (2005) 'Grounding Local Peace Organizations. A Case Study of Southern Sudan', *Journal of Modern Africa Studies*, 43(4): 537–563.

Hilhorst, D. and M. Serrano (2010) 'The Humanitarian Arena in Angola, 1975–2008', *Disasters*, 34(S2): S183–S201.

Hilhorst, D., I. Christoplos and G. van der Haar (2011) 'Reconstruction from Below. Magic Bullet or Shooting from the Hip?', *Third World Quarterly*, 31(7): 1107–1124.

Hilhorst, D., L. Weijers and M. van Wessel (2012) 'Aid Relations and Aid Legitimacy. Mutual Imaging of Aid Workers and Recipients in Nepal', *Third World Quarterly*, 33(8): 1439–1457.

Hutt, M. (2003) *Unbecoming Citizens; Culture, Nationhood, and the Flight of Refugees from Bhutan*, Oxford: University Press.

Hyndman, J. (2000) *Managing Displacement: Refugees and the Politics of Humanitarianism*, Minneapolis MN: University of Minnesota Press.

Jansen, B. (2011) *The Accidental City: Violence, Economy and Humanitarianism in Kakuma Refugee Camp Kenya*, Wageningen: Wageningen University.

Kibreab, G. (2004) 'Pulling the Wool over the Eyes of the Strangers: Refugee Deceit and Trickery in Insitutionalized Settings', *Journal of Refugee Studies*, 17(1): 1–26.

Lister, S. (2003) 'NGO Legitimacy: Technical Issue or Social Construct?', *Critique of Anthropology*, 23(2): 175–192.

Long, N. (2001) *Development Sociology. Actor Perspectives*, London: Routledge.

Madut Jok, J. (1996) 'Information Exchange in the Disaster Zone: Interaction Between Aid Workers and Recipients in South Sudan', *Disasters*, 20(3): 206–215.

Malkki, L. (1995) *Purity and Exile, Violence, Memory and National Cosmology among Hutu Refugees in Tanzania*, Chicago, IL: Chicago University Press.

Péchayre, M. (2011) *Humanitarian Action in Pakistan 2005–2010: Challenges, Principles, and Politics*, Medford, MA: Feinstein International Center. 13.

Potter, J. and M. Wetherell (1987) *Discourse and Social Psychology; Beyond Attitudes and Behaviour*, London: Sage.

Sandvik, K. (2008) 'The Physicality of Legal Consciousness: Suffering and the Production of Credibility in Refugee Resettlement', in R. Brown and R. Wilson, *Humanitarianism and Suffering: The Mobilization of Empathy*, Cambridge: Cambridge University Press. 223–244.

Slim, H. (2002) *By What Authority? The Legitimacy and Accountability of Non-governmental Organisations* at http://www.jha.ac/articles/a082.htm, accessed 15 February 2012.

Utas, M. (2005) 'Victimcy, Girlfriending, Soldiering: Tactic Agency in a Young Women's Social Navigation of the Liberian War Zone', *Anthropological Quarterly*, 78(2): 403–430.

Van Exel, J. and G. de Graaf (2005) 'Q methodology: a Sneak Preview', at http://qmethod.org/articles/vanExel.pdf, accessed 2 February 2011.

Webler, T., S. Danielson and C. Tuler (2009) 'Using Q Method to Reveal Social Perspectives in Environmental Research', Greenfield: Social and Environmental Research Institute, at http://www.seri-us.org/sites/default/files/Qprimer.pdf, accessed 14 February 2012.

Wood, G. (1985) *Labelling in Development Policy*, London: Sage.

Zetter, R. (1991) 'Labelling Refugees: Forming and Transforming a Bureaucratic Identity', *Journal of Refugee Studies*, 4(1): 39–62.

Index